REVOLUTION IS LOVE

A YEAR OF BLACK TRANS LIBERATION

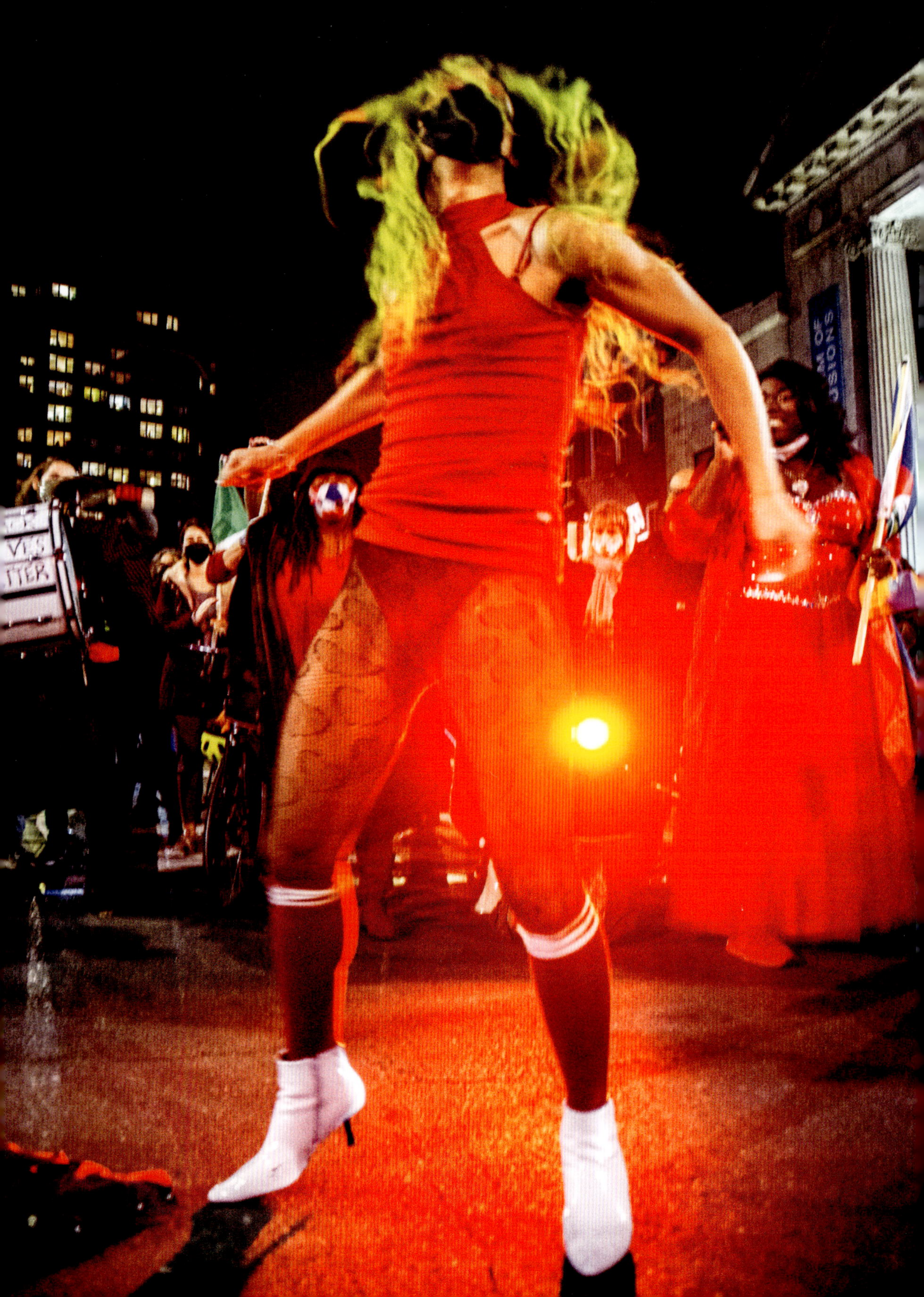

REVOLUTION IS LOVE

Featuring images and text by 24 photographers

Text contributions by Qween Jean, Joela Rivera, Mikelle Street, and Raquel Willis

A YEAR OF BLACK TRANS LIBERATION

aperture

Ramie Ahmed
Lucy Baptiste
Budi
Brandon English
Deb Fong
Snake Garcia
Stas Ginzburg
Katie Godowski
Robert Hamada
Chae Kihn
Zak Krevitt
Erica Lansner
Daniel Lehrhaupt
Caroline Mardok
Ryan McGinley
Josh Pacheco
Jarrett Robertson
Phoenix Robles
Souls of a Movement
Madison Swart
Cindy Trinh
Sean Waltrous
Ruvan Wijesooriya
David Zung

Introduction
Qween Jean

Iyanna Dior was twenty years old when she was attacked and beaten up by a community of people in Minnesota. She ran to a bodega for help. The owners declined to help and pushed her out. She recalled, "If I'm going to die, I'm going to die on camera . . . I wanted people to actually know what happened." These traumatic stories and videos are all too common for Black trans women. Dior's attack took place on June 1, 2020: the beginning of Pride Month and first rally I attended at the Stonewall Inn.

At our first march two weeks later, on June 18, 2020, I returned to the steps near the Stonewall Inn with a message that was fighting to escape my body. It was necessary to acknowledge Black queer trans folks during the Black Lives Matter revolution. Past movements had ignored the contributions of our TGNC ancestors: Marsha P. Johnson and Sylvia Rivera. This connection was undeniable and felt utterly divine. The Stonewall Protests was born, and Black Trans Liberation was the mission.

Our purpose became clearer every week as more people came out and the collective grew. There were a few resilient bikers the first time who took up space on the West Side Highway. We continued to march with a ferocious fervor of passion and rage, an army of lovers ready for change and a new day. We had the right to assemble, and the right to fight for our freedom. Marginalized folks don't need to prove they deserve respect; we demand it! We were not alone, and for the first time, it felt real.

I would start each rally with activist Raquel Willis's mantra:

I believe in my power
I believe in your power
I believe in our power
I believe in Black queer power
I believe in Black trans power

Her words became a testimony that electrified the crowd. That power would lead us into jubilation.

When I think about our Stonewall community, I think of family. Despite pain, trauma, or abuse, the community was there to nourish, heal, and make you feel whole. Black queer and trans folks were supported and embraced as we are, in our vibrant fullness. Our chosen family held space for the possibility of transformation. Someone could evolve over time and grow more comfortable to express their true selves. Our cis-het community members also learned language and ways to better support us. To understand that trans women are in fact women and Black trans people deserve the utmost respect and protection. Our diversity was instrumental in growth and understanding intersectional liberation.

Our history is rooted in violence; our ancestors were raided and looted. Yet they persevered and radically dreamed of freedom. We stand tall on the shoulders of sex workers, drag queens, healers, queer writers, storytellers, community leaders, abolitionists, and courageous Black women, who had to fight injustice and prove that they belonged. So we, too, continue to fight, knowing that we had power all along. The power of our beauty, joy, and vision for Black Trans Liberation!

The rallies consisted of teachings, brave offerings, stories of our history, and powerful vigils for the siblings we'd lost to racism and transphobic violence. There were core themes, subjects, and dates that dictated the tone for each action, including Black Angels Ball, Homegoing Services, Trans Day of Visibility, Sex Workers' March, African Diasporic History, World AIDS Day, and In Solidarity with ICE Detainees. Audre Lorde says that "without community, there is no liberation." And I feel that without service, there is no community. The actions were rooted in community building, mutual aid, and advocacy for trans wellness and vitality. We consistently met up with other organizations throughout the week to support other actions involving women's health, LGBTQ refugees and asylum seekers, housing discrimination, AAPI hate, Free Palestine, sex-workers' rights, and many more. Clothing drives during the winter, self-defense training sessions, food drives, and meal distributions were essential to the mission. Holiday celebrations like Transgiving, Transmas, and toy drives created space dedicated to chosen family and fellowship. The community modeled that change doesn't have to take a lifetime. We have the ability and capacity to generate a sustainable future, and trans women have been providing for their communities all this time.

I realized we needed a way to release. Instinctively I called for us to "open it up," and the percussion beats guided us into a circle. Inspired by our ancestors, one could enter the circle and relinquish the burdens they may have been carrying as a way to heal. An ecstatic roar of love from the crowd would erupt as the individual danced, vogued, or strutted with no fear. Artists can use their gifts to heal and to reclaim their power and ultimately change this world. Who could deny the power of Black joy as resistance?

Malcolm X reminds us that "the press is so powerful in its image-making role, it can make the criminal look like he's the victim and make the victim look like he's the criminal." We would hold space while navigating transphobia and unprecedented violence from the police. Physical assaults, including punching, hair-pulling, choking, holding us in headlocks, pulling out their guns, unlawful arrests, misgendering, bullying, and abductions of our comrades. This level of abuse and mistreatment was sadly condoned by our public officials, including former Mayor Bill DeBlasio. No one should be treated with this egregious behavior while simply trying to fight for their freedom. I can only imagine how our ancestors felt when they were hosed, bitten by dogs, and beaten with batons in past movements.

Revolution is often depicted as a pastoral memory or event from the past, seen in paintings, folktales, novels, or even film. The reality is that real revolution exists when real people come together and demand change. We revolt against the systems that attempt to suppress and silence us. This revolution is dedicated to uprooting white supremacy and dismantling its relatives: racism, homophobia, transphobia, and misogyny. The work will prevail. They can't stop the revolution. And I'm not tired yet.

Qween Jean and Raquel Willis in Conversation

Raquel Willis:
Could you place us in the environment of young Qween Jean, and the journey that laid the foundation for you to become so invested in Black Trans Liberation?

Qween Jean:
To set the world for young Qween is difficult. She faced a lot of issues with self-worth, value, and wanting to belong, a lot of which was tied to faith and spirituality. My household was rooted in faith and discipline, and focused on preservation and appearance. How are we viewed as a family? Will we make our parents proud? But in the end, those ideals and visions didn't really include me, all of me, the full parts of myself. I thought, If this is family, I don't want it. Because I can't be myself here, I can't dress the way that I want here. I have to constantly conform myself and shift, code-switch into this being, into this boy.

RW:
I resonate so much with that feeling of not belonging and not having a space of salvation. Church is often a safe haven for Black families and communities, but I wasn't in a "Black church," I was in a Catholic church. So as a Black family in the South, there were multiple layers of feeling we're not where we're supposed to be. And I'm not who I'm supposed to be. As a kid, I felt all these questions of, What is the rulebook? What is this script that seemingly works for everyone else that I just cannot get the lines and blocking down for? I think the points that hurt the most were when I knew that I was queer or that I was gender nonconforming, and I really wanted to own it, but I didn't because I wanted to save face for my family and for all the people that I was supposed to represent. But I was never going to stay silent. I was silent for too long. It just got to a point in high school where I knew, this is the point of no return, honey.

QJ:

High school was a big turning point for me as well. It is when I started my physical journey into femininity, into womanness, into Qween. And honestly, if I didn't do something, it would have been a thorn in my side. The point of no return: I'm ooout! And I'm proud!

RW:

Exactly. I'm out. So what are we gonna do about it now? Because I've had to navigate and strategize for my own survival up until this point, so you figure out the rest, because I'm not going to live with this secret anymore.

QJ:

Before I started reading stories of Black queerness, seeing Black queer elders, seeing other young trans women, I spent a lot of years in turmoil, angry and conflicted. The first time I saw a Black trans woman, I was in a flea market with my mother. There was definitely a disdain for her presence from the other Southern Black women. But for me, there was complete eruption of joy to see myself, essentially. Moments like this have inspired me to ensure that young people don't feel ostracized or less than because they're different, because they're heavyset, because they're dark-skinned, because they're disabled, because they love Sailor Moon, for any reason.

RW:

Well, you are the evangelist, honey. Every time I see you, I hear you speak, I hear you sing, there is a testimony. What is that testimony that led you to activism and to the Stonewall Protests?

QJ:

Wow, yes! It is a testimony. Personally, I believe that God doesn't give me the spirit of fear, so why should I be afraid? There have been so many things in my life that I have navigated, dealt with, am still struggling with, that didn't kill me. And so why should I not sing? Why should I not fight? I always come back to the phrase "come as you are." There's such power in that idea: to come with your experience, your struggles, your burdens, all the trespasses that have been made against you, to show up and still have faith and to still know, without a shadow of a doubt, that you will win, that you will persevere. I, and all queer people, experience moments where we feel we are alone or will no longer be accepted, that we won't be loved, that we won't make it. And I'm here to say we are. And we will.

RW:

And we have!

QJ:
And we have. Because the reality is, we've always been here. We have been at every moment of history, we've been at every fight, at every social justice movement. We've existed.

RW:
I think about how depleted so many of us were in June 2020 after the murders of Ahmaud Arbery, George Floyd, Breonna Taylor, and then of course the overlooked Black trans murders: our brother Tony McDade in Tallahassee by police, Nina Pop and Monika Diamond, Dominique "Rem'mie" Fells and Riah Milton. We were depleted but still managed to organize and to show up for the first Brooklyn Liberation march on June 14, 2020, which became one of the largest marches for Black trans lives in history.

QJ:
The Brooklyn Liberation march in 2020 has been one of the most powerful moments in my entire life. I think that people are going to talk about that day for the rest of eternity, truly. Because we saw so many people come out who were depleted, who felt like, Is this ever going to end? The violence is just not stopping. But there was so much love and joy in that space. It truly was an alternate reality. And that was liberation. It was a space of liberation, where people felt seen, held, celebrated. We were with our living deities. What a gift.

RW:
Liberation is so speculative and can feel impossible. You're literally writing fiction in your head when you're thinking about liberation. But that day when upwards of twenty thousand folks came out—a whole congregation of folks who weren't necessarily Black, who weren't necessarily trans—it felt possible.

QJ:
I will never forget being able to turn any direction and see so many beautiful kinsmen, kin sisters, kin siblings who had also come out to receive that blessing. So many people that I admire and look up to testified that day about love, about community, about taking pride in the self, about standing up to your enemy, to your oppressor, and saying to them, "You will not win." It was a benediction for me. It gave me marching orders and gave me direction. I recited the benediction every chance I could, because it was a way for me to connect back to that moment of liberation.

RW:

It's divine inspiration. Whenever it feels impossible for us to reach liberation, I have that moment, that day, to look back on. With the Stonewall Protests, you have so many moments to look back on from that year because you gathered every week after Brooklyn Liberation. What is that like for you, to be living with those glimpses? And what does that make you hungry for now?

QJ:

At the Stonewall Protests, we came out to seek truth: emotional truth, the overwhelming political truth that exists within our world, and personal truth. And we needed space. Week after week in 2020, more of our Black trans siblings were being killed, and we needed a way to heal, to escape and gather, to scream it out, to march it out, to rejoice, to join in fellowship and to dance. And to truly be connected and fortified. It was like church in so many ways.

RW:

And a ball. It was everything at one time.

QJ:

The community was so powerful. We were ultimately coined an army of lovers. People from all walks of life, from all backgrounds, all ages, all intersections of race and culture and religion. We held space, and we gave reverence, and we all understood the role that we had to play in that moment. We had to combat and to speak out against injustice, the ongoing racism, transphobic violence, transphobia, homophobia that exists in all of the subcultures that we know, that we come from, and all the communities that we shy away from, where we don't feel safe, where we don't feel accepted. This was a space where we could belong. And I want that to be a permanent space. I want to create a place of worship for queer people, for trans and nonbinary-identified folks. We deserve a trans choir! So many of our people have an anointed gift. Young queer people, we need a space to just have, to hold, to call our own. That is something that I know in my destiny has to happen. In so many ways, the Stonewall Protests was the church experience that I wish I could have had as a child. I prayed that I could have met up with community once a week in my Sunday best and come with a spirit and a fervor for truth.

RW:

I love that you have documentation of what was happening from week to week, that the photographers were present and part of the community.

QJ:
At the Stonewall Protests, we had such dedicated and passionate community members who are storytellers, photojournalists, archivists, muralists, who would show up. No one's getting paid for this. No one is earning a salary to fight for Black lives. We are doing this so that we don't have to in the future. We're doing this so that we can have liberation now. To feel it, to exist in it. The documentarians who showed up for us have made such an impact. For me, it's an offering. For our movement to not only have been recorded but to be shared and amplified, for other queer people to bear witness or to be able to hear it, who don't necessarily have the access to community, to a weekly protest. That truly has been a huge gift and, I hope, something to mark our fight, to show it wasn't just a onetime thing, that it's still happening.

RW:
When we think about the Civil Rights movement, we think about images and film from the [1963] March on Washington, from Selma and the Edmund Pettus Bridge. And the grueling moments, like [the murder of] Emmett Till and other victims of lynching. We have the benefit of looking at past generations and understanding how important visual documentation is for the next ones coming up. But, something we grapple with as Black trans and queer people is that we often weren't in the frame, both physically and metaphorically, and so we continuously are excavating ourselves and our direct ancestors in these stories and histories. What are your thoughts on the importance of documenting what's happening in real time?

QJ:
I think it is so important and necessary to document, period. If we don't know where we've come from, we won't have the full knowledge to take us to where we need to go. But I completely agree that it often feels like excavation work. We are literally trying to find the fossils of our Black trans history. Trying to find any recollection, any relic that connects us to our past. I often think about the photographs and video footage of Black people being hosed or beaten by batons, things that are now archetypes of Black American experience and culture, unfortunately. So what does it mean to see Black trans people celebrating, having joy, being in community with one another, being able to rejoice, to not only mourn another sibling's life but to celebrate it in the way that Black people do? That is part of our culture, to have a repass that does not just exist in a home, that truly carries out onto the street, that alerts and informs the entire neighborhood that Black trans lives are valuable, that so many of our siblings deserved better. They deserve to be alive, quite frankly. So I'm grateful that this visual documentation allows for this message to continue, to keep these names, faces, and lives in print, in vogue, in conversation as part of our culture.

We often talk about this moment as the visibility era for trans people. But I'm eager to see us find new ways to express ourselves that don't have to check off any more boxes. Visibility is a double-edged sword. It's not all shiny and glamorous, and it shouldn't have to be. We shouldn't have to look or sound a certain way, be educated in a certain way, have a platform or microphone, or have a specific type of body to be visible and respected.

QJ:

Just as our Blackness is varied and beautiful, so is our transness, our queerness. In the present day, we are still fighting, even for our own community to fully see us. And not just to tolerate us, but accept us and truly respect us as Black trans individuals. How do you see visibility and representation in our fight?

RW:

I think visibility and representation obviously are important, but visibility was never going to save us in a world that still isn't ready for us. Ultimately, I think the most important thing is vitality. The most important goal is, how can we keep our people healthy, safe, and alive, and how can we improve their lives? And that means all our people, not just the ones who have been accepted as exceptional. But we've always done that, so it's in us. It's innate. We've just got to listen to those voices and to each other.

QJ:

That is such a powerful credo, but it is a very tough thing to do. But like you said, we've been doing it, and we've been doing it without a Greenbook of our own. We've been literally building our foundation and building our own grassroots pathway towards liberation. And that is exciting.

RW:

Something I think about is: How do I leave the door open wider for the next person? And how do I make it so that they don't have to check off as many boxes as I had to? How do I acknowledge the intersection of my own privileges, my personal will and hard work, and the foundation of my ancestors that all played a role in me getting to where I am? And that was one of the beautiful things about the Brooklyn Liberation march. That day felt like ego death, you know? This amazing high in which I didn't feel a separation of myself from the collective. I want to continue to be a part of making those moments happen.

QJ:

I also think about Marsha P. Johnson often: the impact she had, the lives that she will continue to change. It's so important to tell these stories. It is so important for us to excavate and unearth our past, as we have in this conversation. I've been really moved by that tonight, so thank you for that.

RW:

Thank you! I'm sure Marsha would be very proud.

QJ:

I'm grateful to be surrounded by so many other fearless, powerful community leaders and icons. We don't always get to see the full breadth of life for us, the painful truth is that the life expectancy for Black trans people is thirty-five years. And so it is necessary to uplift the joy that I associate with us as a Black queer community. That is how I would first define us, that we are joy. Not pain, not death. We are truly joy.

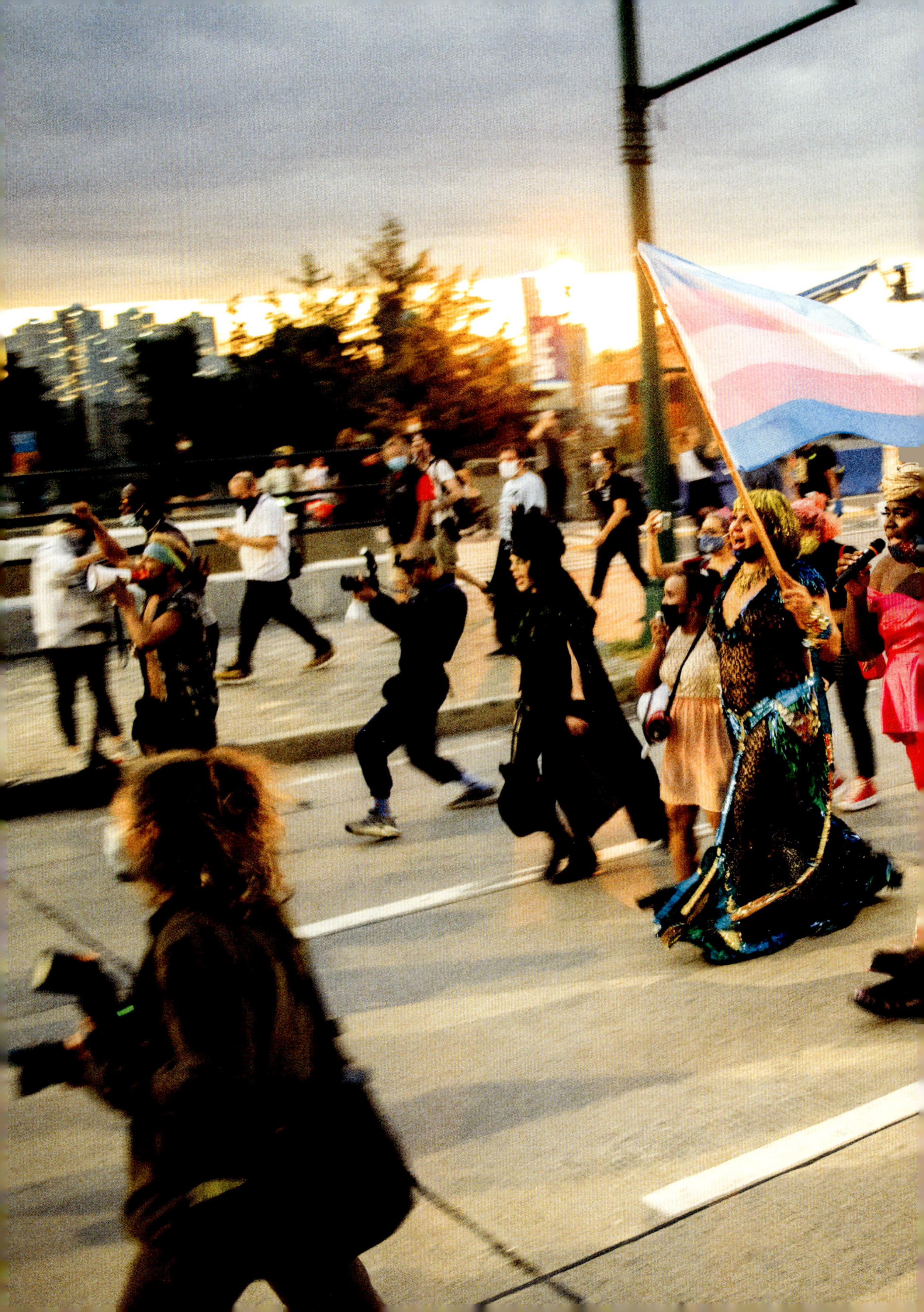

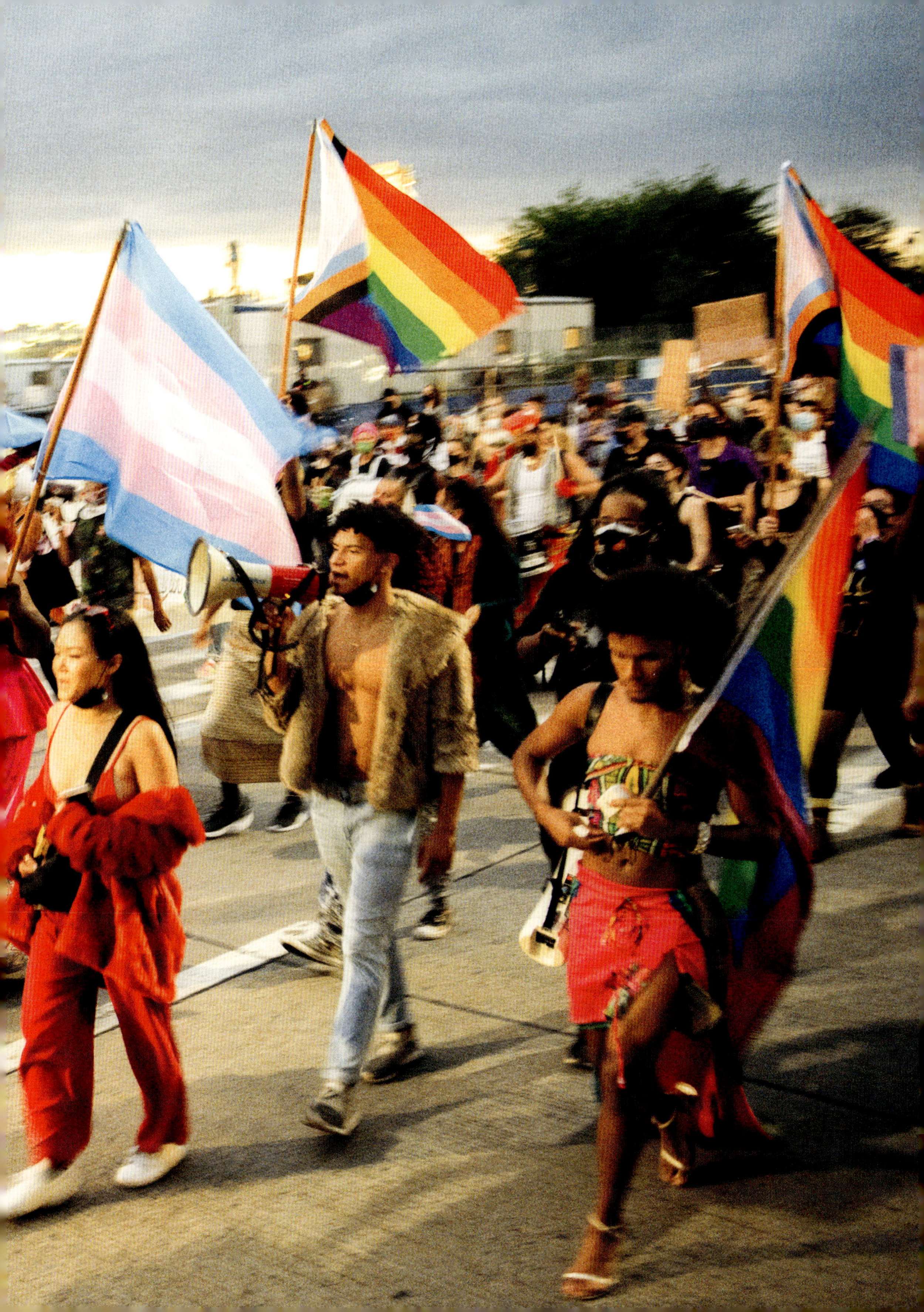

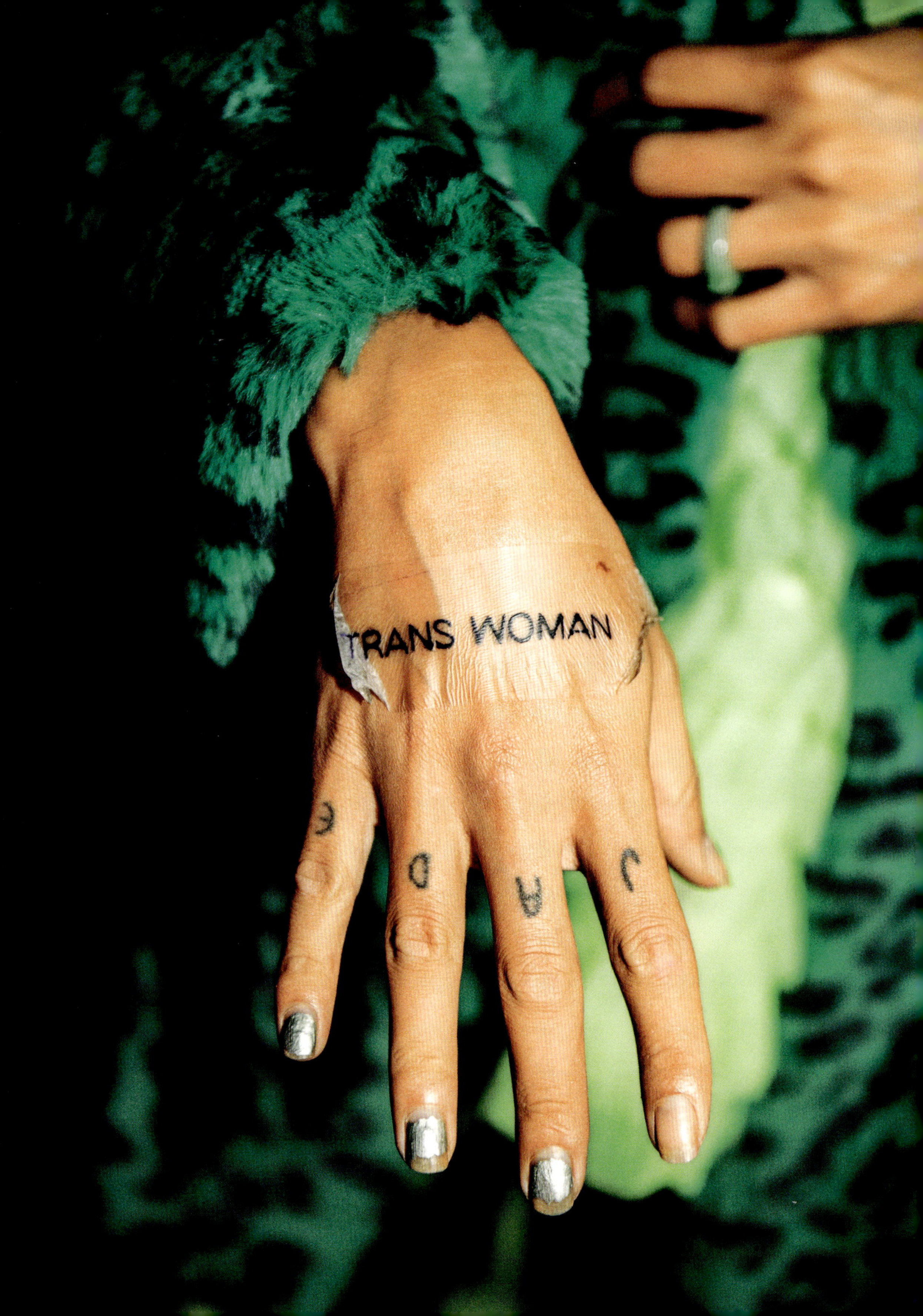
TRANS WOMAN

While the seasons changed, Stonewall was a constant. Every Thursday evening we awaited the grand entry of Qween Jean and Joela Rivera. When we heard the call, "BLACK LIVES . . . MATTER," everyone came to attention at the steps of 55 Christopher Street to begin another night of collective passion, joy, learning, and healing.

—Erica Lansner

Ryan McGinley
Black Trans History Ball
February 2021

PREVIOUS SPREAD:
Ryan McGinley
Liberation Not Deportation
October 2020

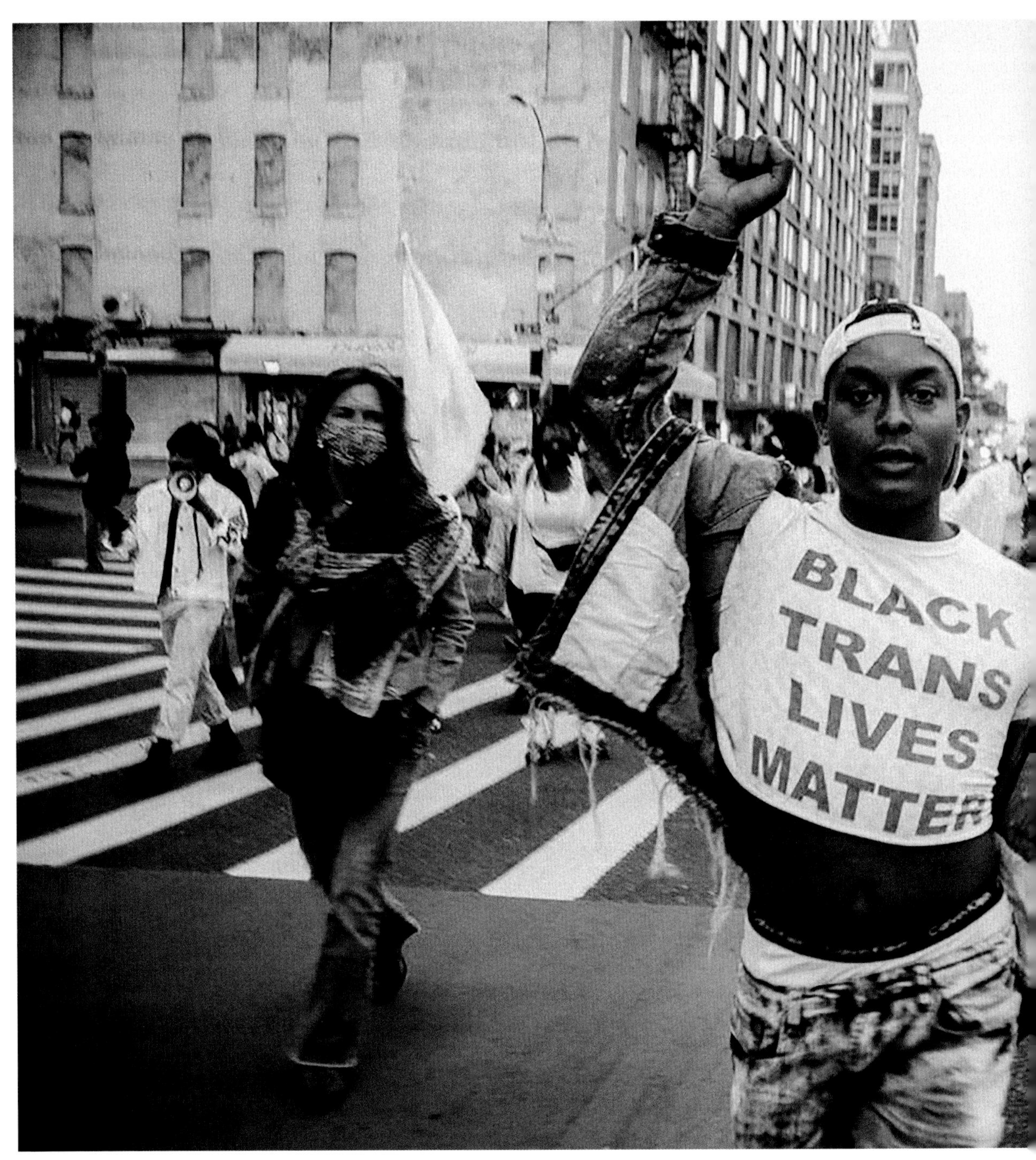

Madison Swart
Trans Visibility March
October 2020

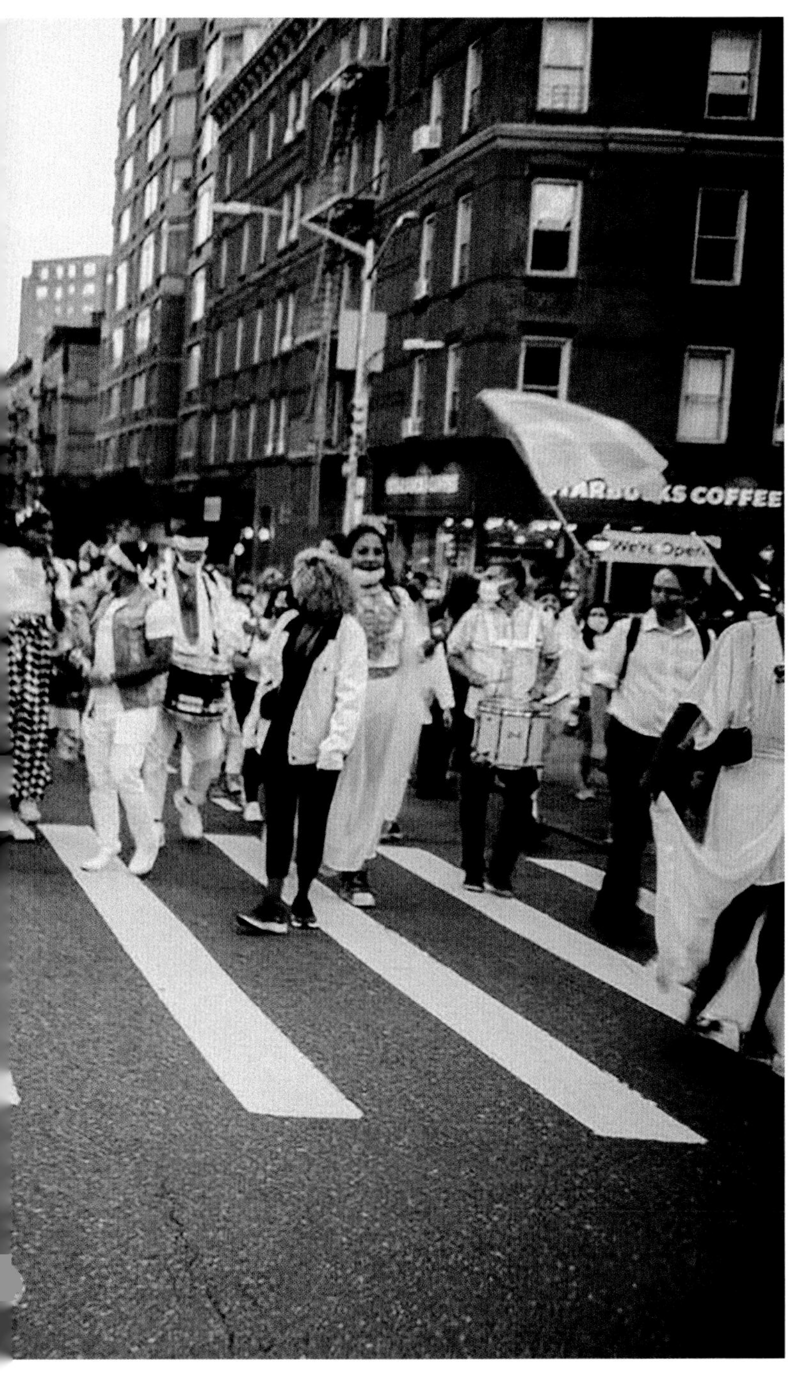

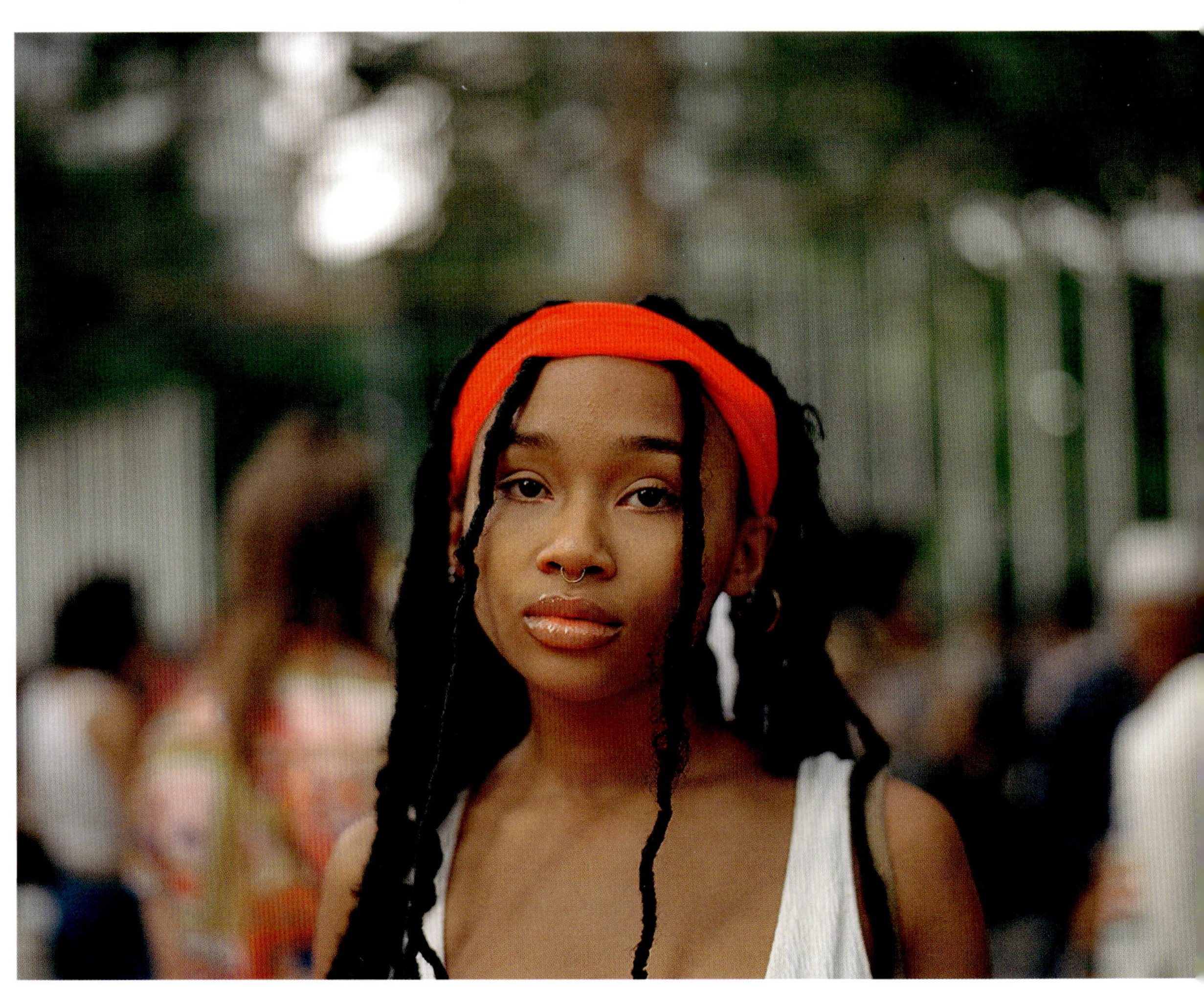

Ramie Ahmed
July 2021

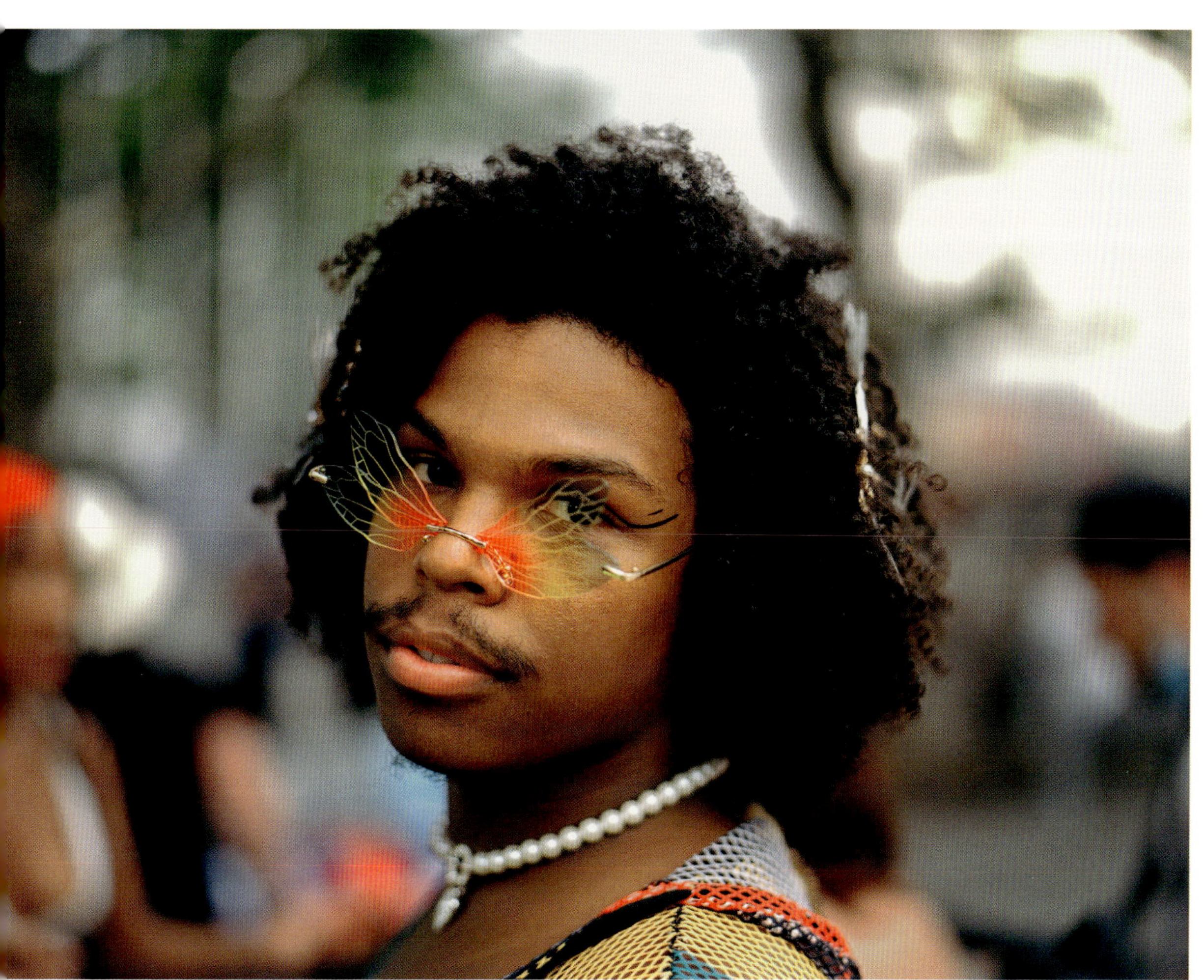

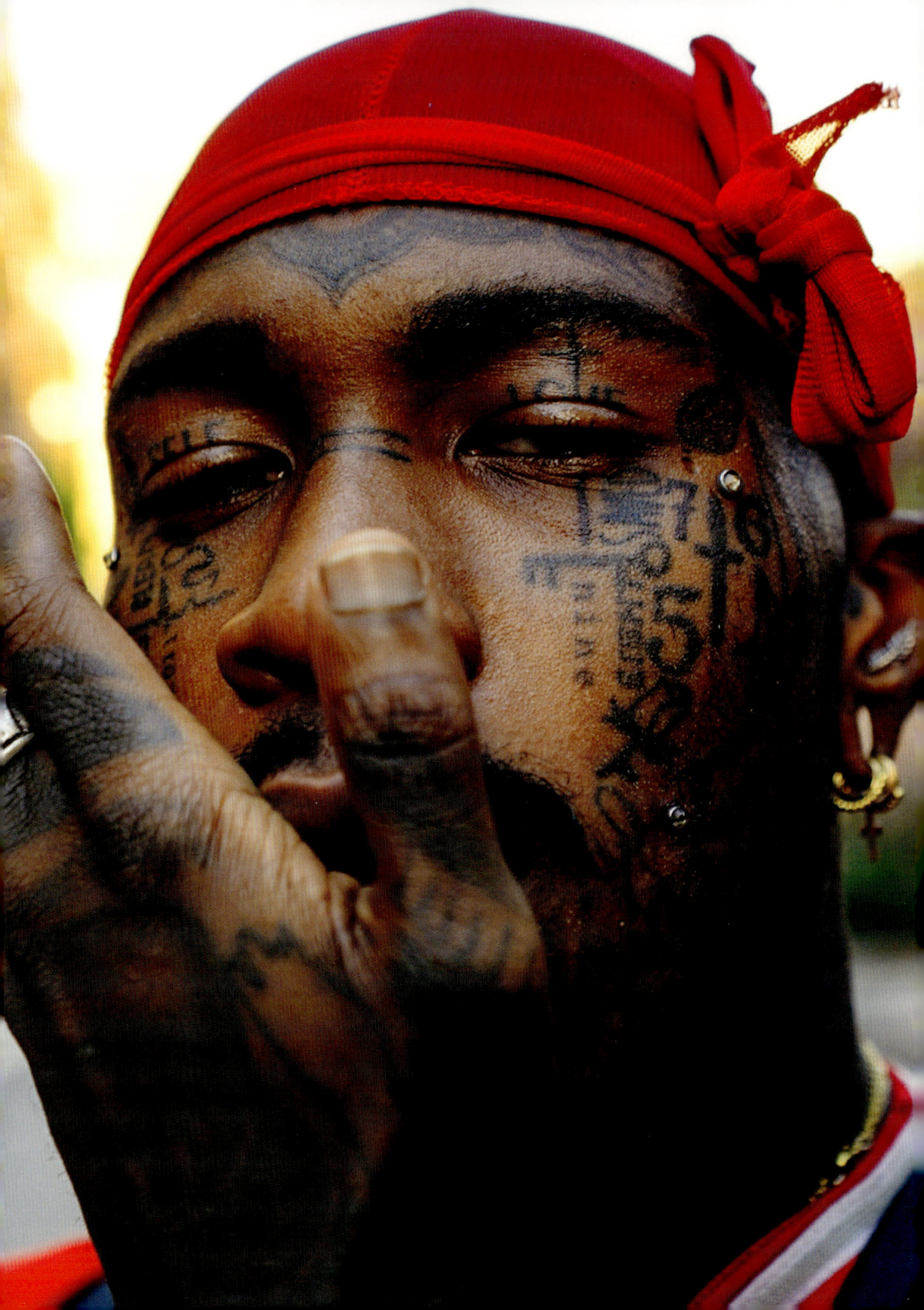

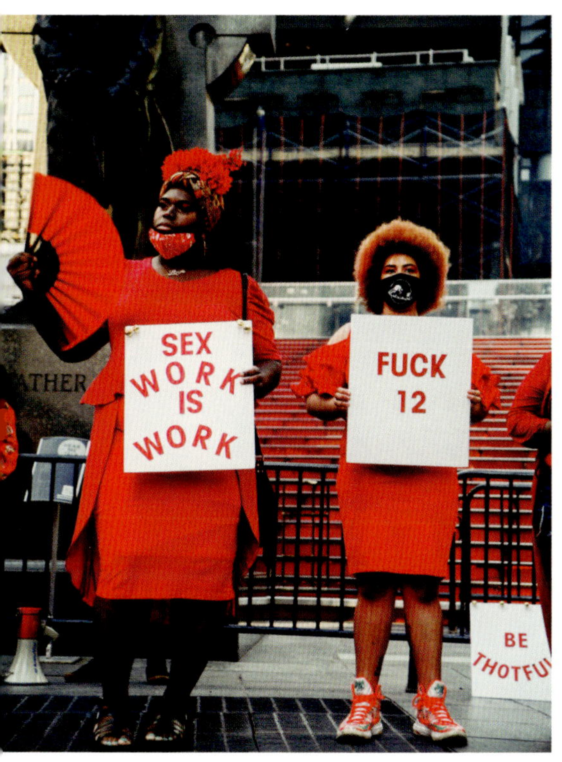

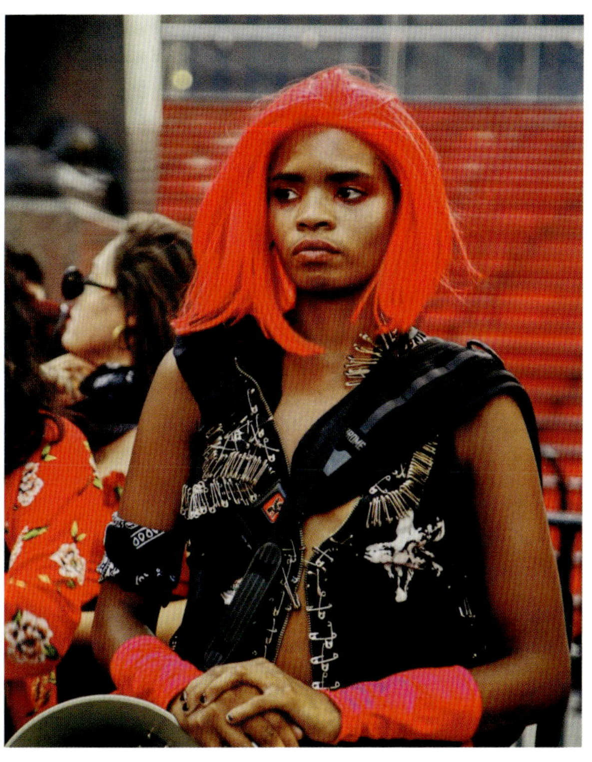

OPPOSITE:
Budi
October 2021

Madison Swart
Black Sex Worker Liberation March
August 2020

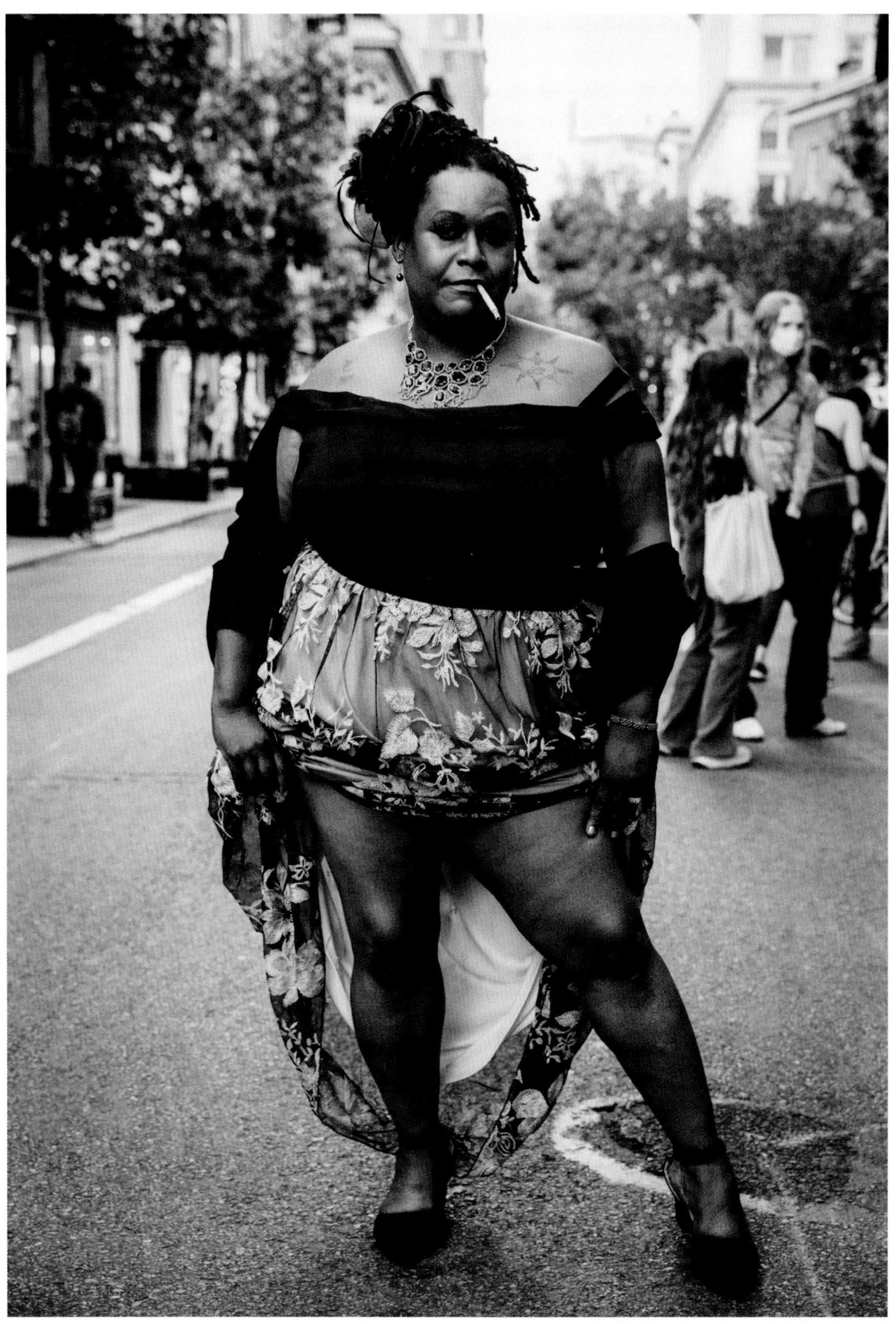

Chae Kihn
September 2020

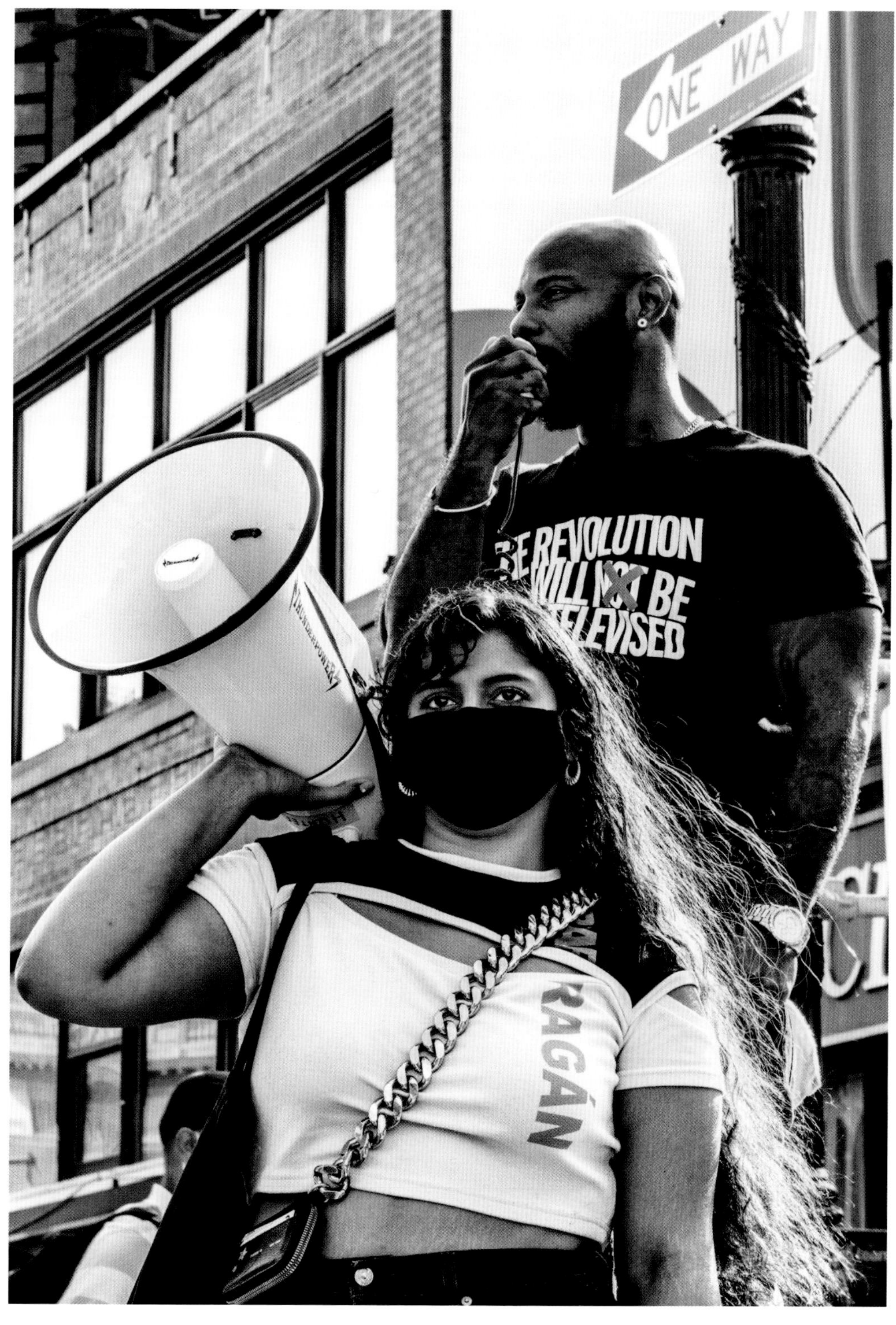
ONE WAY
THE REVOLUTION
WILL NOT BE
TELEVISED
RAGÁN

At the Stonewall Protests everyone had a role. The protestors held signs and banners. The musicians played instruments as we marched and danced. The People's Bodega provided food, and the bikers, under constant threat, created a wall of protection. It was impossible to document this movement without becoming involved. The activists became photographers, and the photographers became activists.

—Chae Kihn

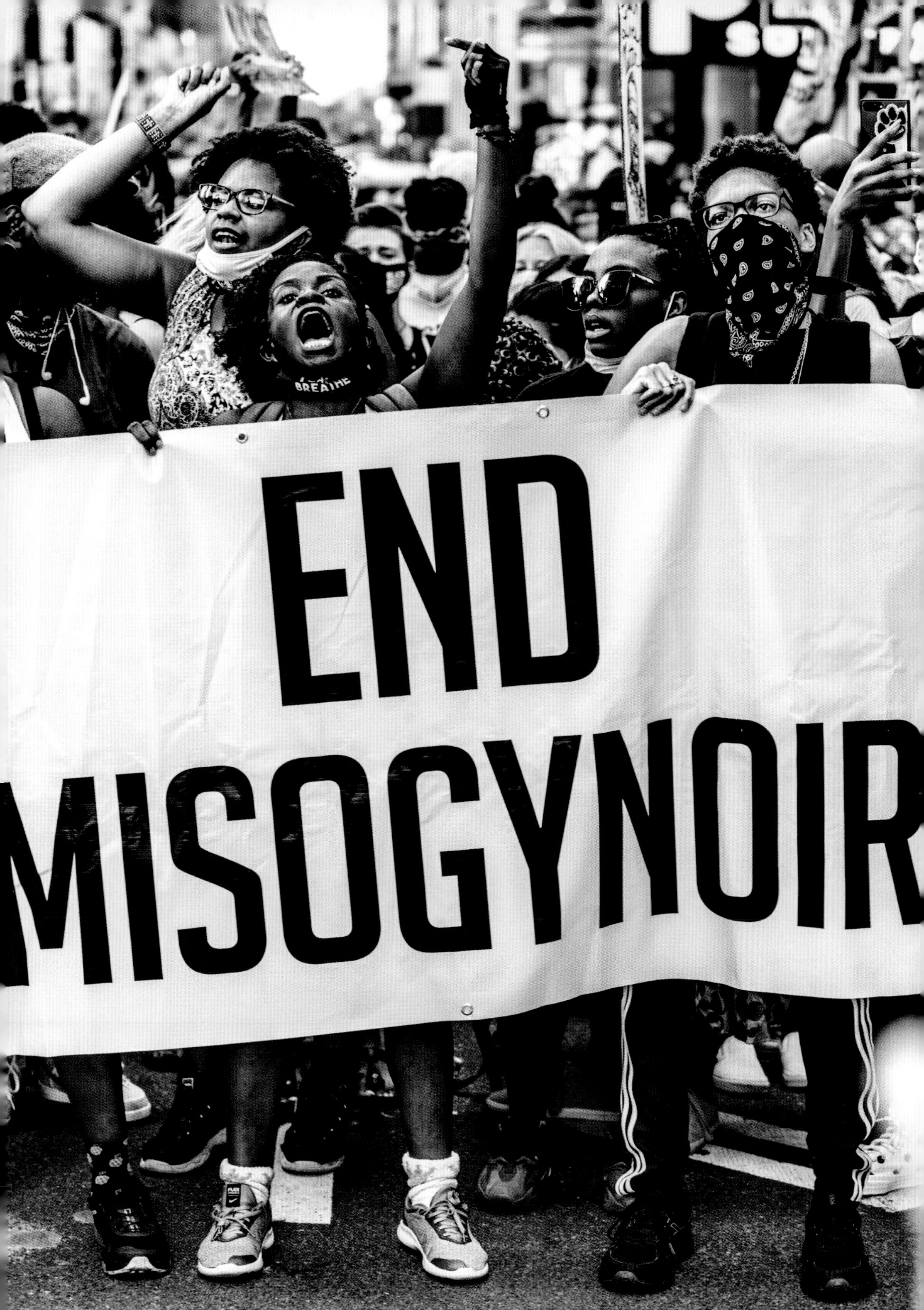
END
MISOGYNOIR
BREATHE

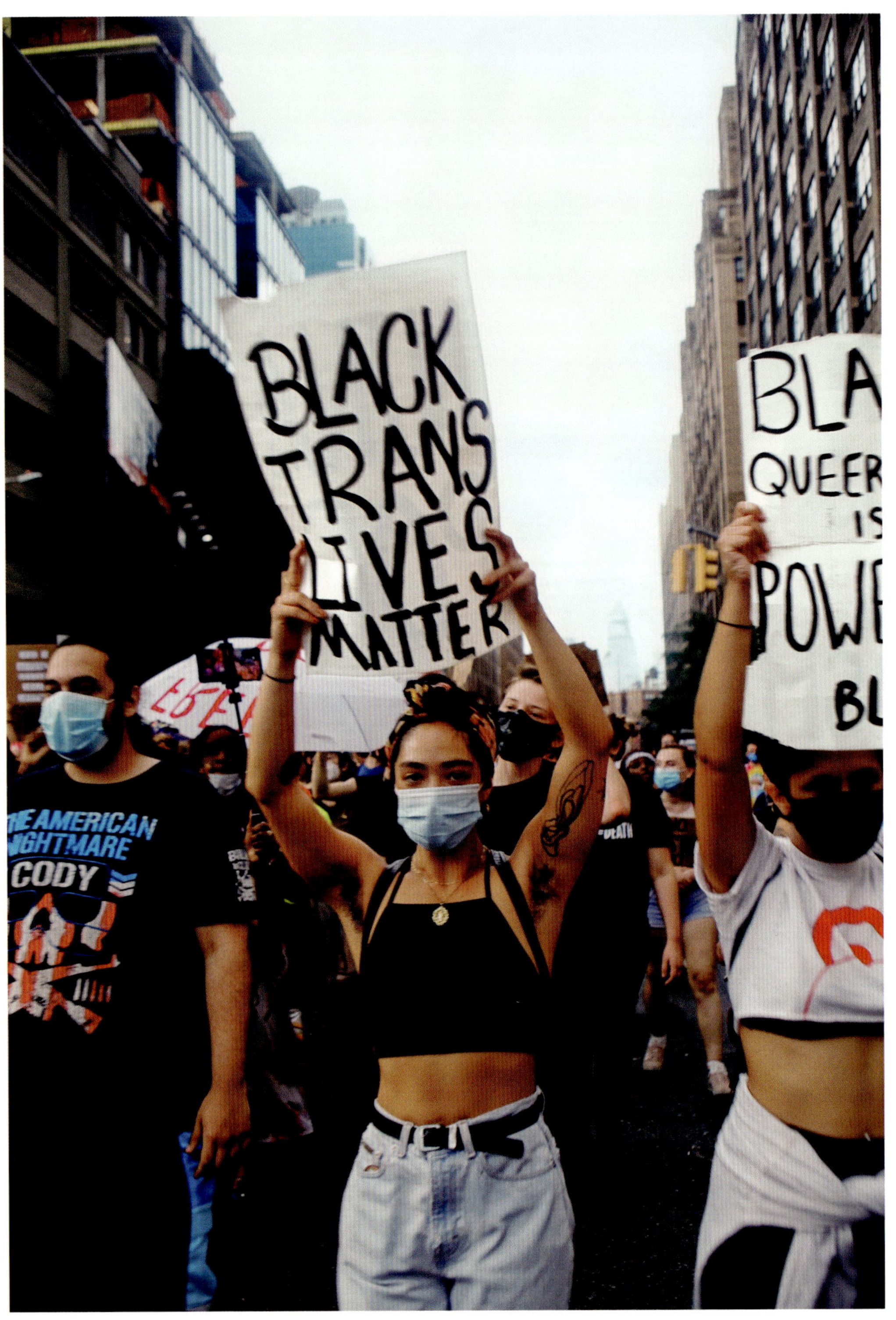

ABOVE AND OPPOSITE TOP:
Madison Swart
Trans Liberation March
July 2020

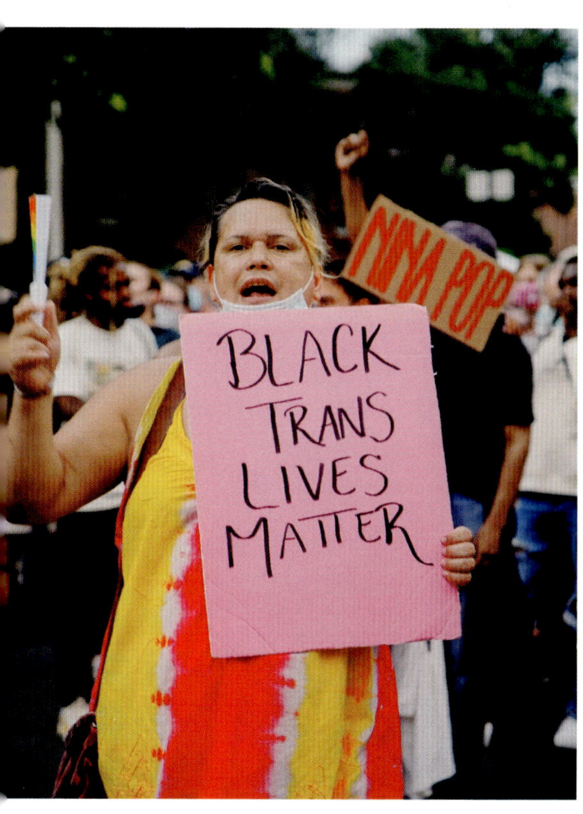

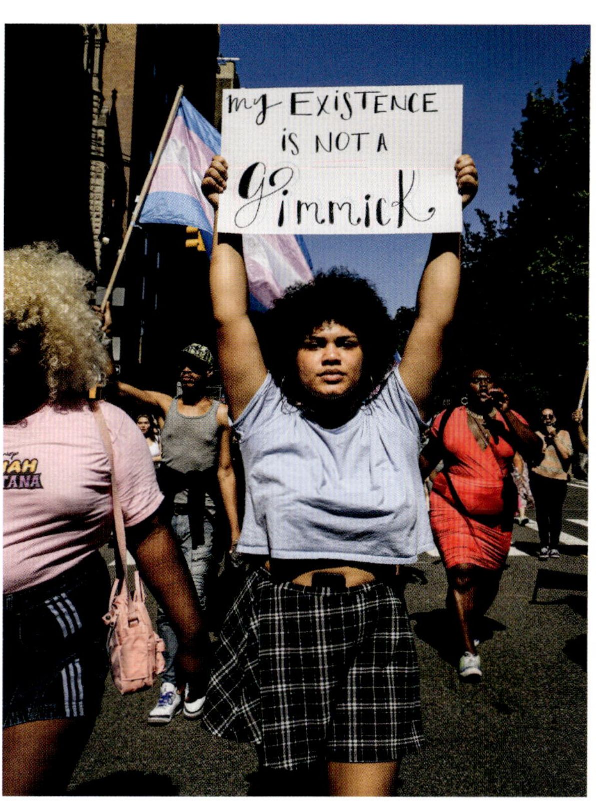

Katie Godowski
September 2021

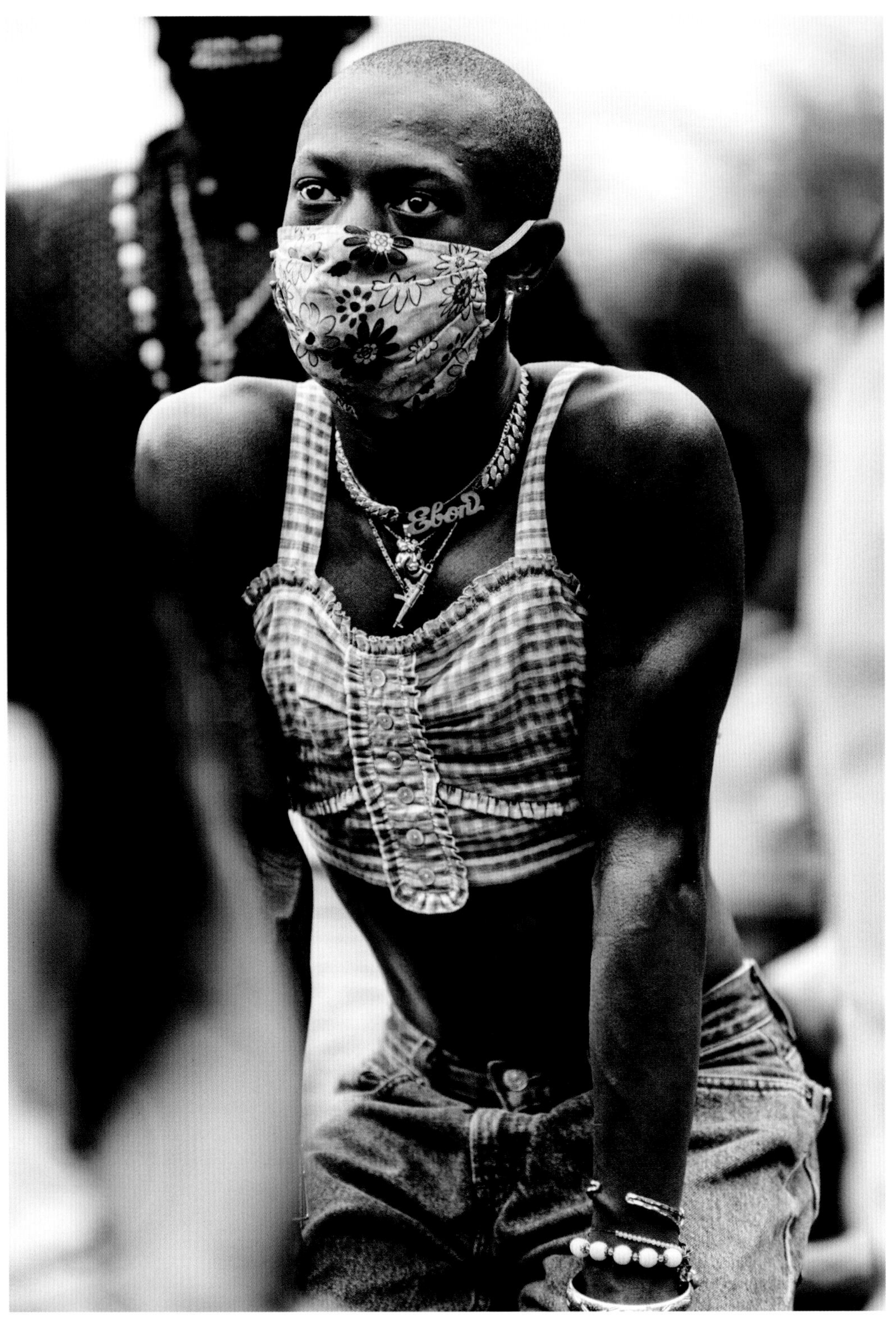

Souls of a Movement
Marsha's March & 75th Birthday
August 2020

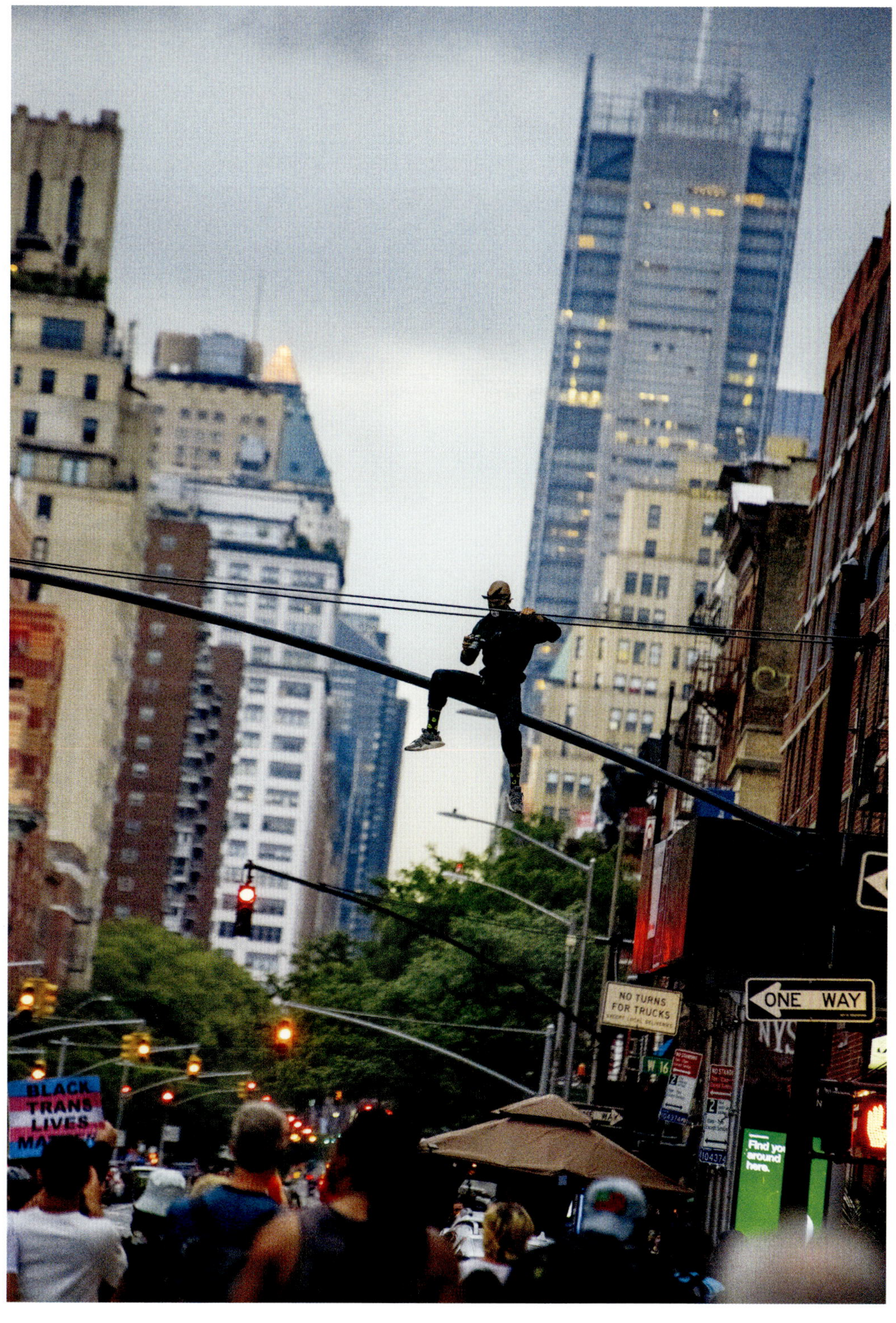

Ryan McGinley
September 2020

NEXT SPREAD:
Souls of a Movement
The Forgotten Children's Youth March
September 2020

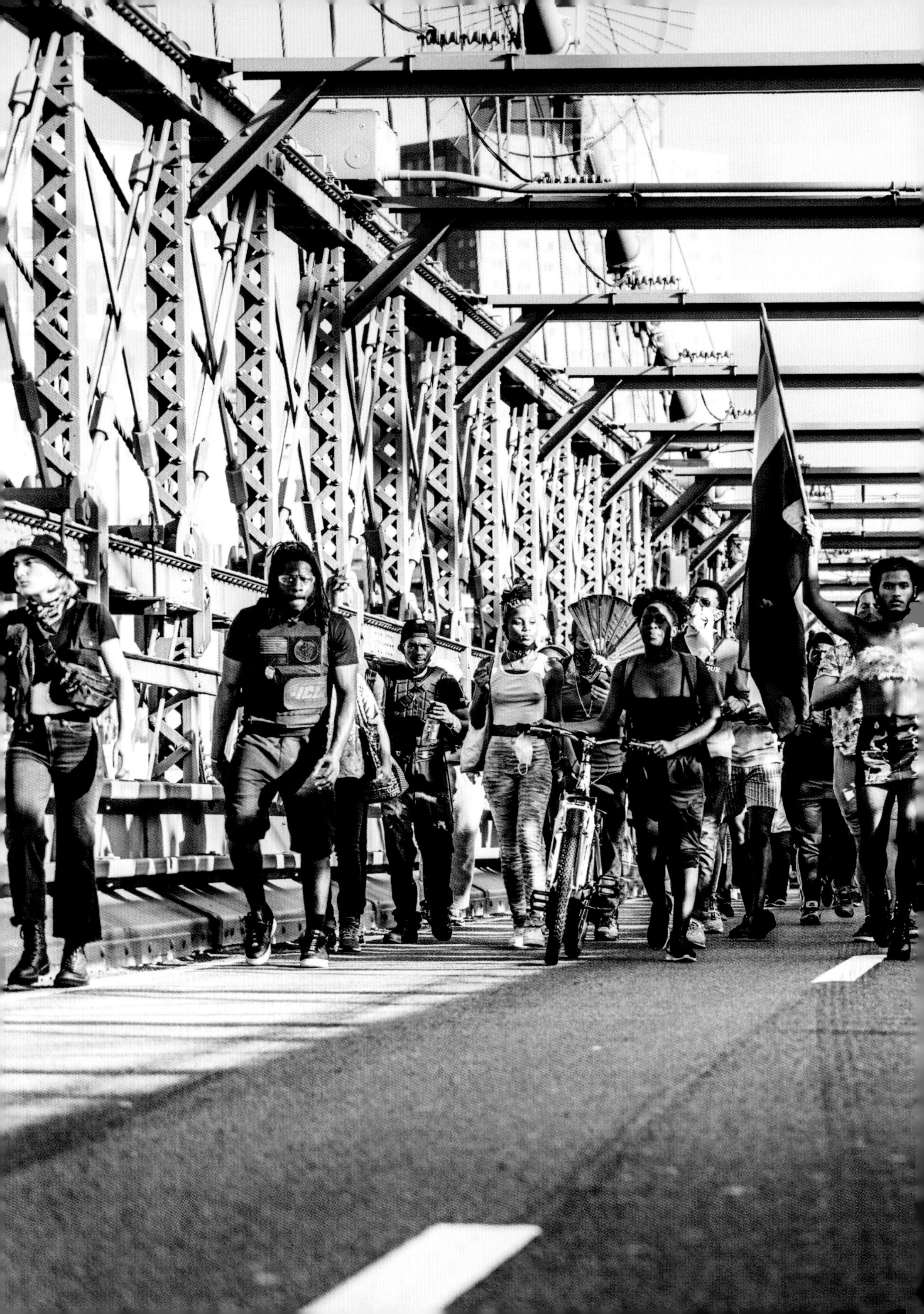

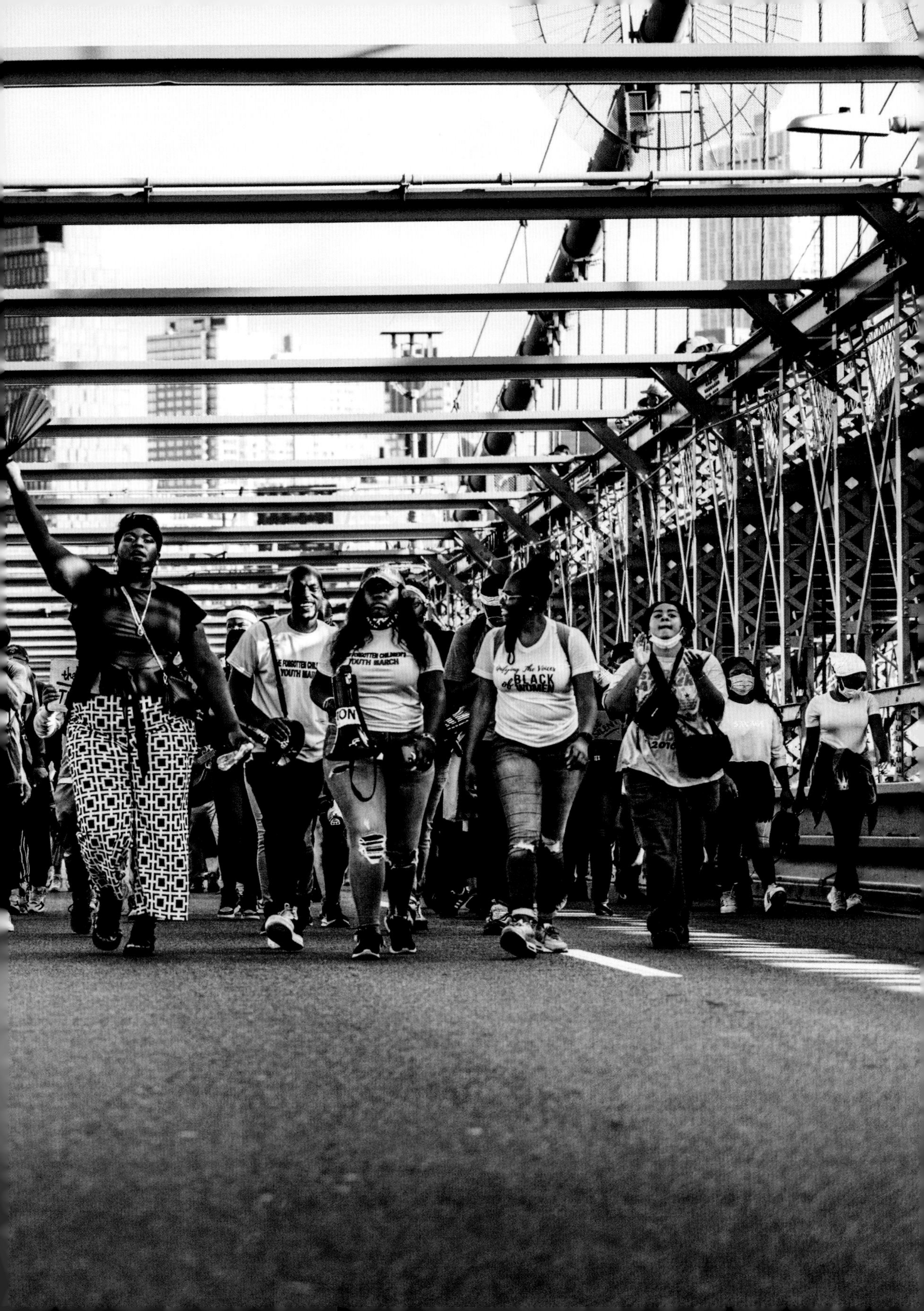

In the face of significant pain, this community exuded brazen bravery and unfiltered joy. Instead of hate, love. Despite despair, hope. From vulnerability, courage. Out of complacency, change.

—Deb Fong

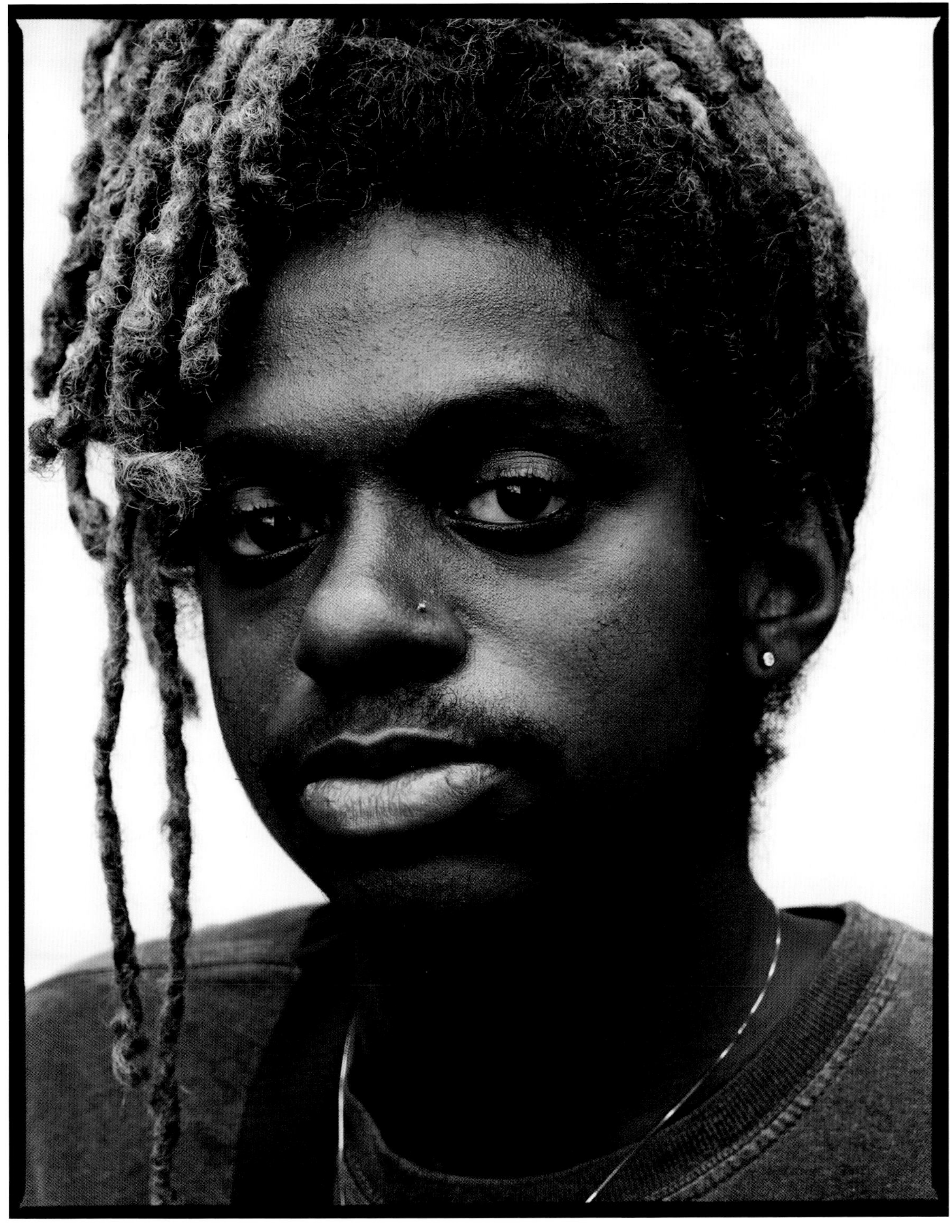

**Stas Ginzburg
The Forgotten Children's Youth March
September 2020**

39

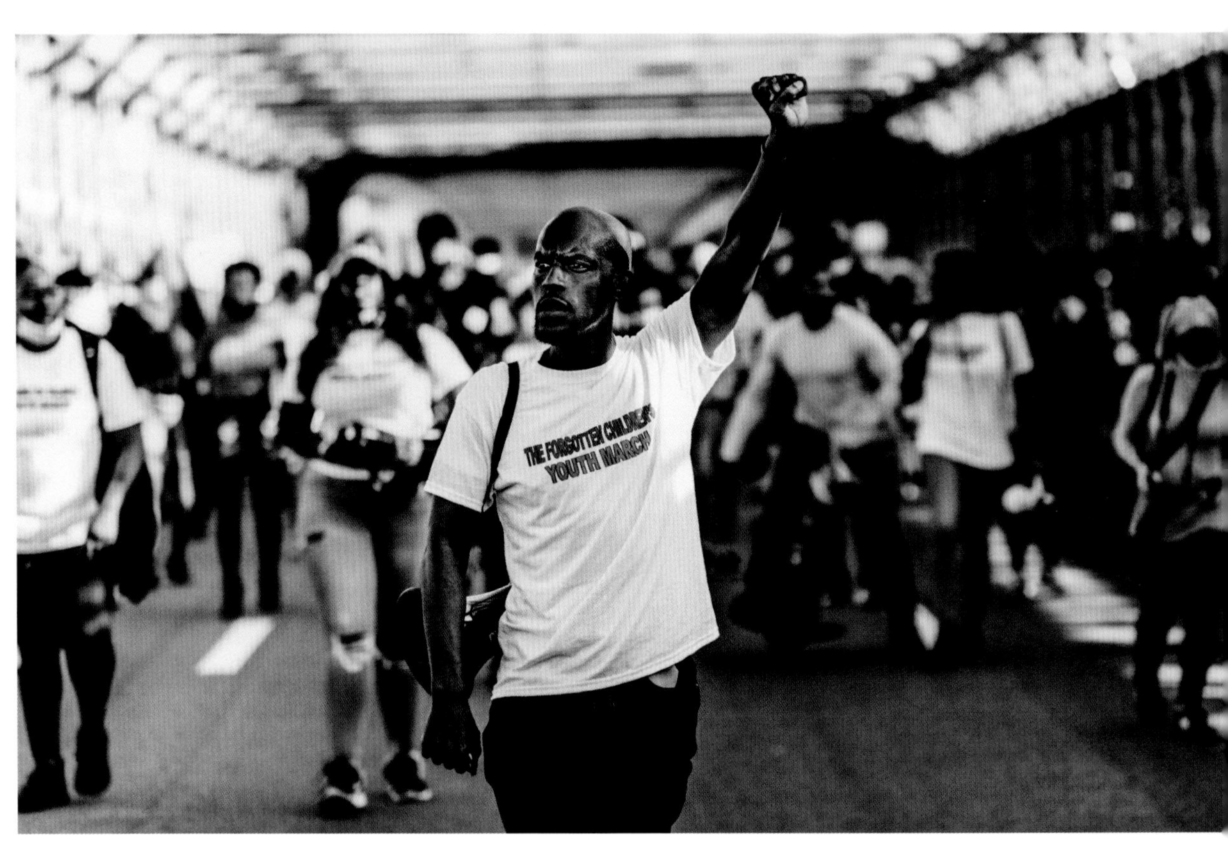

Souls of a Movement
The Forgotten Children's Youth March
September 2020

OPPOSITE:
Cindy Trinh
The Forgotten Children's Youth March
September 2020

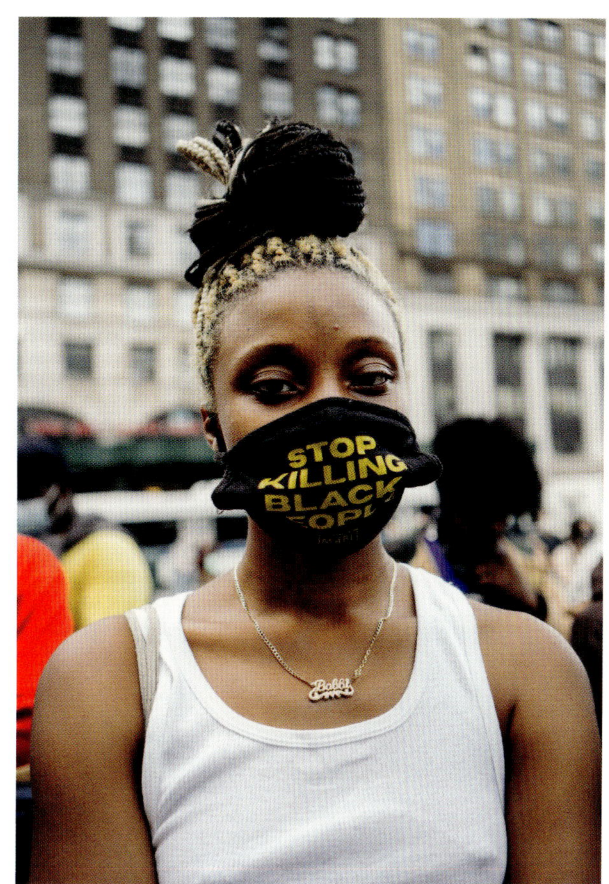

STOP
KILLING
BLACK
PEOPLE

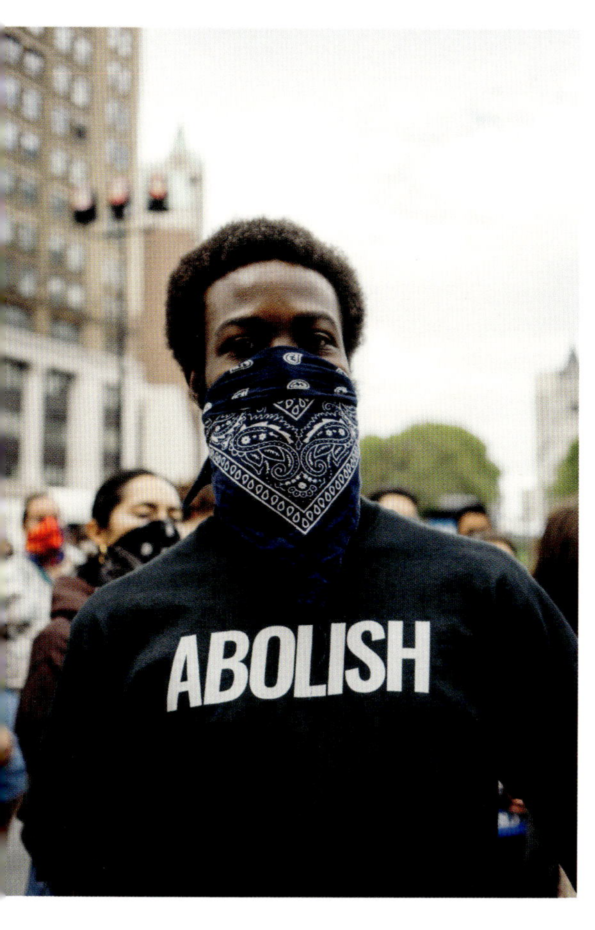

ABOLISH

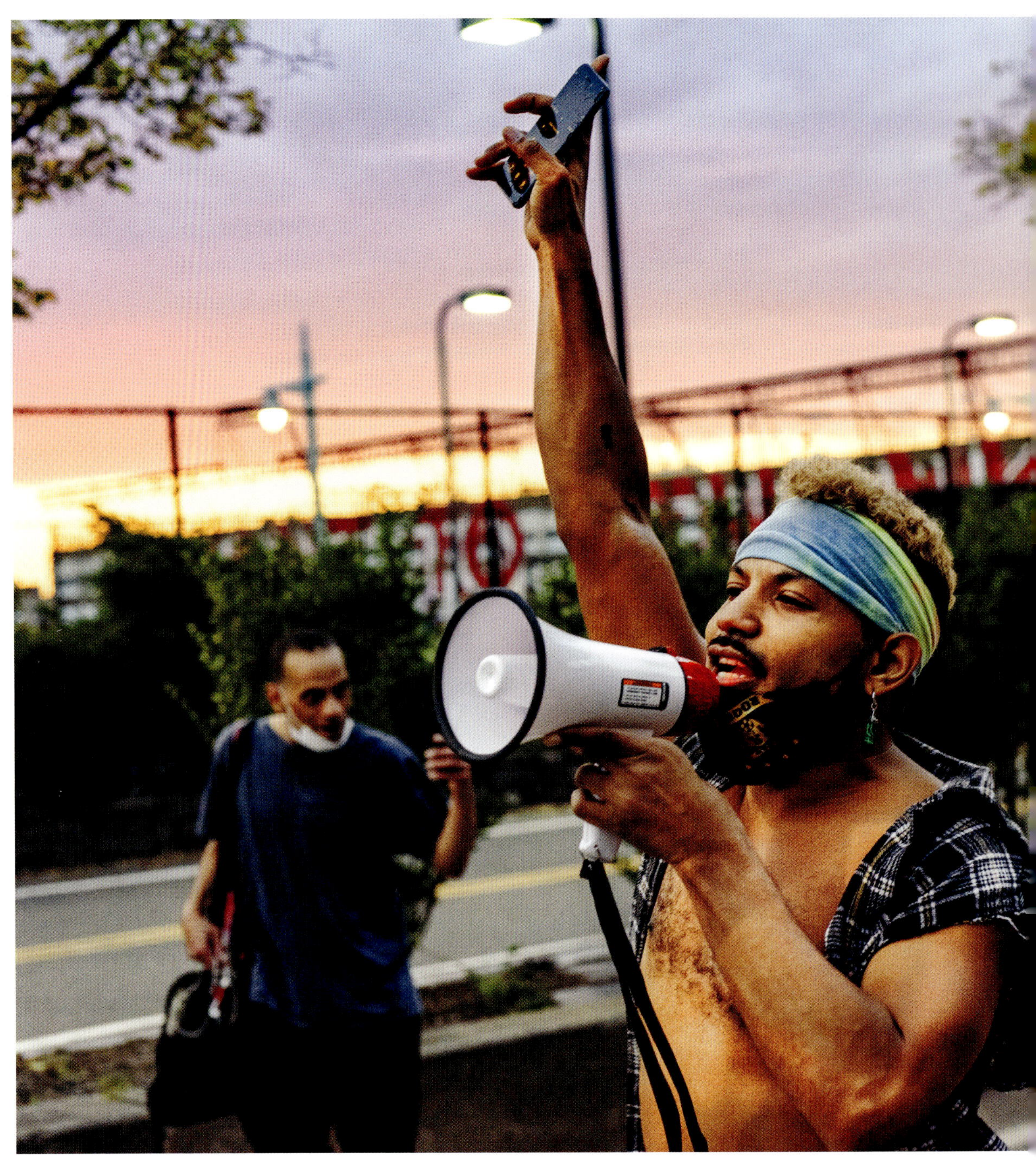

Zak Krevitt
October 2020

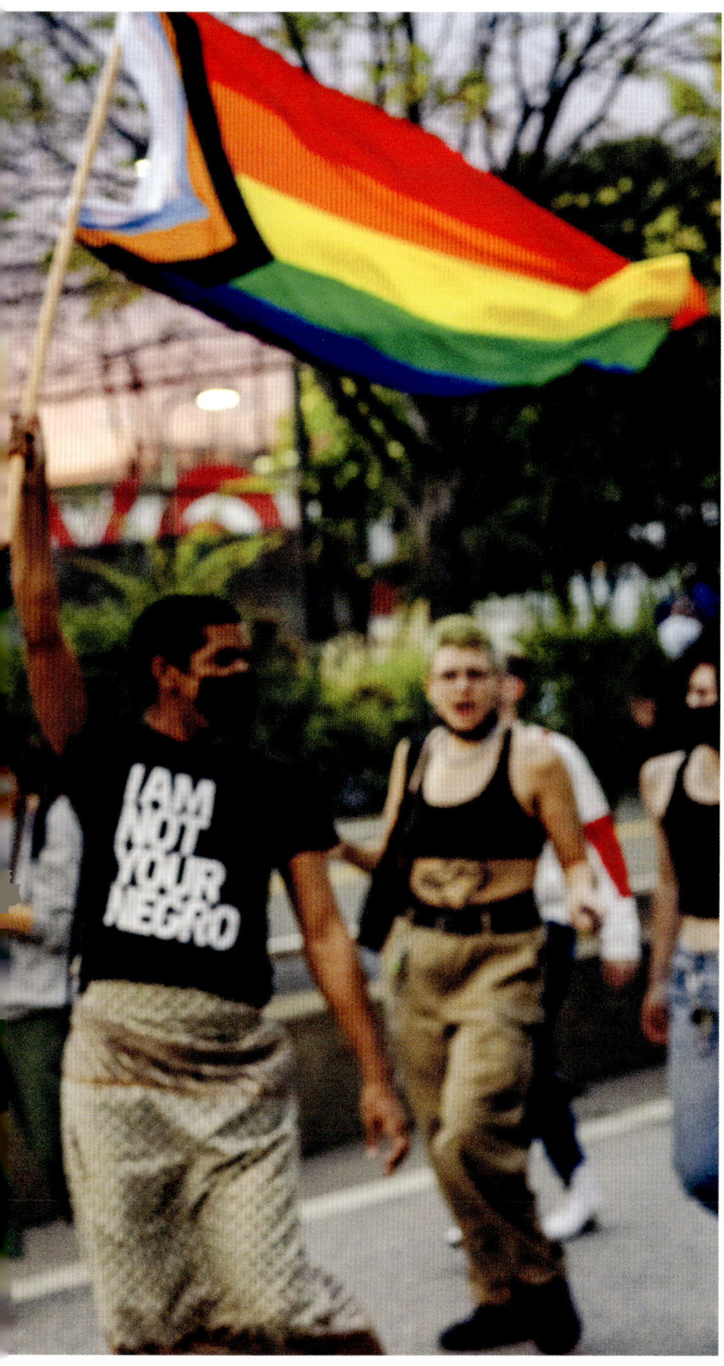

I AM
NOT
YOUR
NEGRO

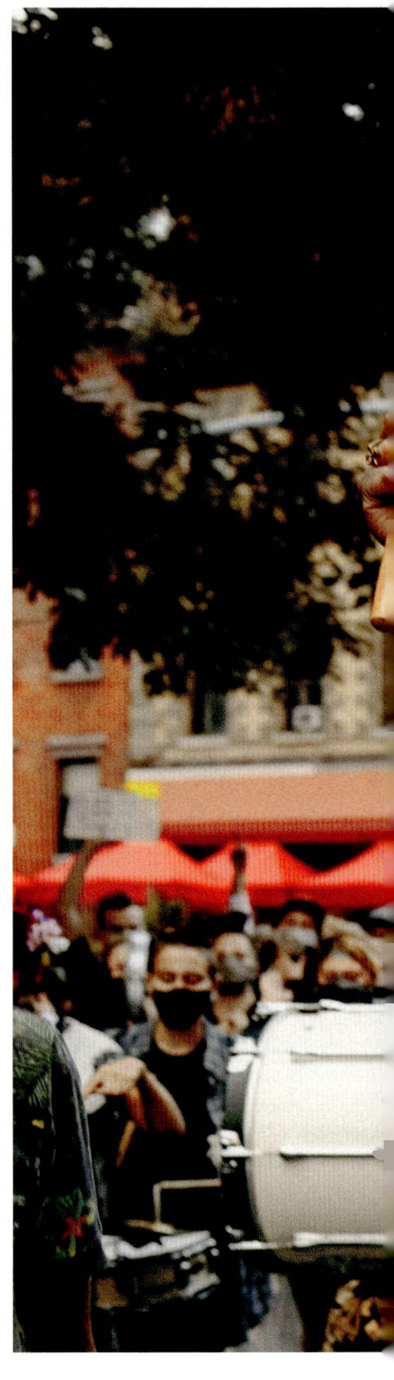

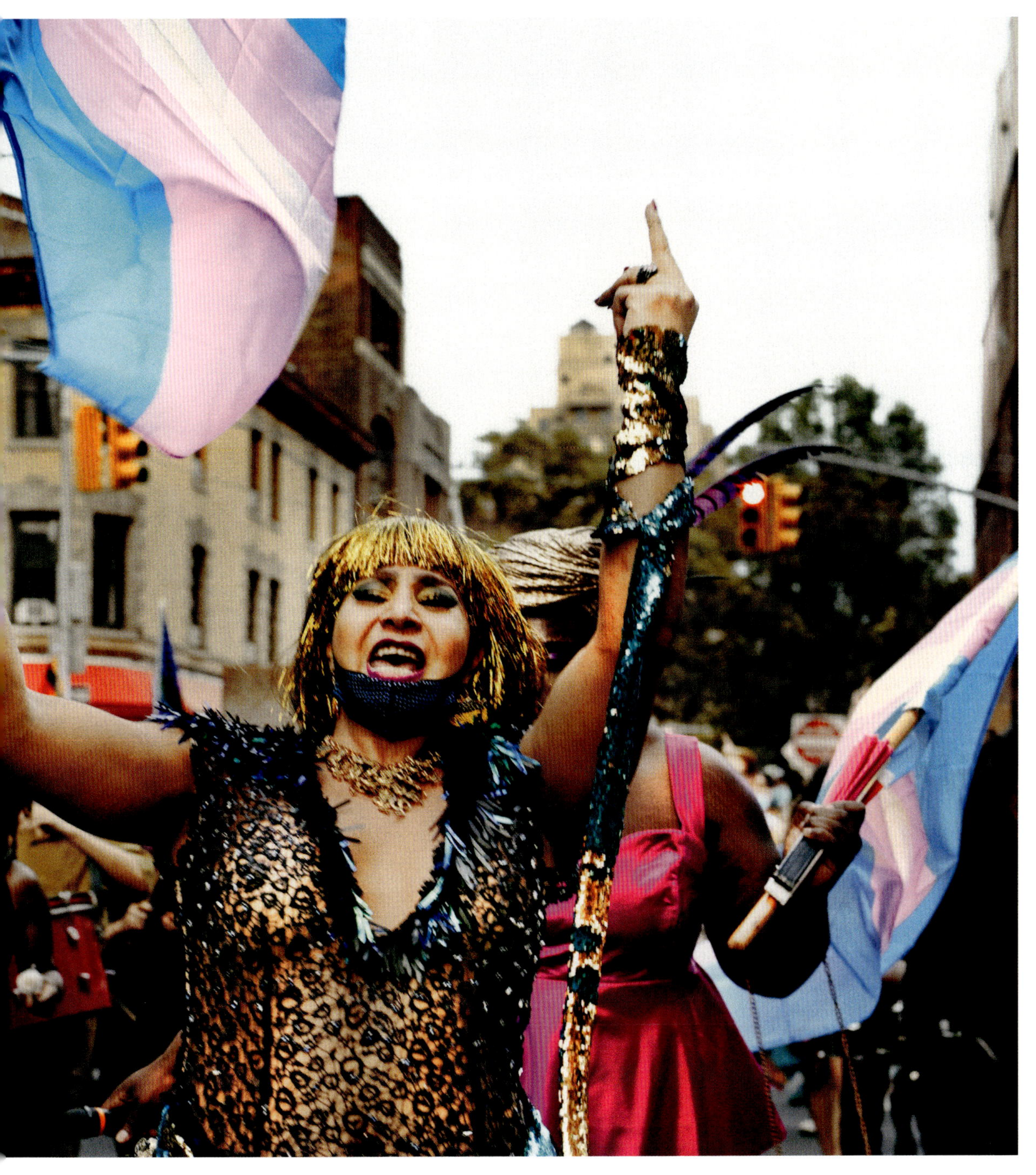

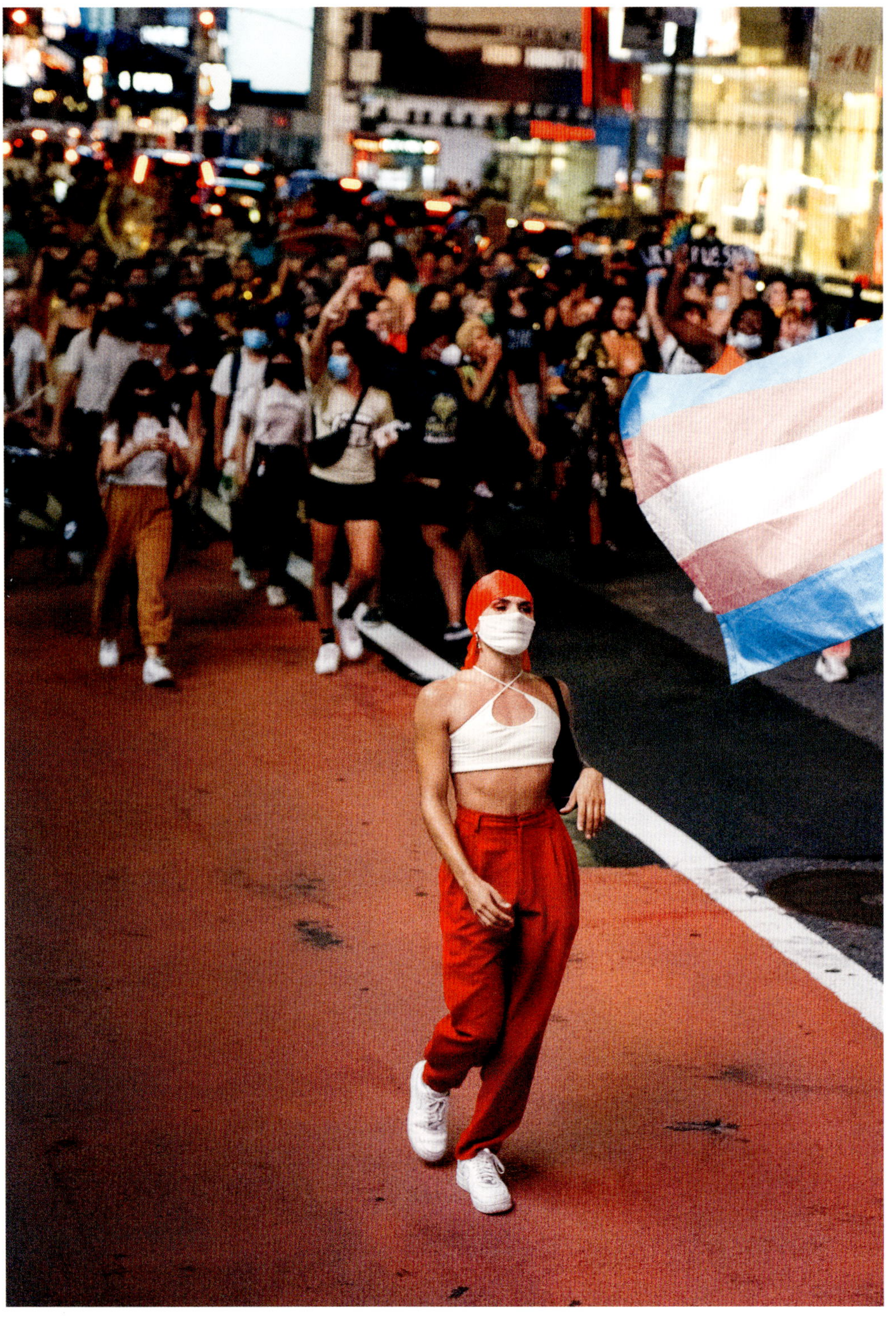

Ryan McGinley
September 2020

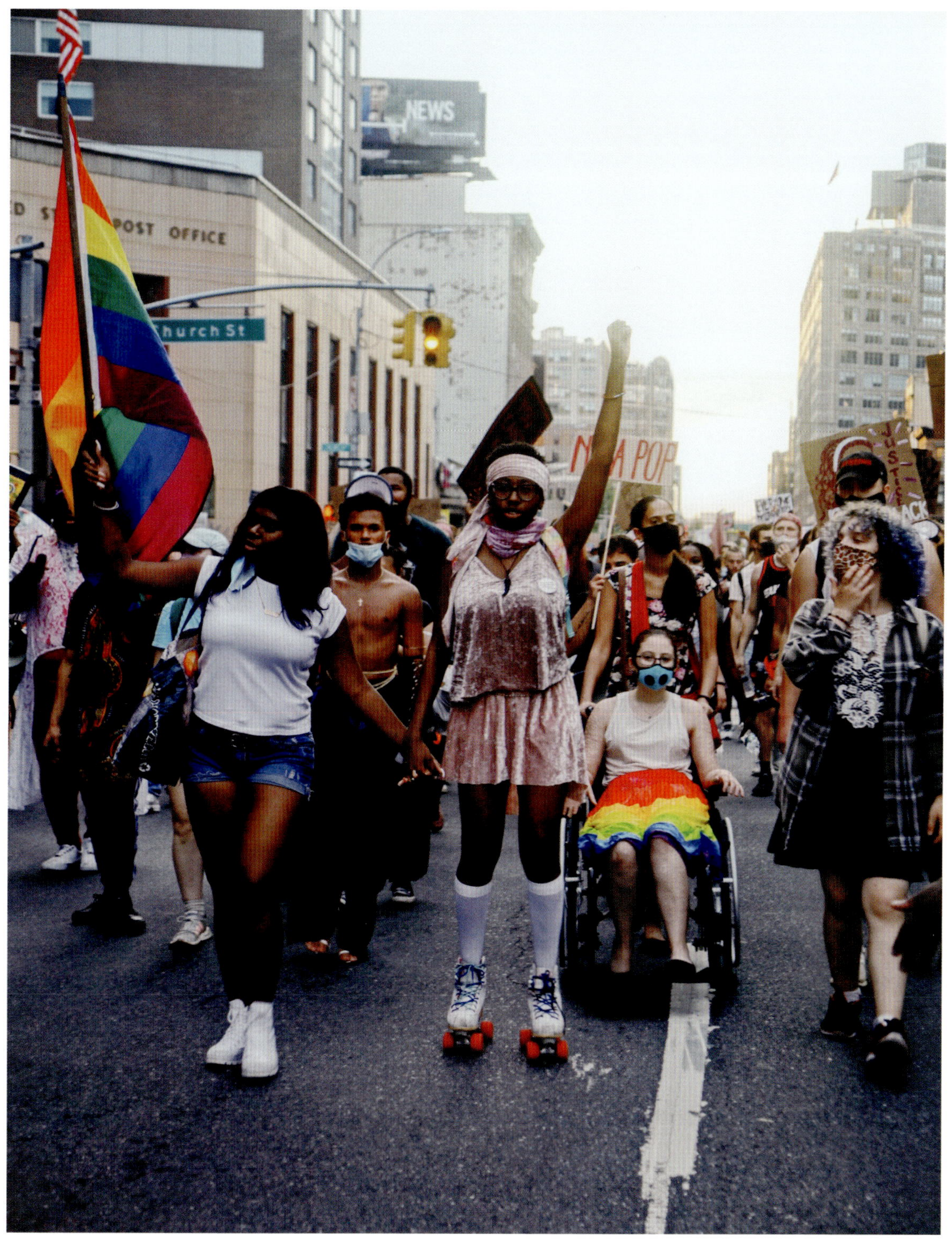

Madison Swart
Trans Liberation March
July 2020

Marching is visibility; it changes hearts and minds. Remember Stonewall was a RI-OT! The photos in this book are seeds for the next queer revolution. I believe in change; I believe that we will win. Black Trans Lives Matter.

—Ryan McGinley

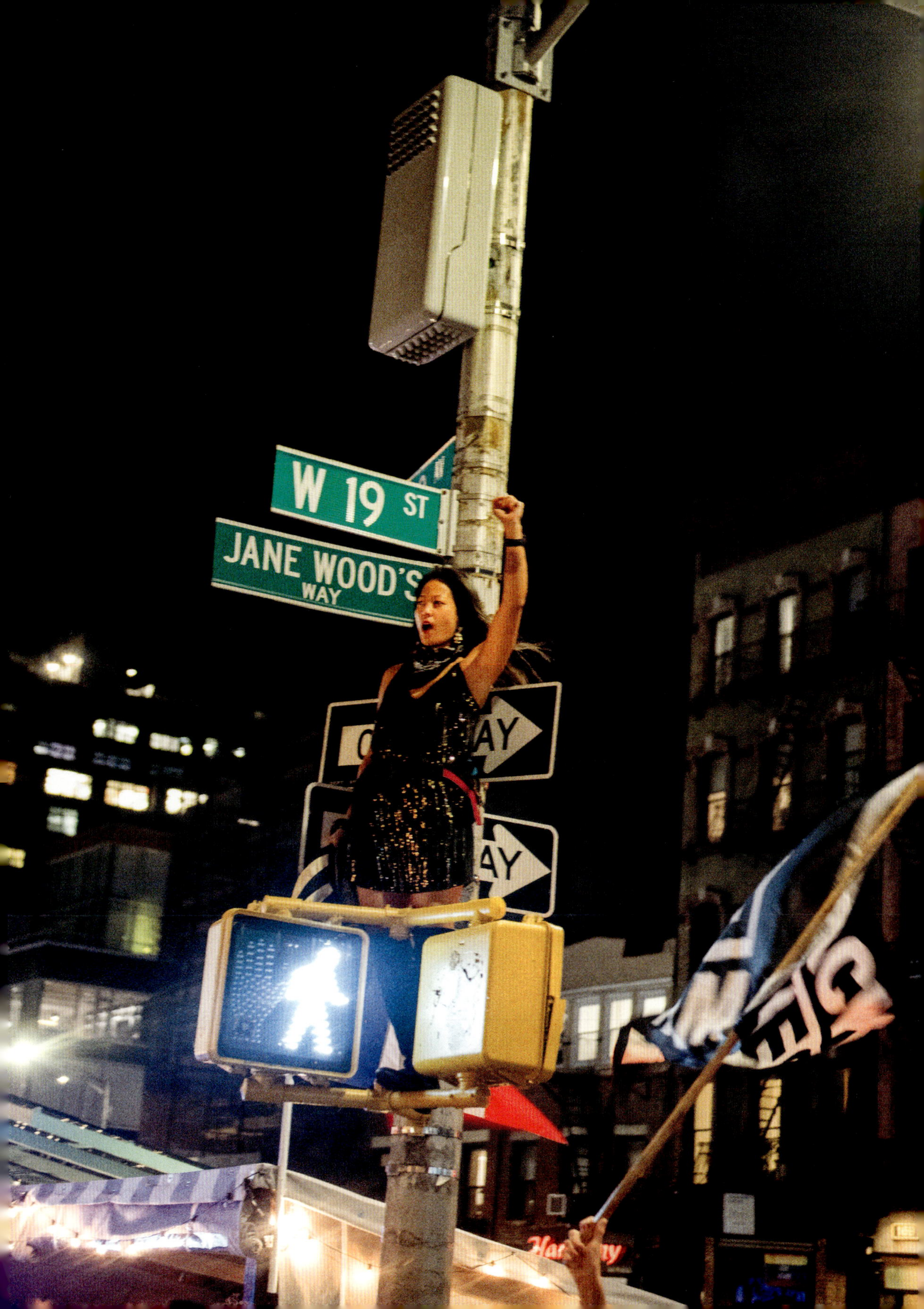

W 19 ST
JANE WOOD'S WAY

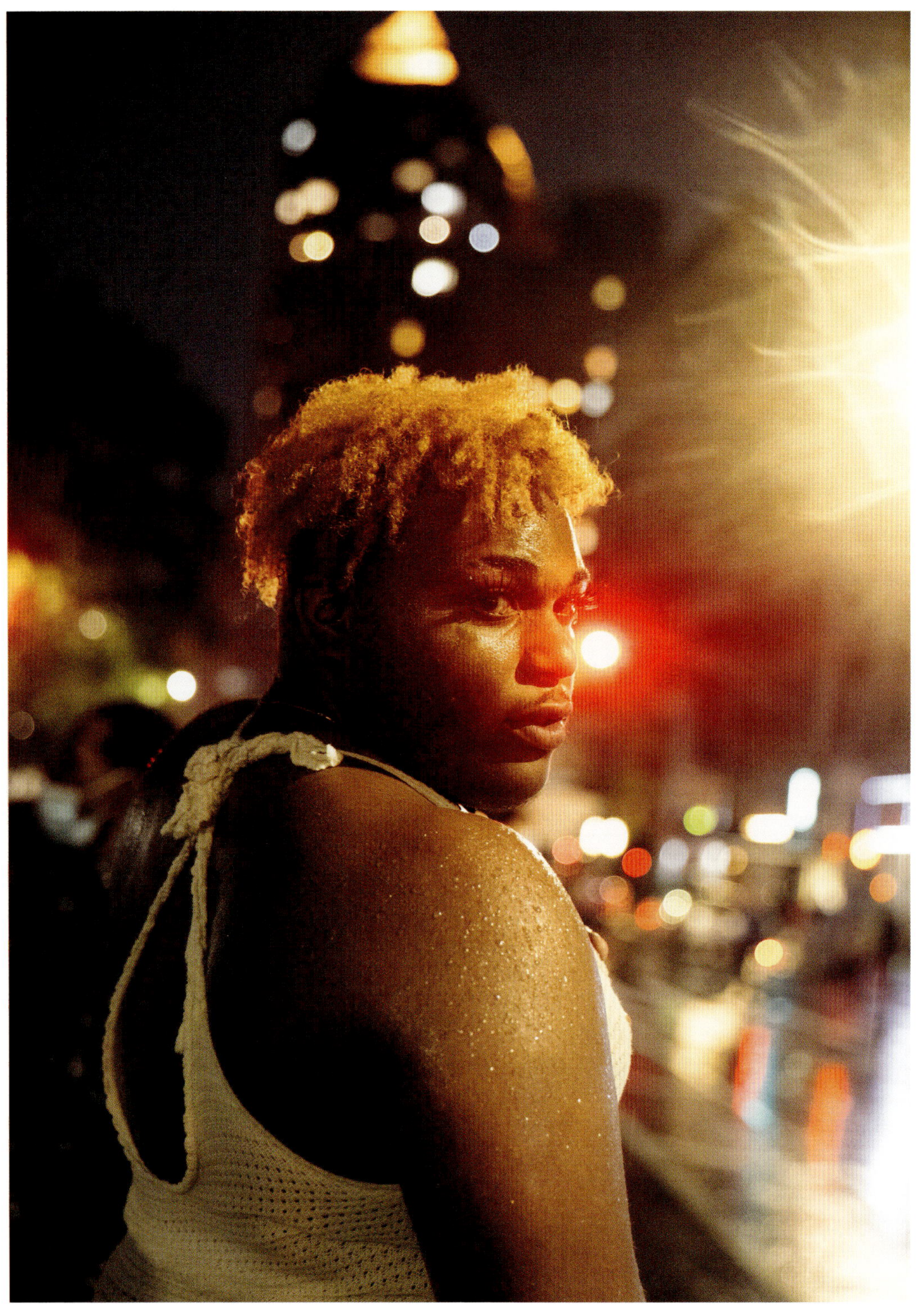

Erica Lansner
We Are Pride
June 2021

Ryan McGinley
Illumination Ball
October 2020

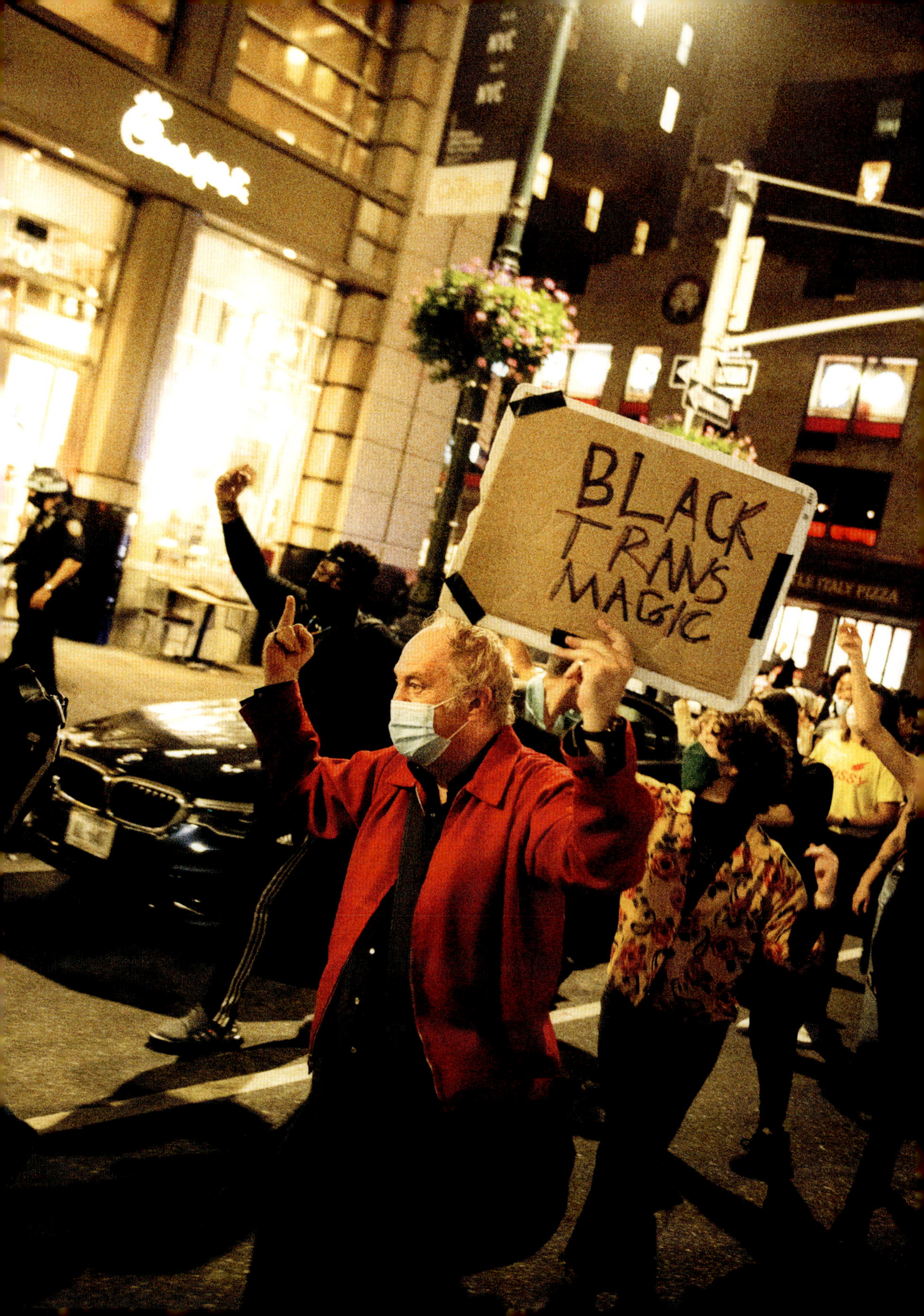
BLACK
TRANS
MAGIC

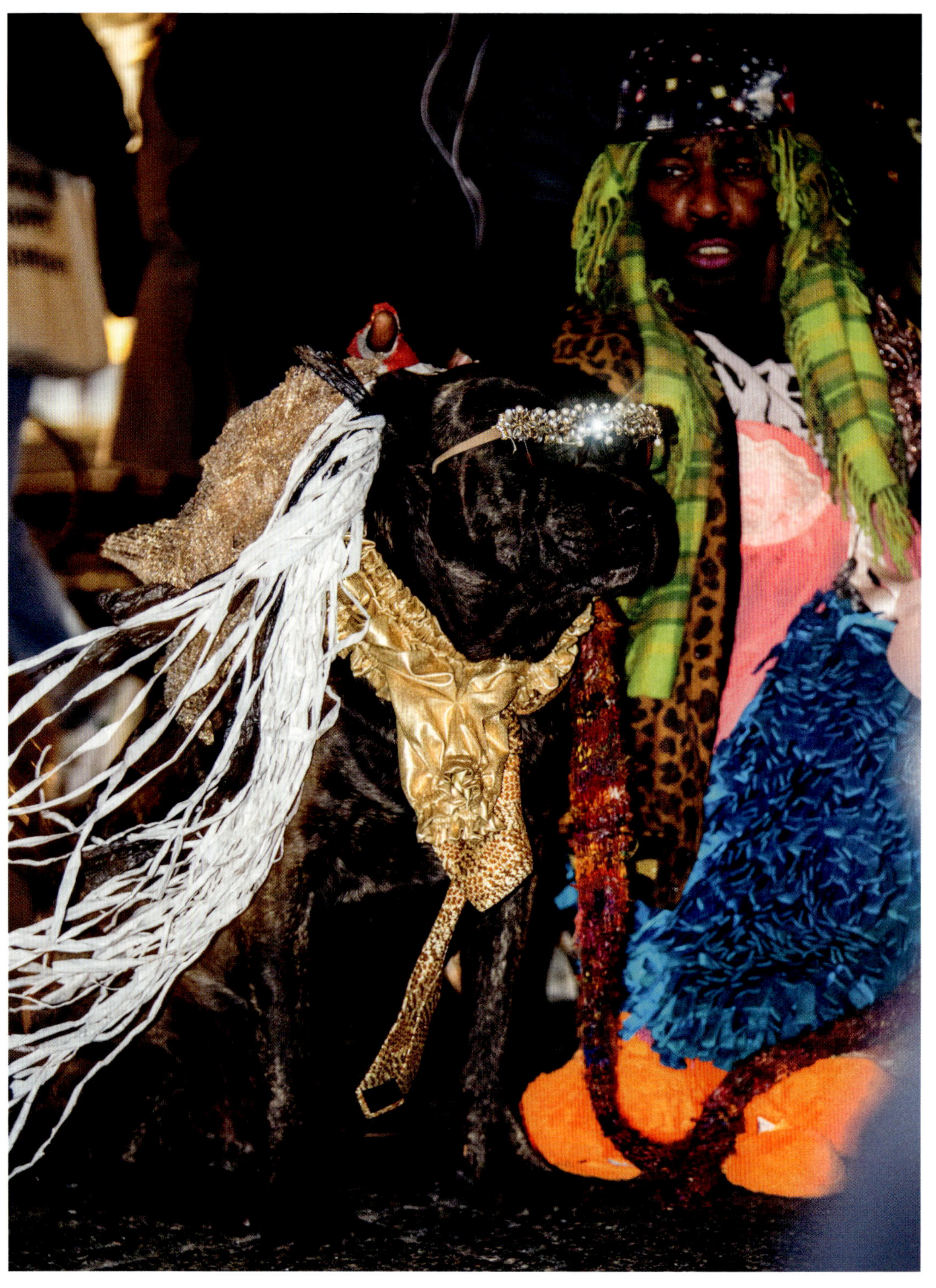

Ruvan Wijesooriya
January 2021

Snake Garcia
May 2021

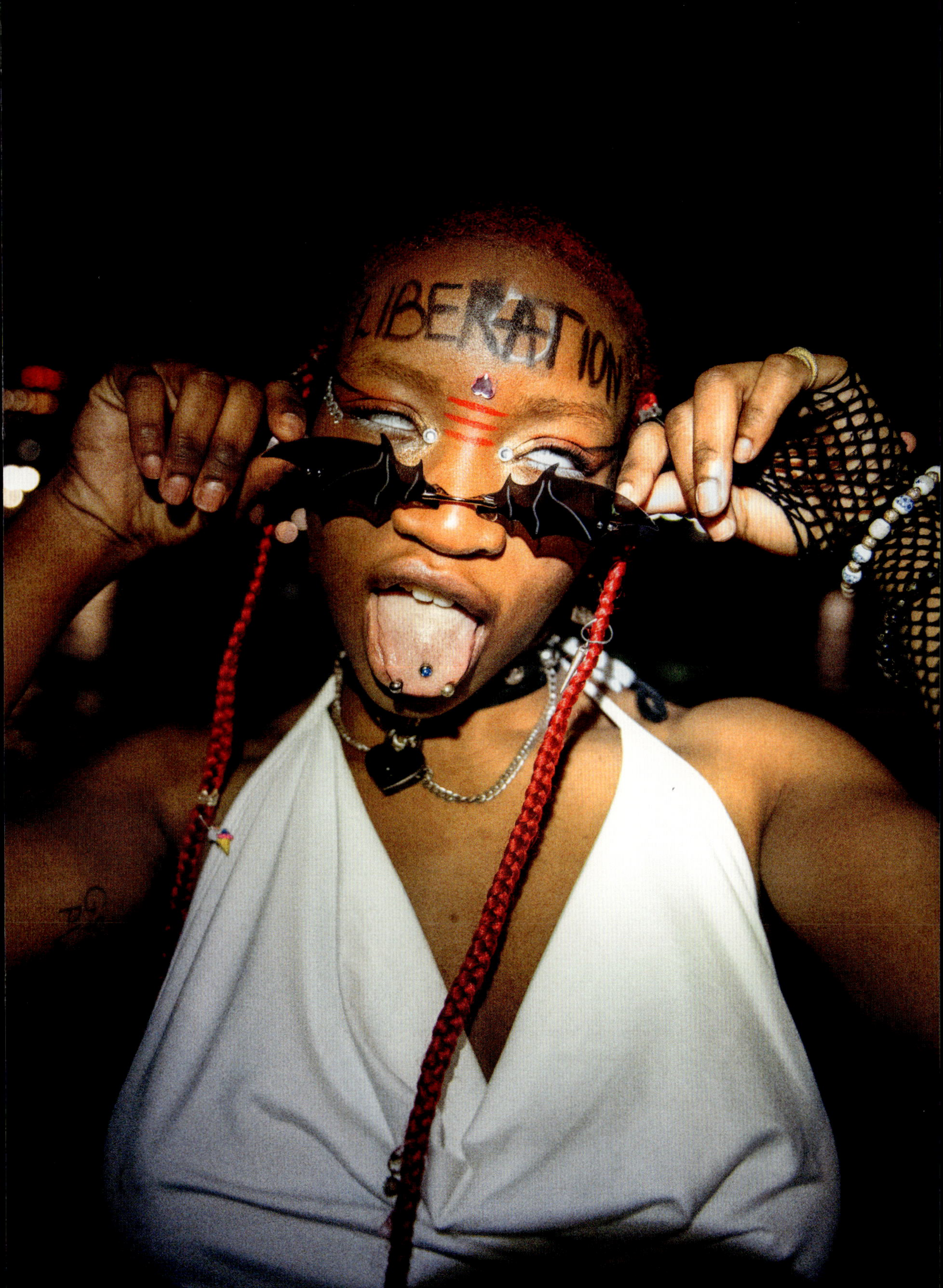

LIBERATION

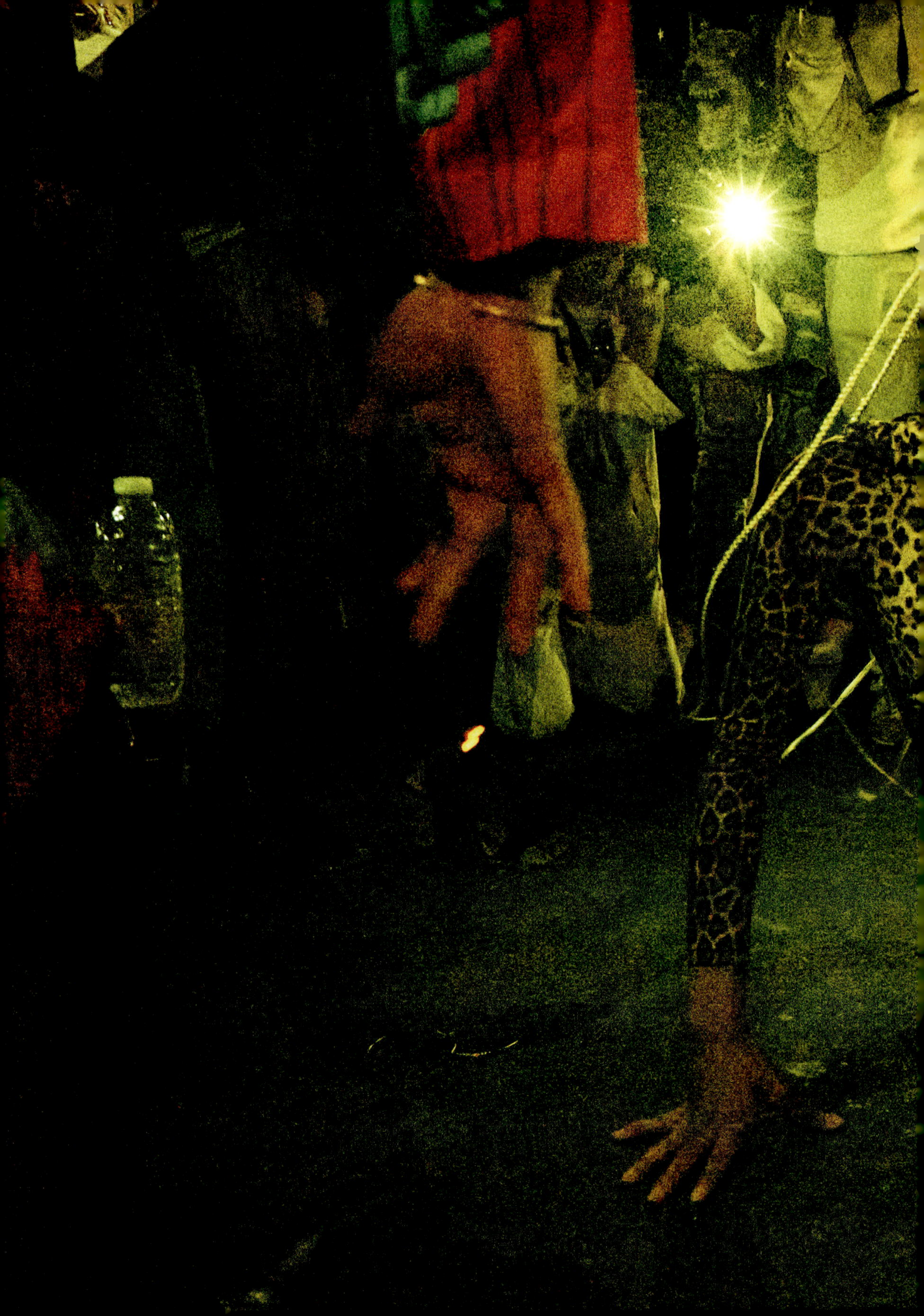

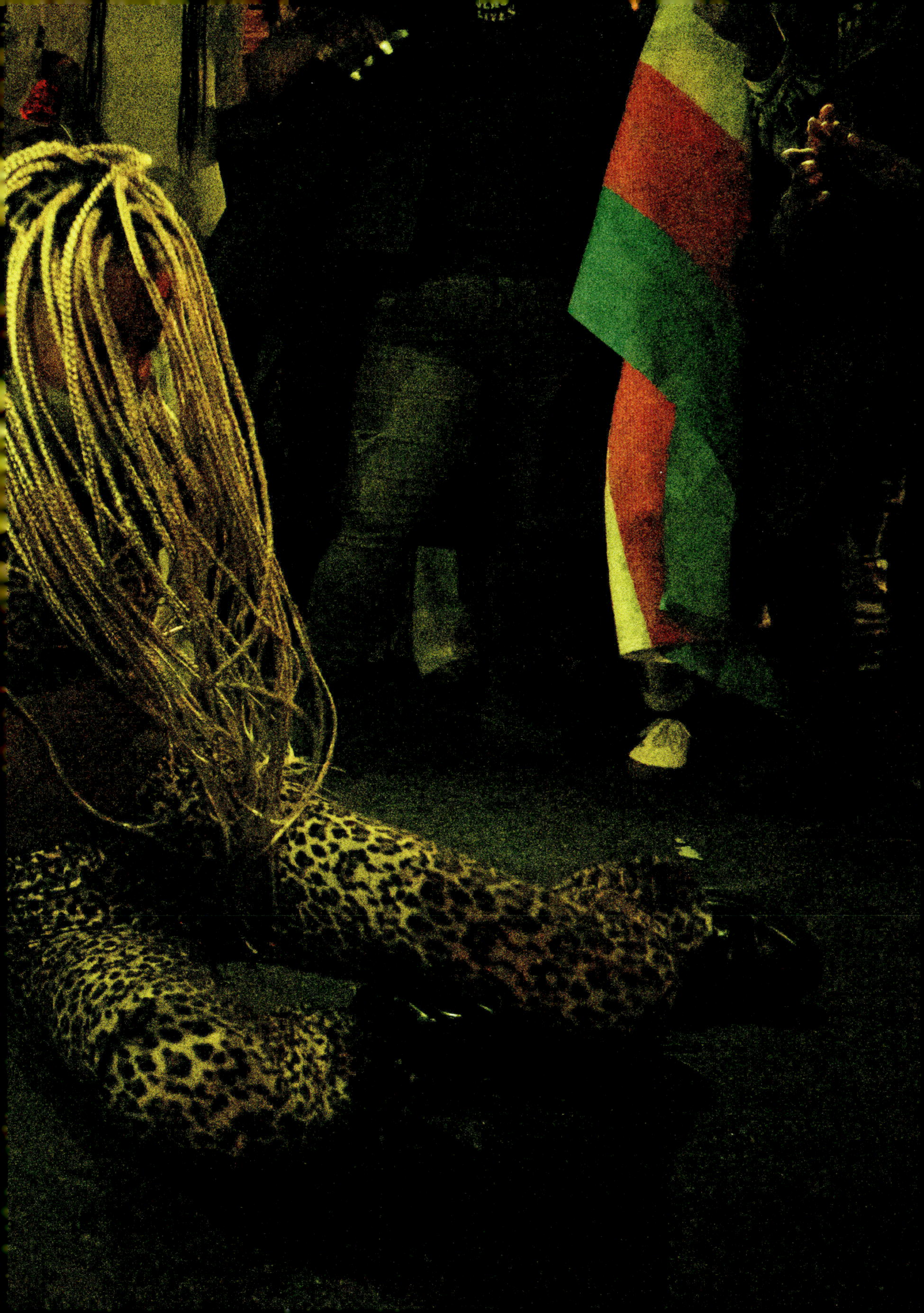

Every Thursday before speeches started, Qween and Joela would turn on the music and dance.
Why dance? As Qween explains, "because there is nothing more powerful than Black joy. It's the freedom and strength to decide to live in joy, not hatred or pain." That is real power; that is real joy.

—Chae Kihn

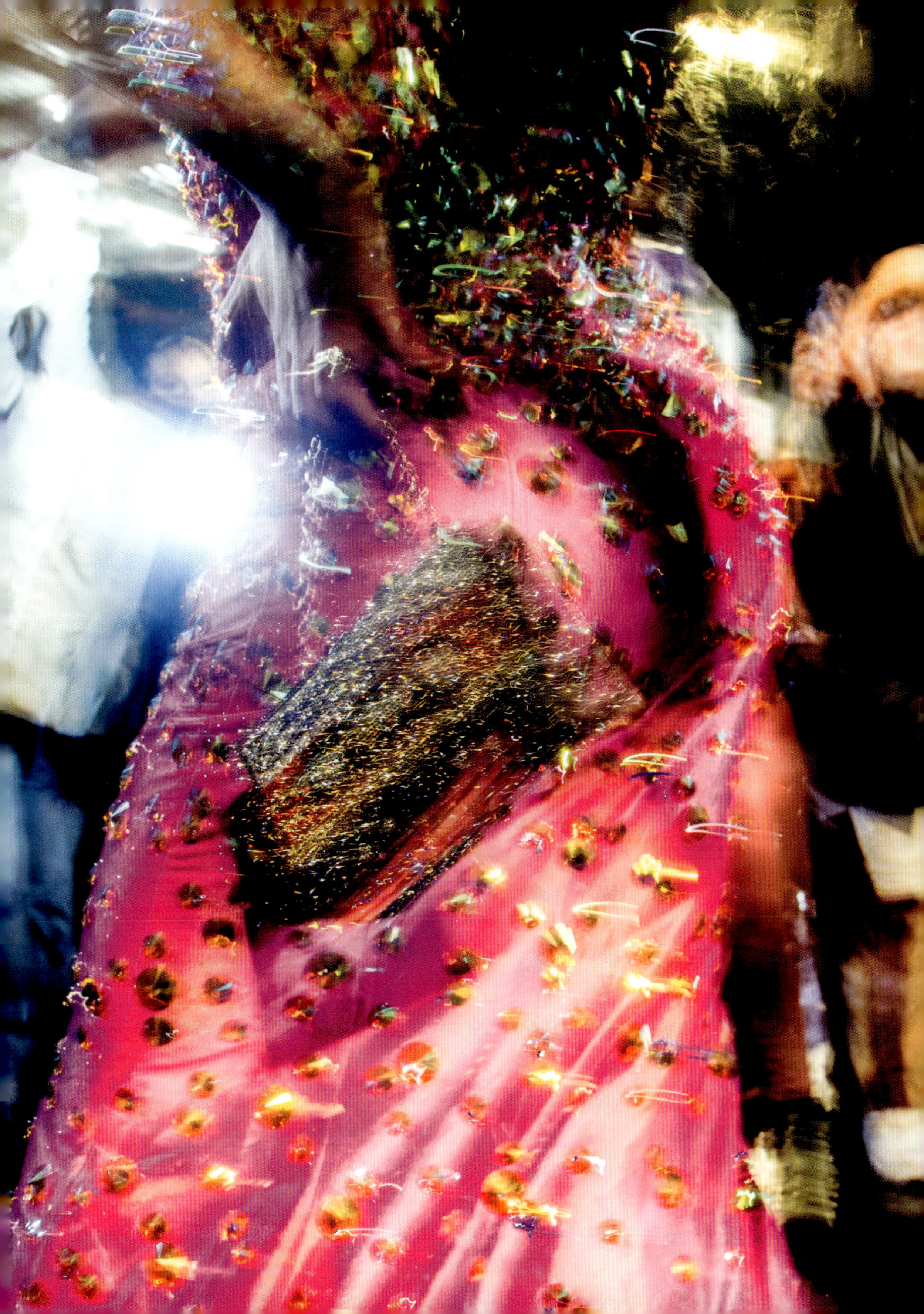

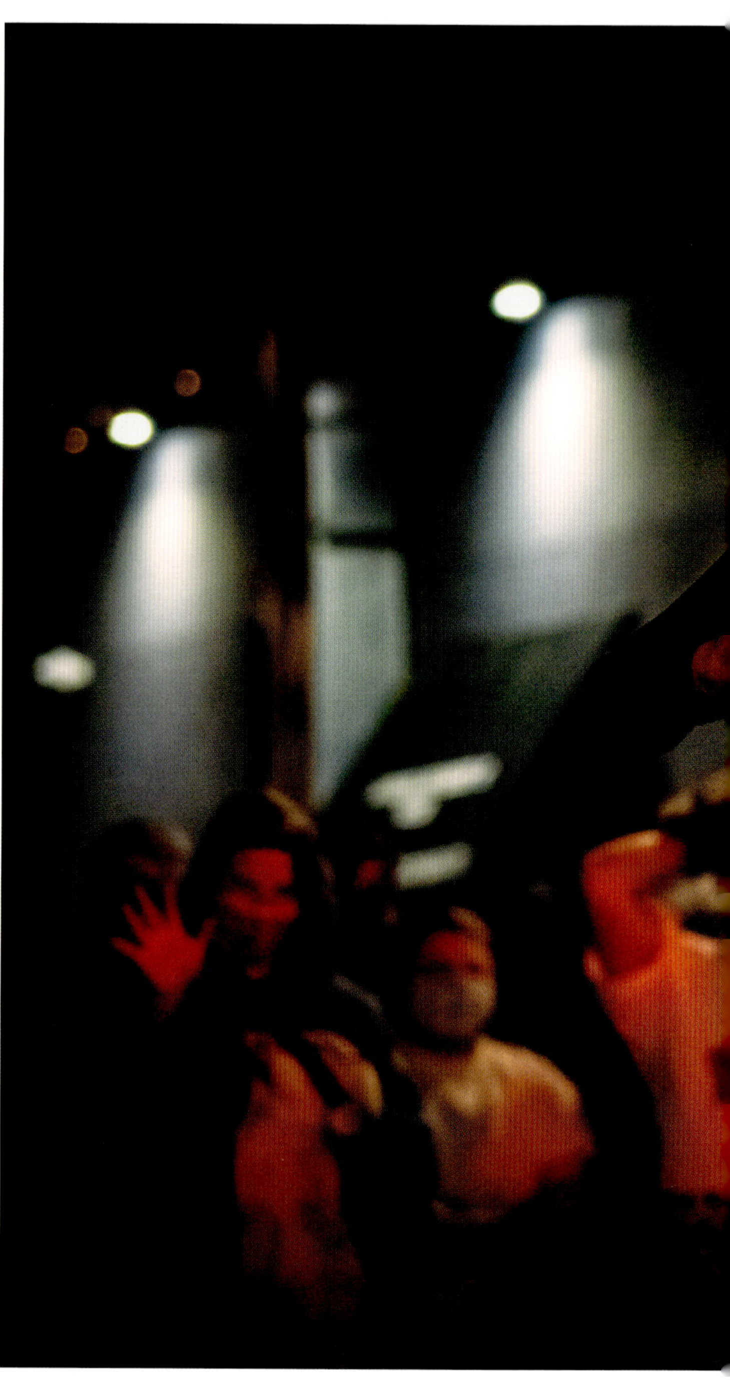

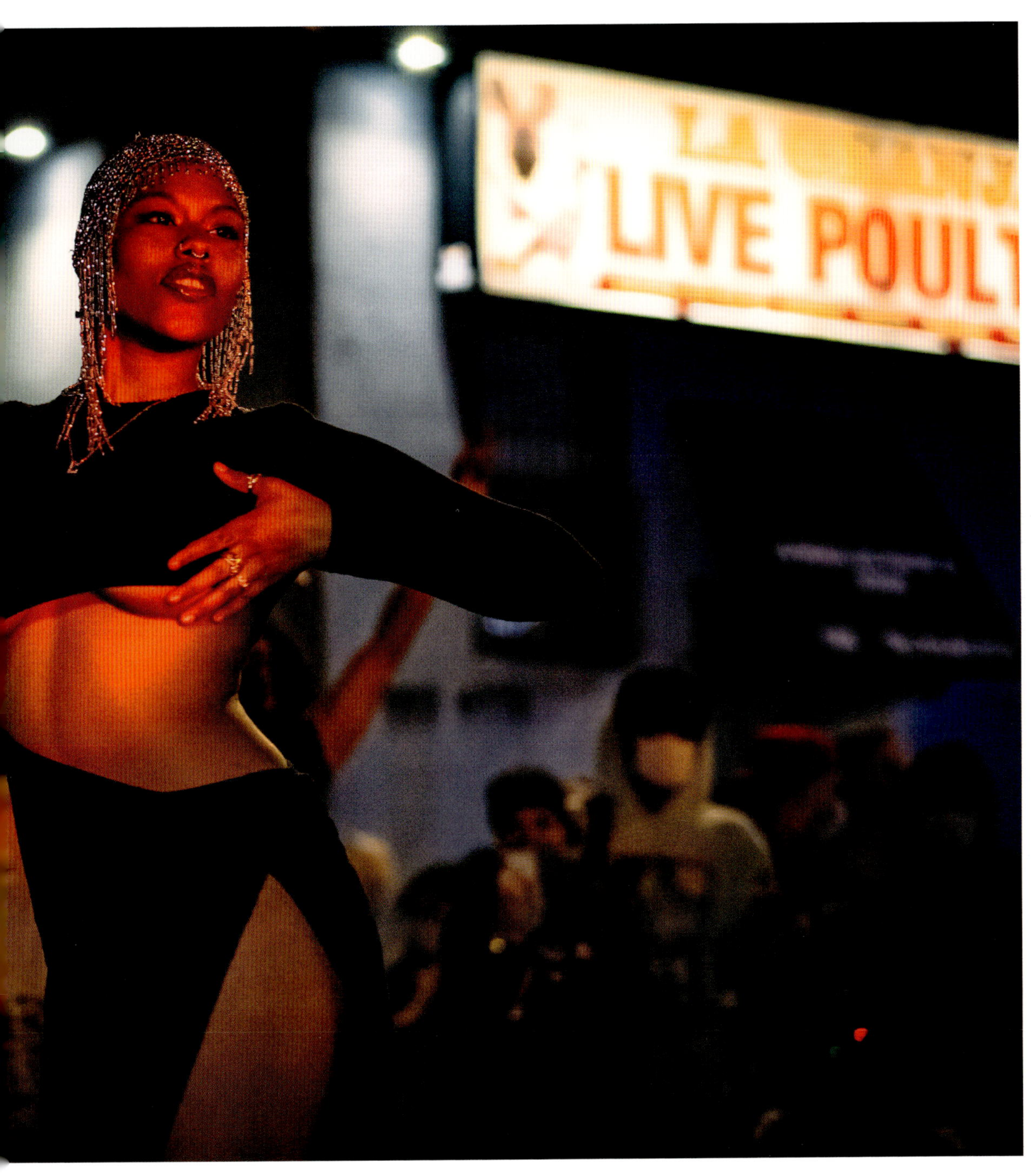

Daniel Lehrhaupt
May 2021

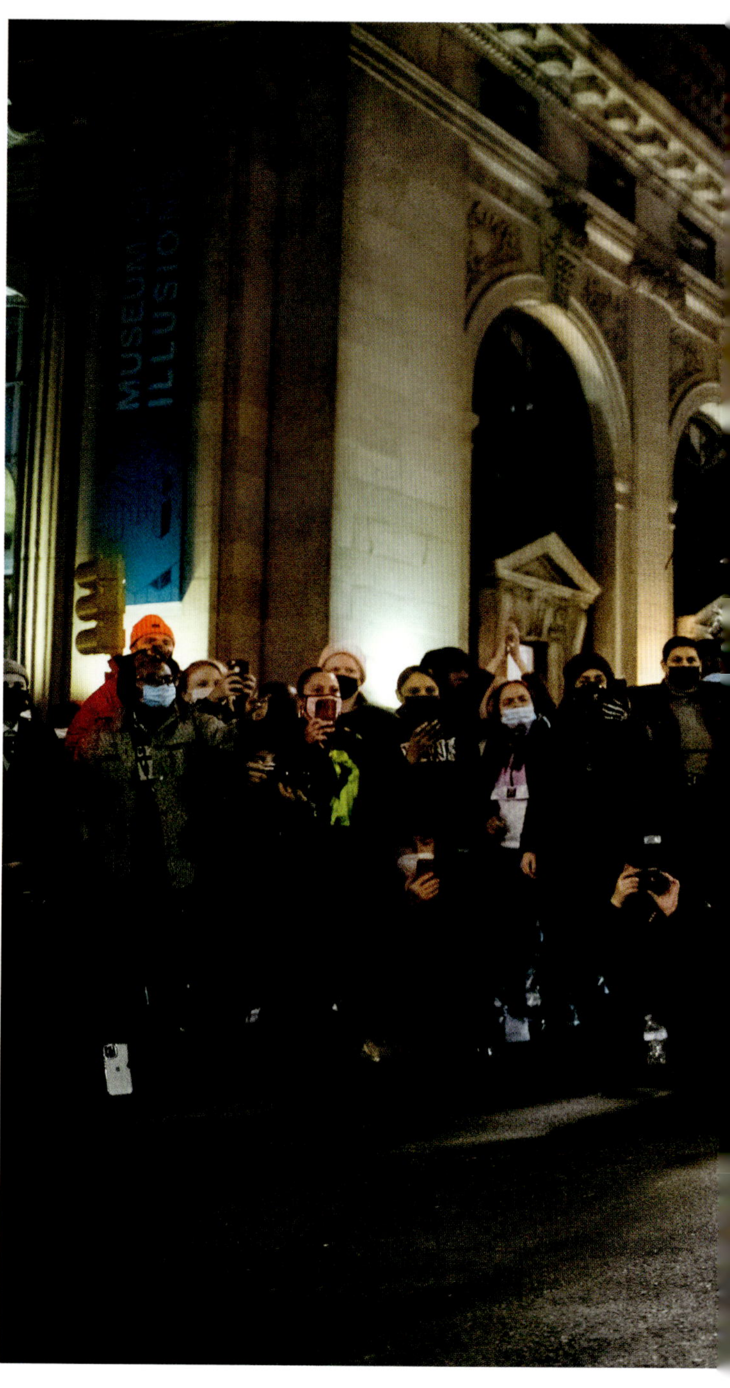

MUSEUM
ILLUSION

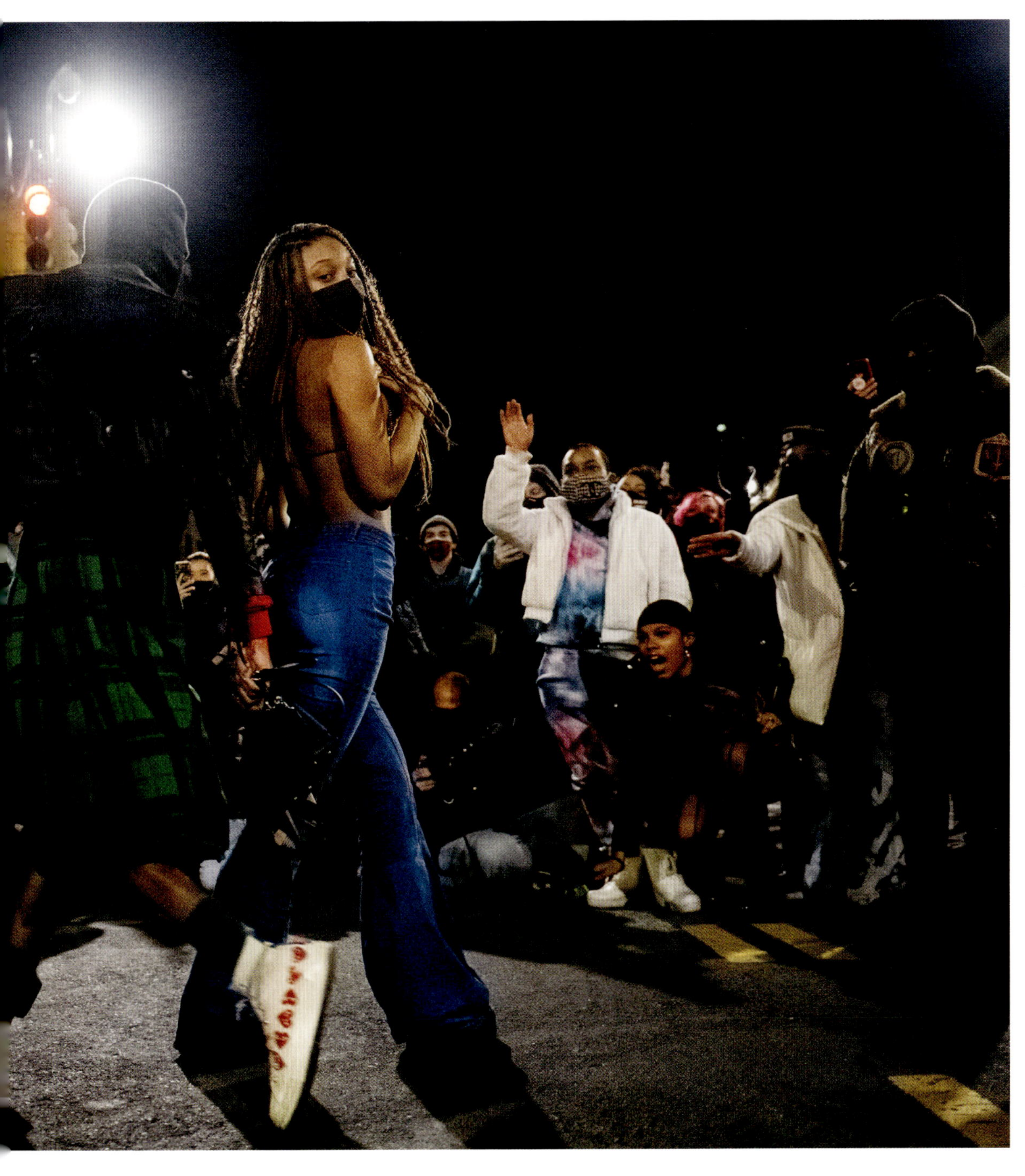

Deb Fong
January 2021

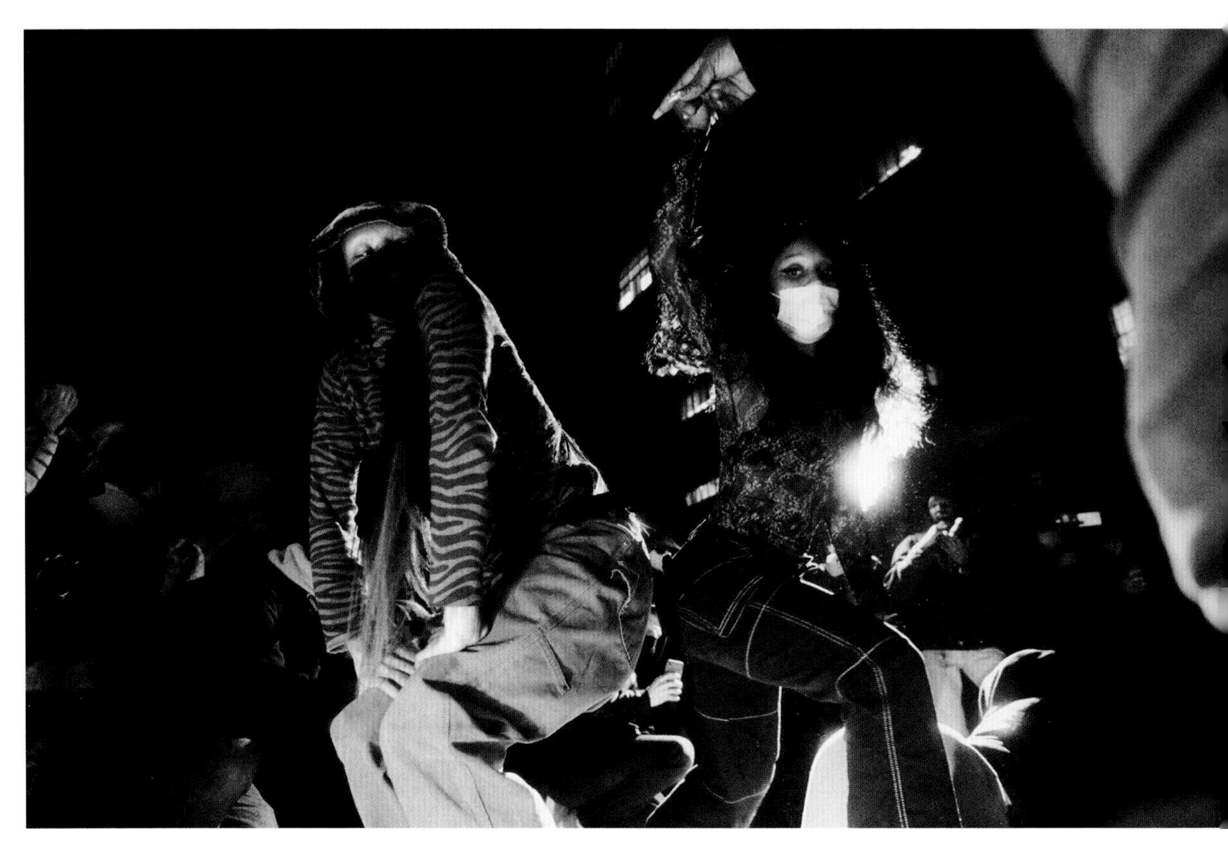

Robert Hamada
Trans Visibility March
October 2020

Robert Hamada
An Honoring of the African
Diaspora
February 2021

Robert Hamada
Who Will Say Their Names
November 2020

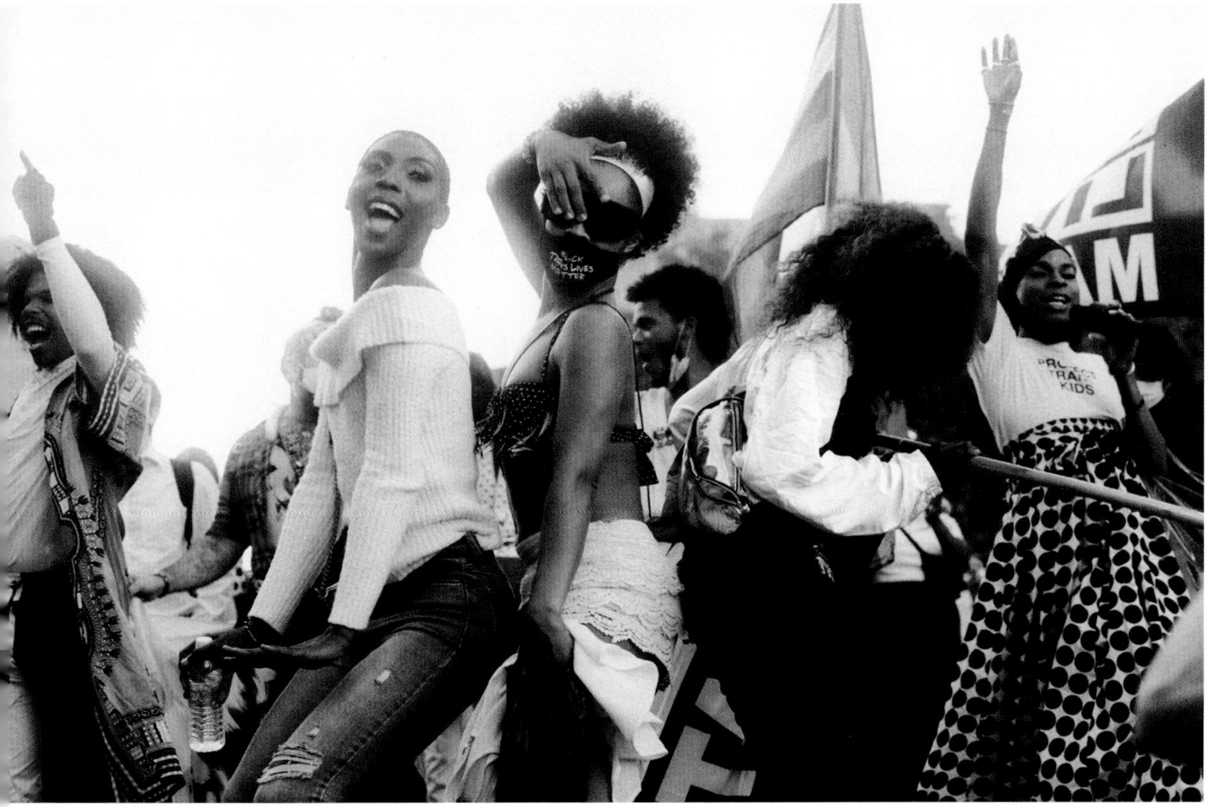

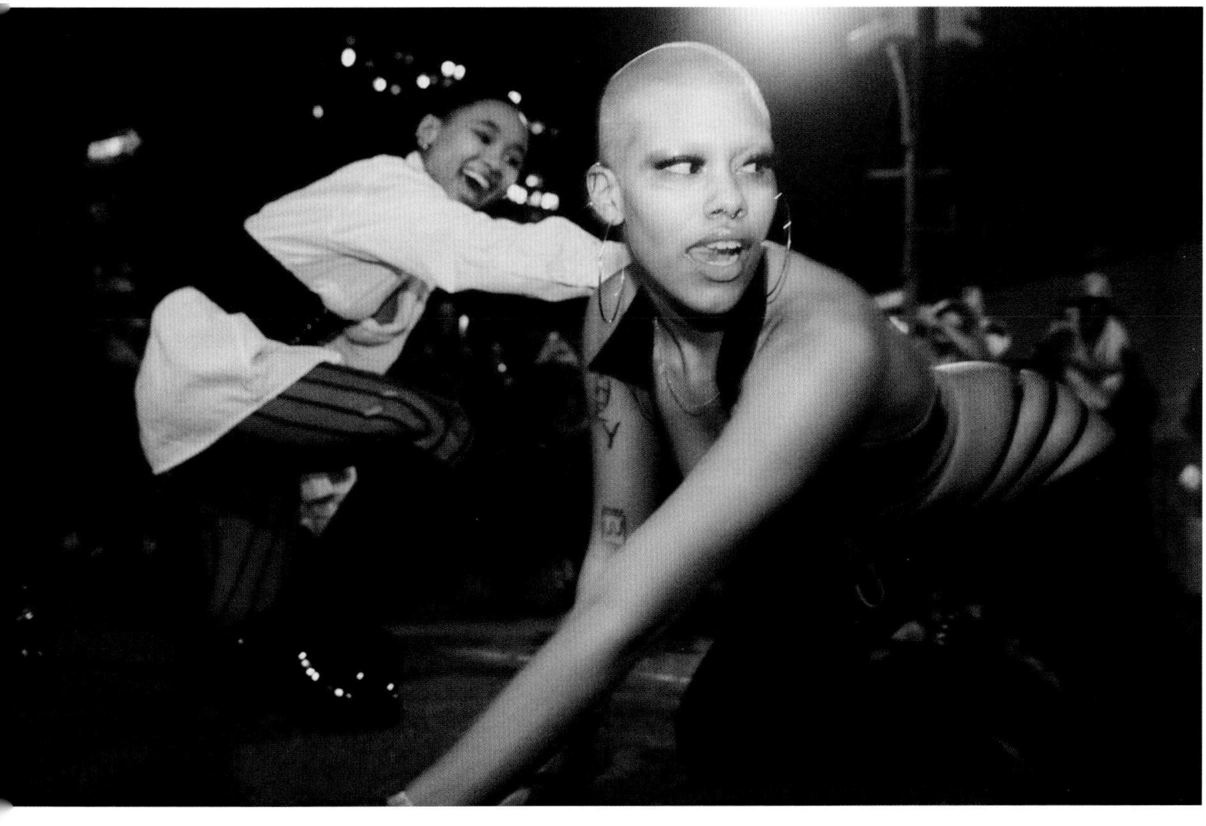

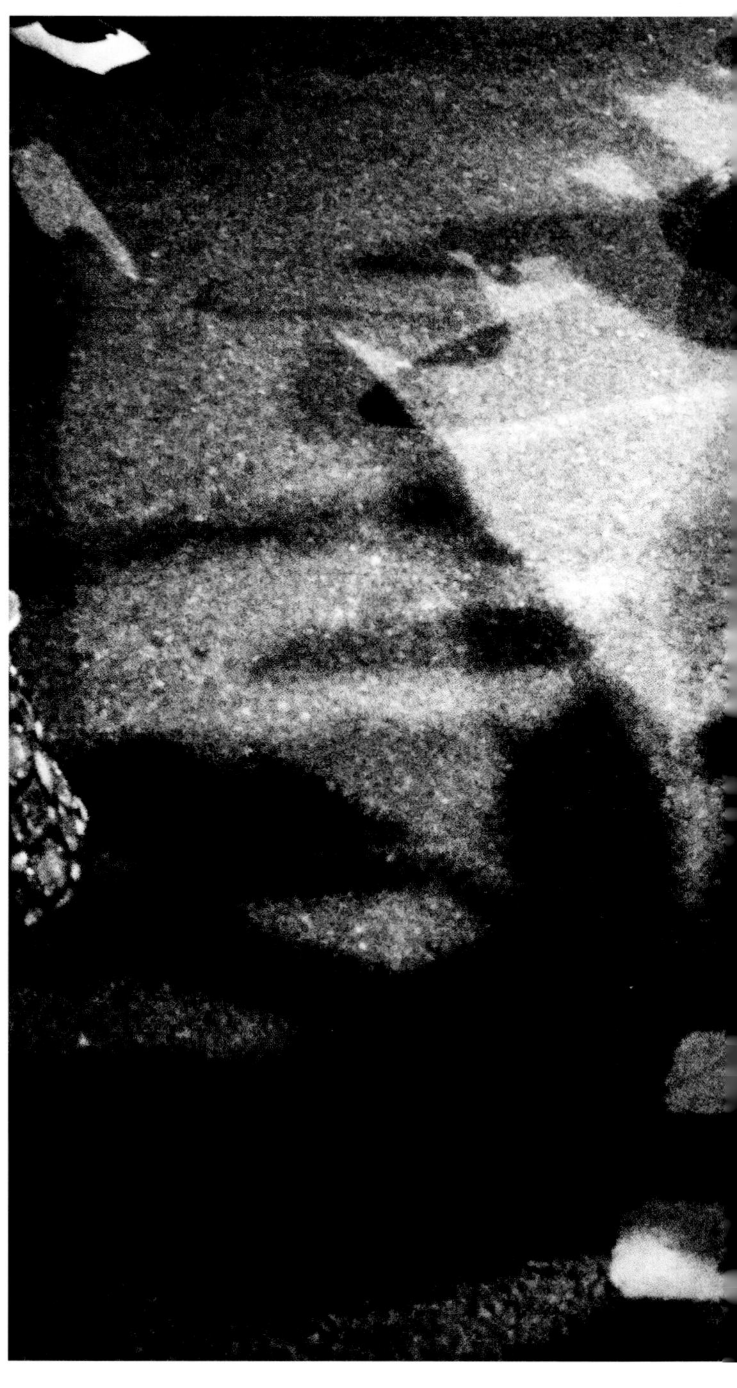

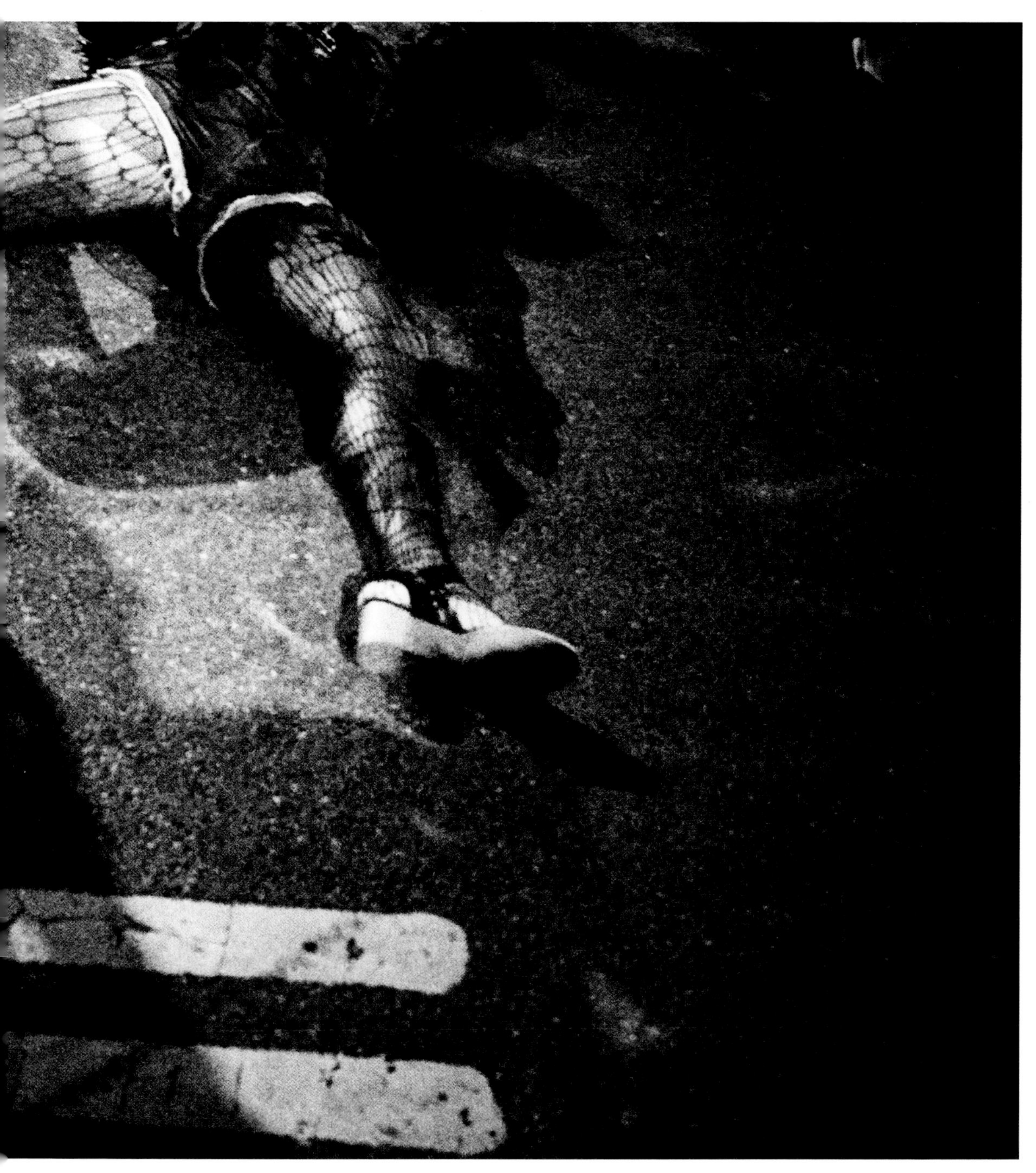

Sean Waltrous
Black Angels Ball
October 2020

As the groups marched, sang, and danced in the middle of active streets, there was this overwhelming sense of joy, freedom, and identity. It was a weekly reminder that community is stronger than oppression.

—Jarrett Robertson

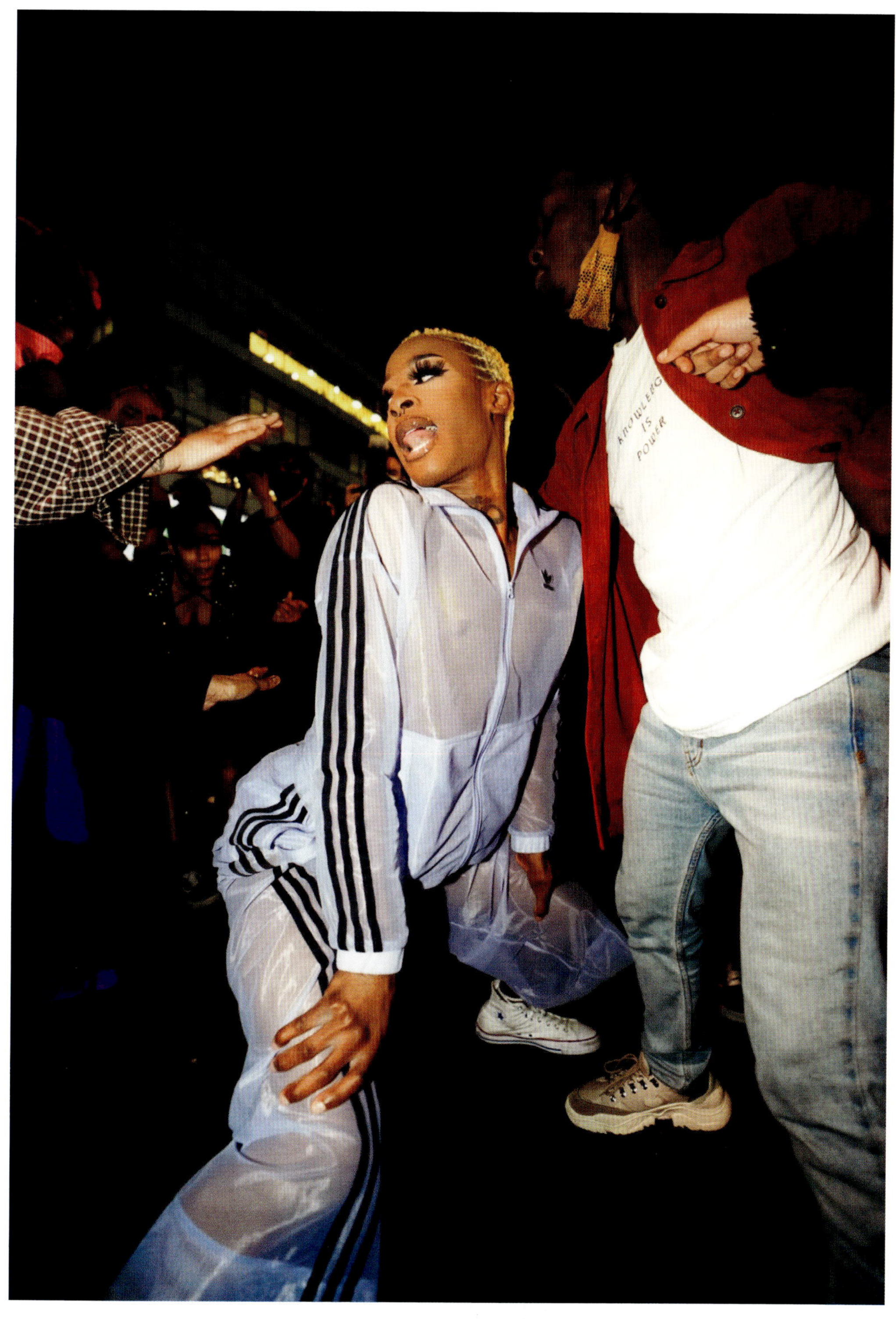

Budi
Black and Asian Solidarity
March 2021

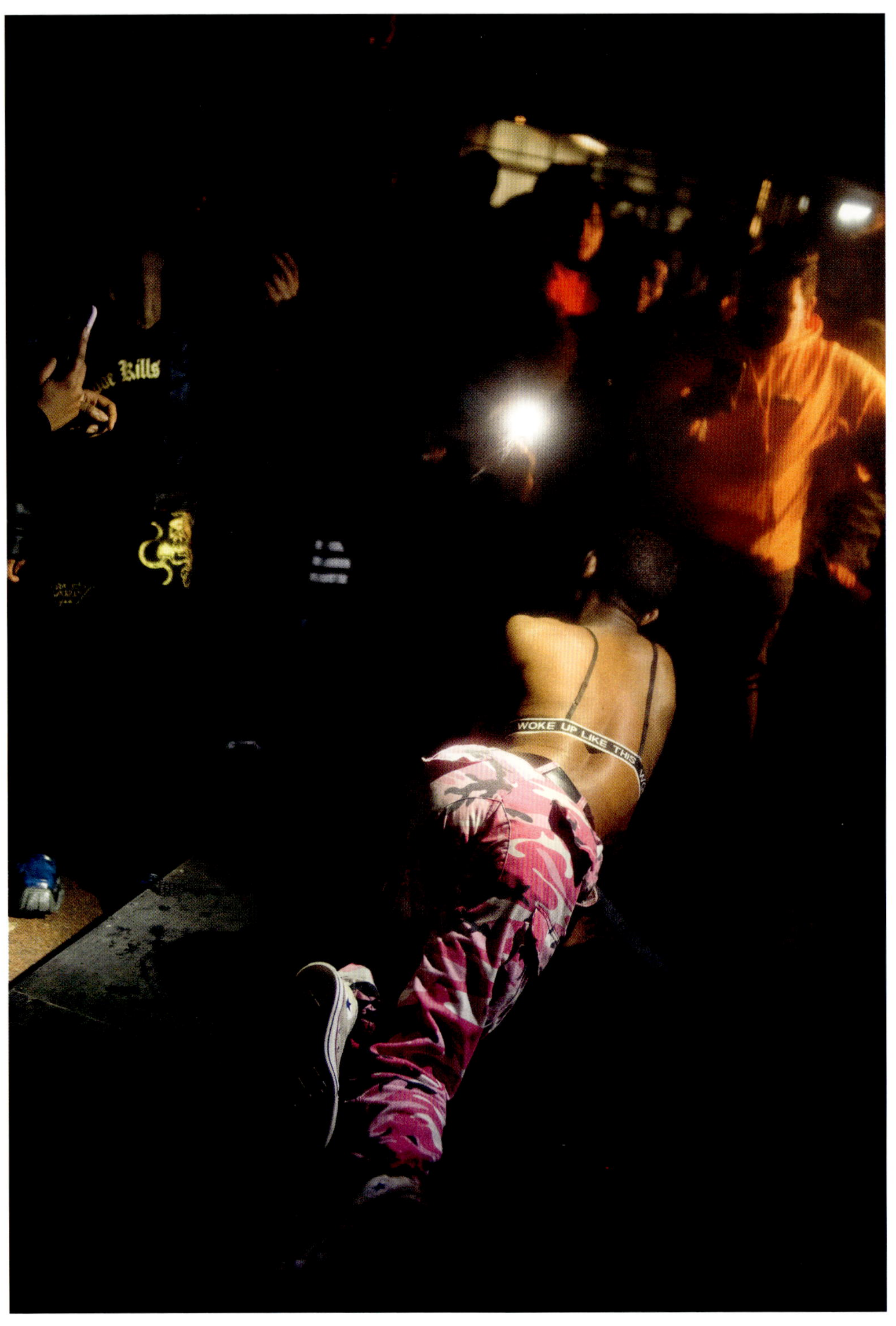

Ryan McGinley
Black Royalty Ball
October 2020

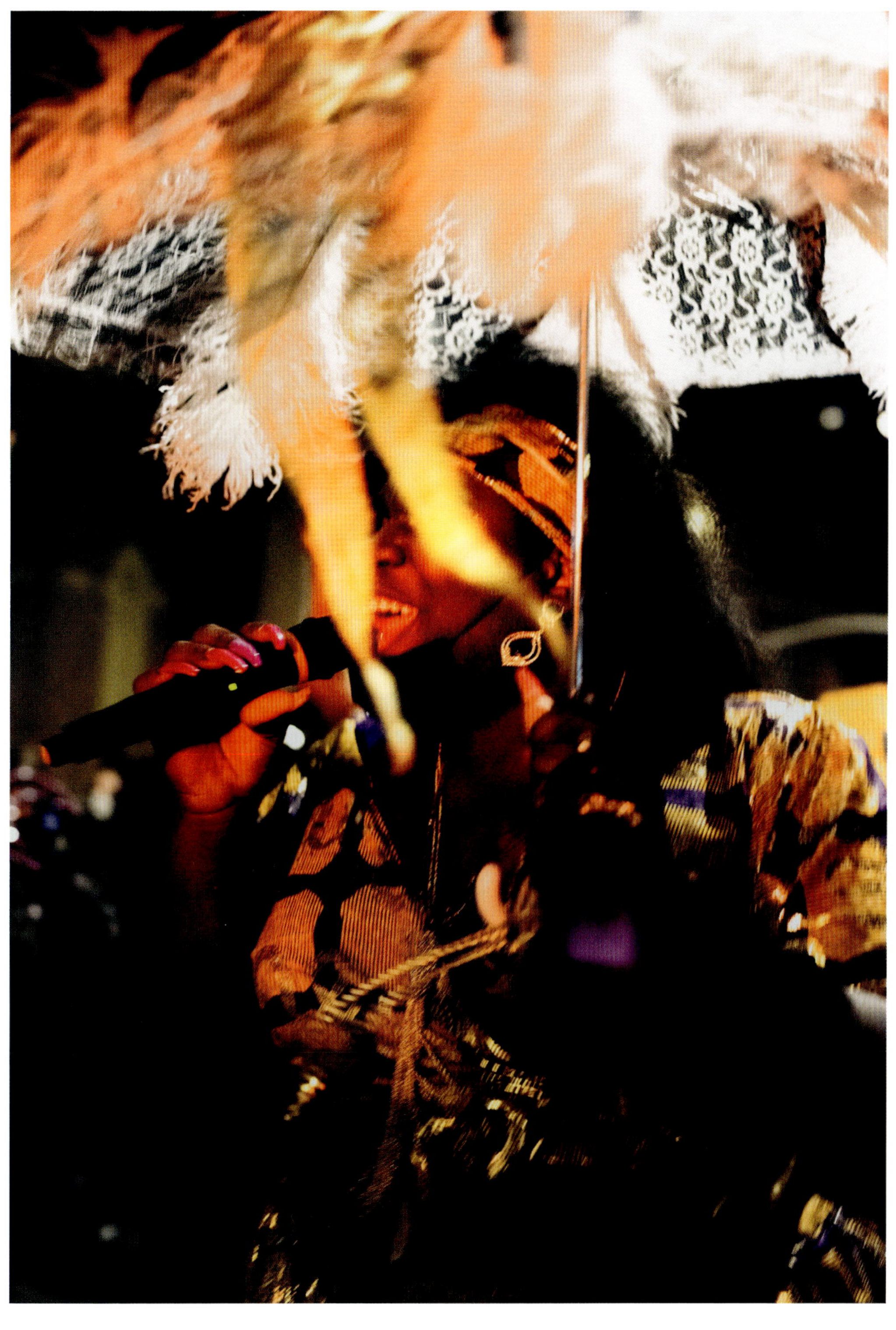

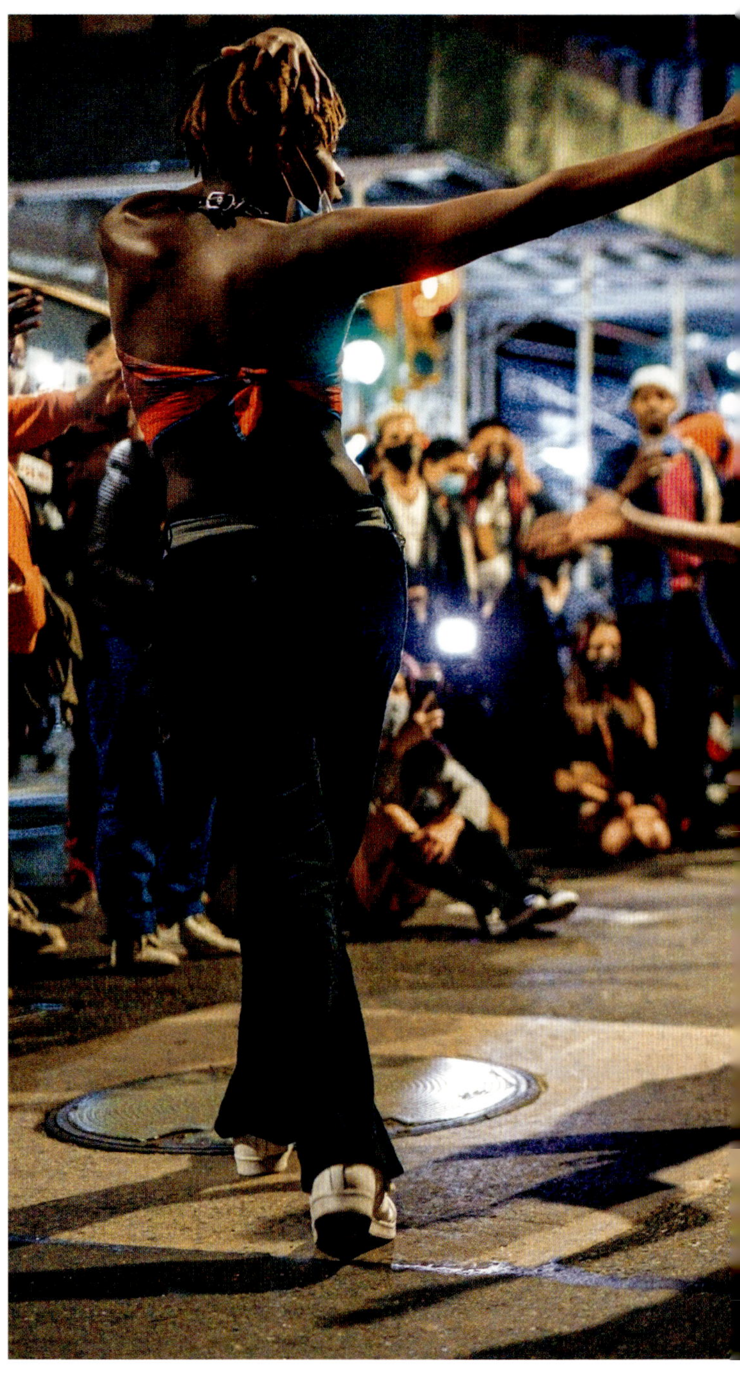

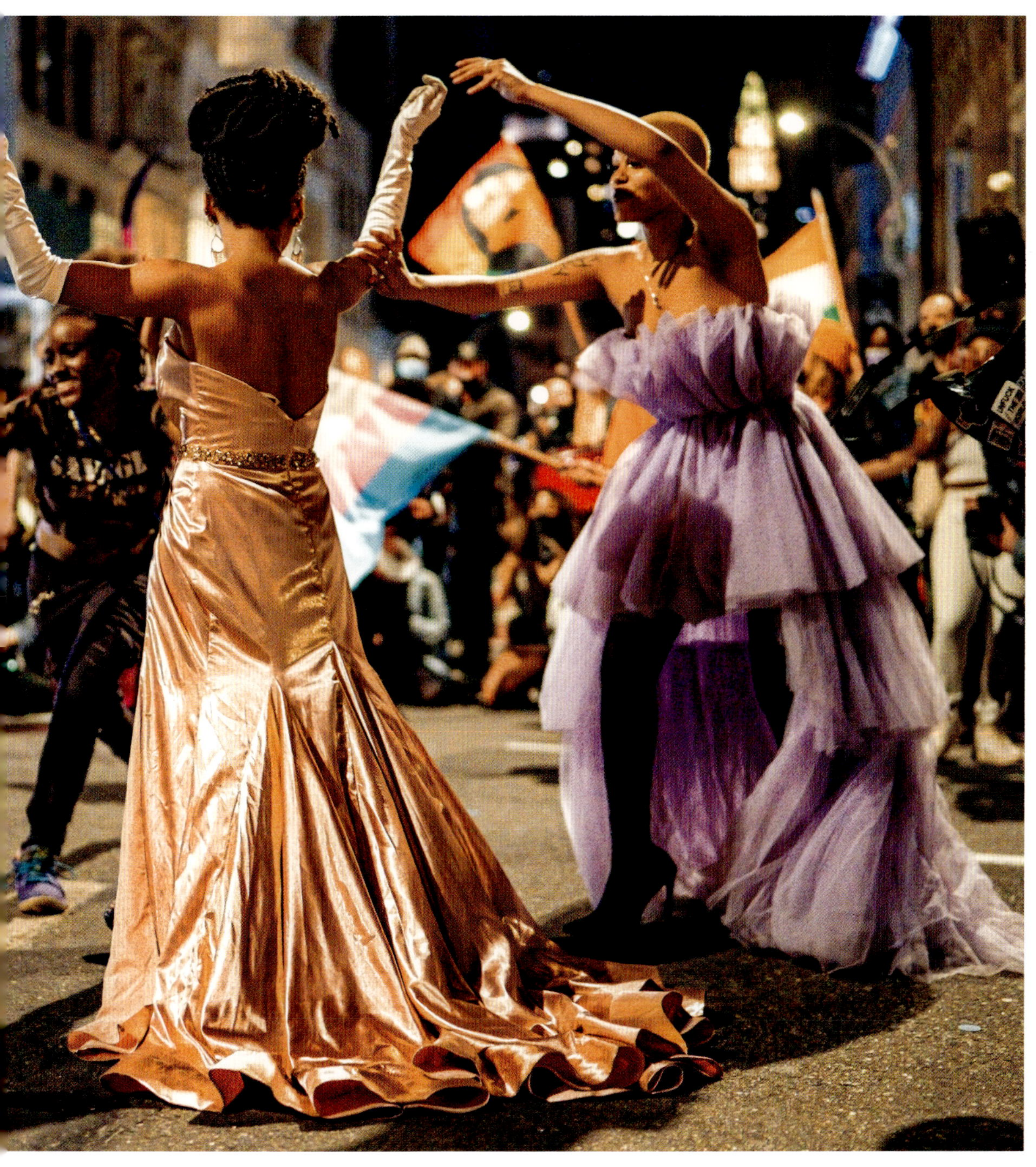

Daniel Lehrhaupt
Community Building Through Intersectionality
April 2021

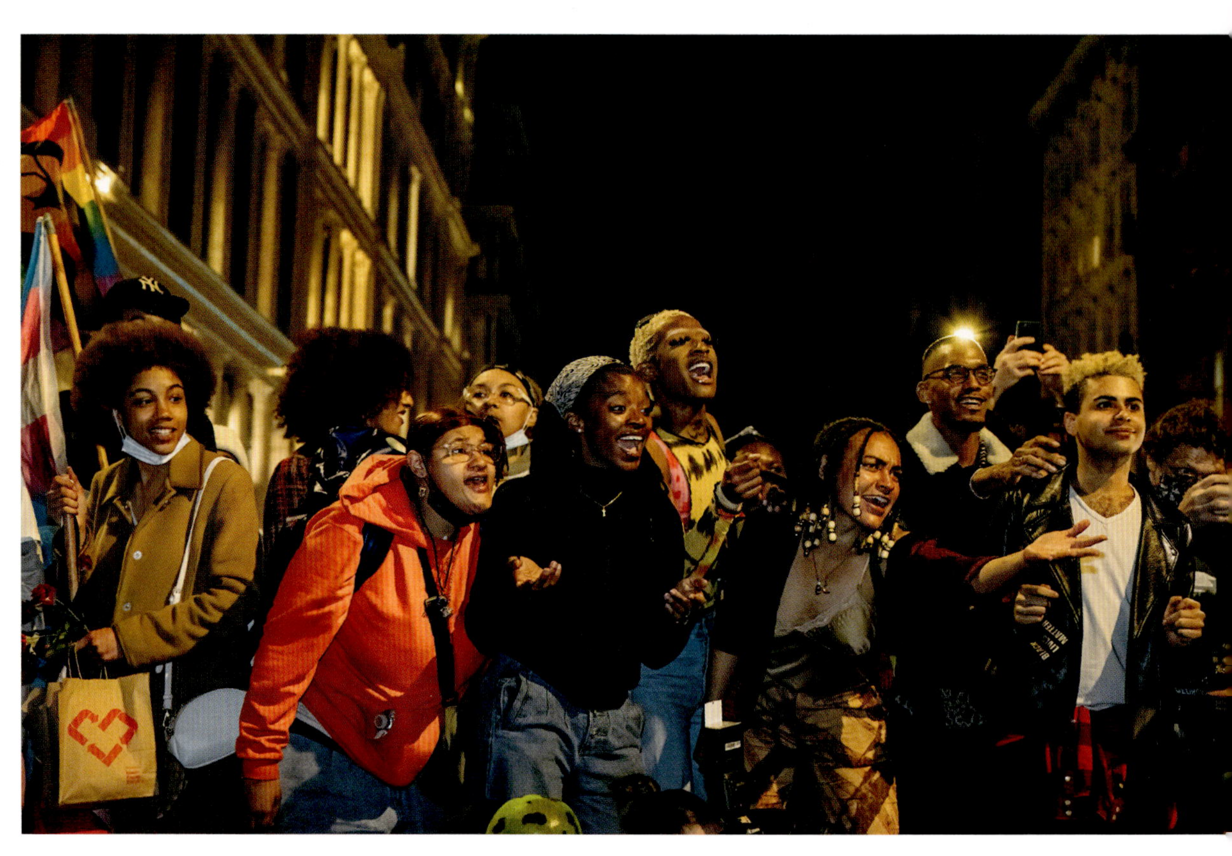

Stas Ginzburg
Community Building Through Intersectionality
April 2021

NEXT SPREAD:
Chae Kihn
Black Royalty Ball
October 2020

Everybody loved the balls—the beat, the outfits, the voguing—the energy was transcendent! All was forgotten; only pure Black joy existed. People lost their inhibitions and melted together. Faces read like an open book. I could not help but feel that we were all connected to each other, to the universe, to God.

—Stas Ginzburg

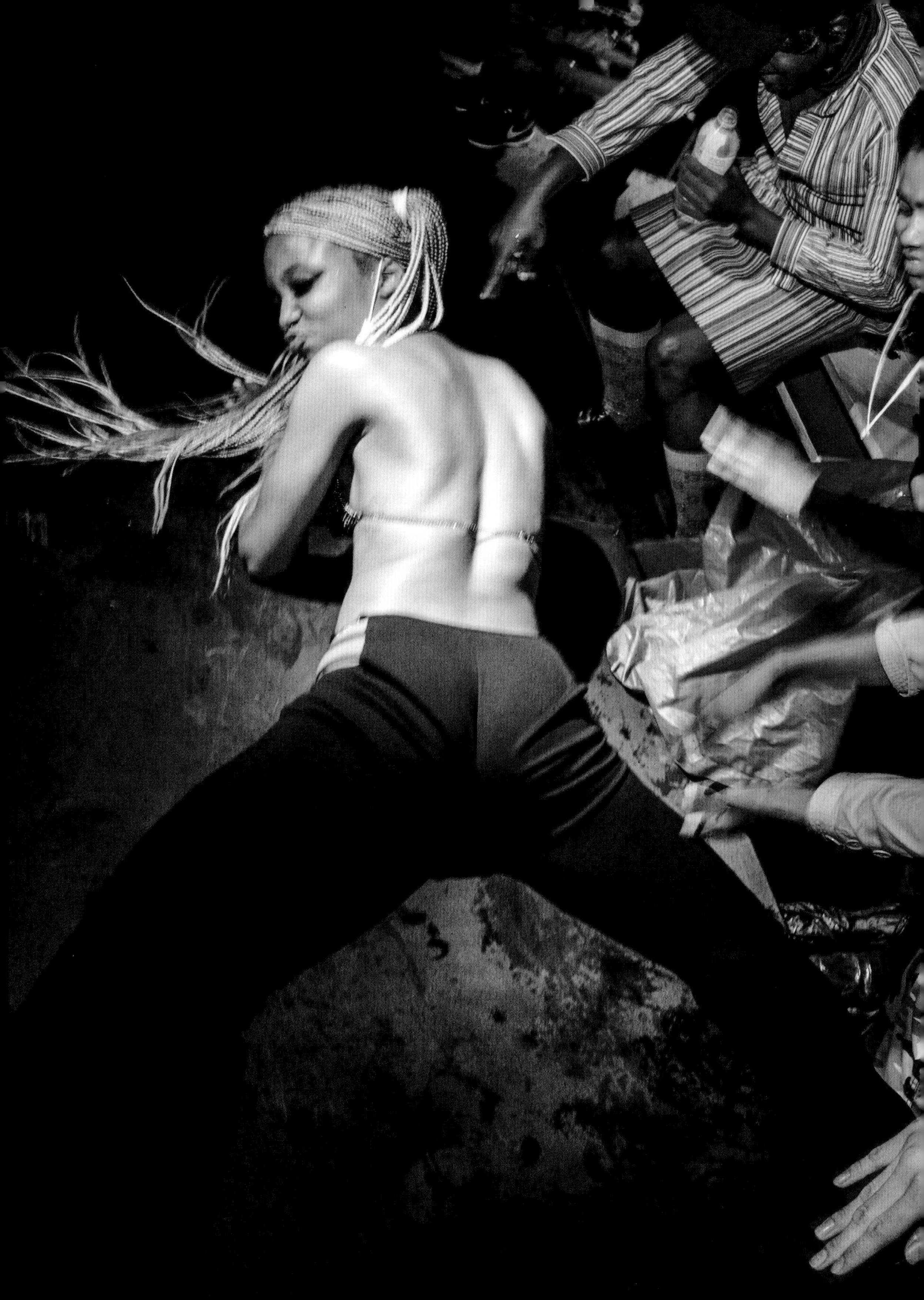

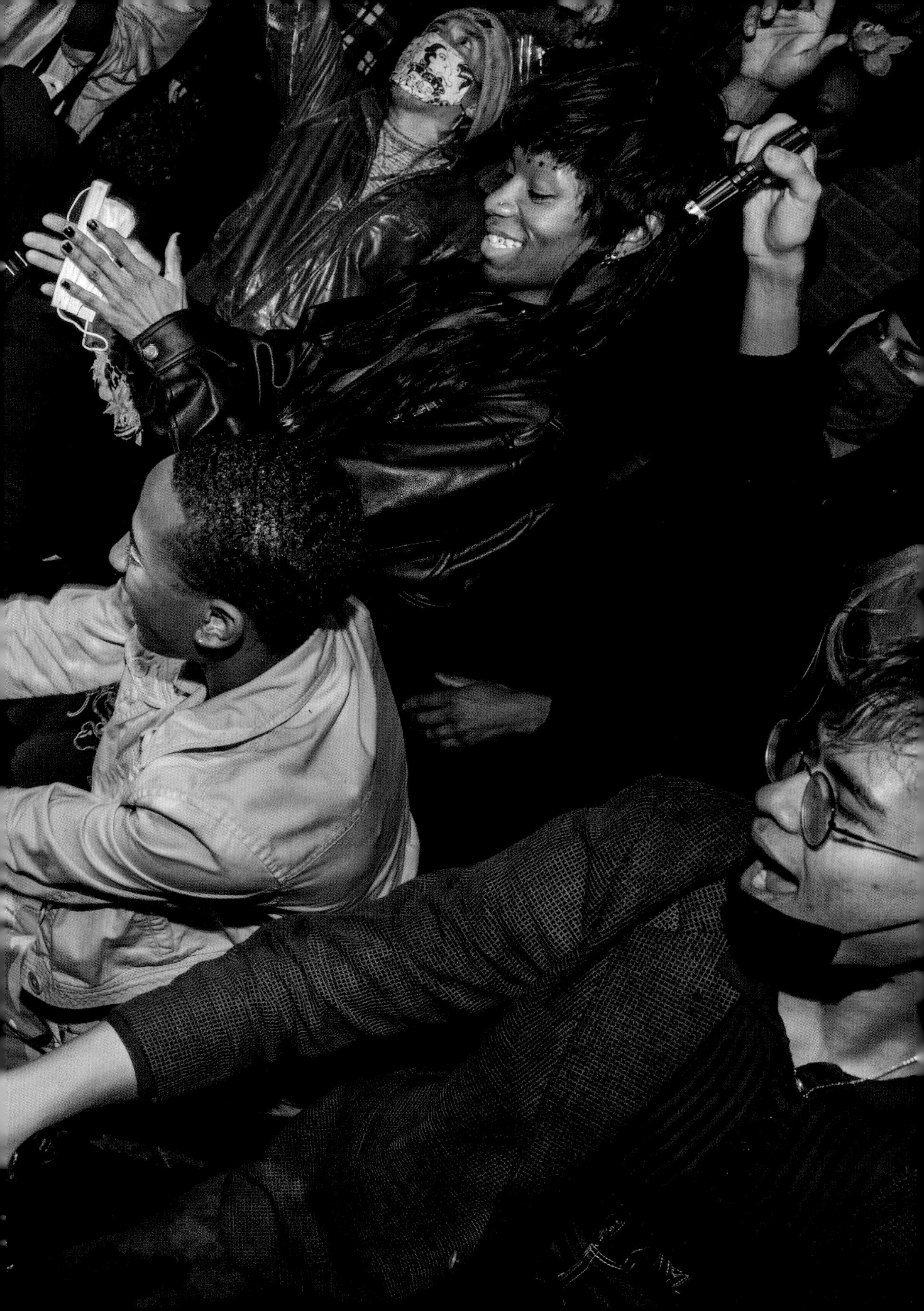

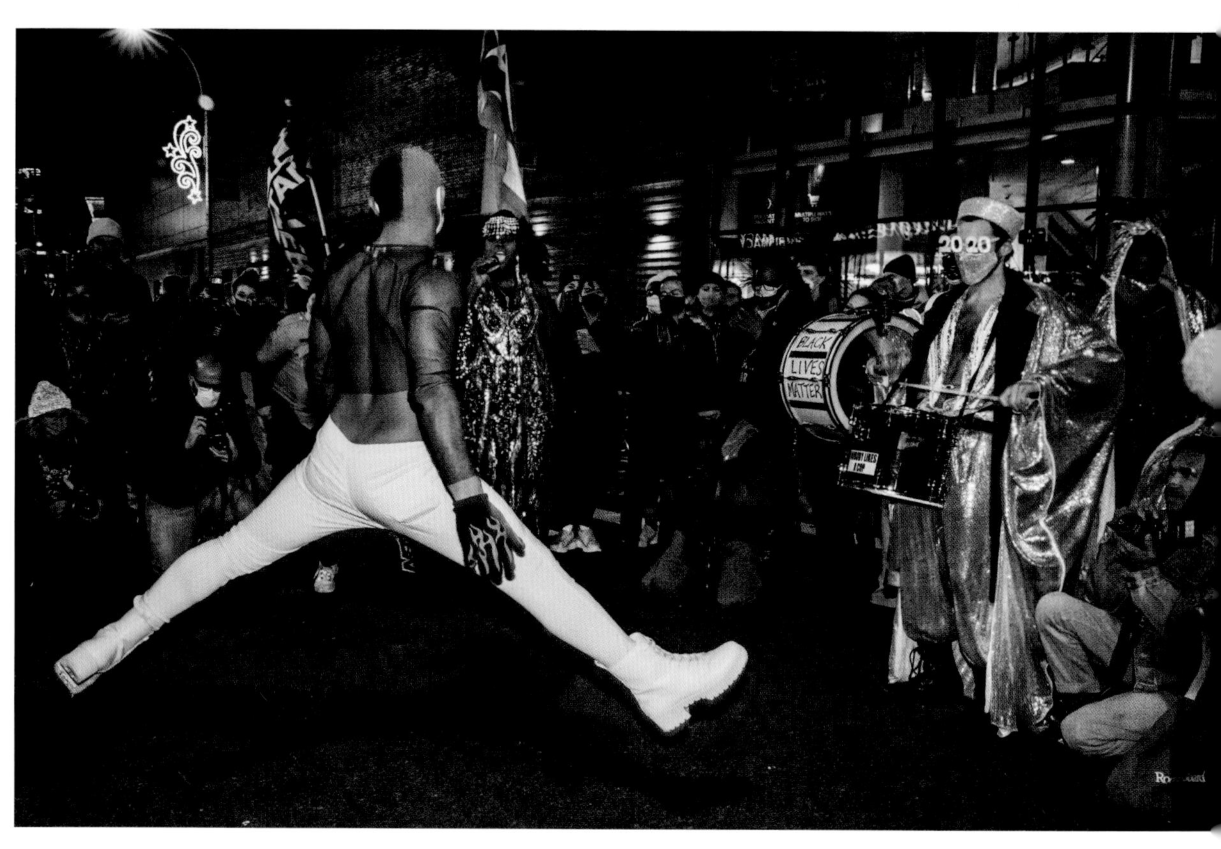

Caroline Mardok
The Last Ball of 2020
December 2020

Sean Waltrous
Who Will Say Their Names
Love Legacy Liberation
November 2020

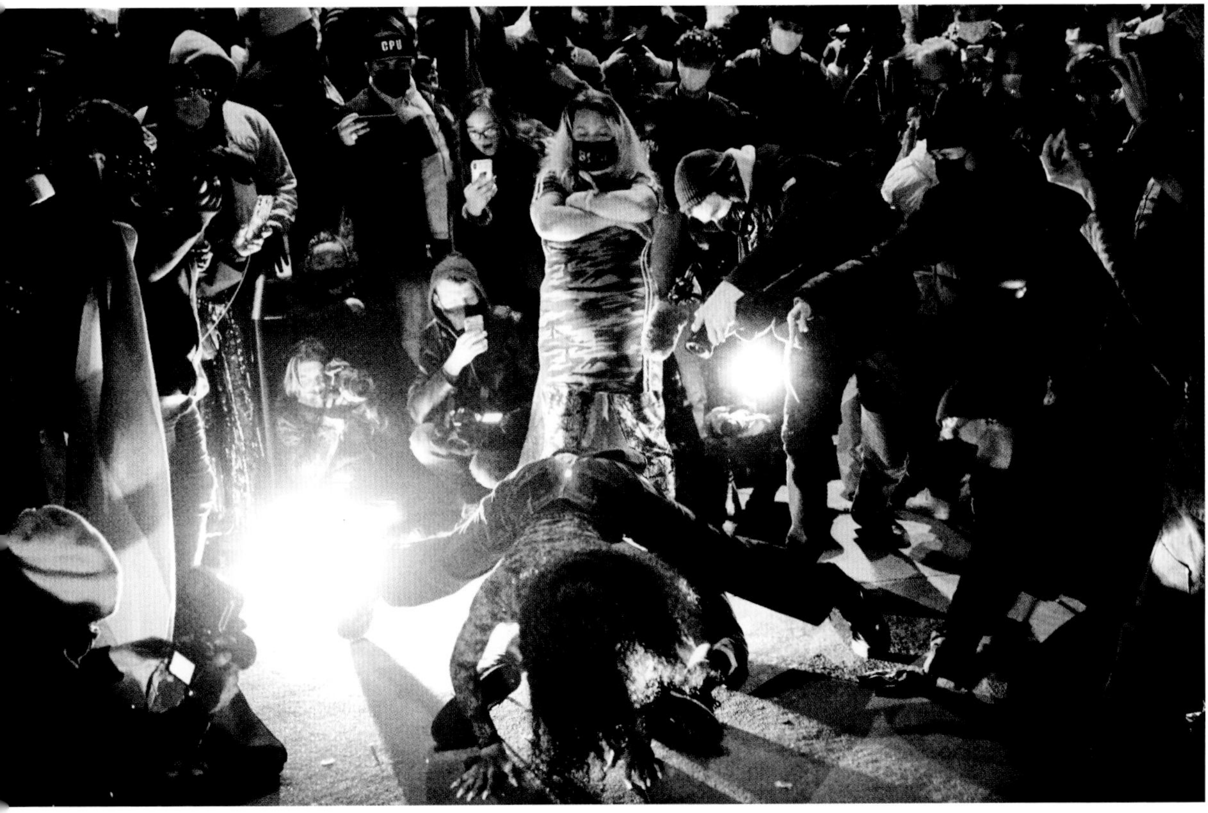

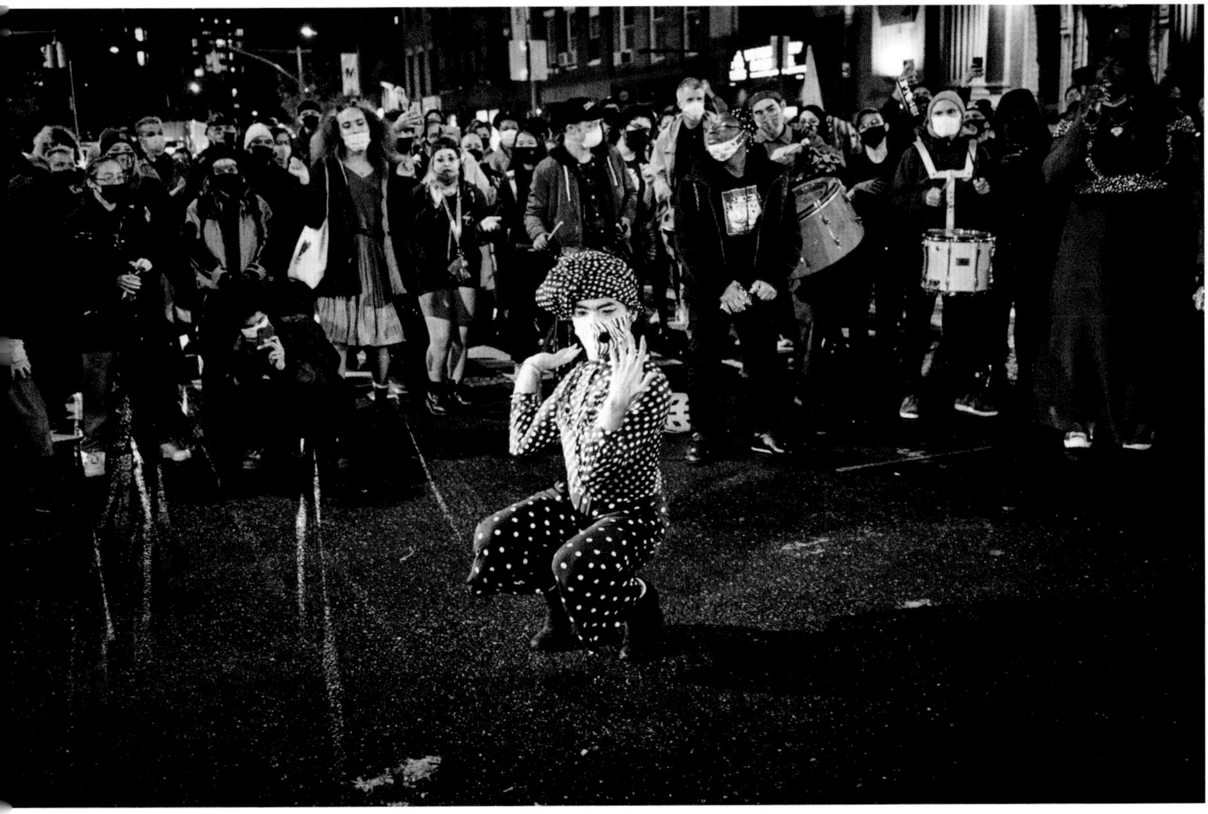

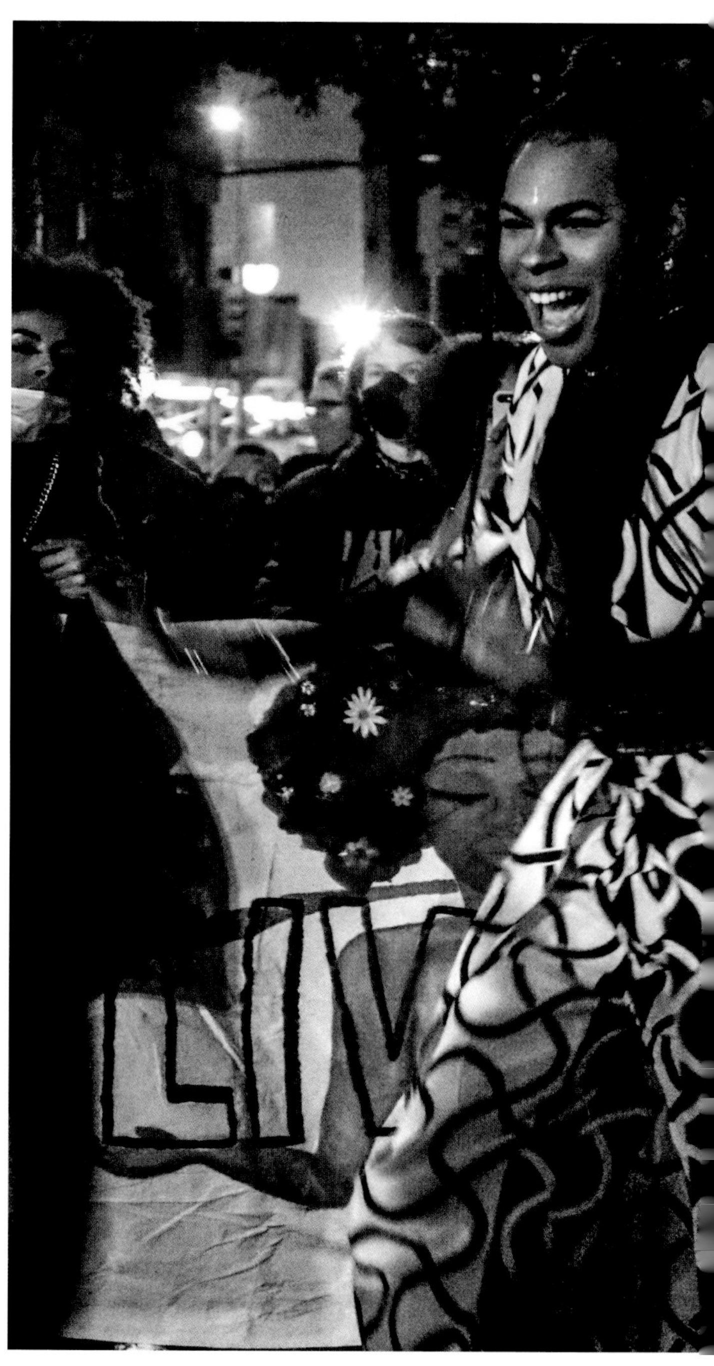

LIV

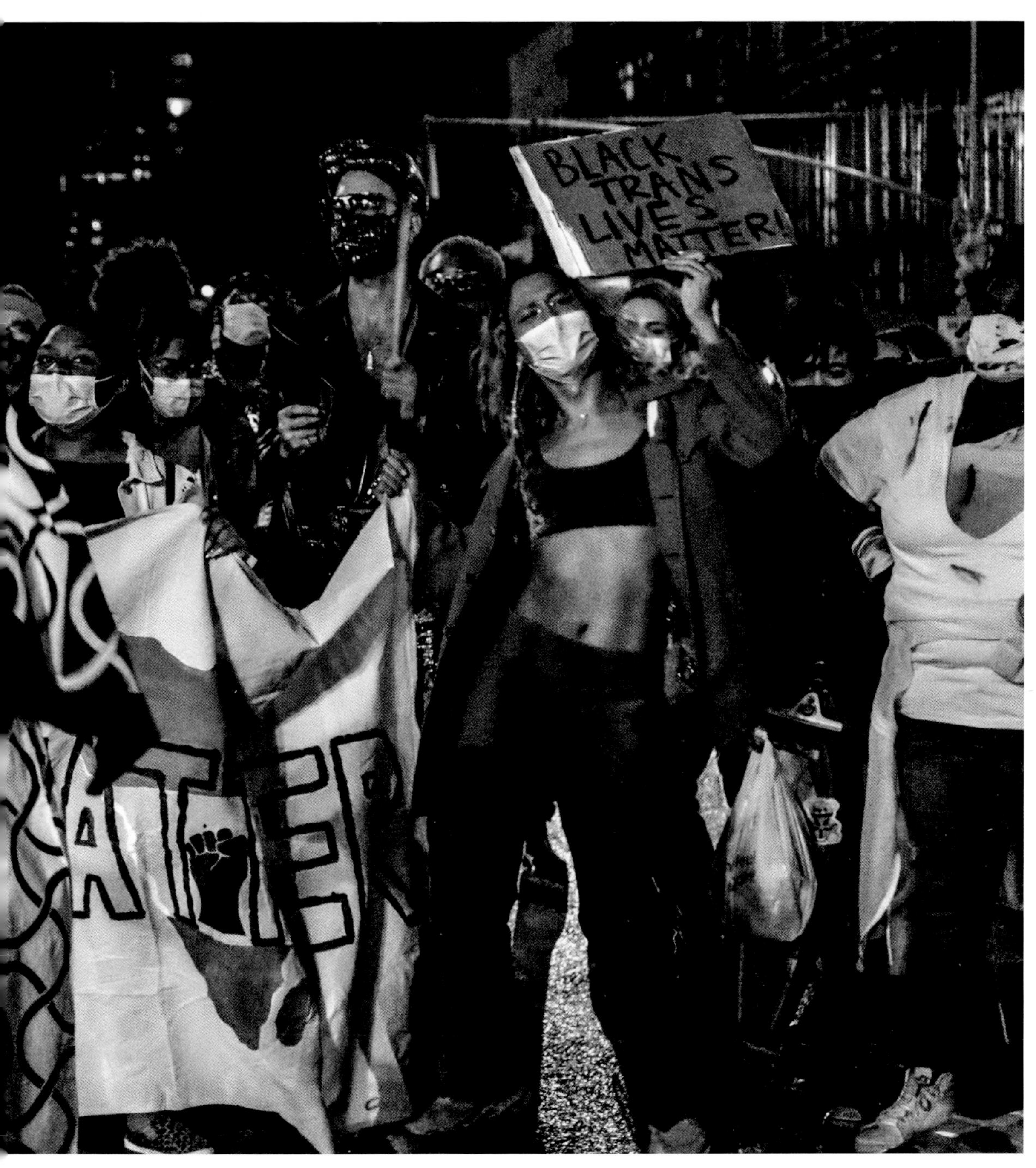

BLACK
TRANS
LIVES
MATTER!

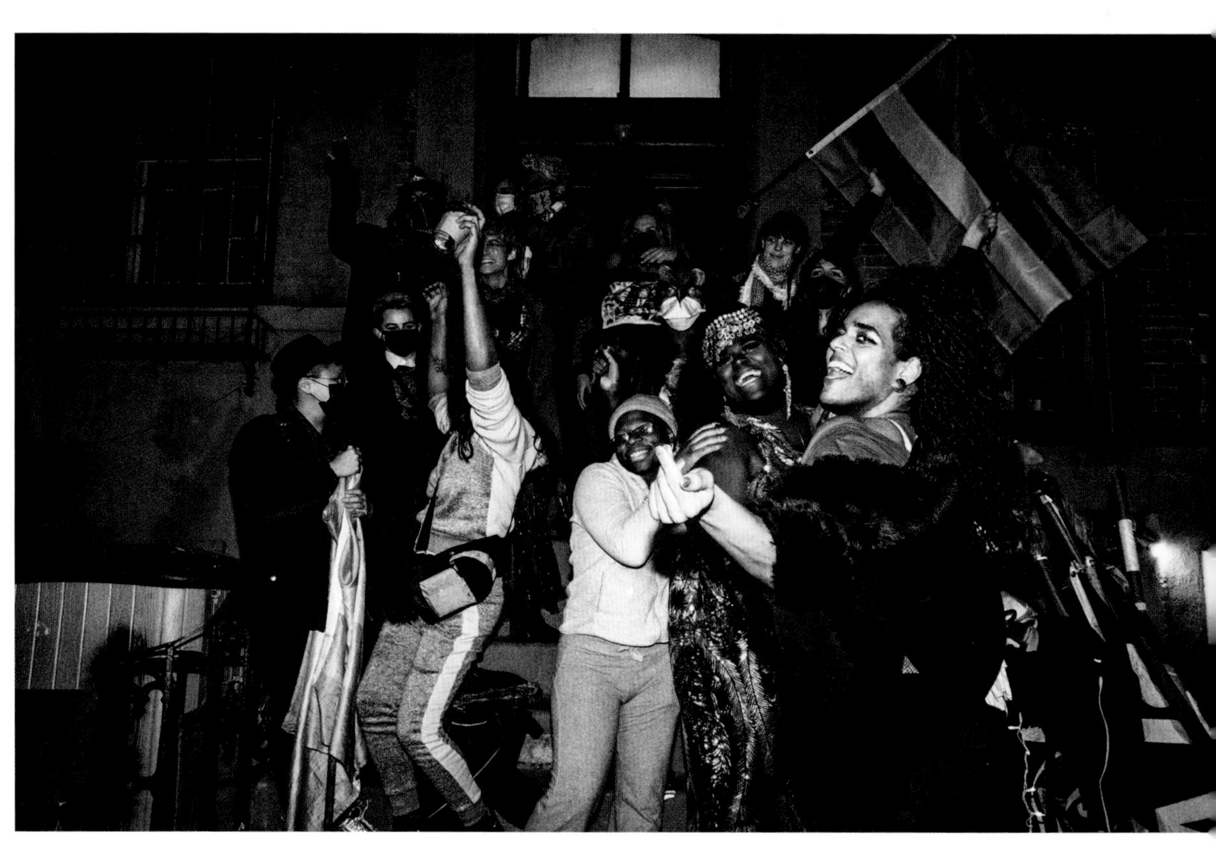

NEXT SPREAD:
Ryan McGinley
Illumination Ball
October 2020

Caroline Mardok
The Last Ball of 2020
December 2020

My favorite moments to photograph
at Stonewall were those of Black
joy. The media has made a habit
and a business of focusing on
Black pain and Black death, but on
Thursdays we took time to mourn
and remember, but also to educate,
dance, love, sing, and express every
emotion together as a community.

—Budi

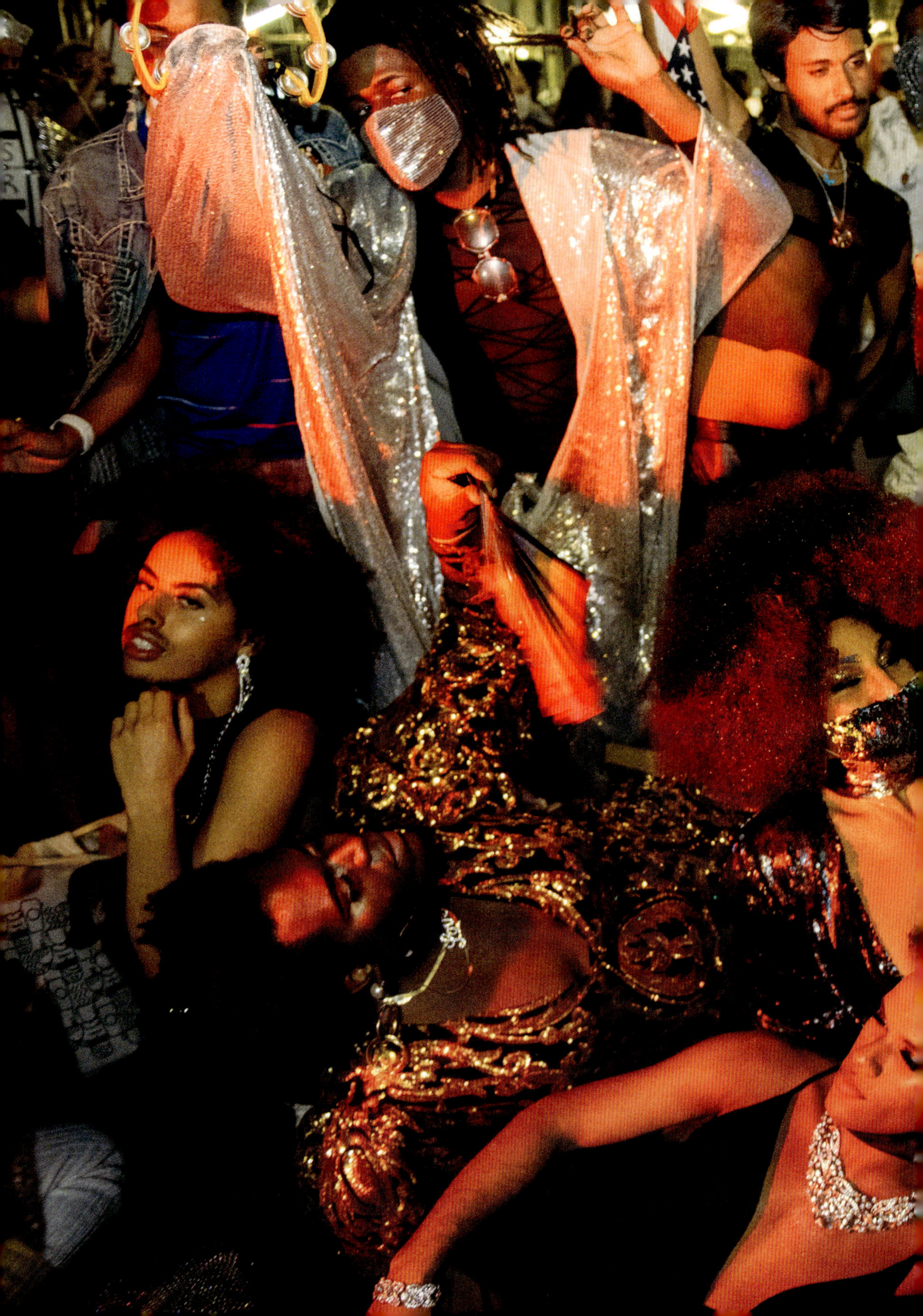

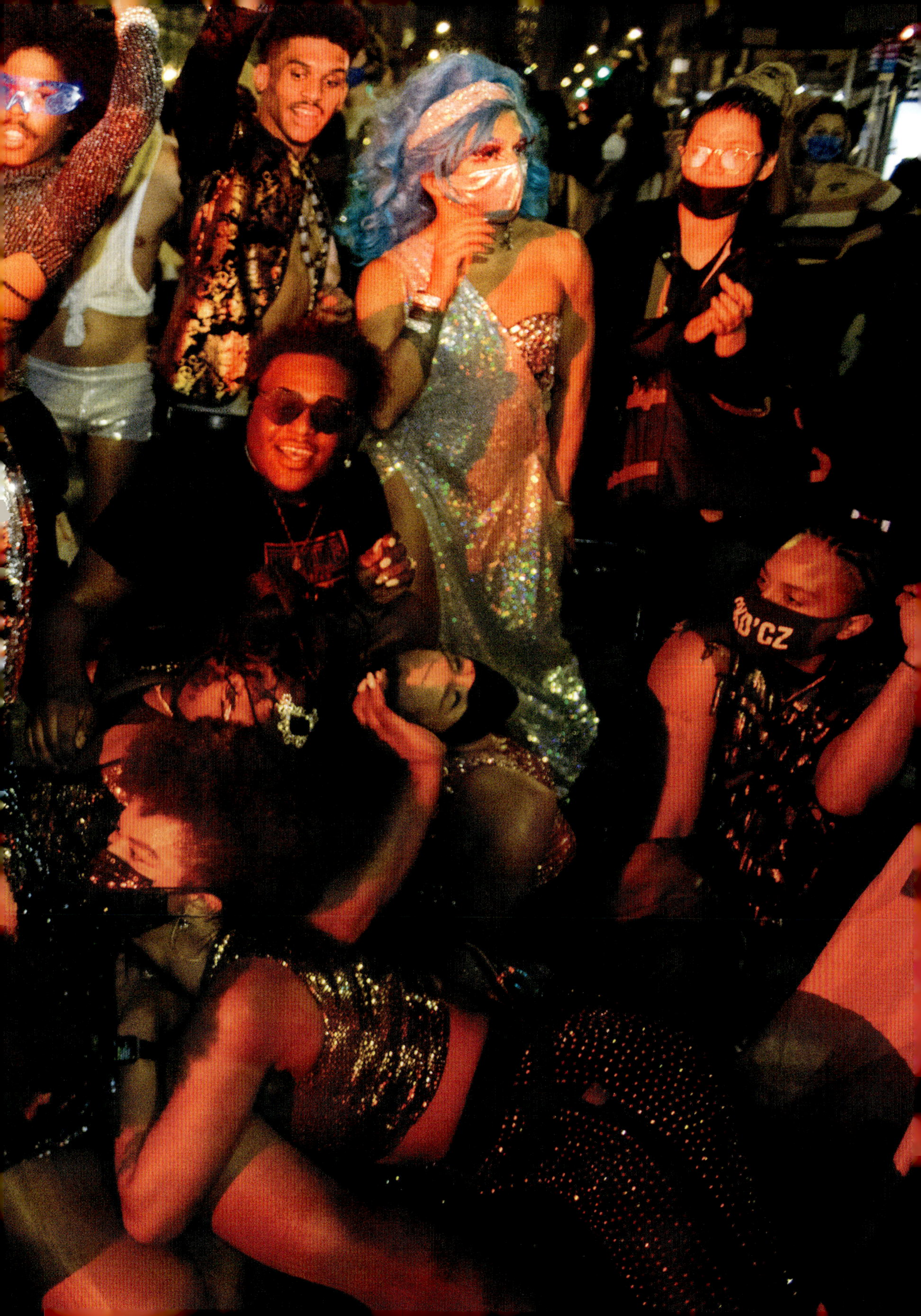

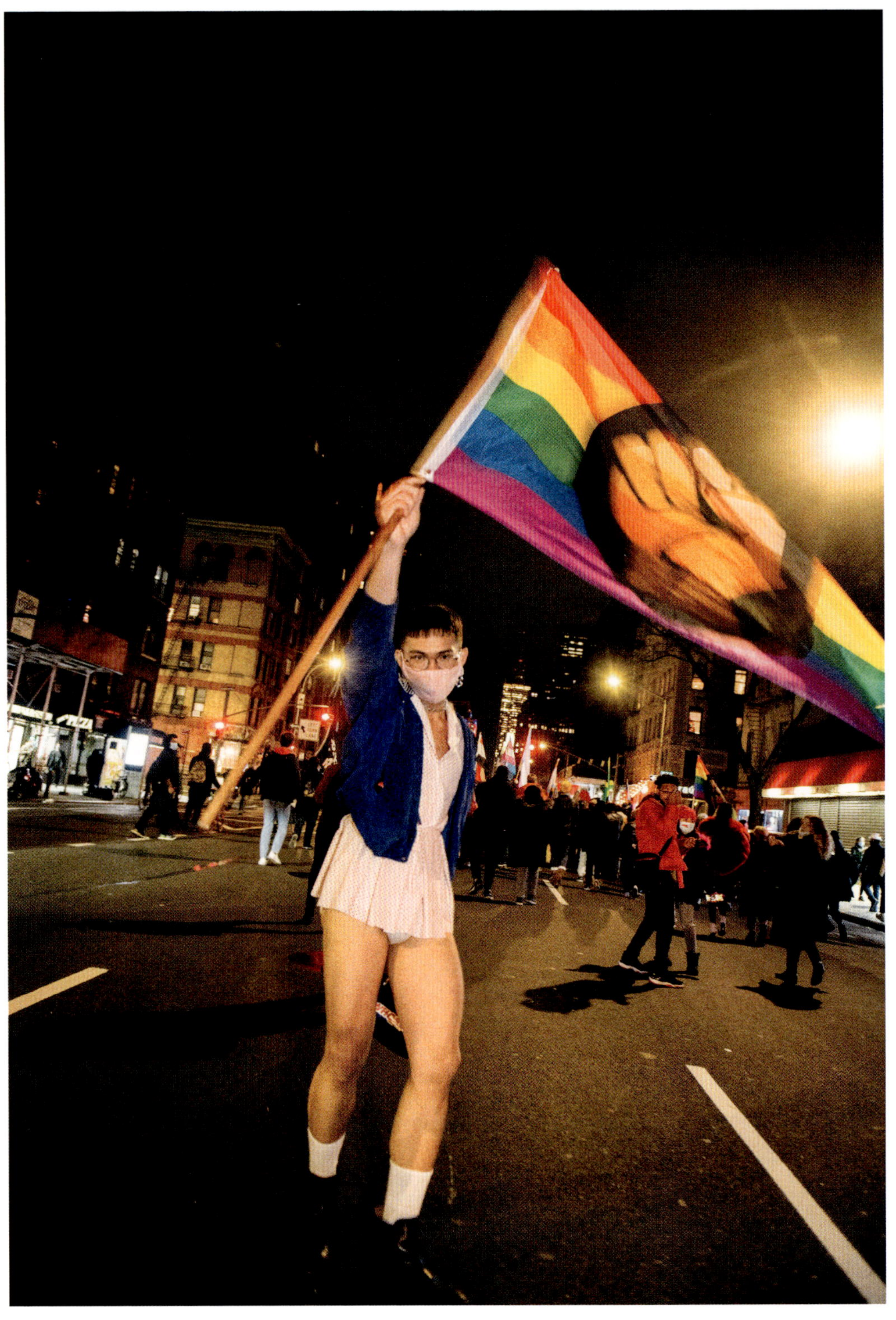

Ryan McGinley
Love Liberation: End the Stigma
December 2020

David Zung
Black and Asian Solidarity
March 2021

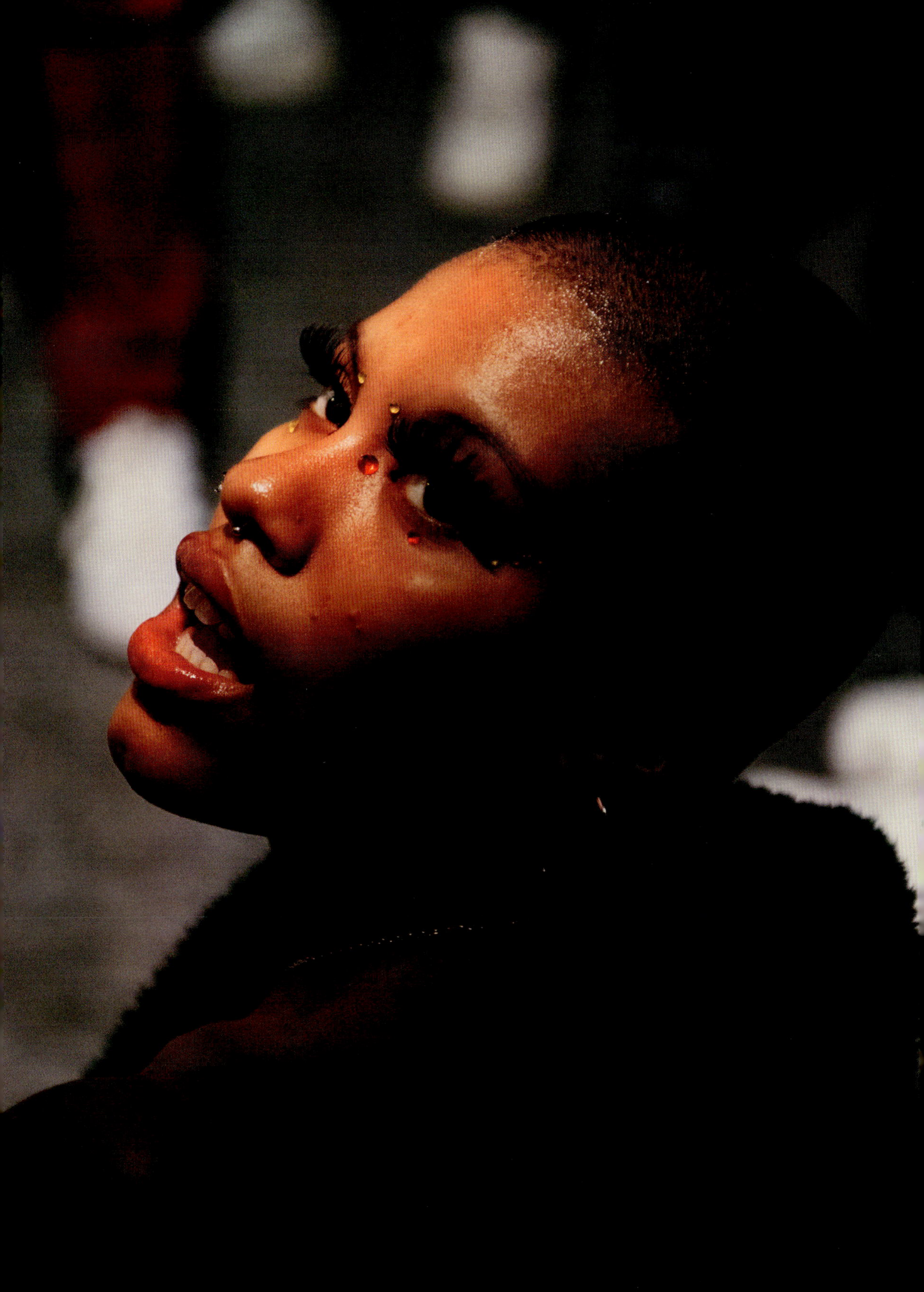

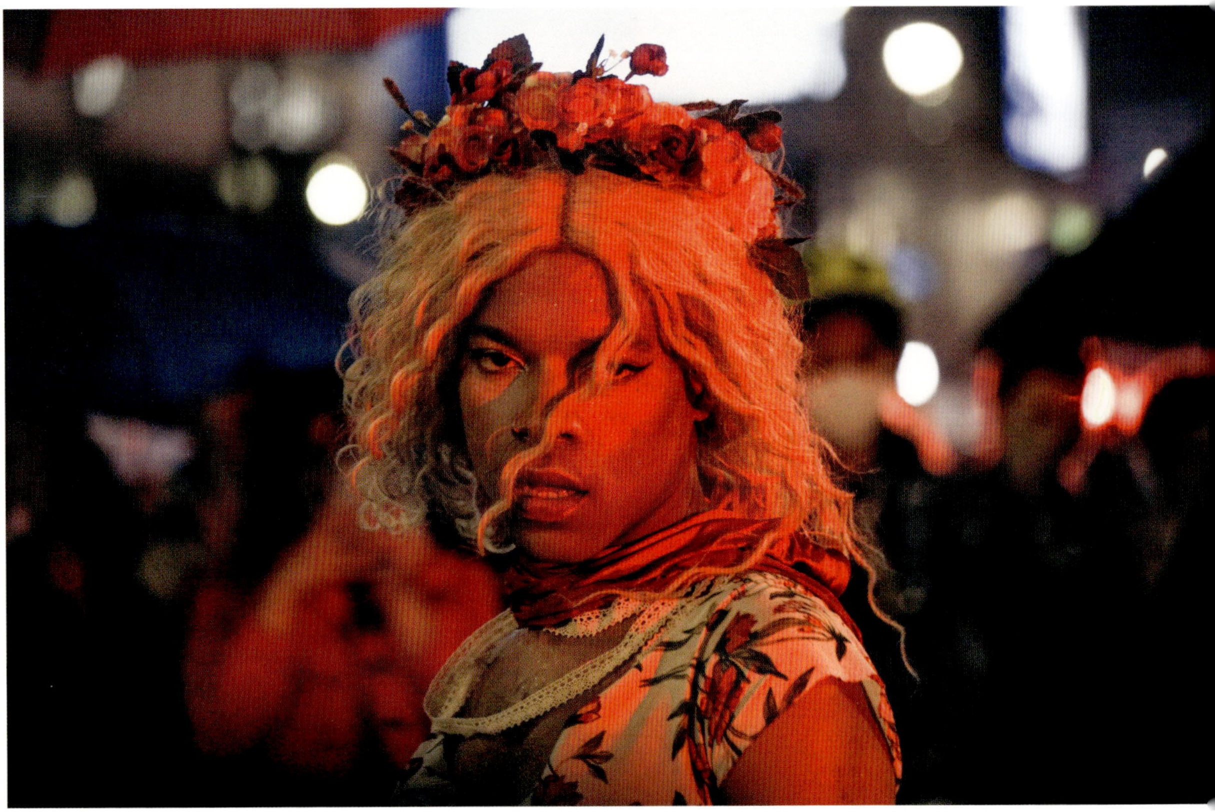

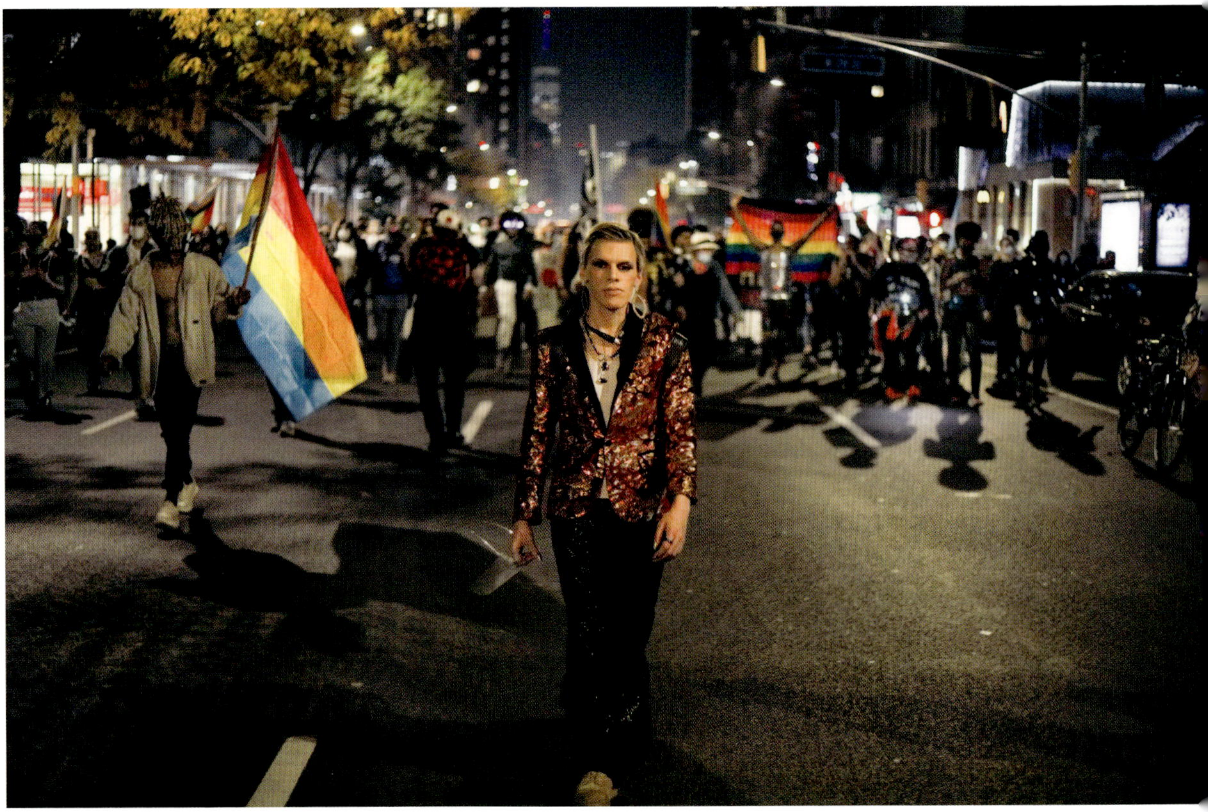

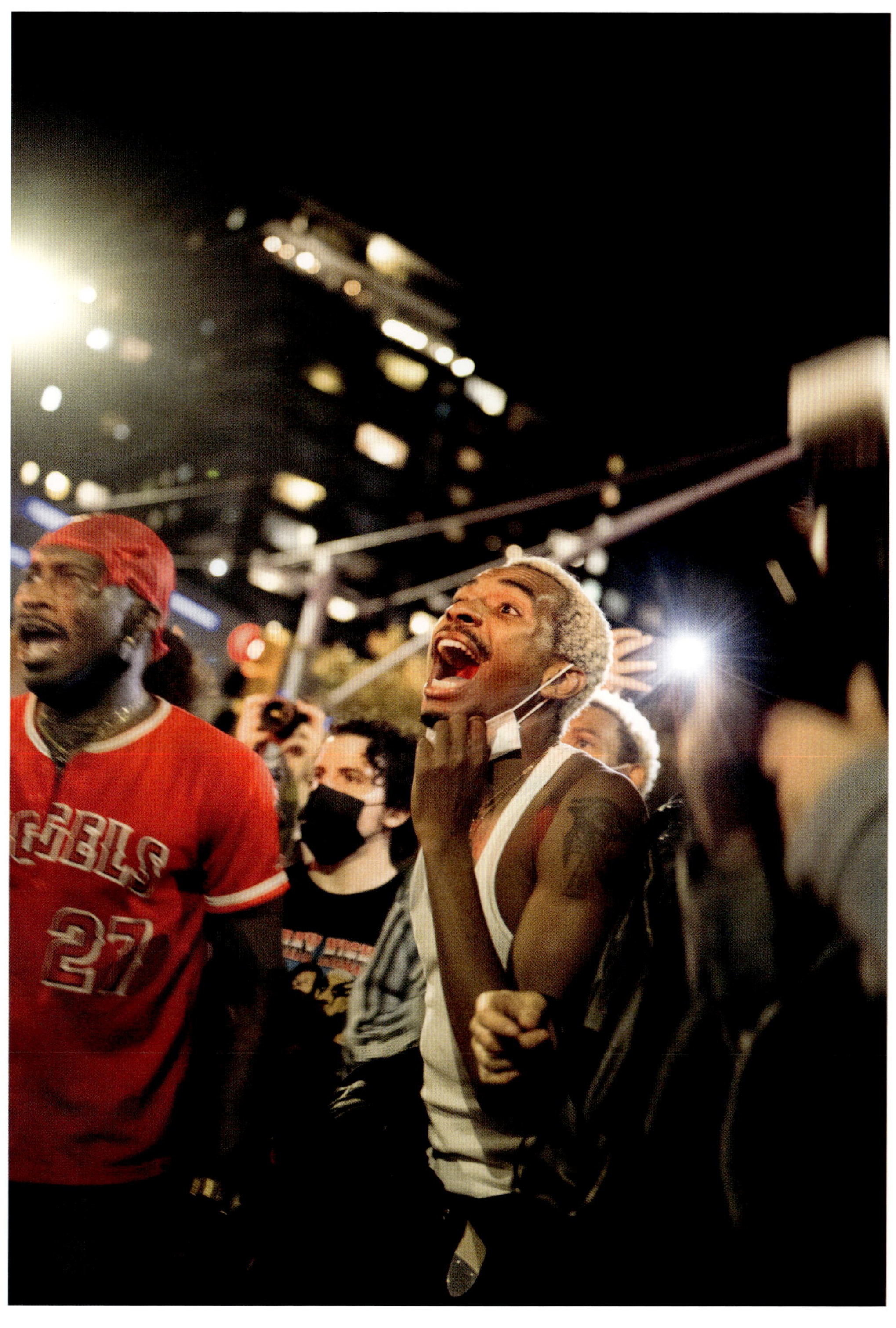

OPPOSITE:
Jarrett Robertson
Black Royalty Ball
Illumination Ball
October 2020

Ryan McGinley
Black Angels Ball
October 2020

In this collective movement I see myself as a contributor to history where I am lucky enough to have and continue to capture moments of Black and Brown joy—especially when there is civil unrest and whenever there is an injustice done to the Black and Brown community.

—Lucy Baptiste

Caroline Mardok
Liberation Not Deportation
October 2020

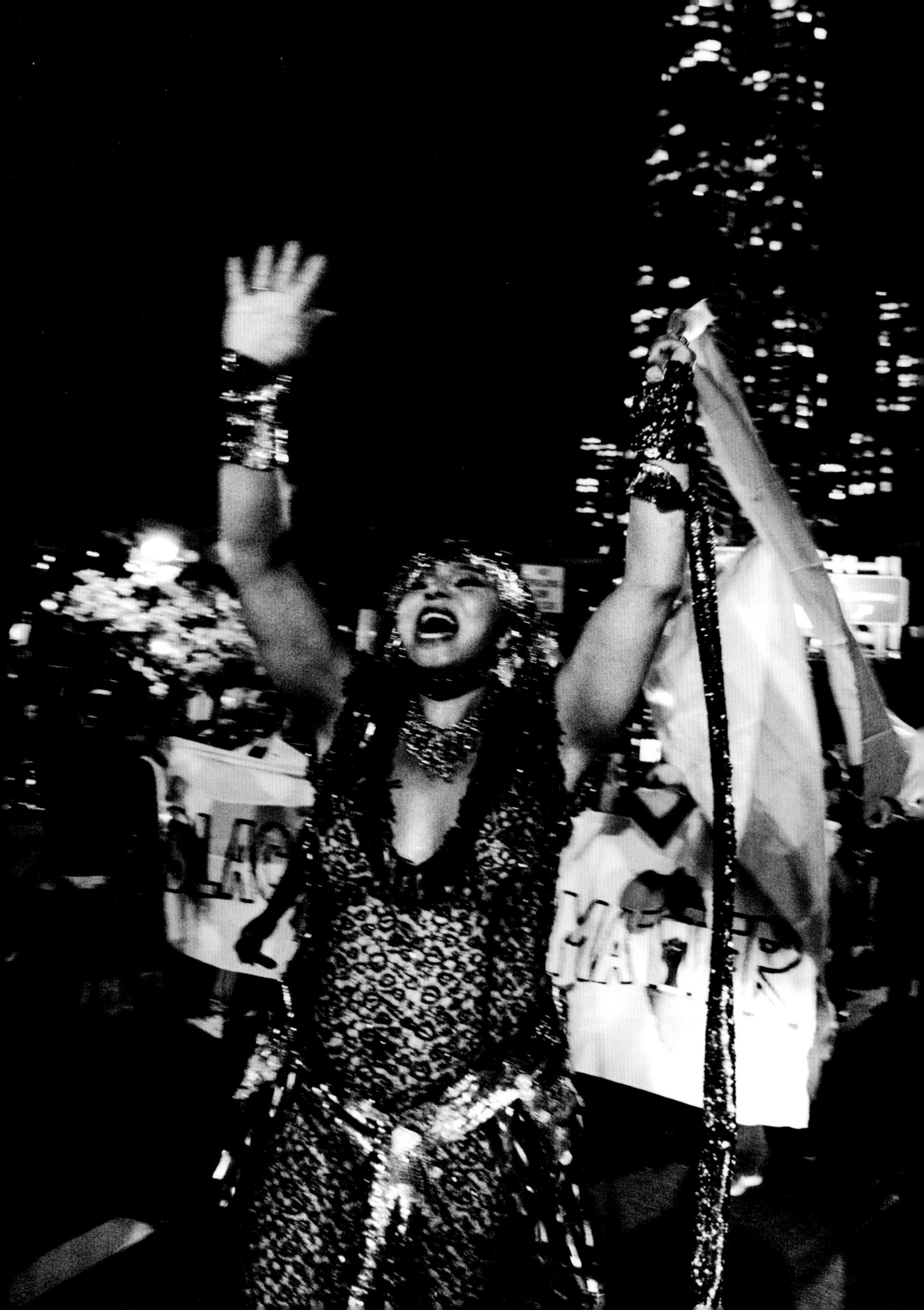

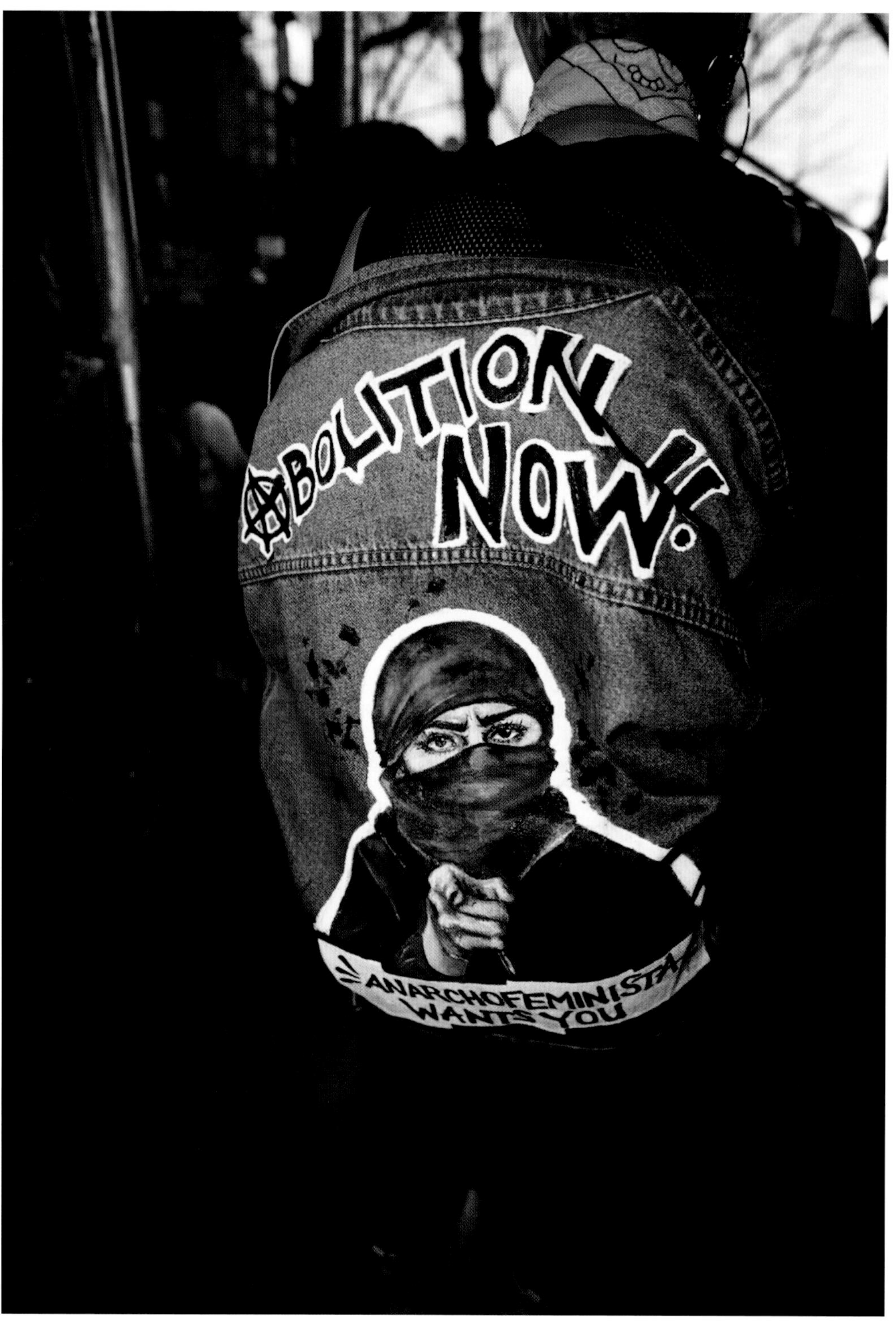

ABOVE AND OPPOSITE:
Budi
Black and Asian Solidarity
March 2021

NEXT SPREAD:
Daniel Lehrhaupt
July 2021

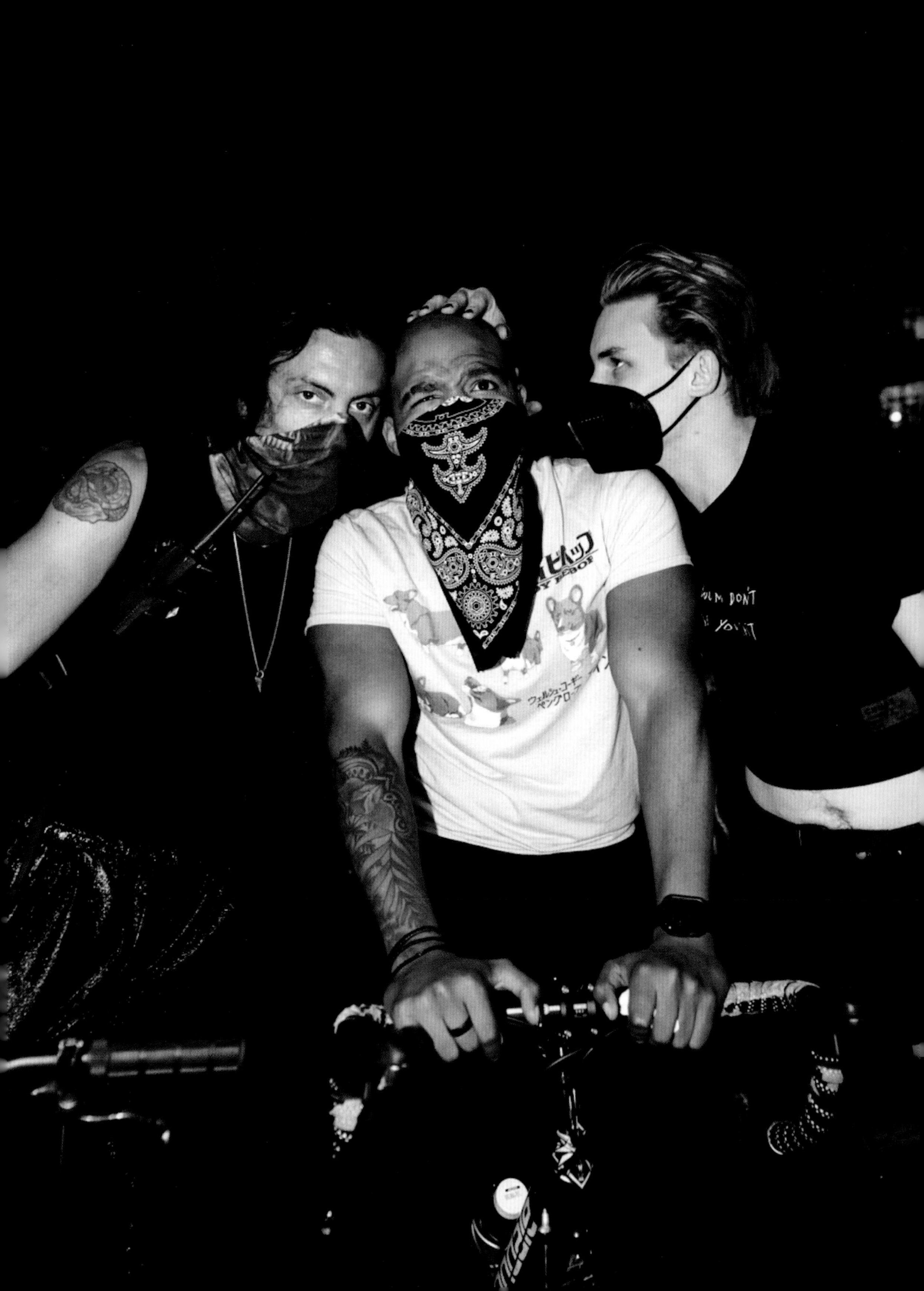

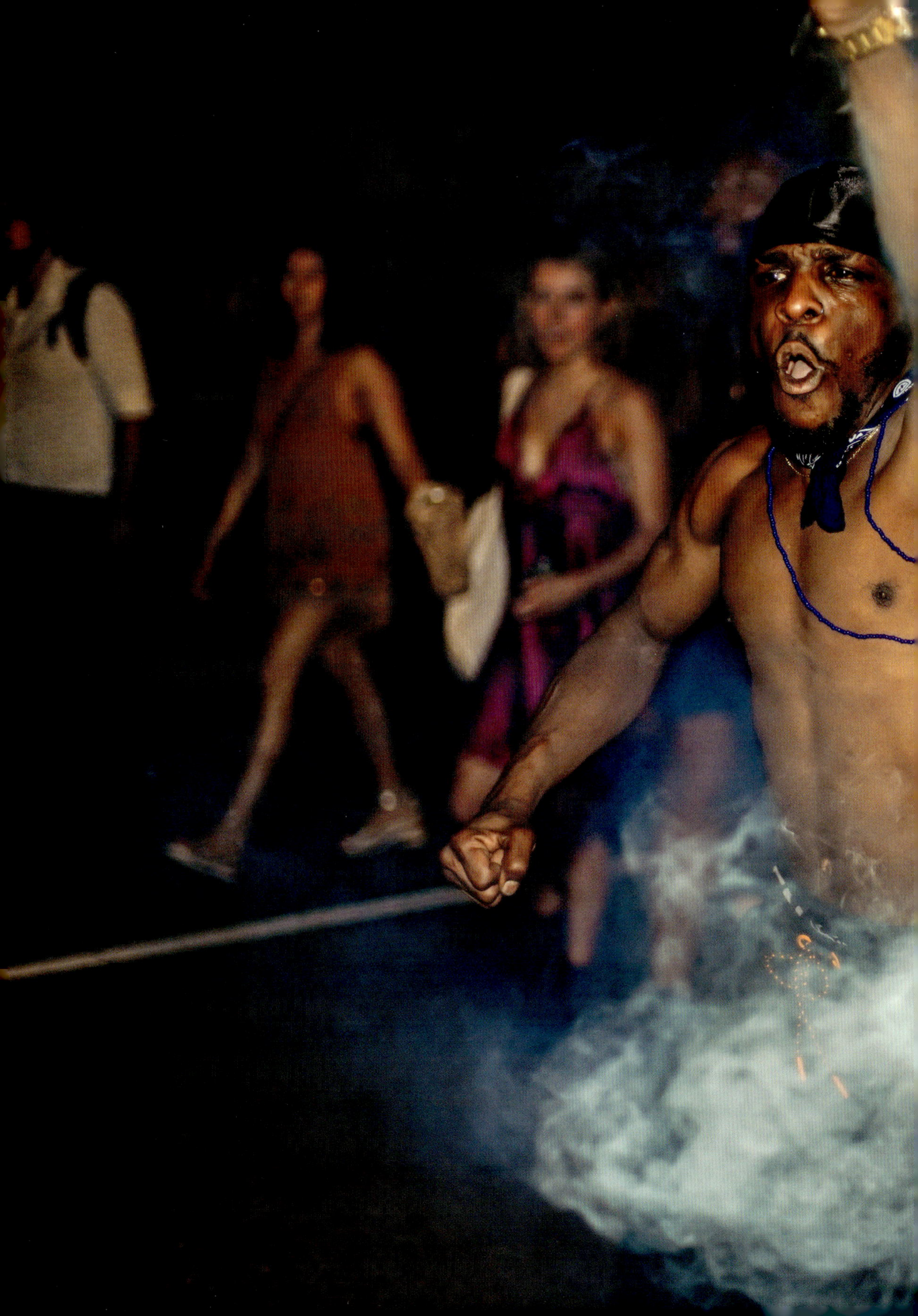

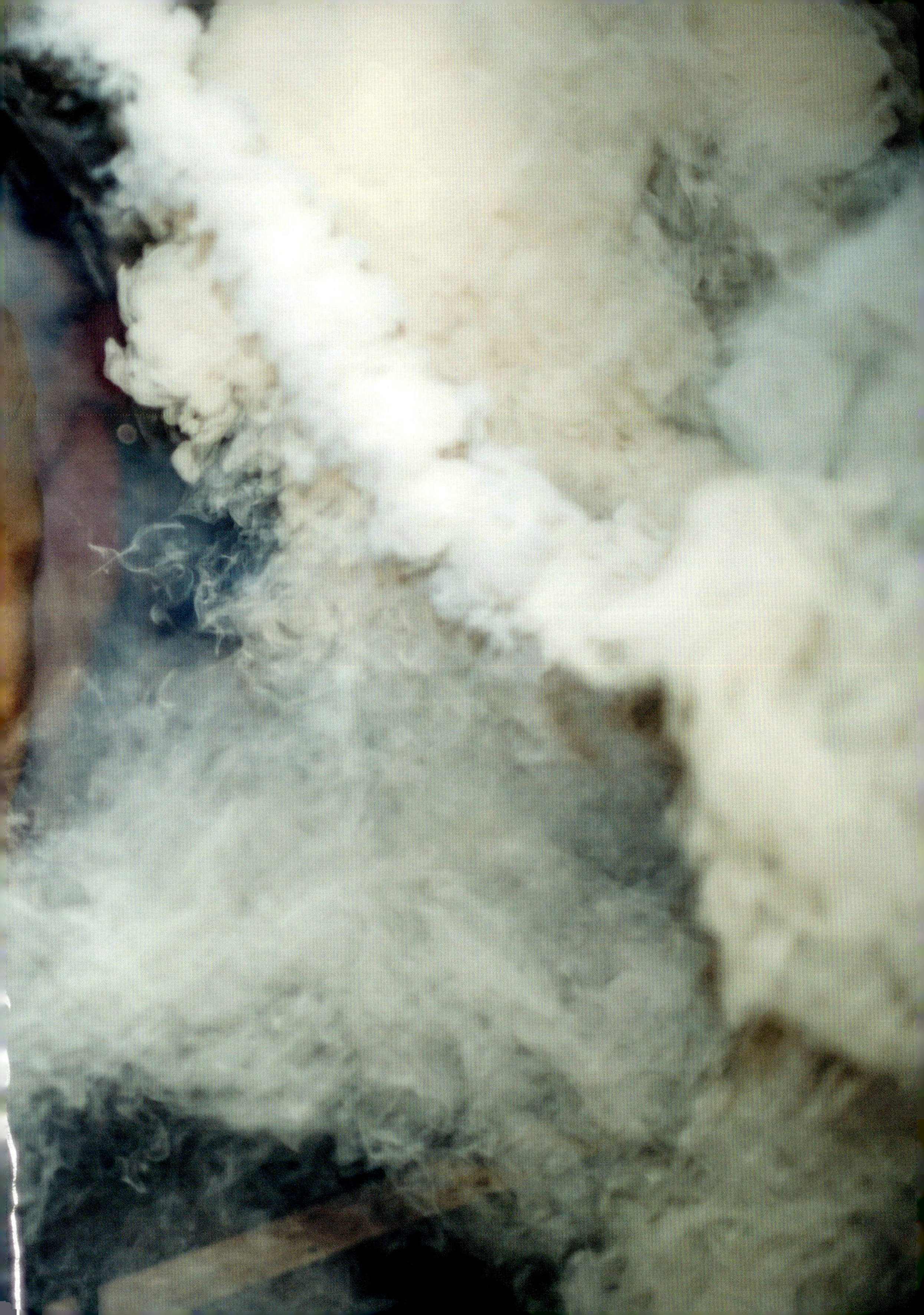

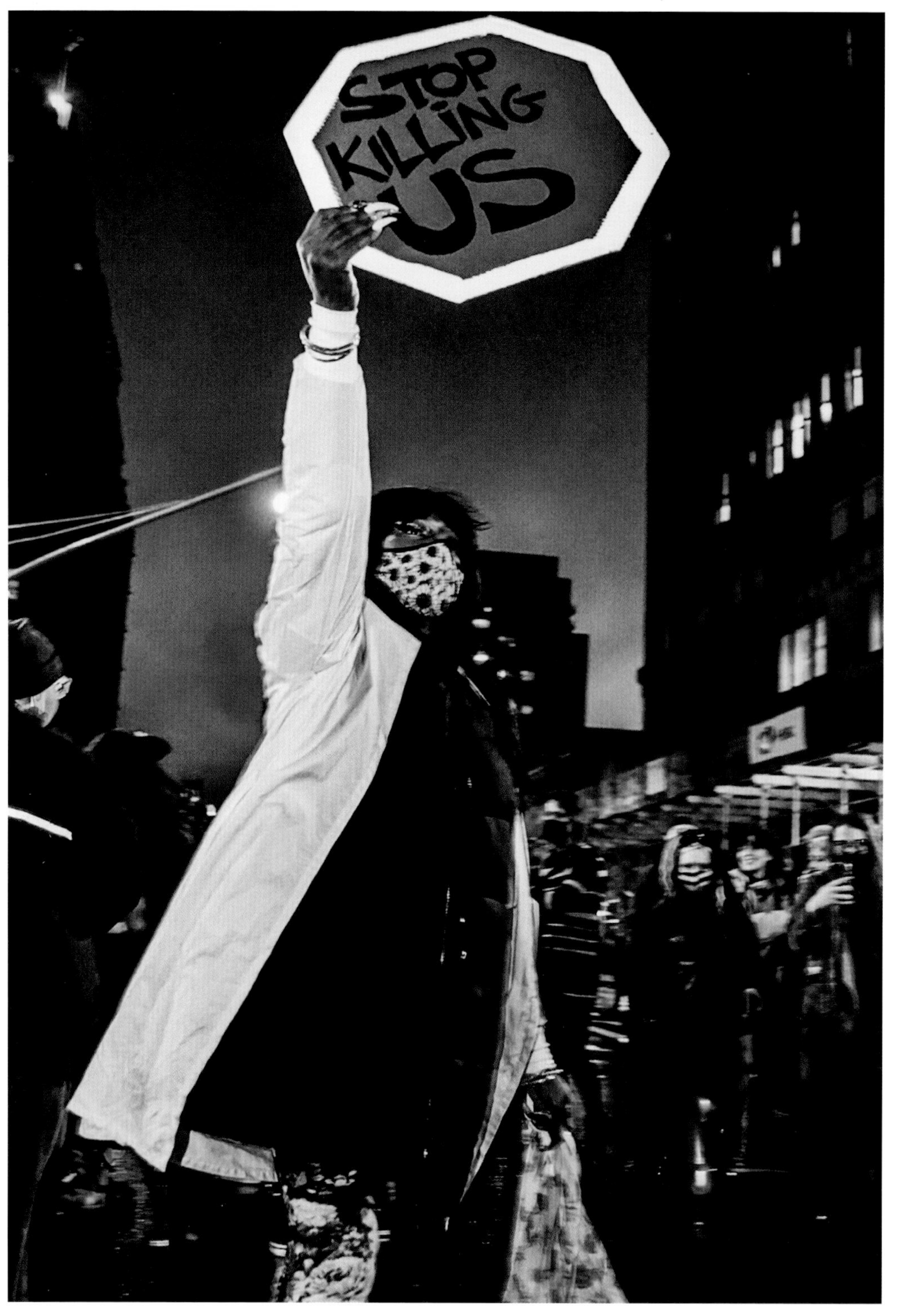

Budi
A Day of Healing for All Black Women
March 2021

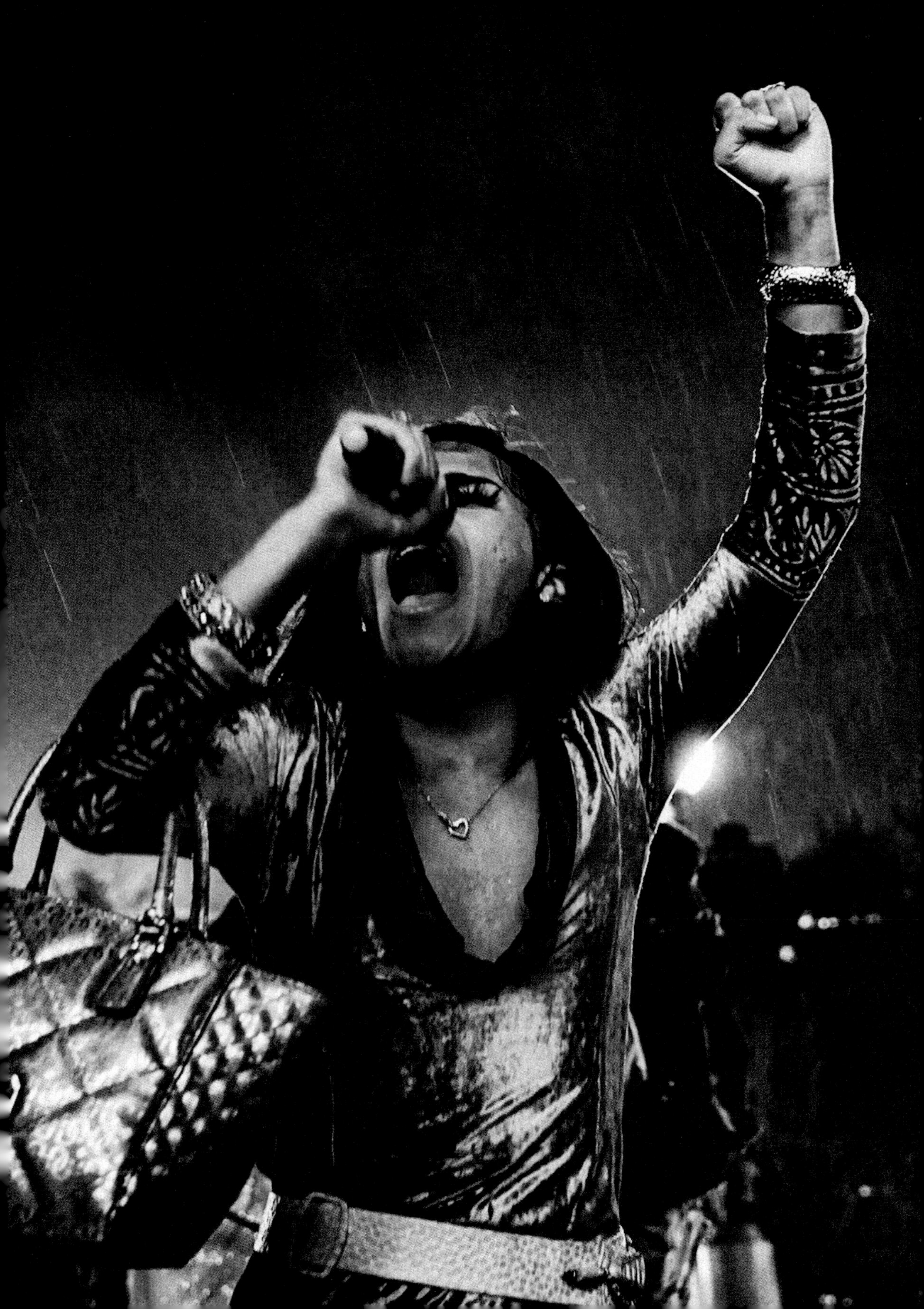

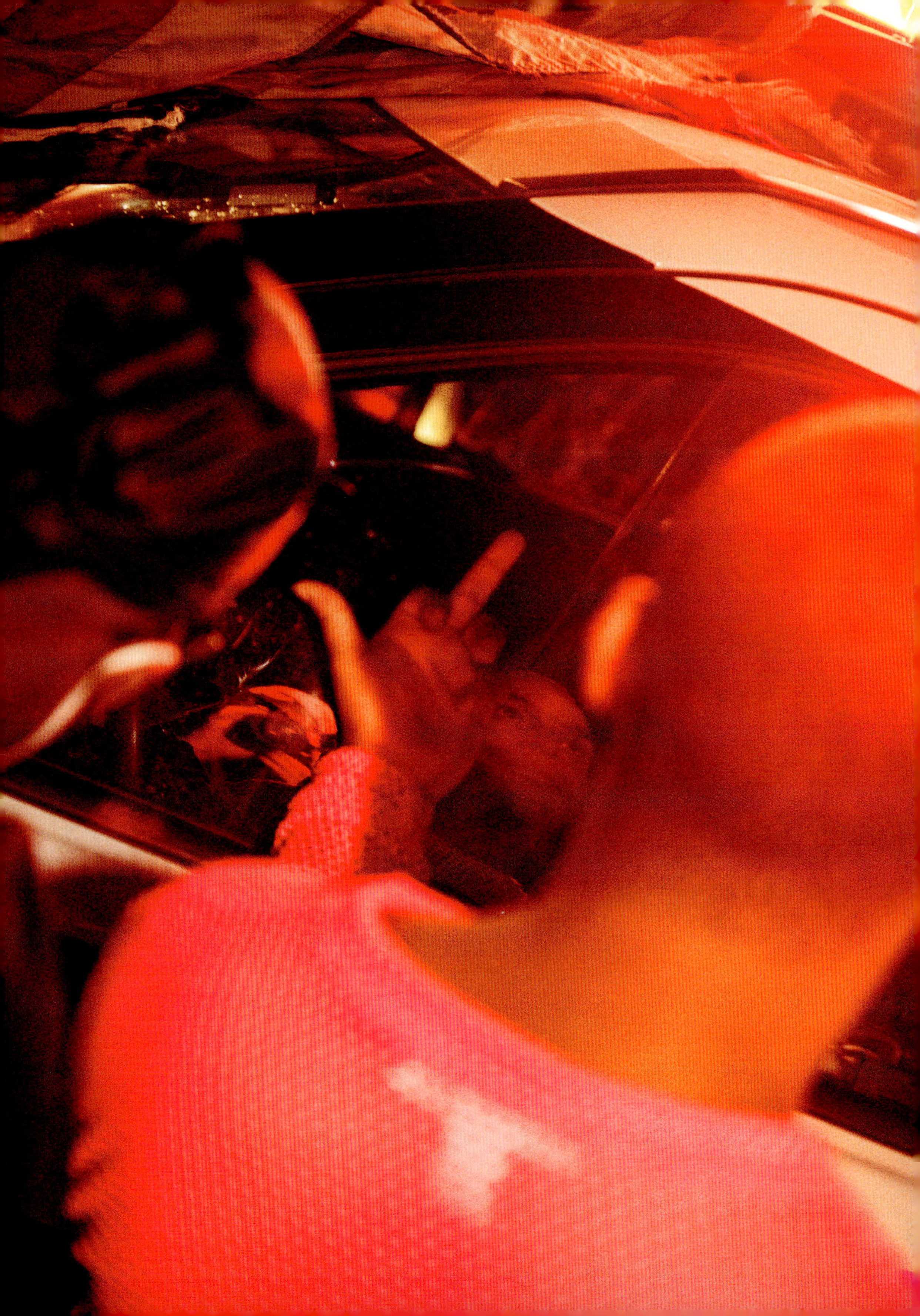

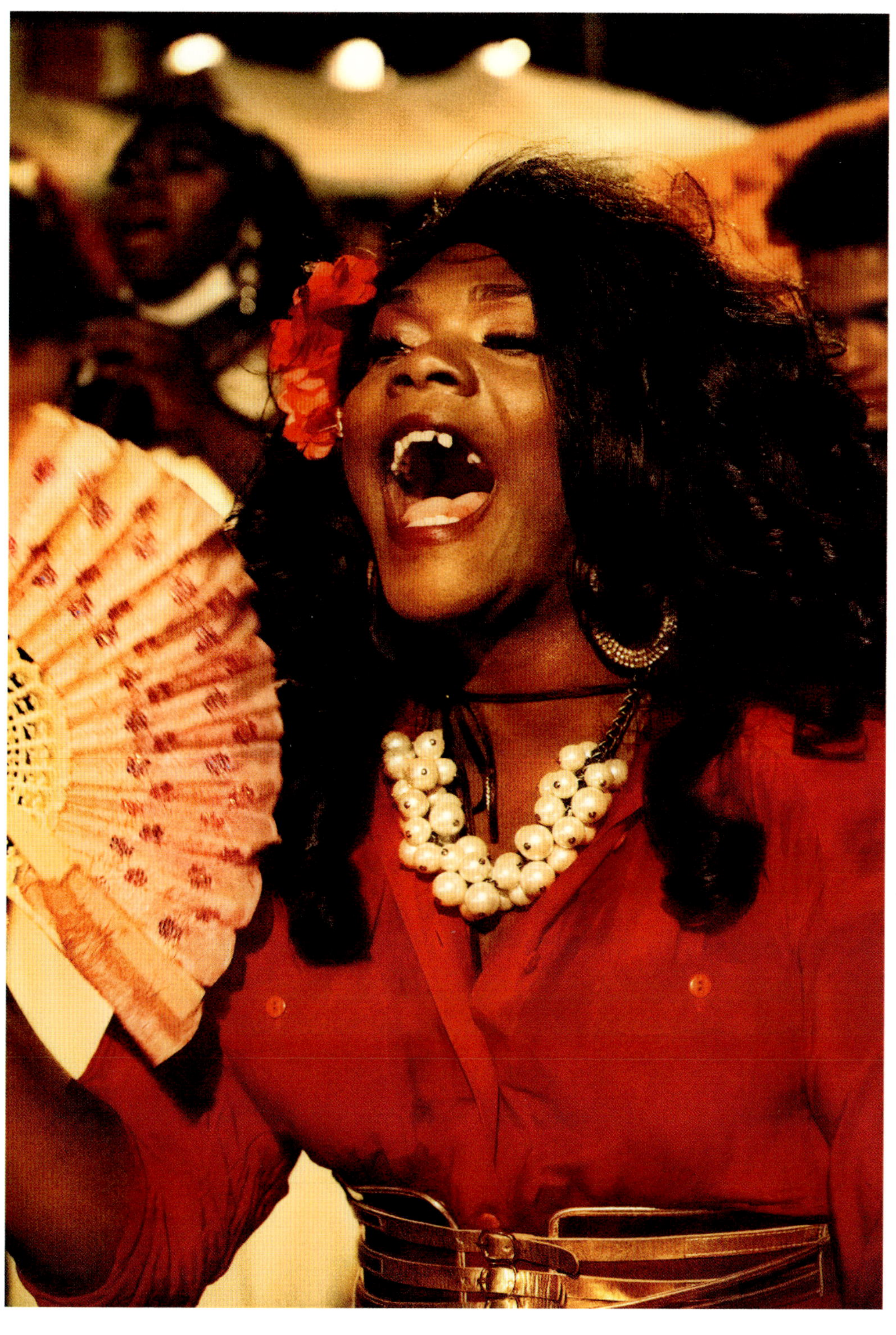

Ryan McGinley
End Transgender Violence
June 2021

Stas Ginzburg
Icons Liberation Ball
October 2020

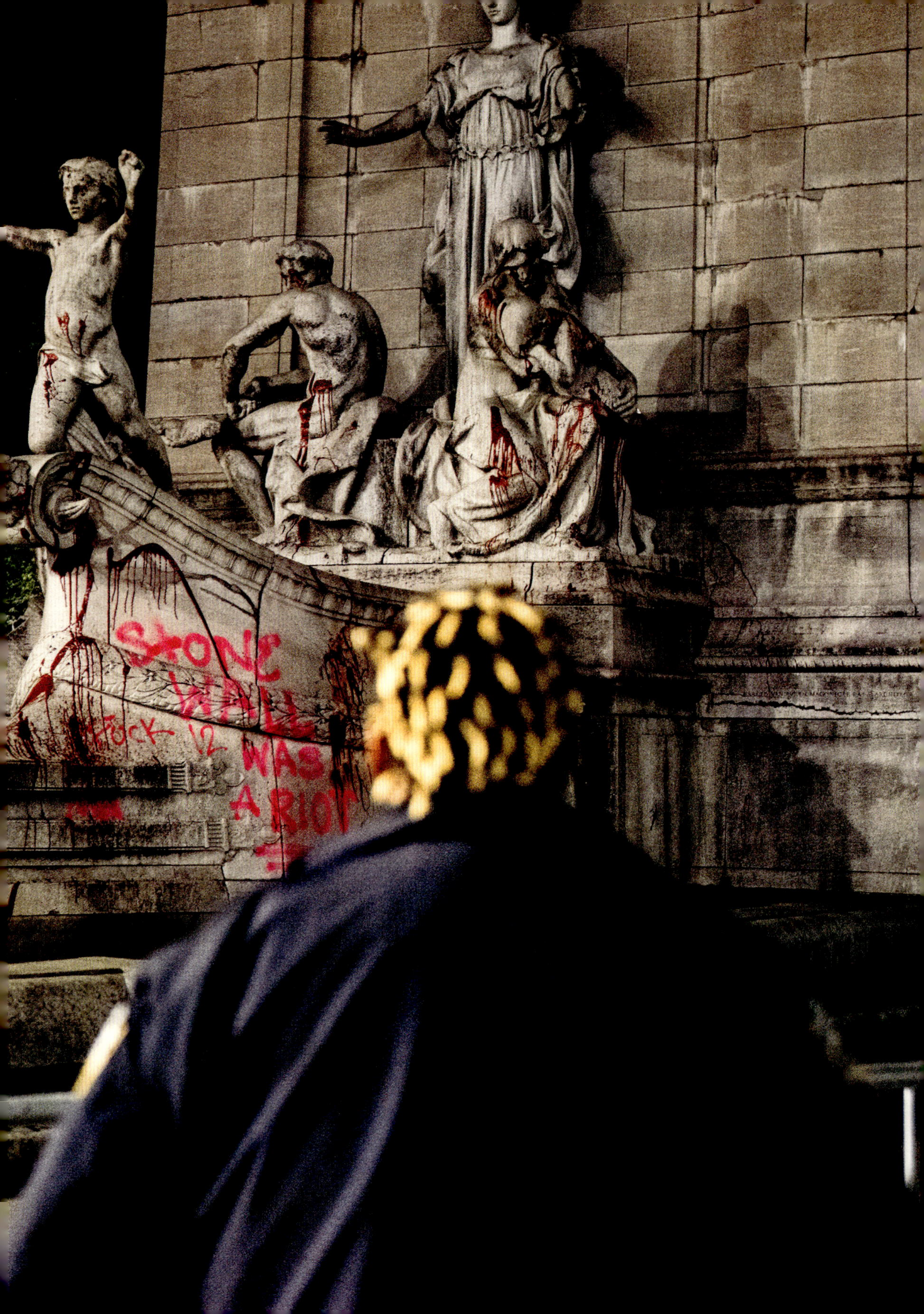

STONE
WALL
FUCK 12 WAS
A RIOT

The Stonewall community returned week after week, together in rain, snow, and heat, relentless and determined. Even in the face of violence, they found the courage to summon joy; in the face of discrimination, the strength to find empowerment; and in the face of oppression, the will to carry on and fight.

—Zak Krevitt

NEXT SPREAD:
Ruvan Wijesooriya
Martin Luther King Jr. Day
January 2021

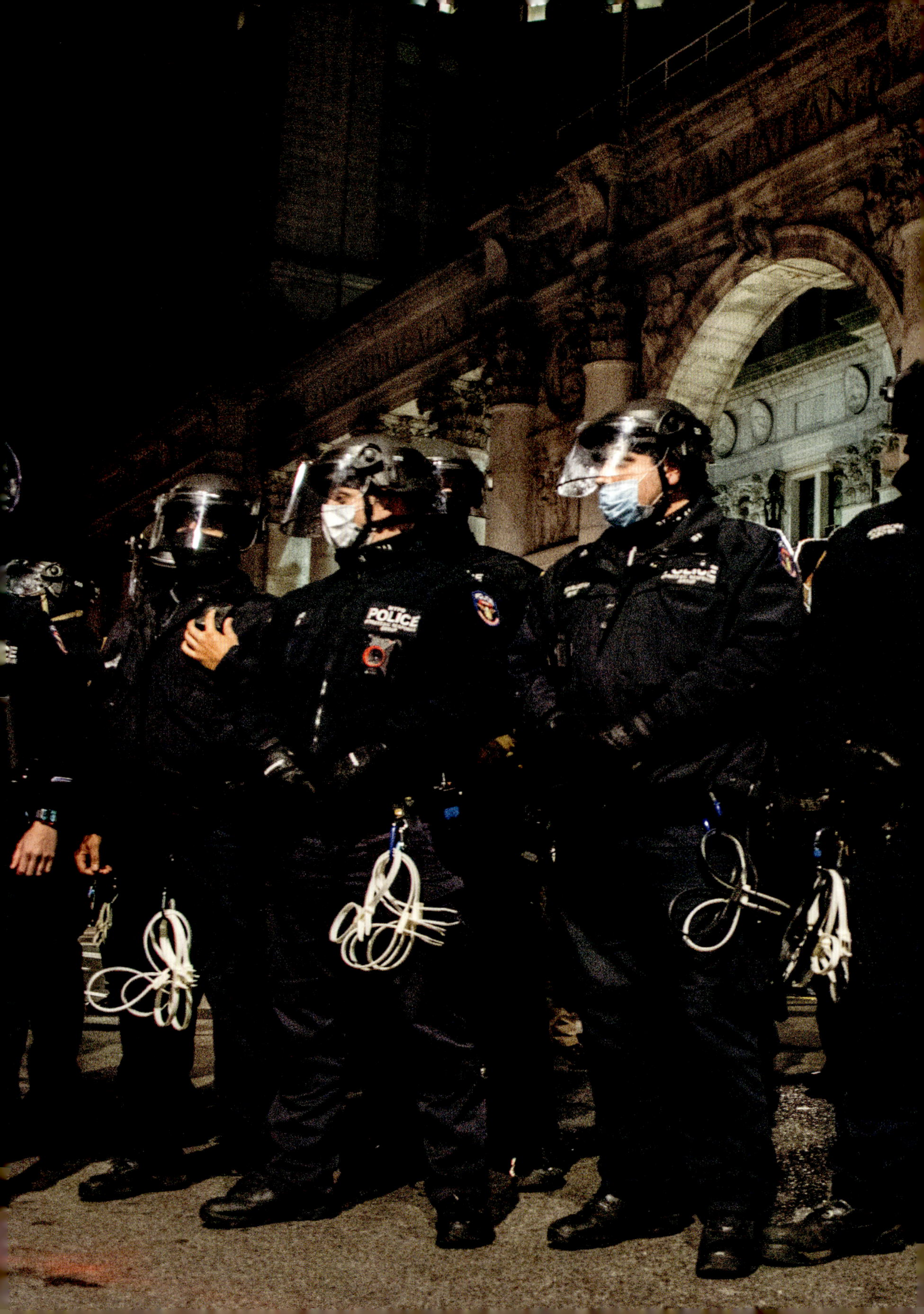

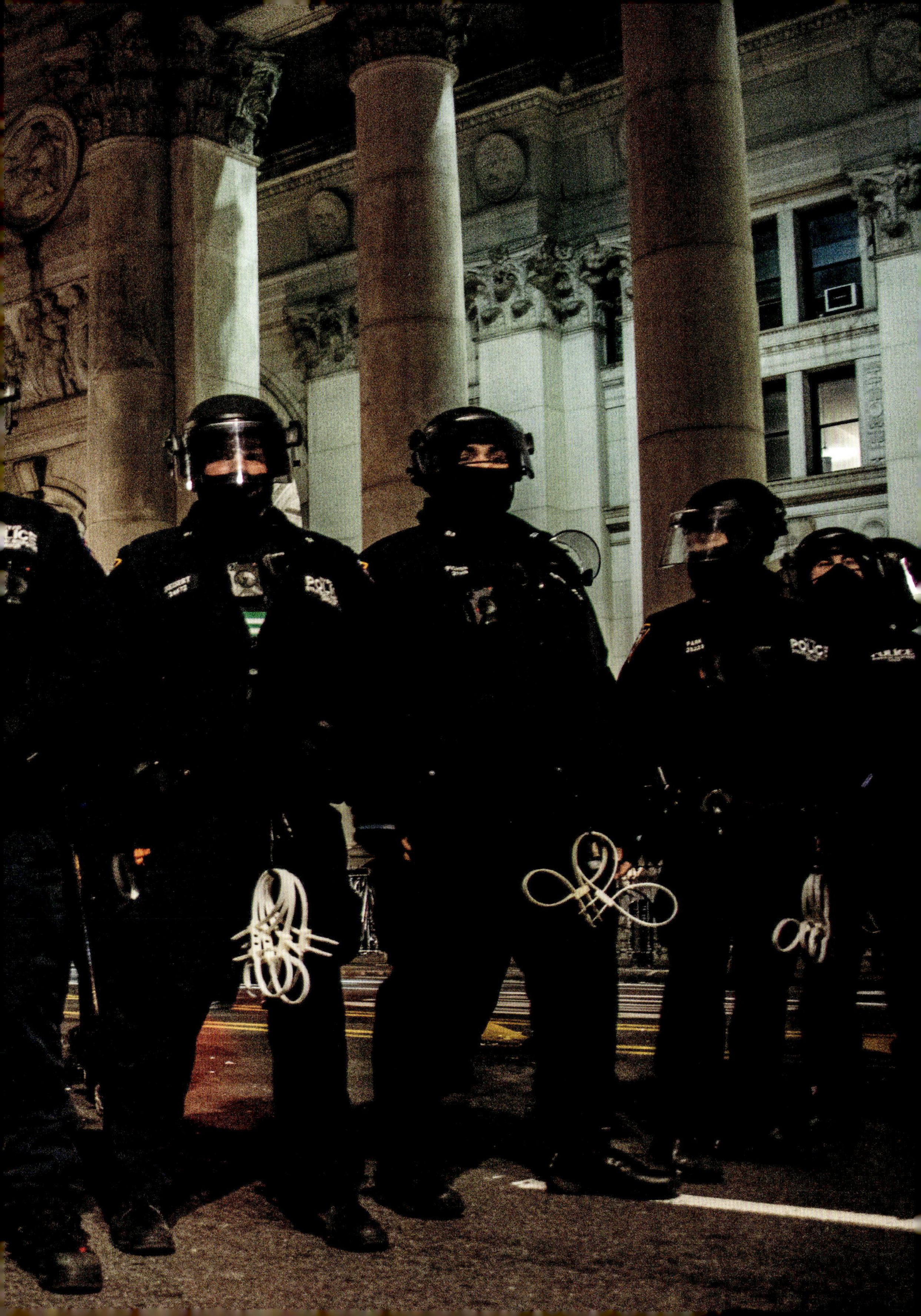

Police have a monopoly on the violence they use disproportionately against Black and trans people. Documenting this culture amplifies the resistance and allows future activists to see they are part of a history.

—Ruvan Wijesooriya

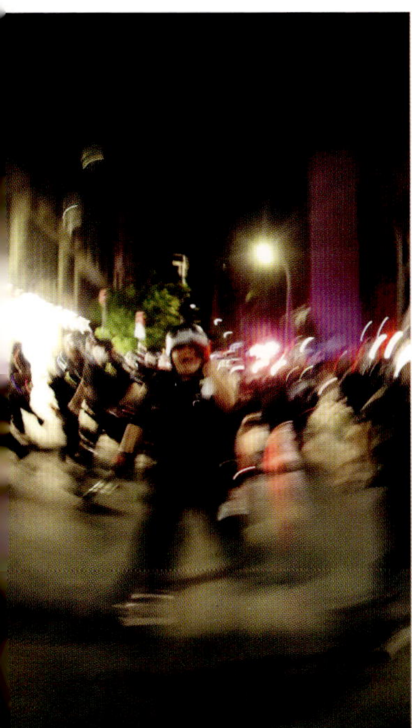 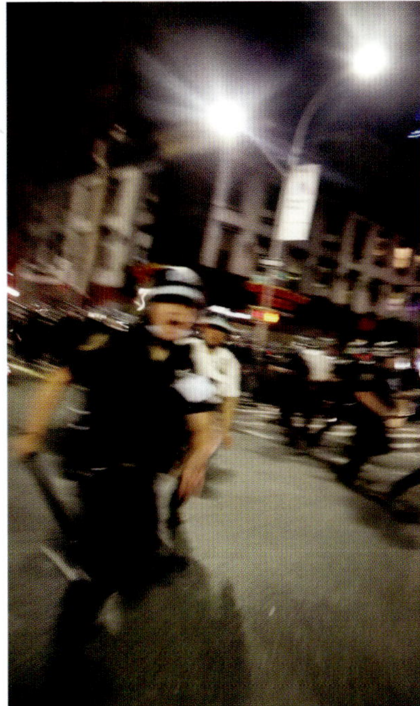 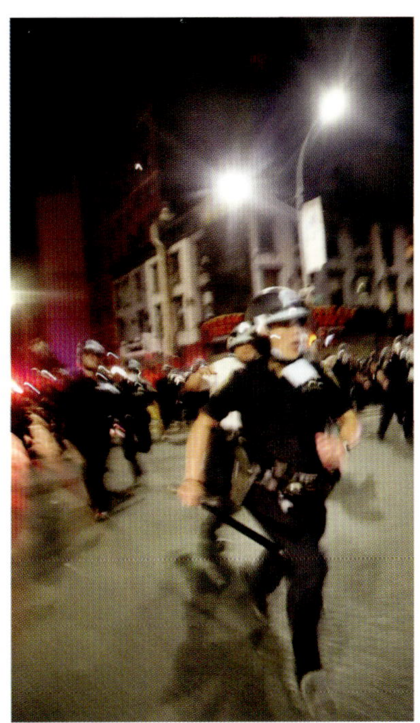
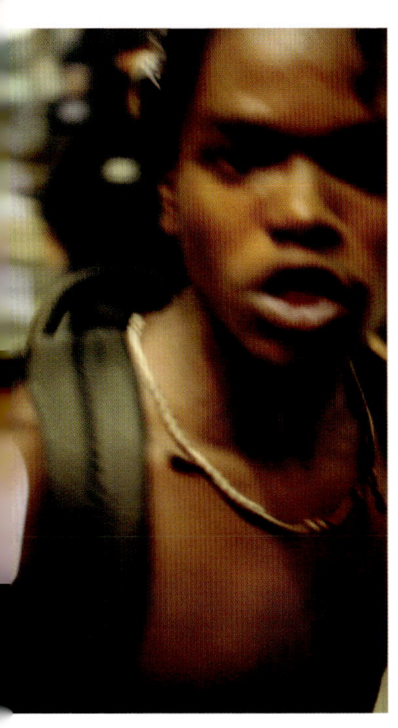 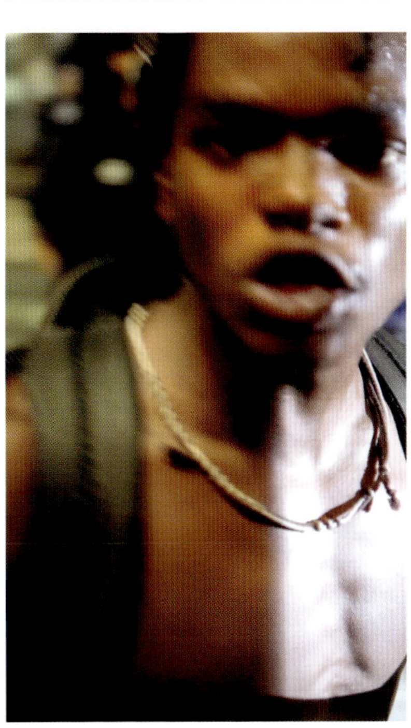 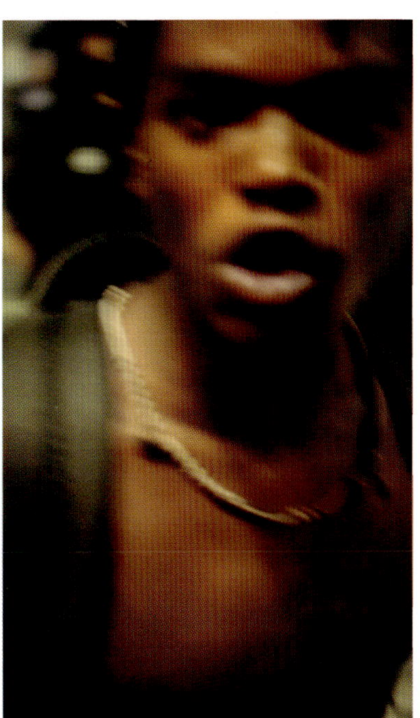

Brandon English
2020

NEXT SPREAD:
Robert Hamada
June 2021

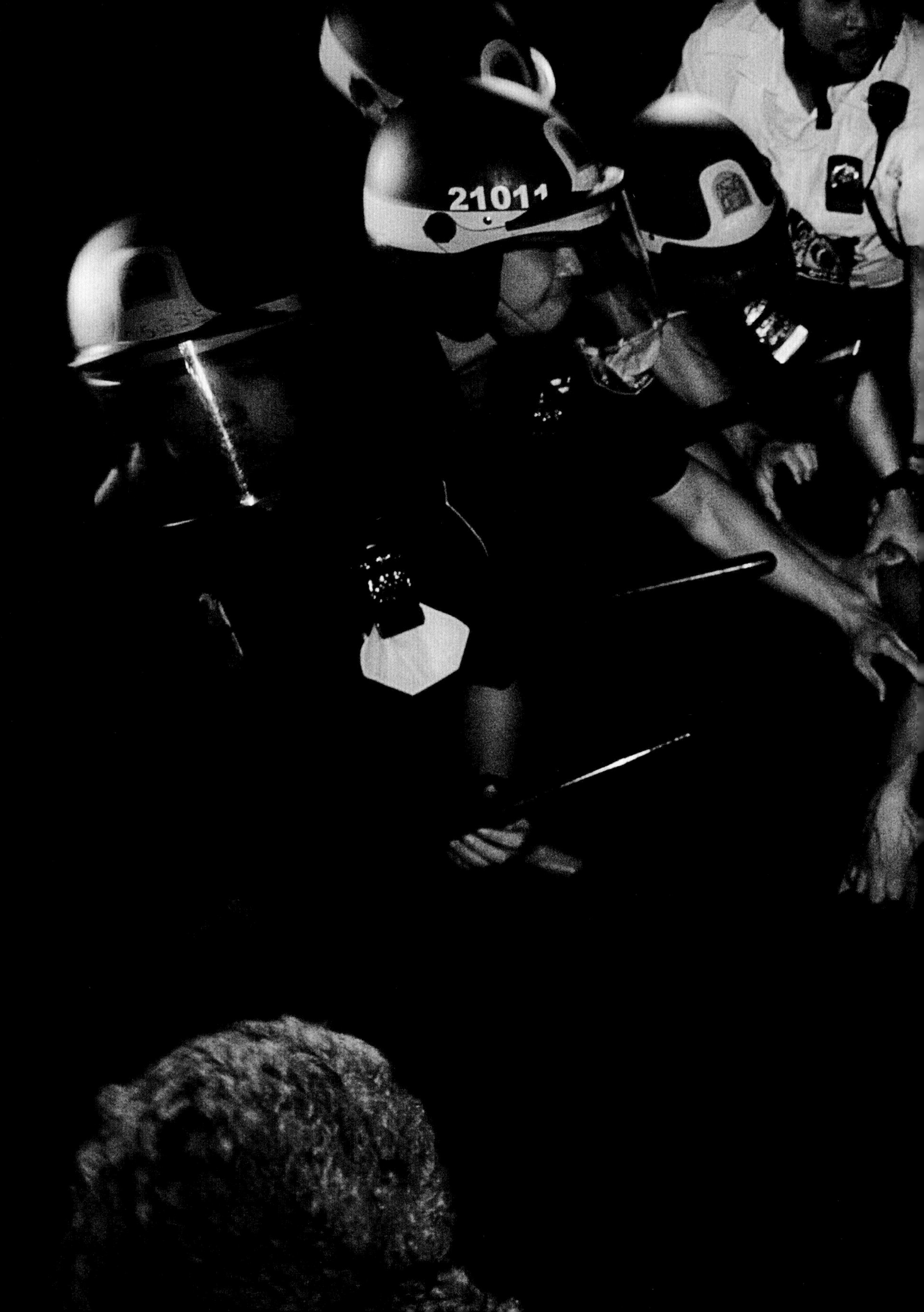

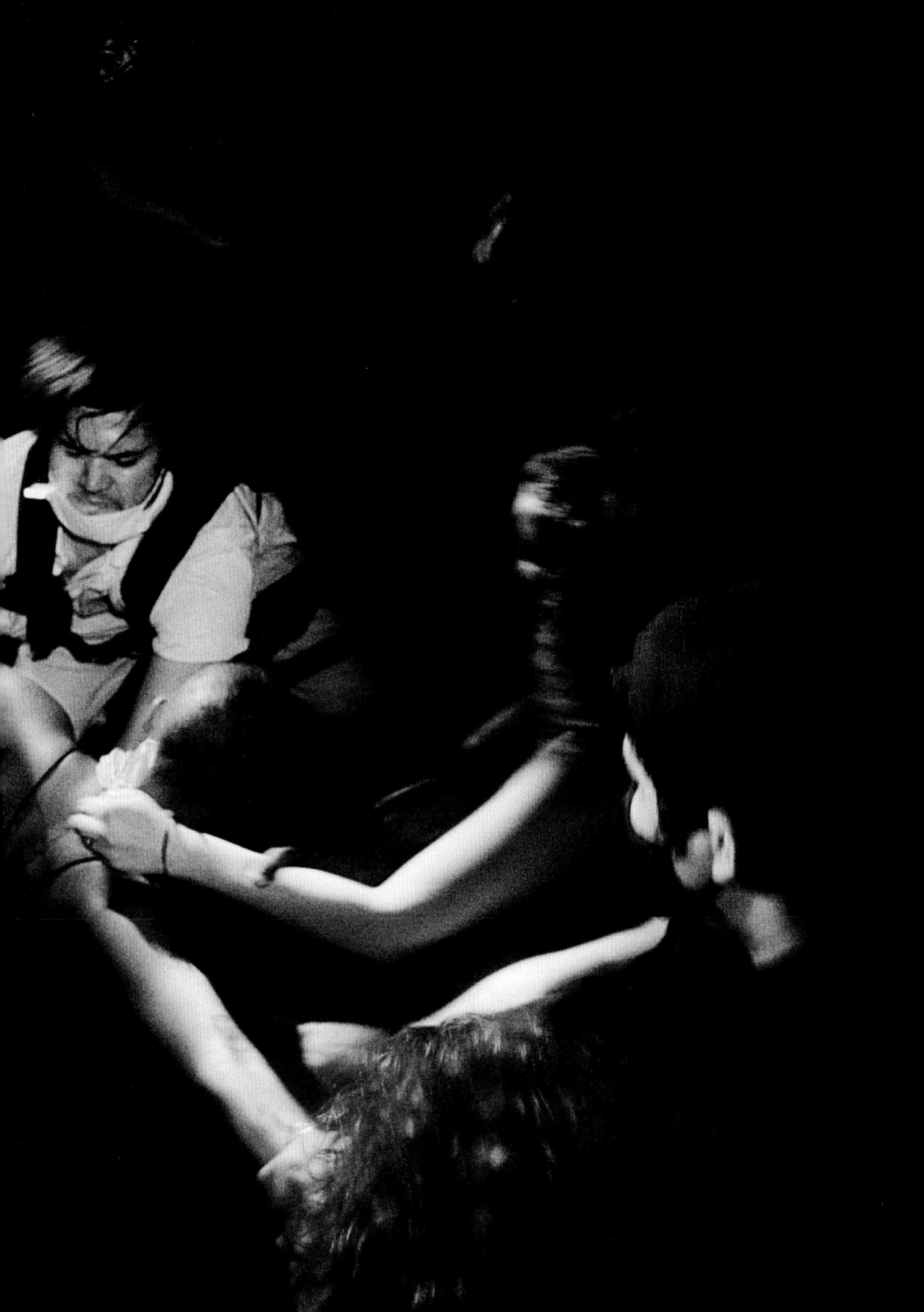

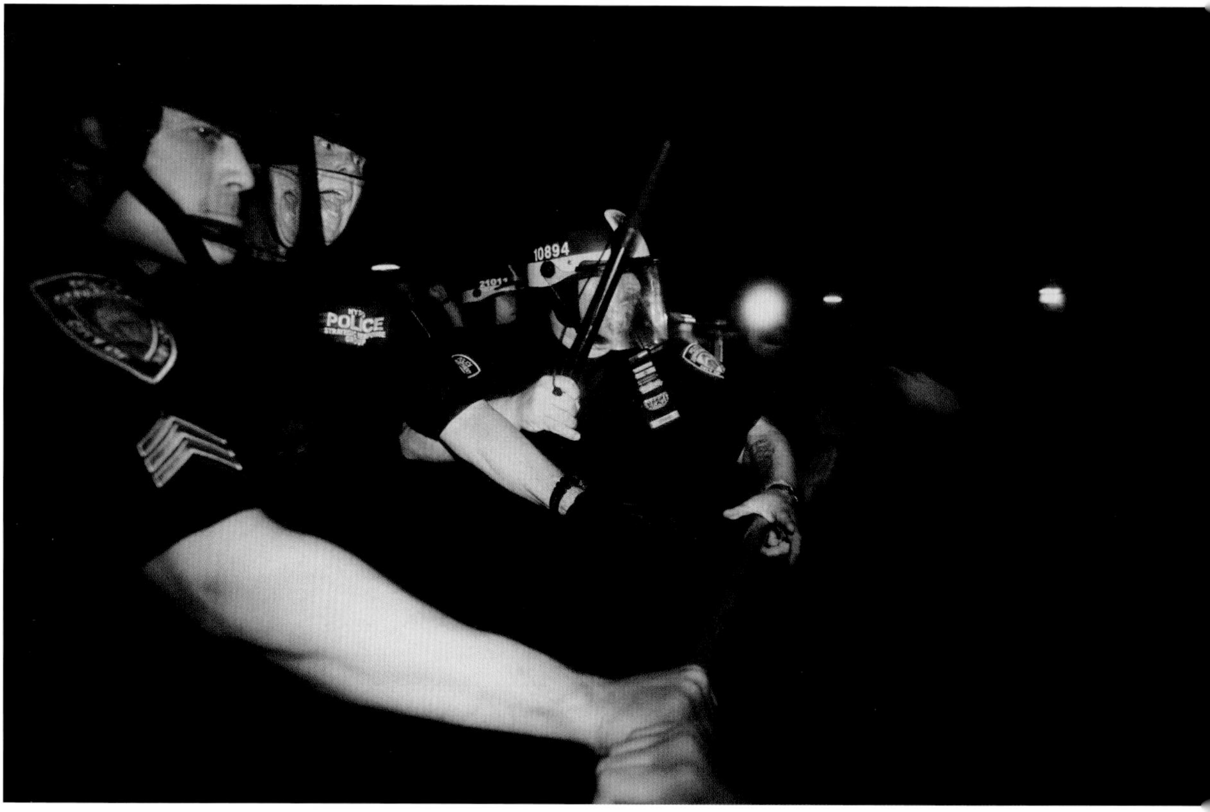

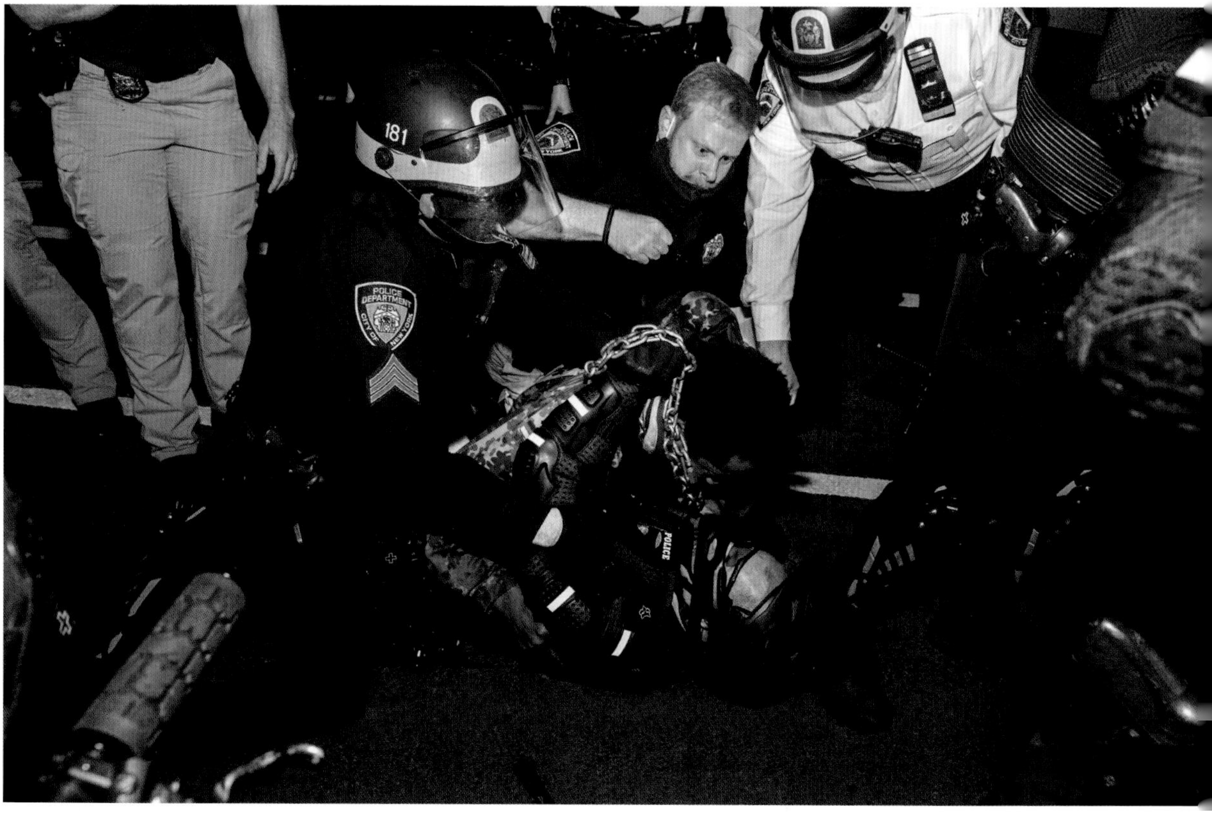

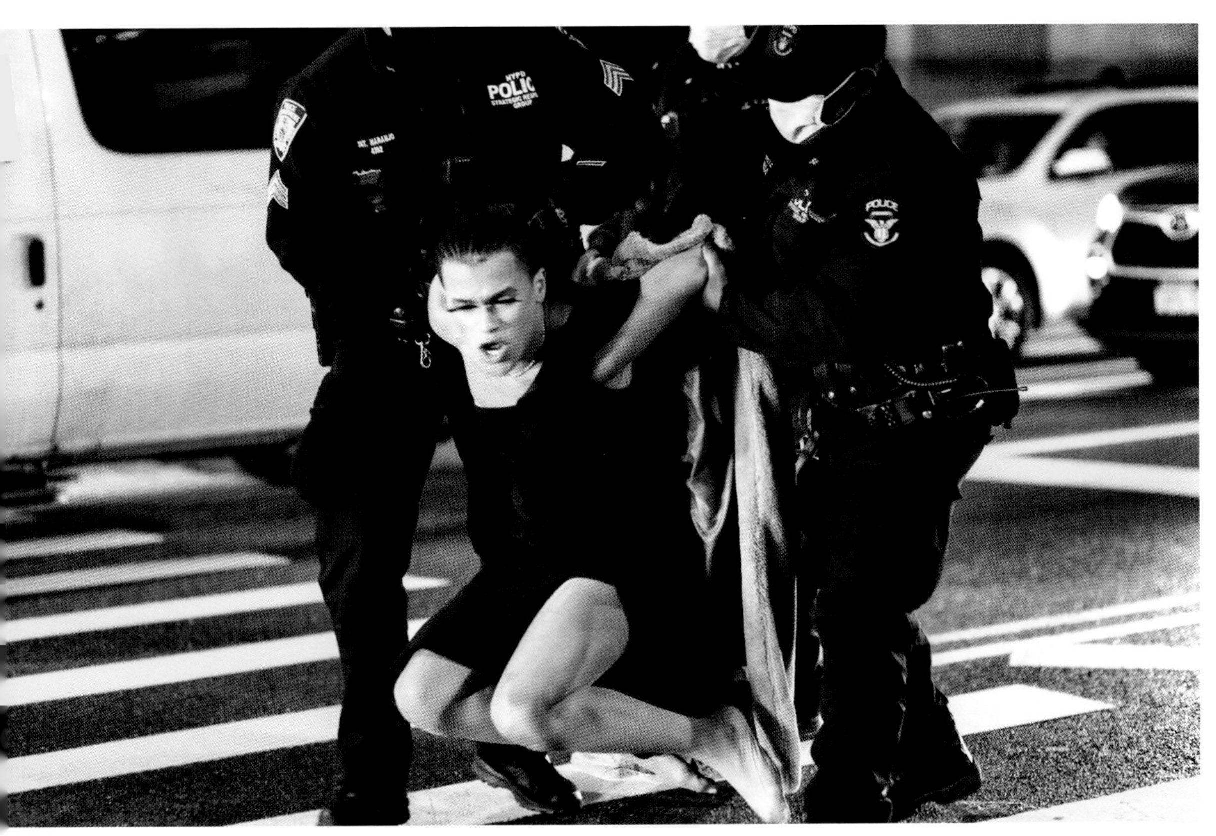

Robert Hamada
June 2021

Chae Kihn
November 2020

Phoenix Robles
Martin Luther King Jr. Day
January 2021

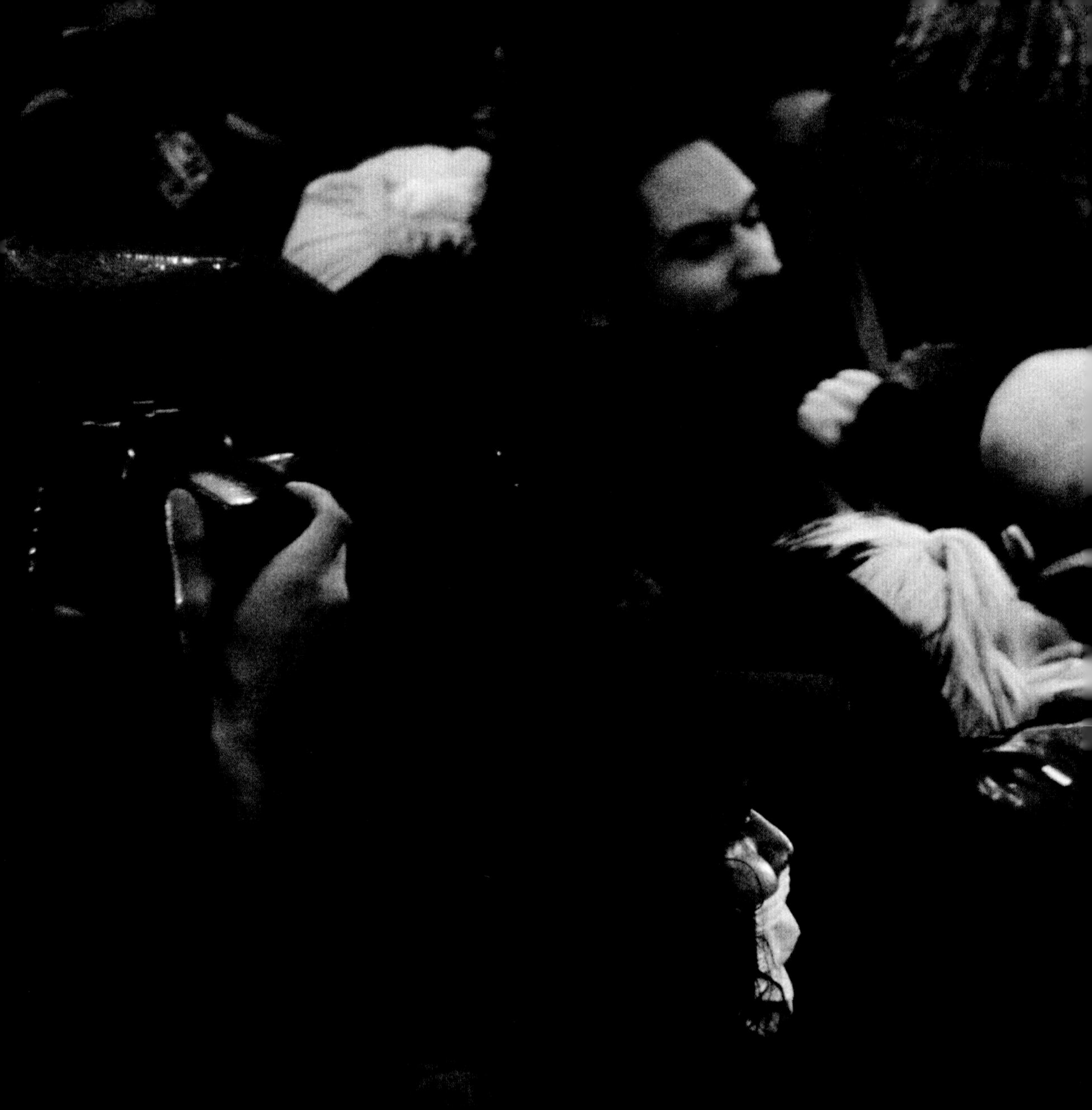

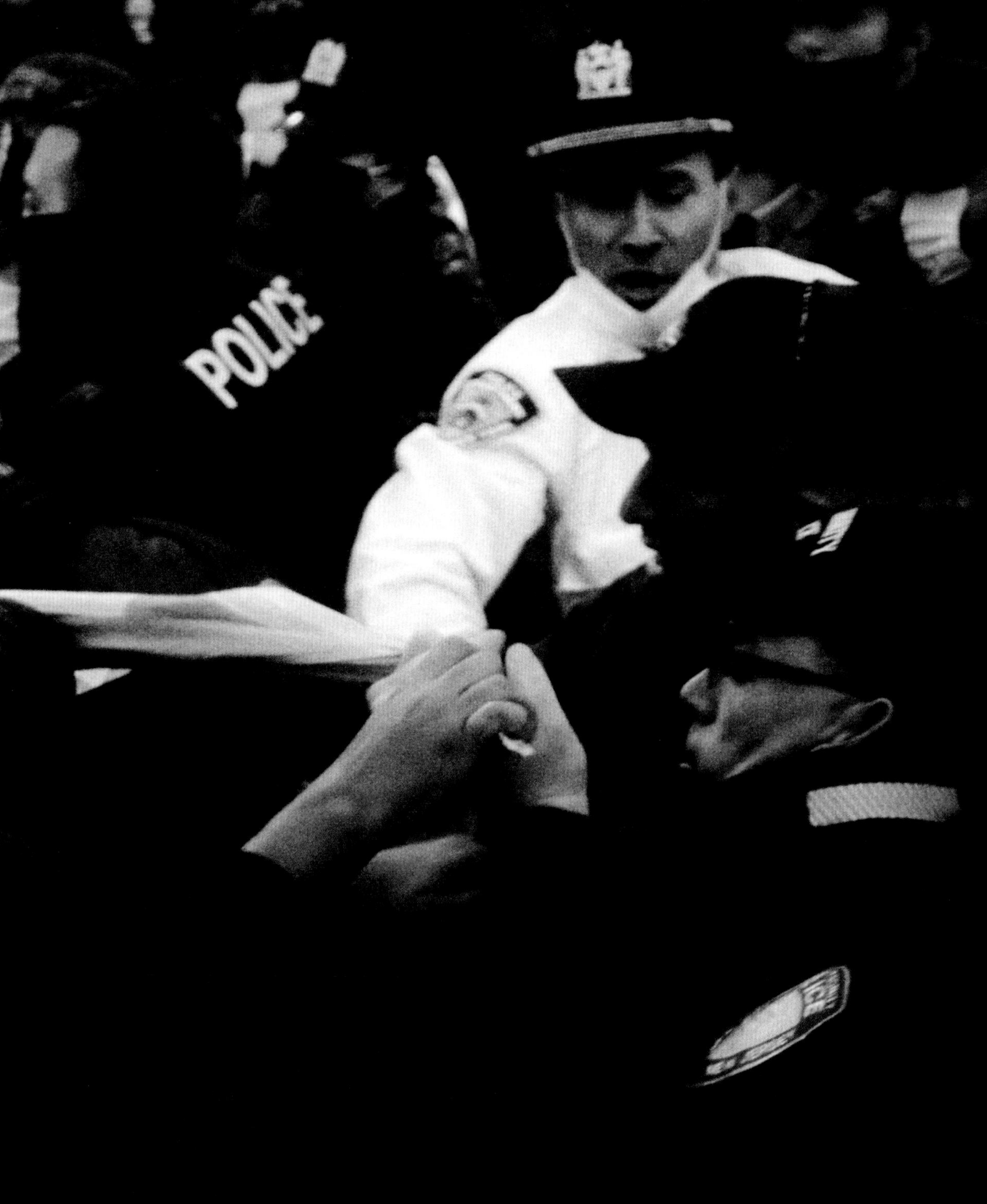

I wholeheartedly believe the legacies Black trans women painstakingly built within the Stonewall Protests will serve as both bedrock and catalyst for future generations toward the fight for justice.

—Brandon English

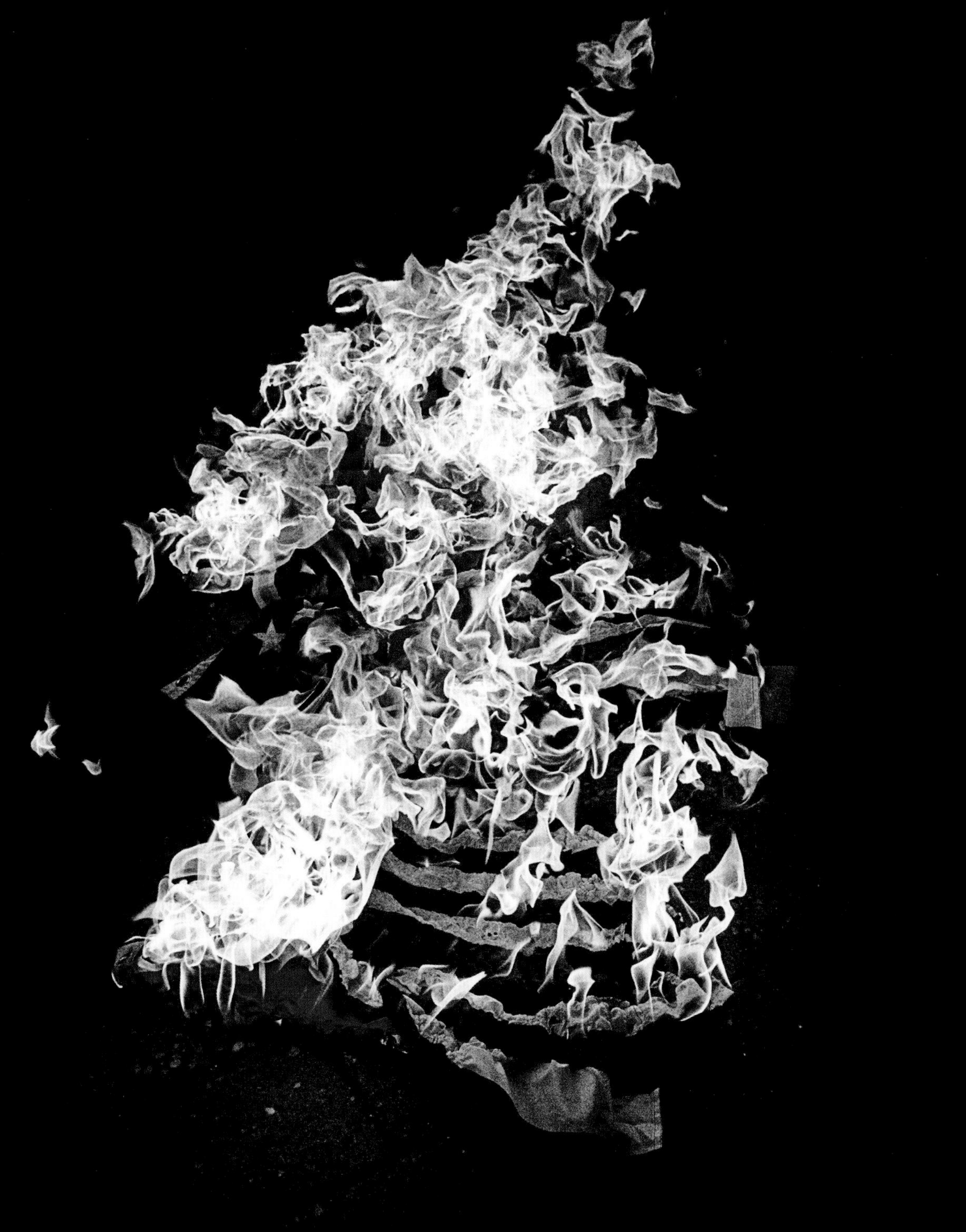

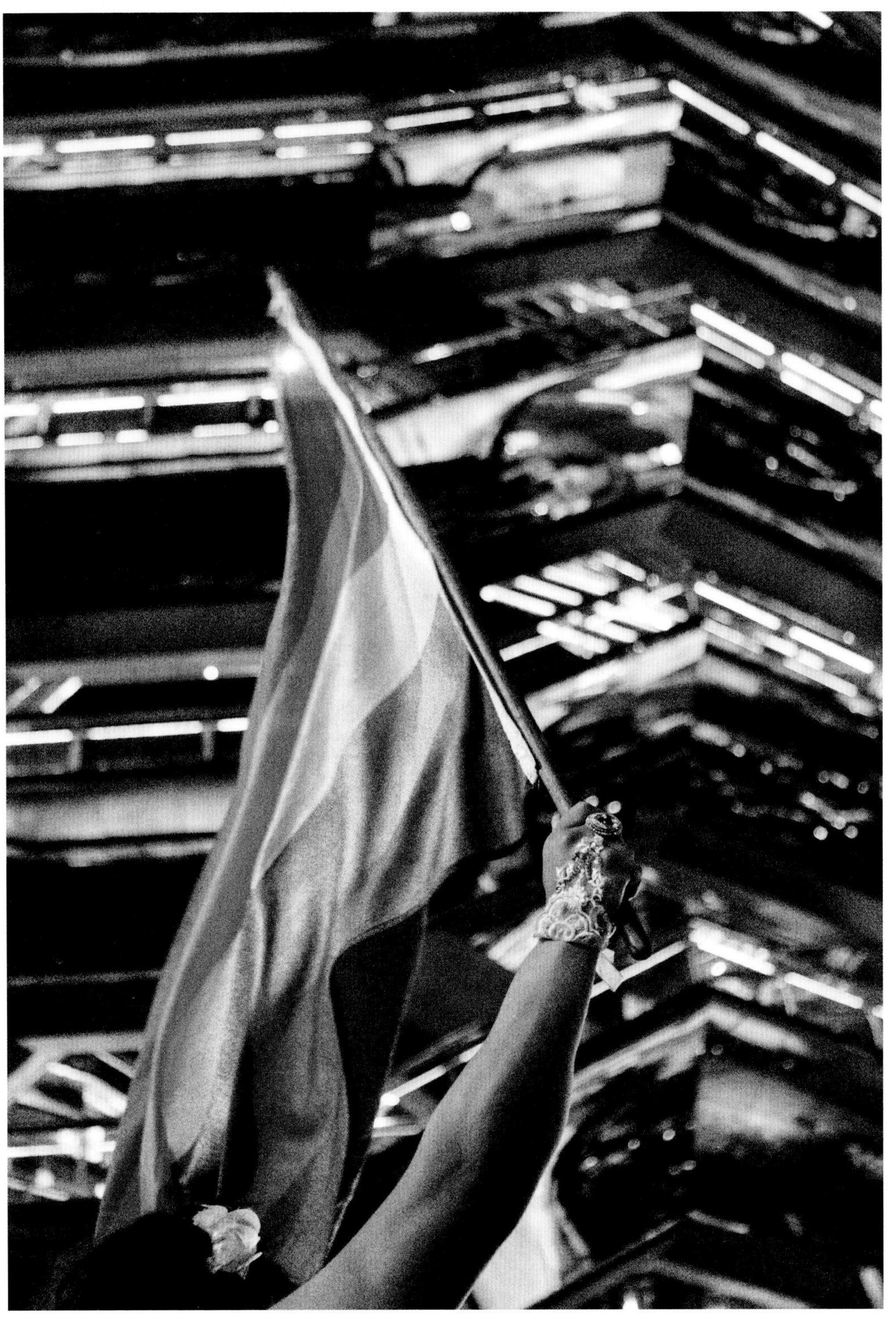

Snake Garcia
Icons Liberation Ball
October 2020

Souls of a Movement
An Honoring of the African Diaspora
February 2021

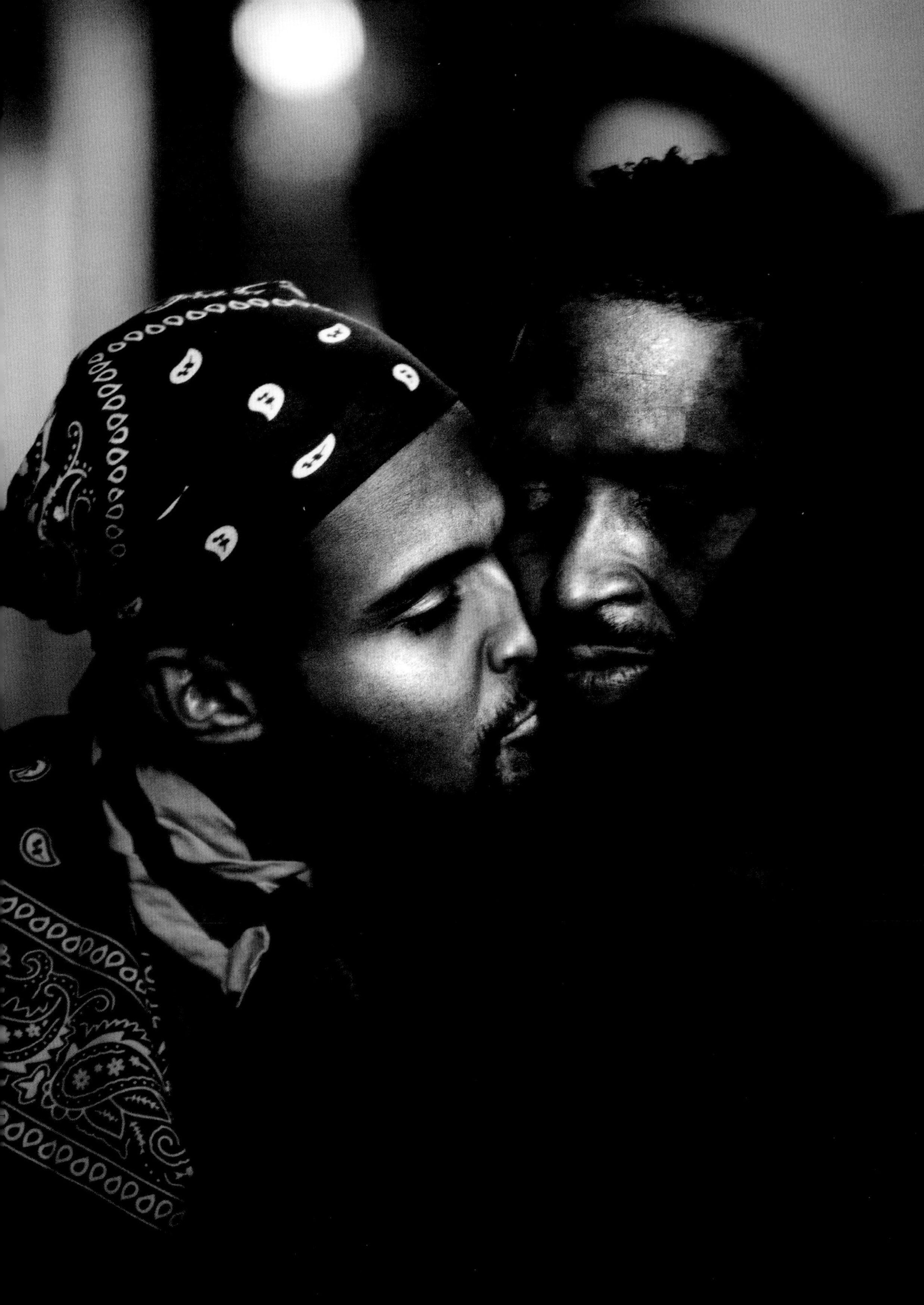

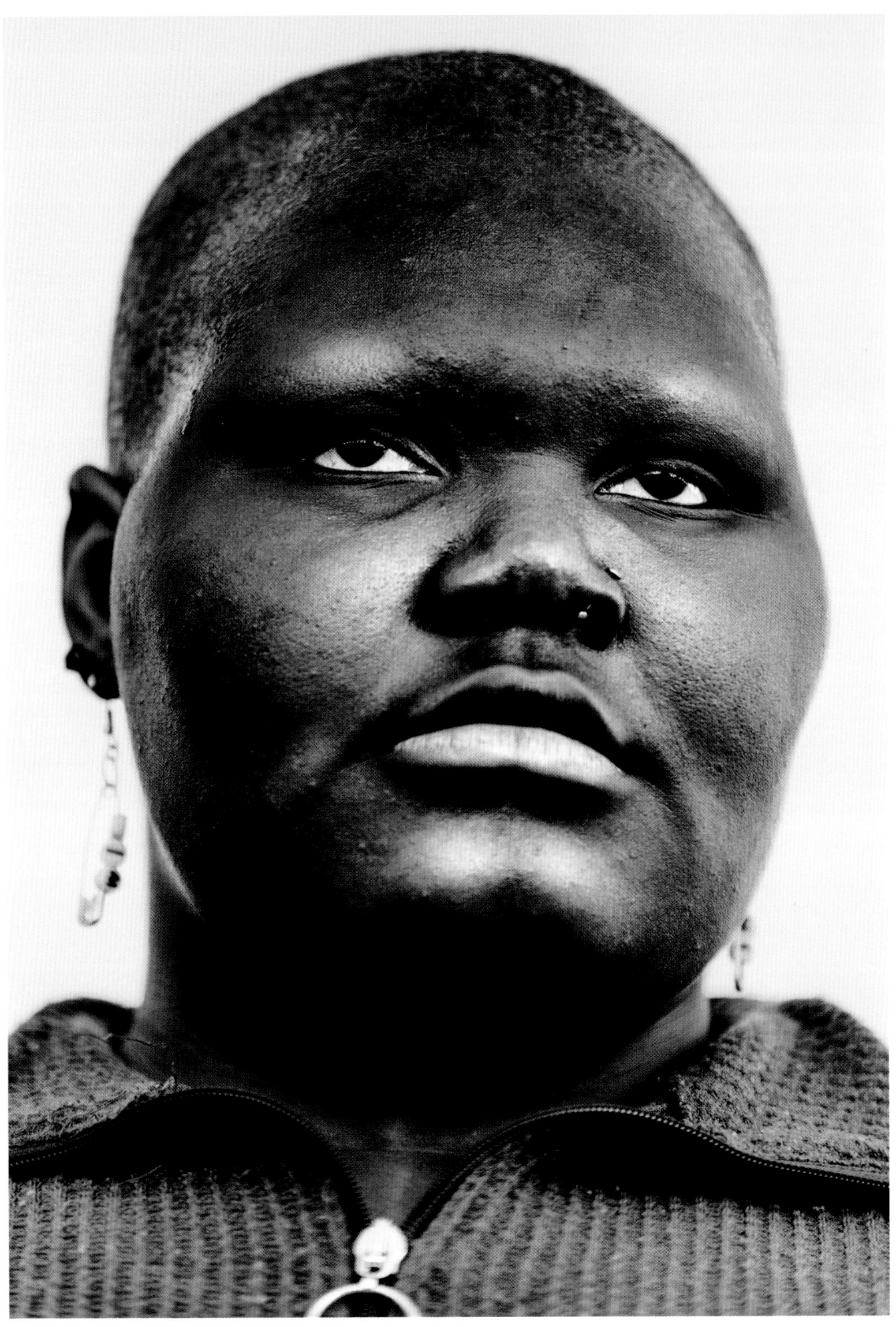

Souls of a Movement
July 2020

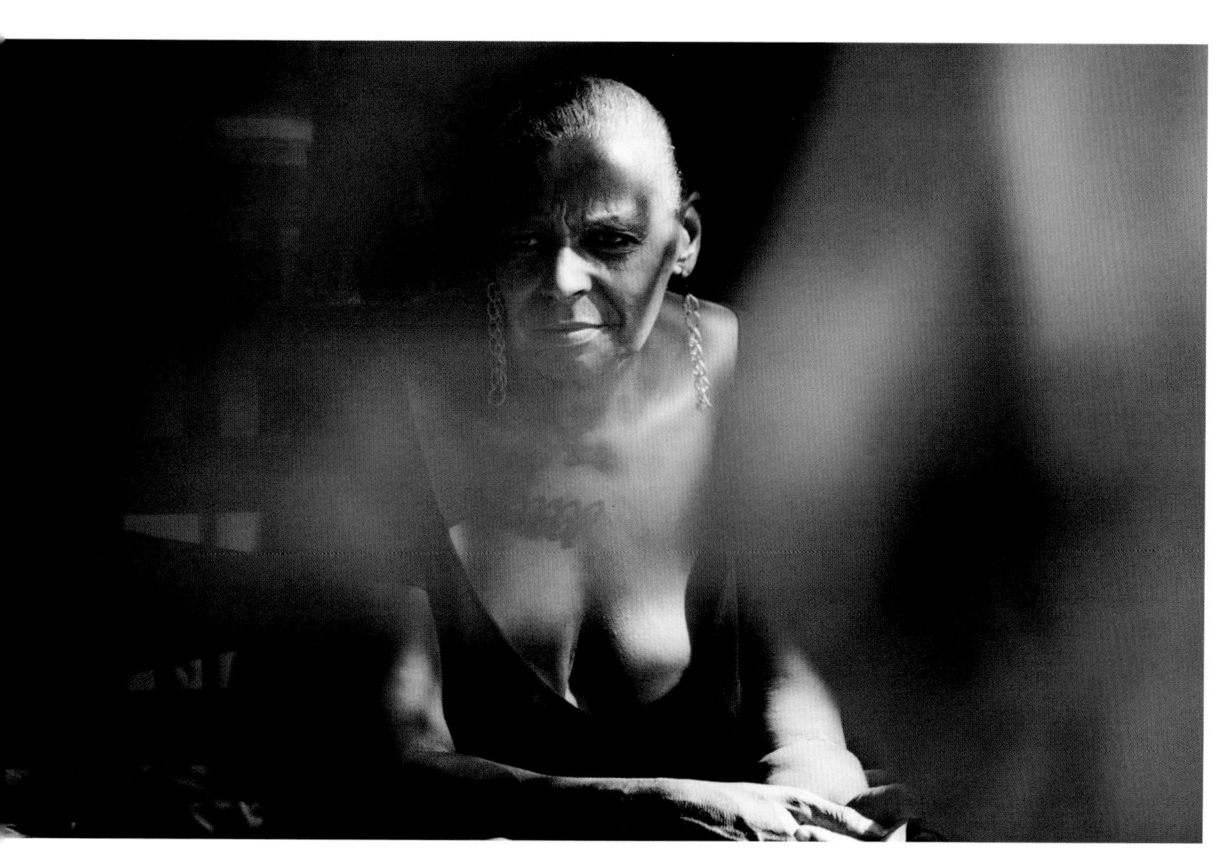

Souls of a Movement
August 2020

115

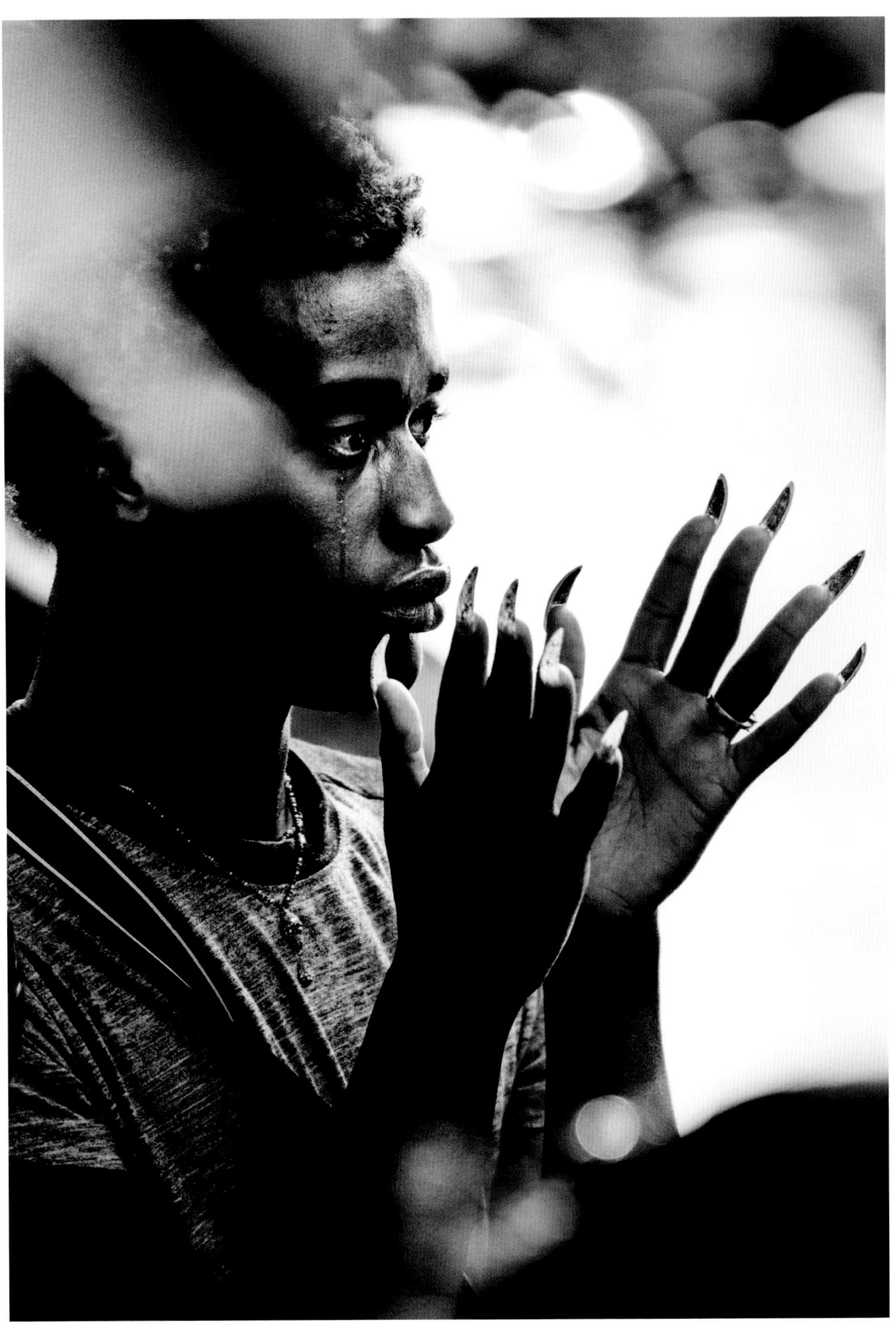

Souls of a Movement
August 2020

We came together to fight for the lives that were not being discussed when talking about the liberation of Black people. The community became a family that you hoped to see every week to acknowledge, mourn, and relate to, but also celebrate Black trans, queer, and nonbinary individuals still living.

—Ramie Ahmed

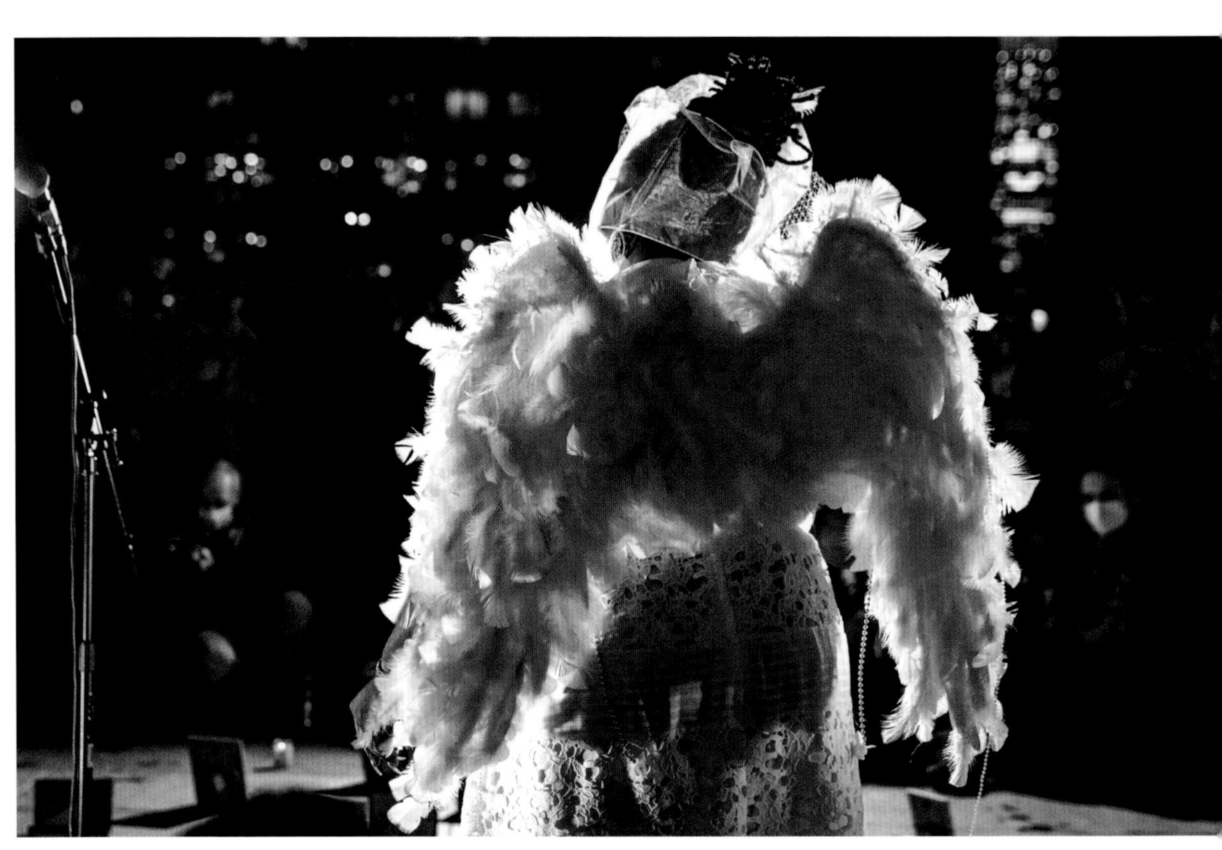

ABOVE AND OPPOSITE TOP:
Chae Kihn
Trans Day of Remembrance
November 2020

Erica Lansner
Trans Day of Remembrance
November 2020

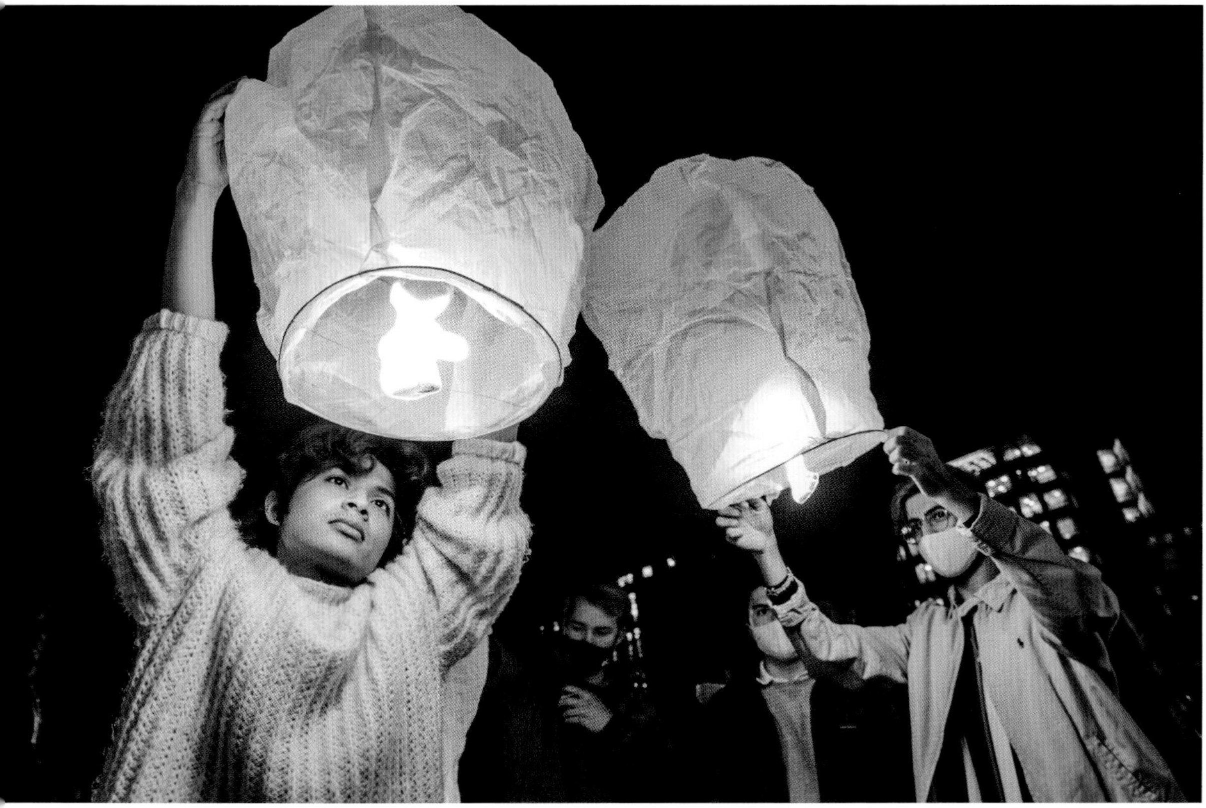

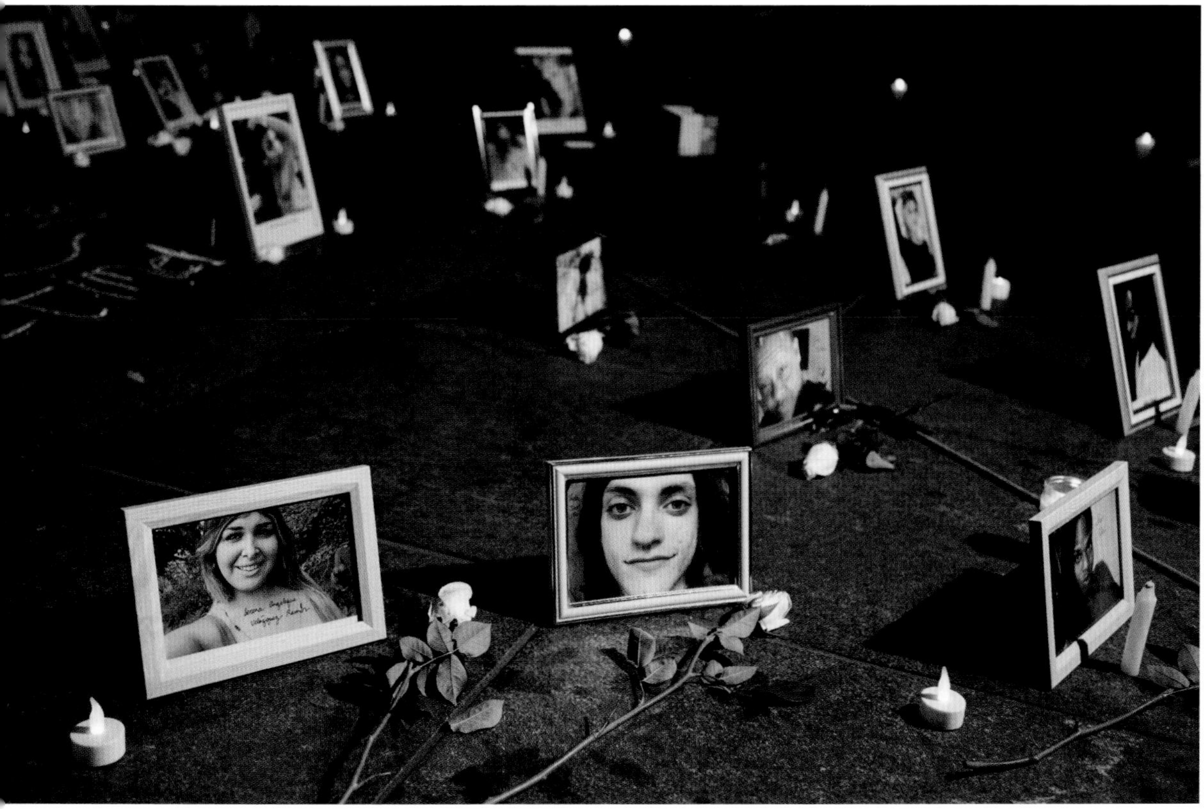

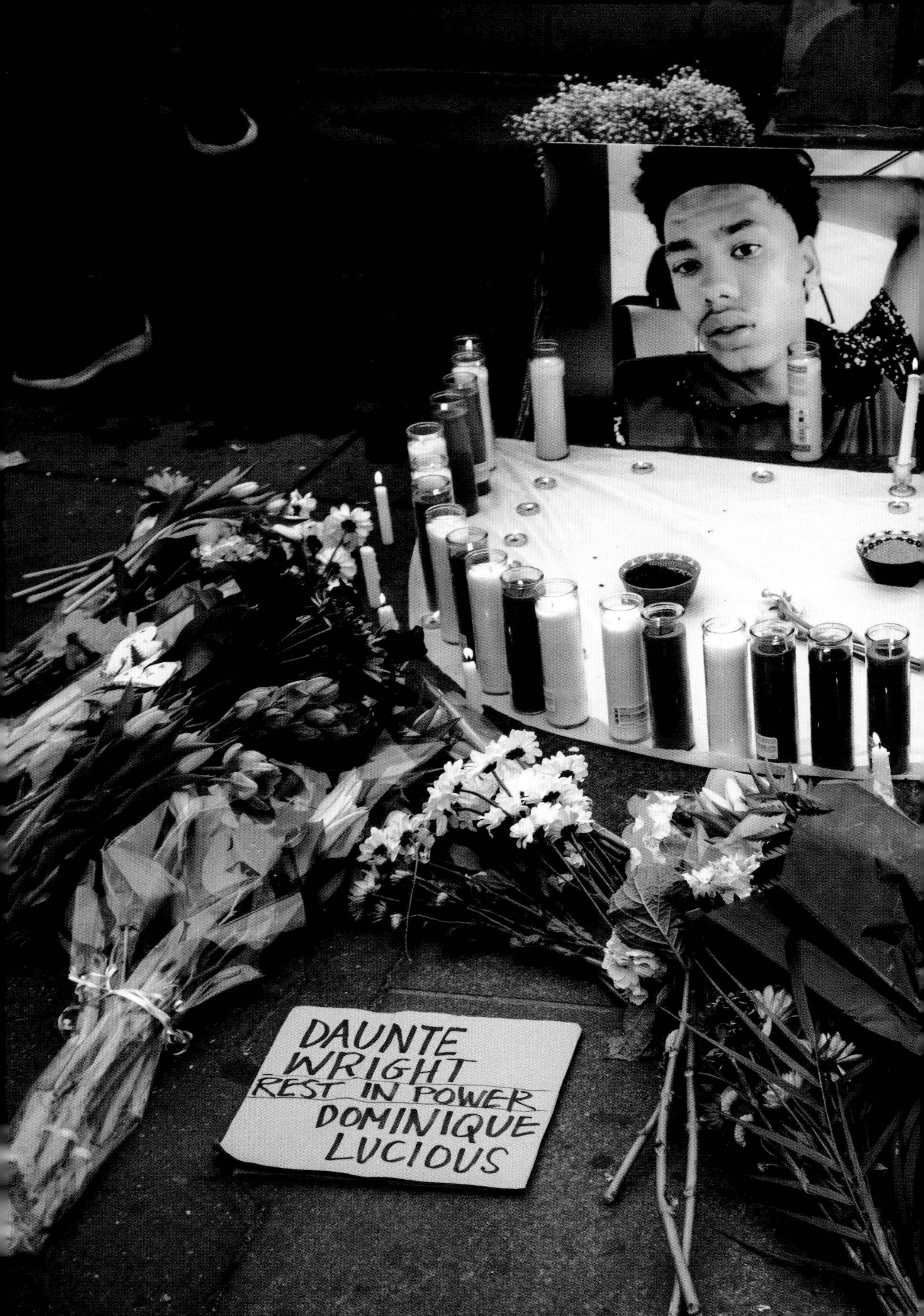

DAUNTE
WRIGHT
REST IN POWER
DOMINIQUE
LUCIOUS

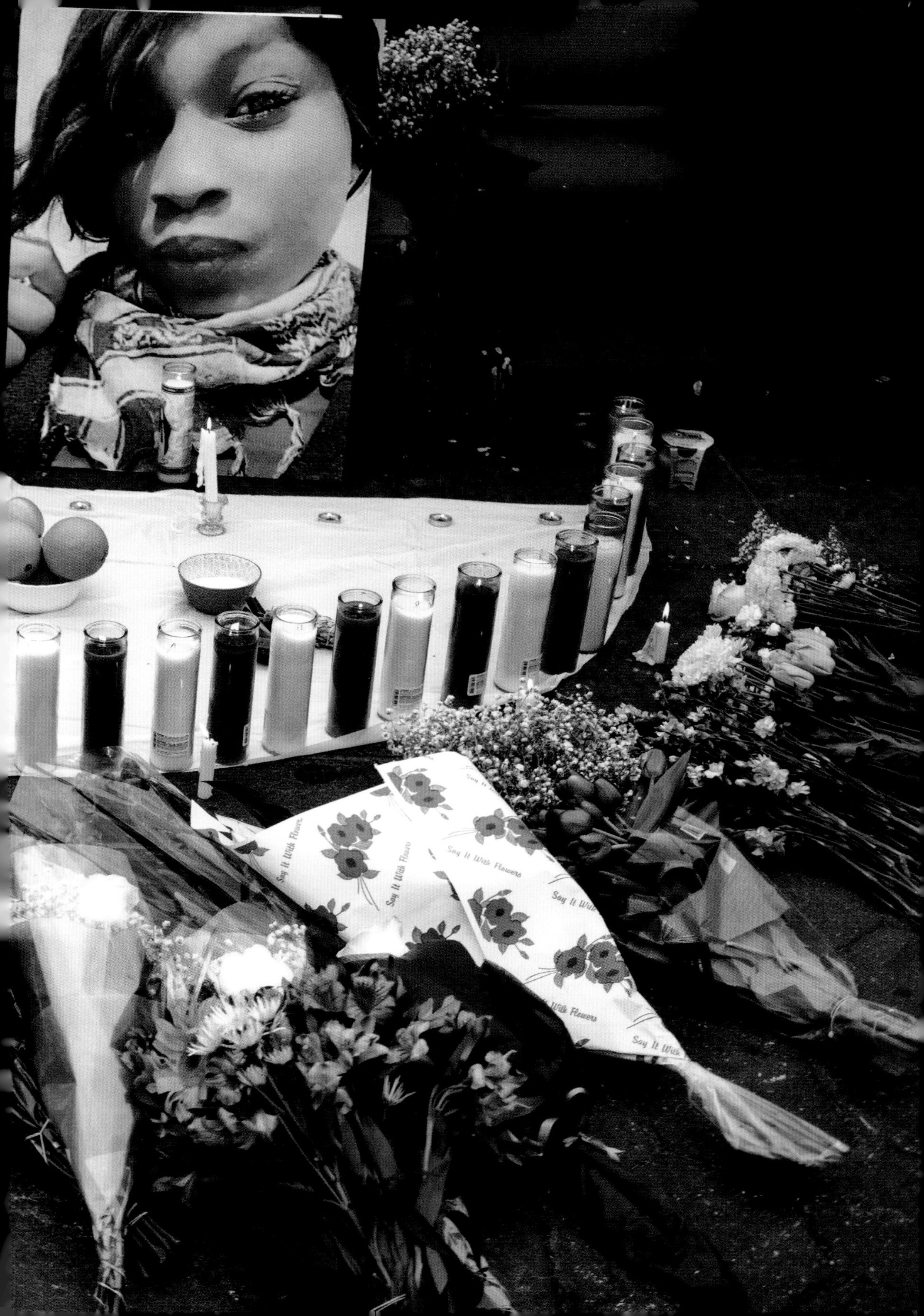

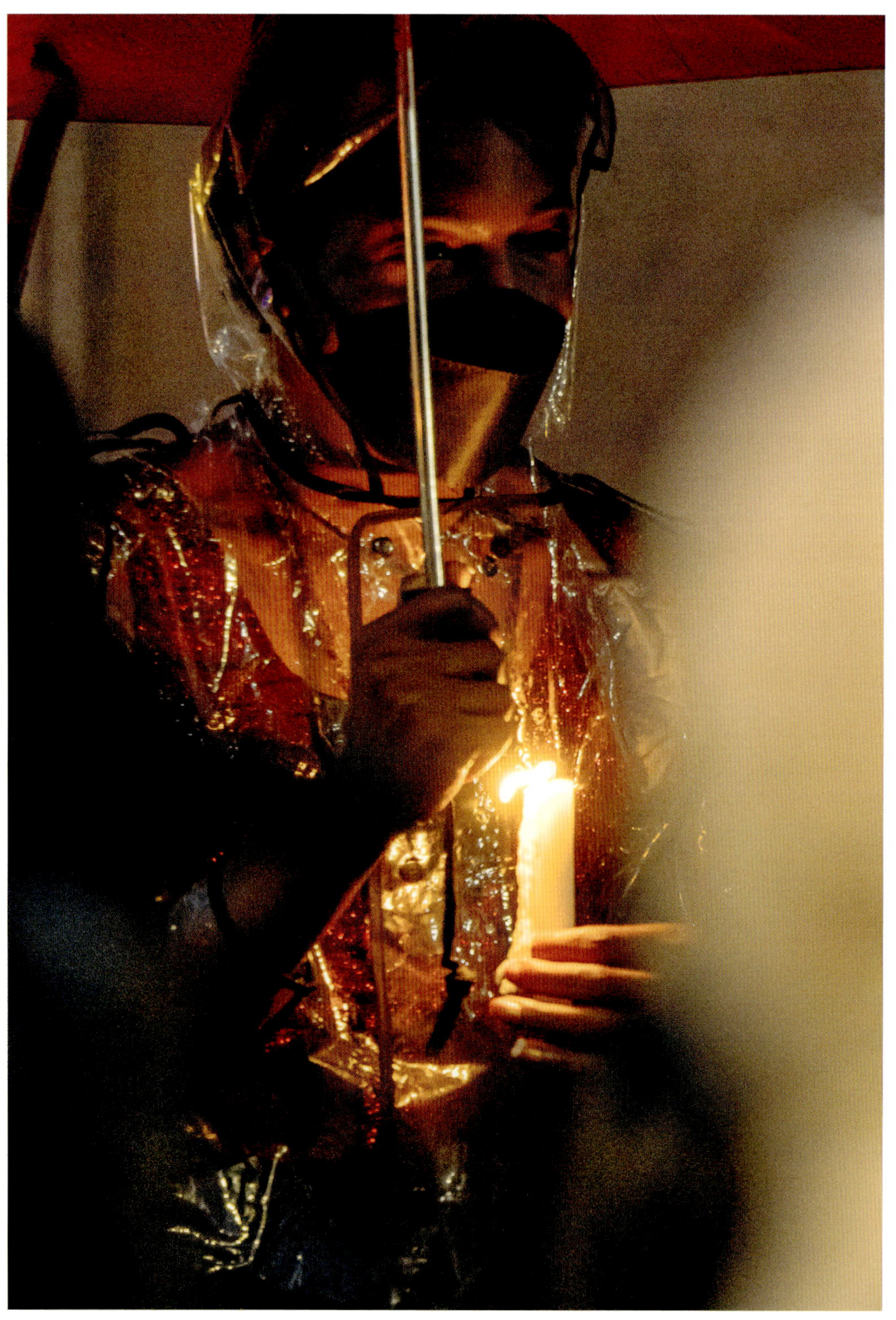

PREVIOUS SPREAD:
Cindy Trinh
Vigil for Daunte Wright & Dominique Lucious
April 2021

Josh Pacheco
Homegoing Service for Daunte & Dominique
April 2021

Princesses and princes of silver asphalt
walk tirelessly through the streets of New York
With no other armor than
the love of a community

Unifying fluid of a suspended city
Their songs and cries awaken the sleeping

To justice for all
Quest for equality of the three sexes
Power to define oneself
By your own
For oneself
Human first

Joy of dance
Joy of defiance
Demanding tolerance
Necessary evolution to a planet
Where being human comes first

Qween and Joela
Rebellious souls who carried us
A whole year
Calling out the names of lost angels
In our memory forever

—Caroline Mardok

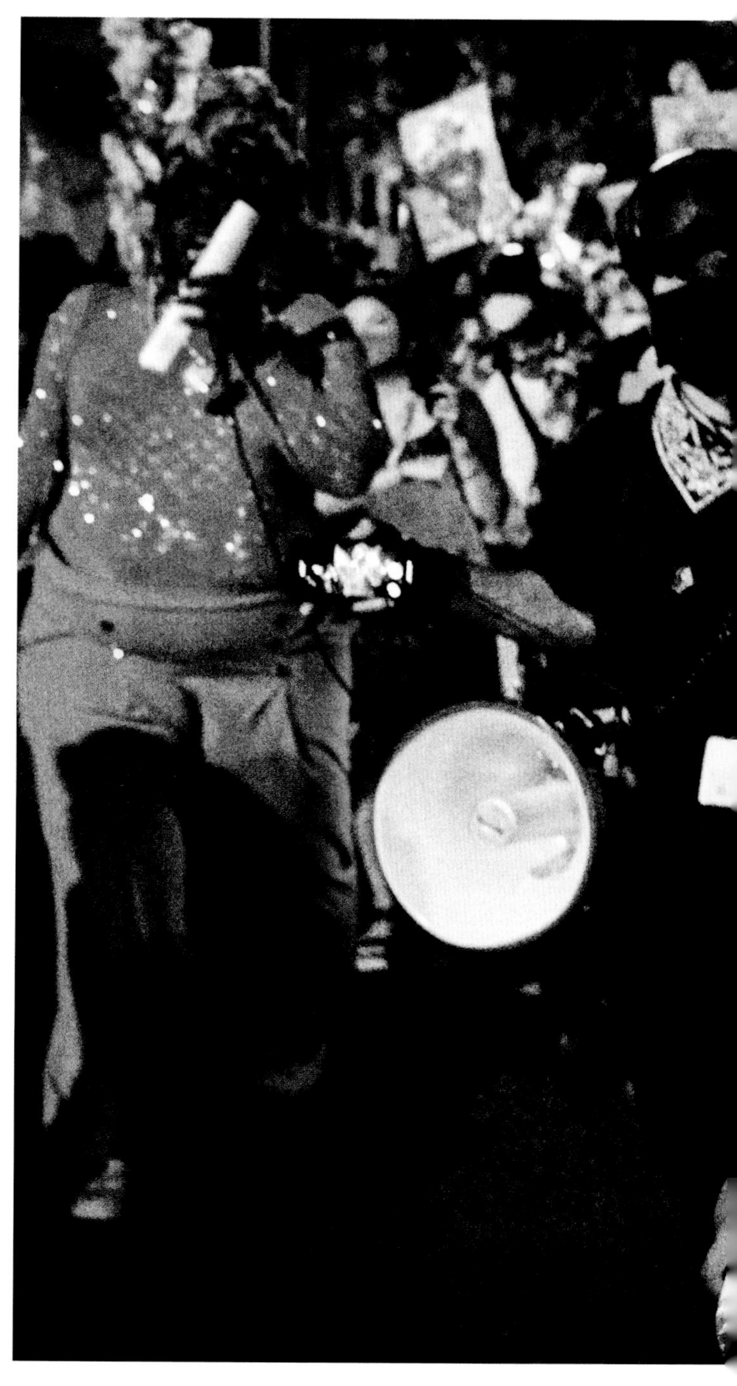

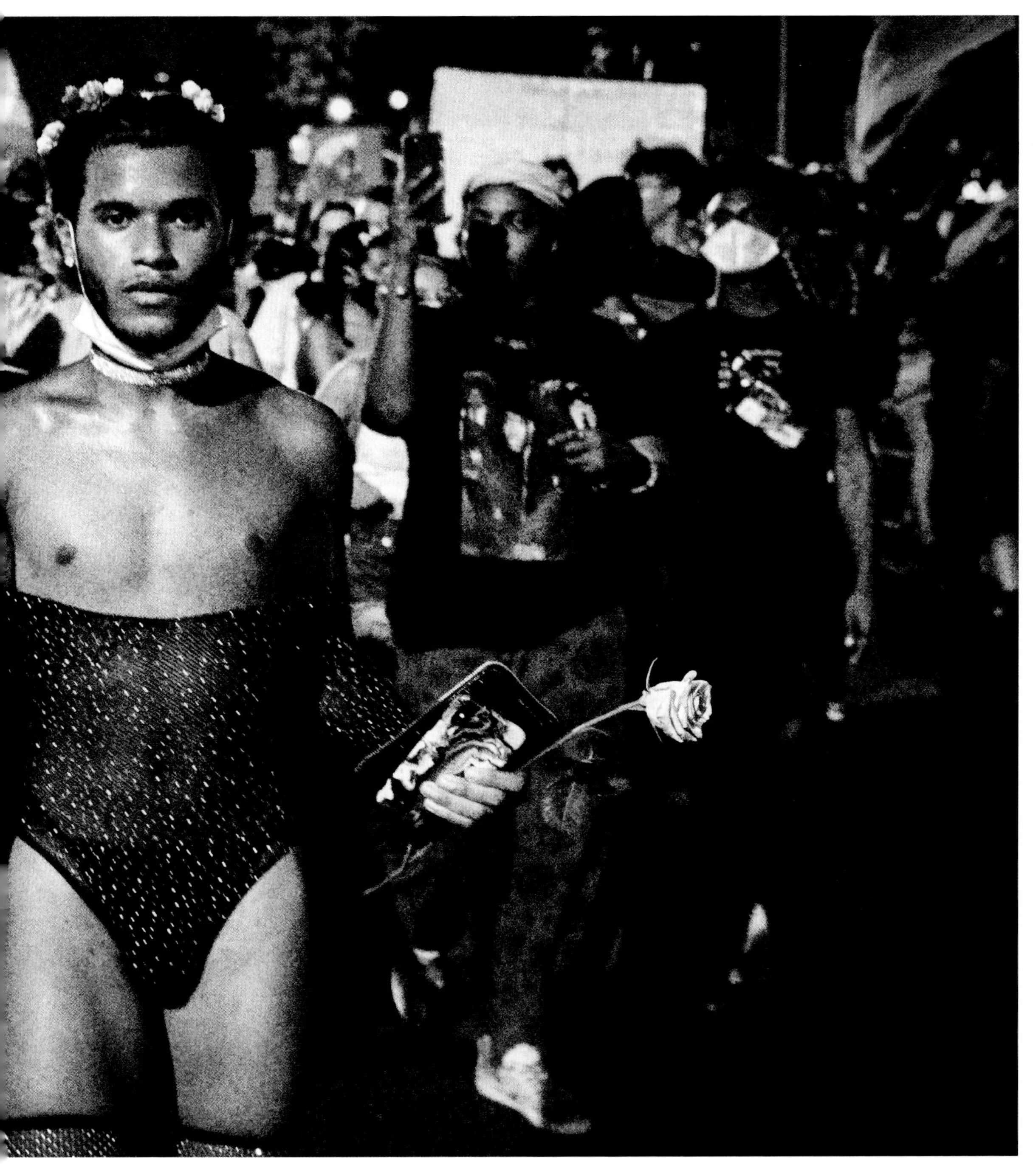

Sean Waltrous
Marsha's March & 75th Birthday
August 2020

125

Souls of a Movement
Illumination Ball
October 2020

NEXT SPREAD:
Stas Ginzburg
Justice for Breonna Taylor
March 2021

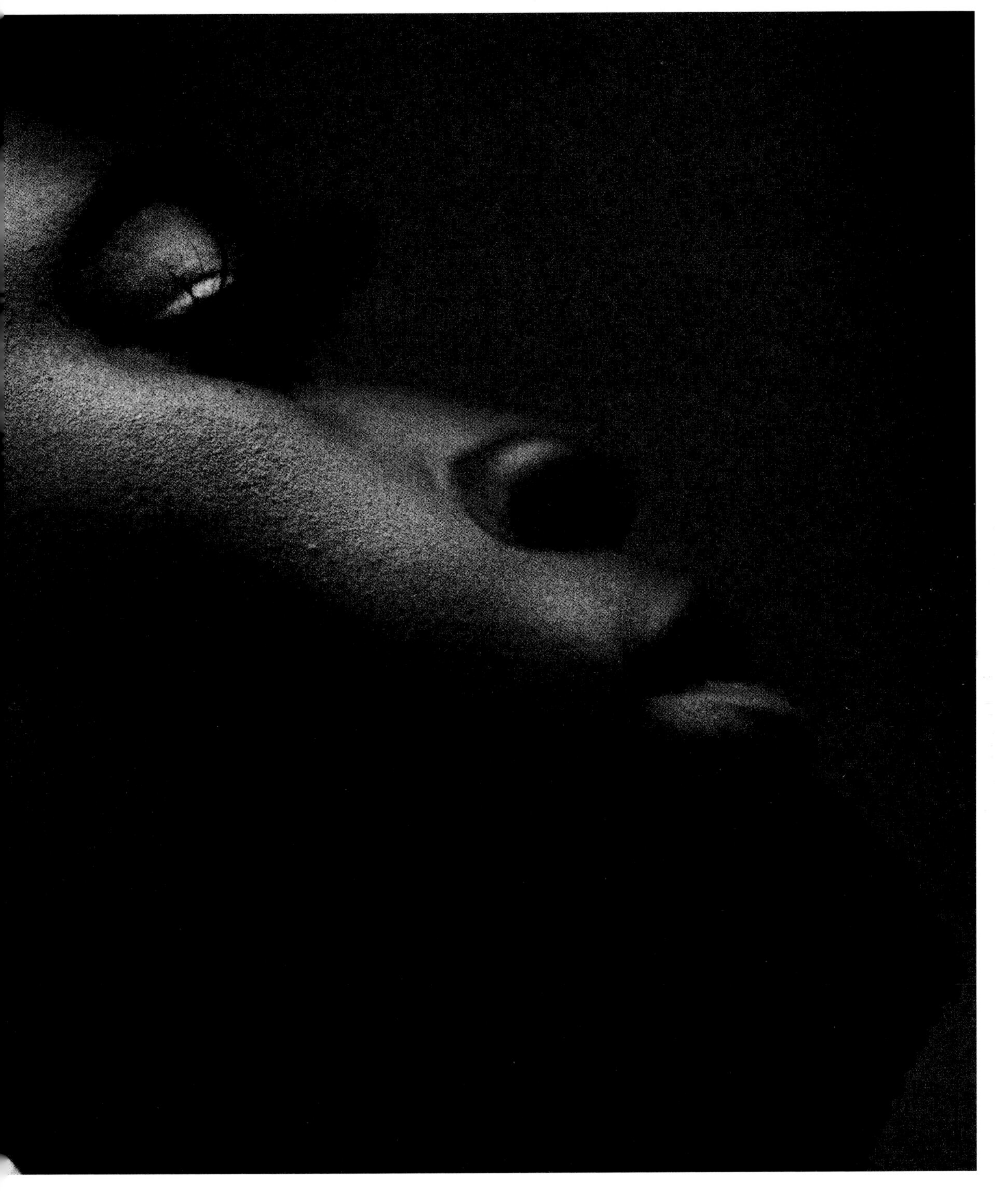

127

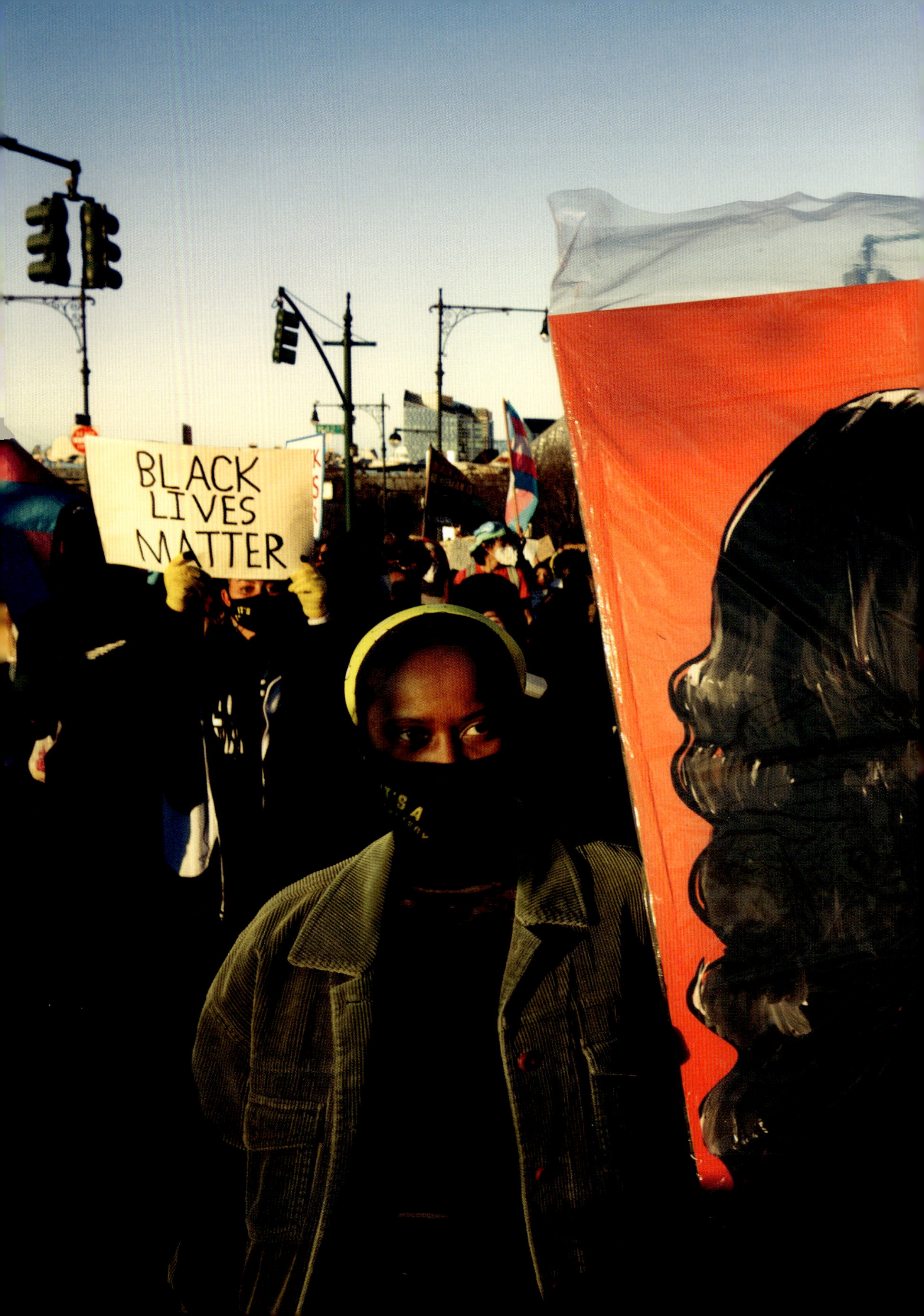
BLACK
LIVES
MATTER

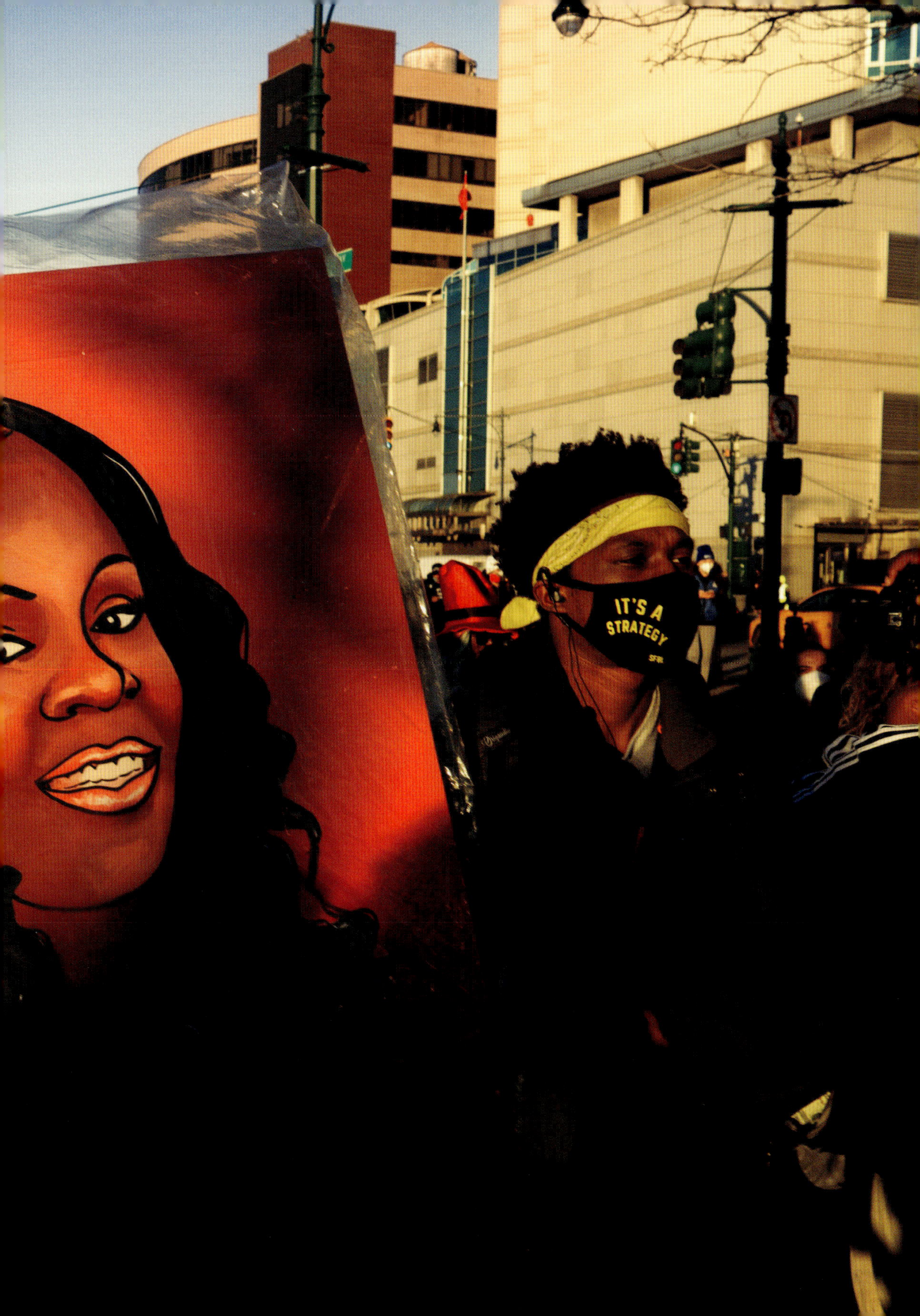

IT'S A
STRATEGY
SFR

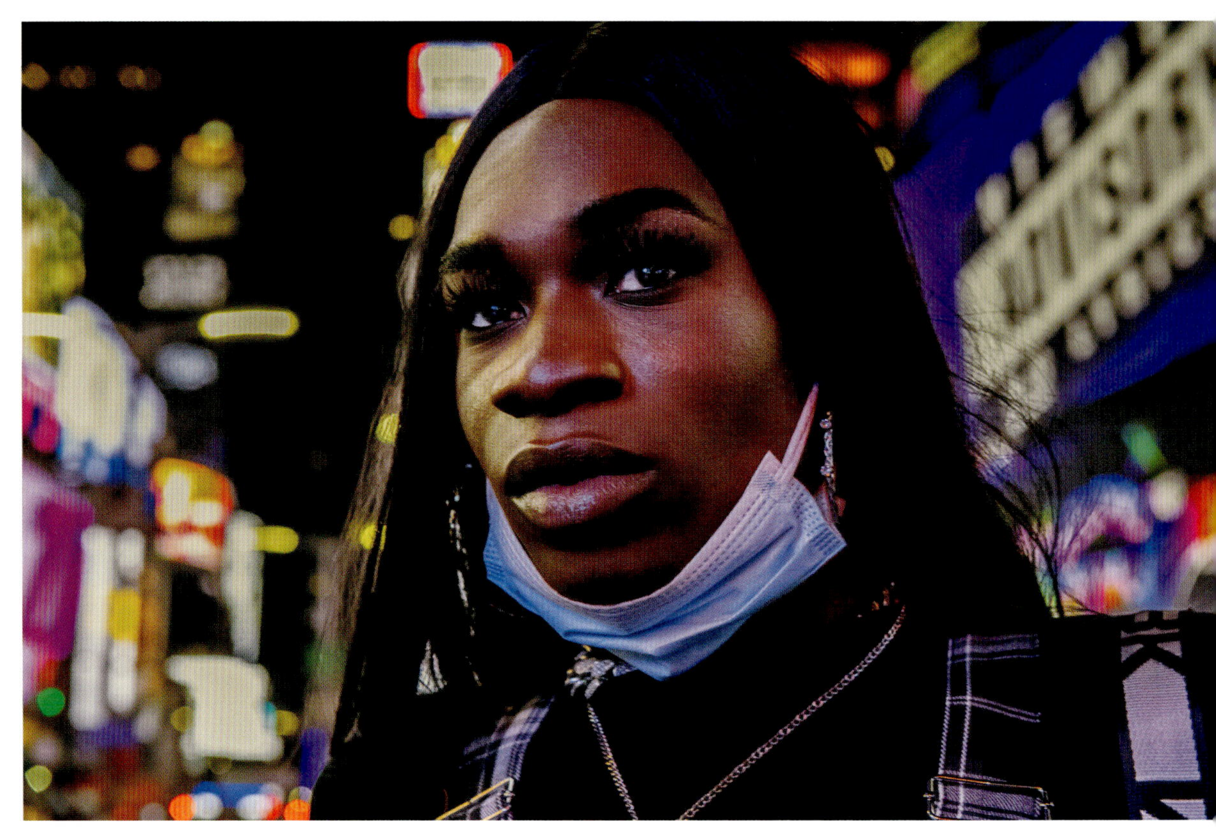

Deb Fong
December 2020

Erica Lansner
Who Will Say Their Names
November 2020

Erica Lansner
People's March for Roxanne Moore
October 2020

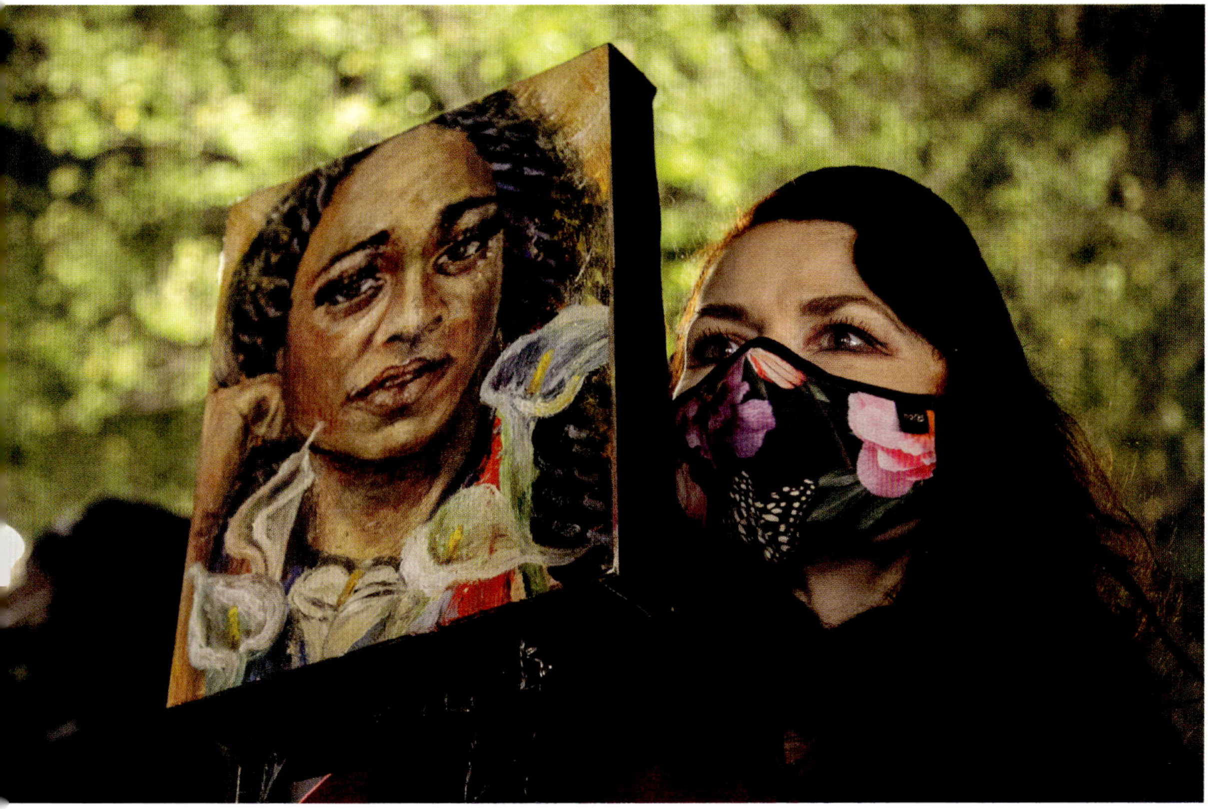

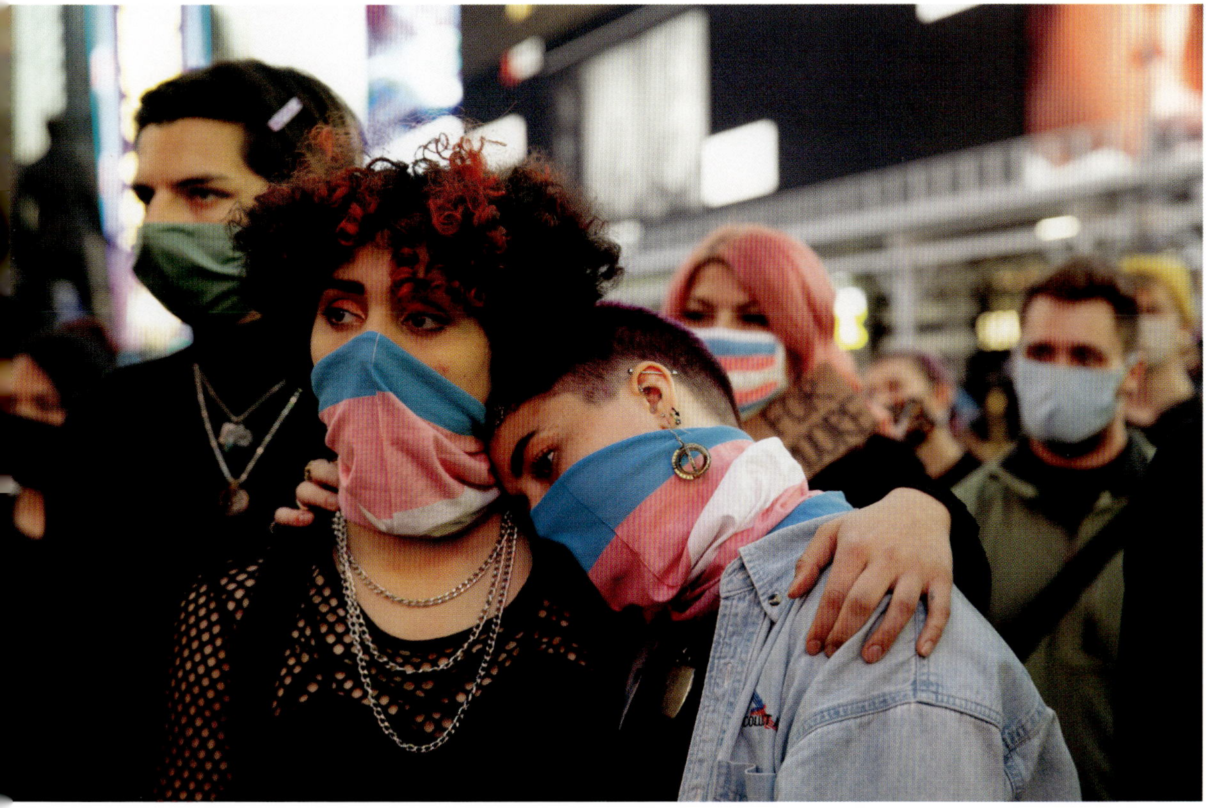

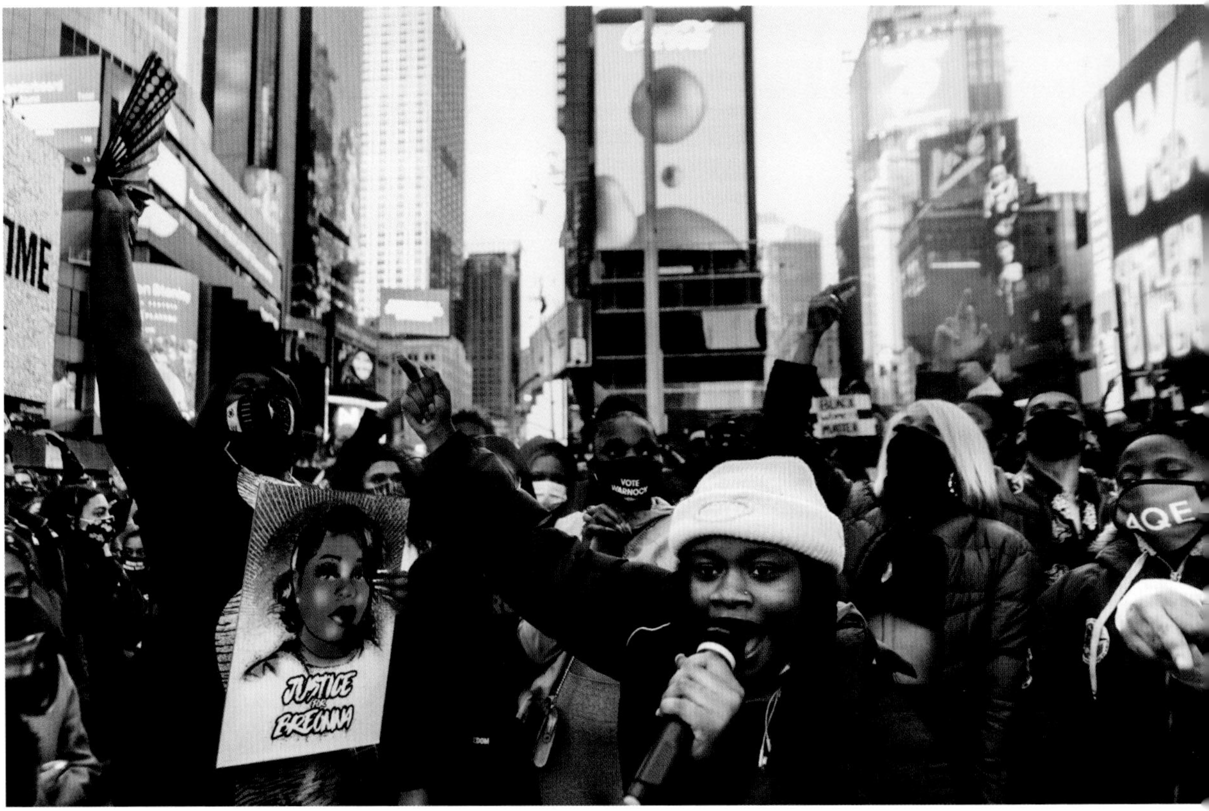

TIME
WE
JUSTICE FOR BREONNA
VOTE WARNOCK
AQE

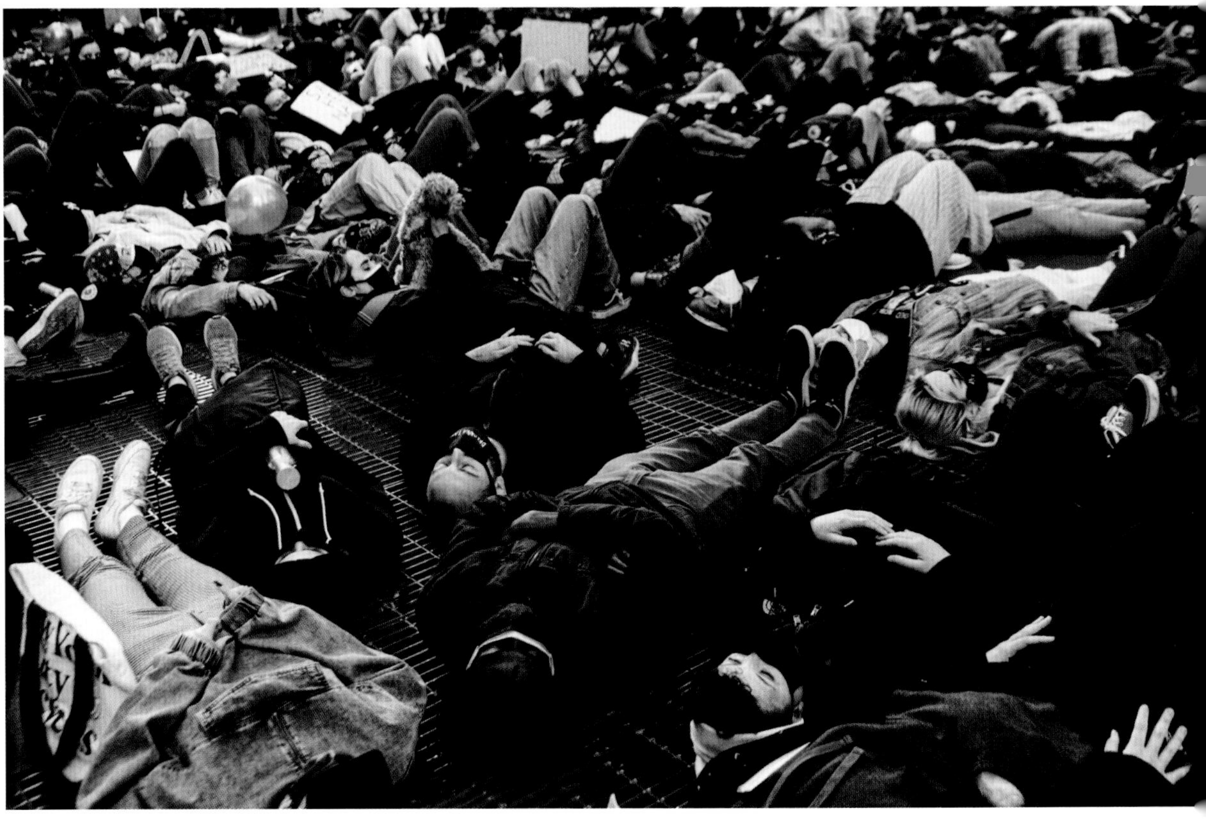

My creativity is too often a replacement for my voice that has been silenced as a Black queer woman in this world. It is also my form of activism—a documentation of existing in a dimension that often sought the demise of Black women. The Stonewall Protests planted seeds of Black unity, so I make it my duty to preserve the correct narrative and the truth that we existed in love, where many others from all walks of life found a home.

—Phoenix Robles

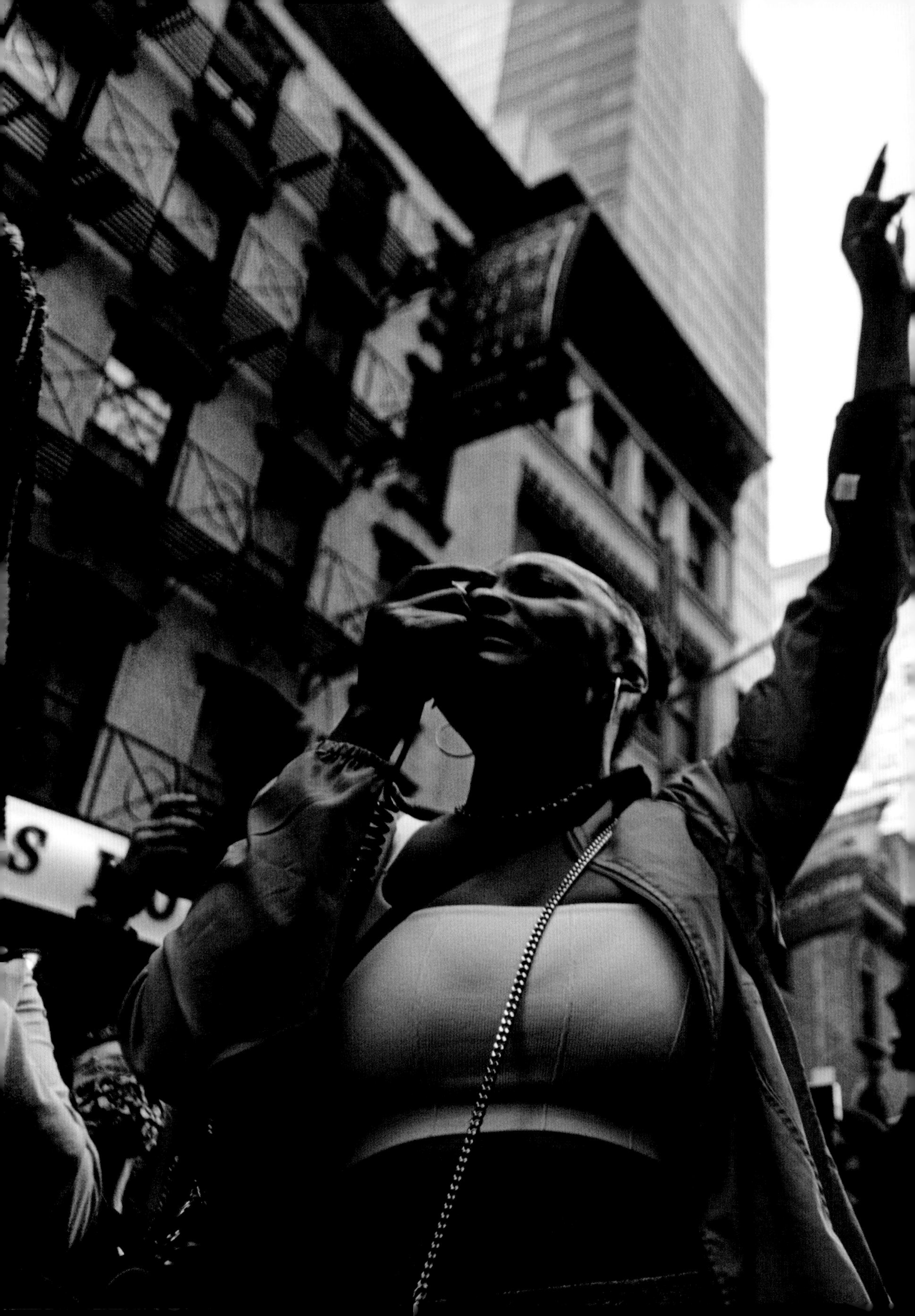

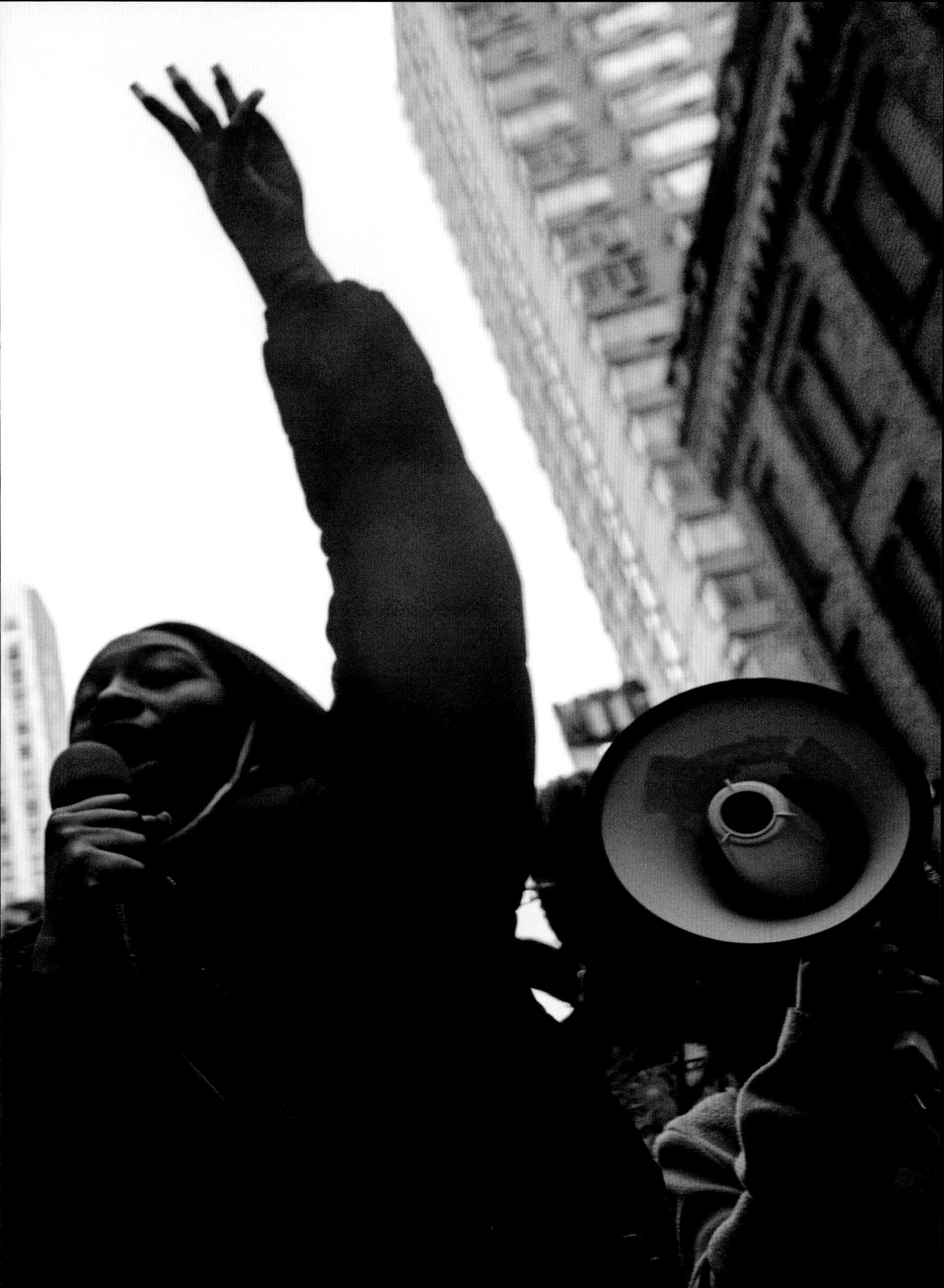

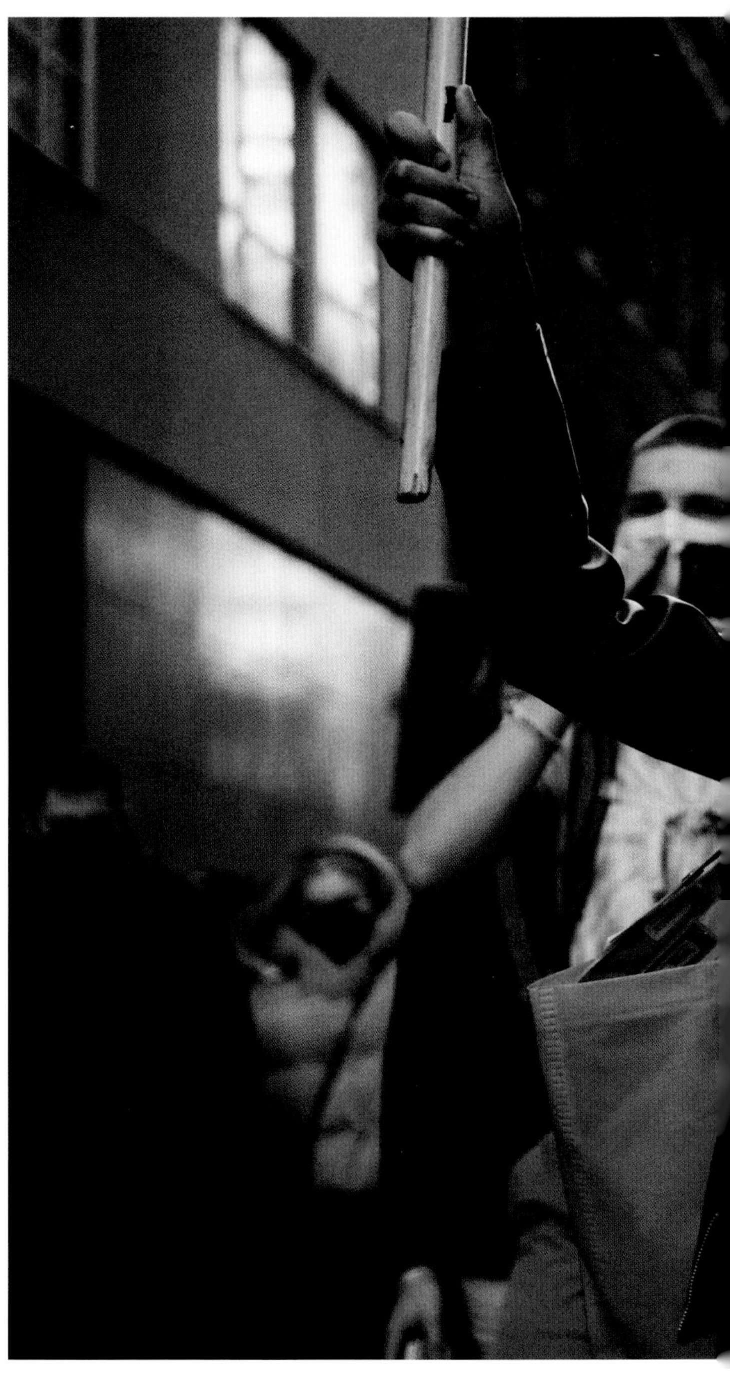

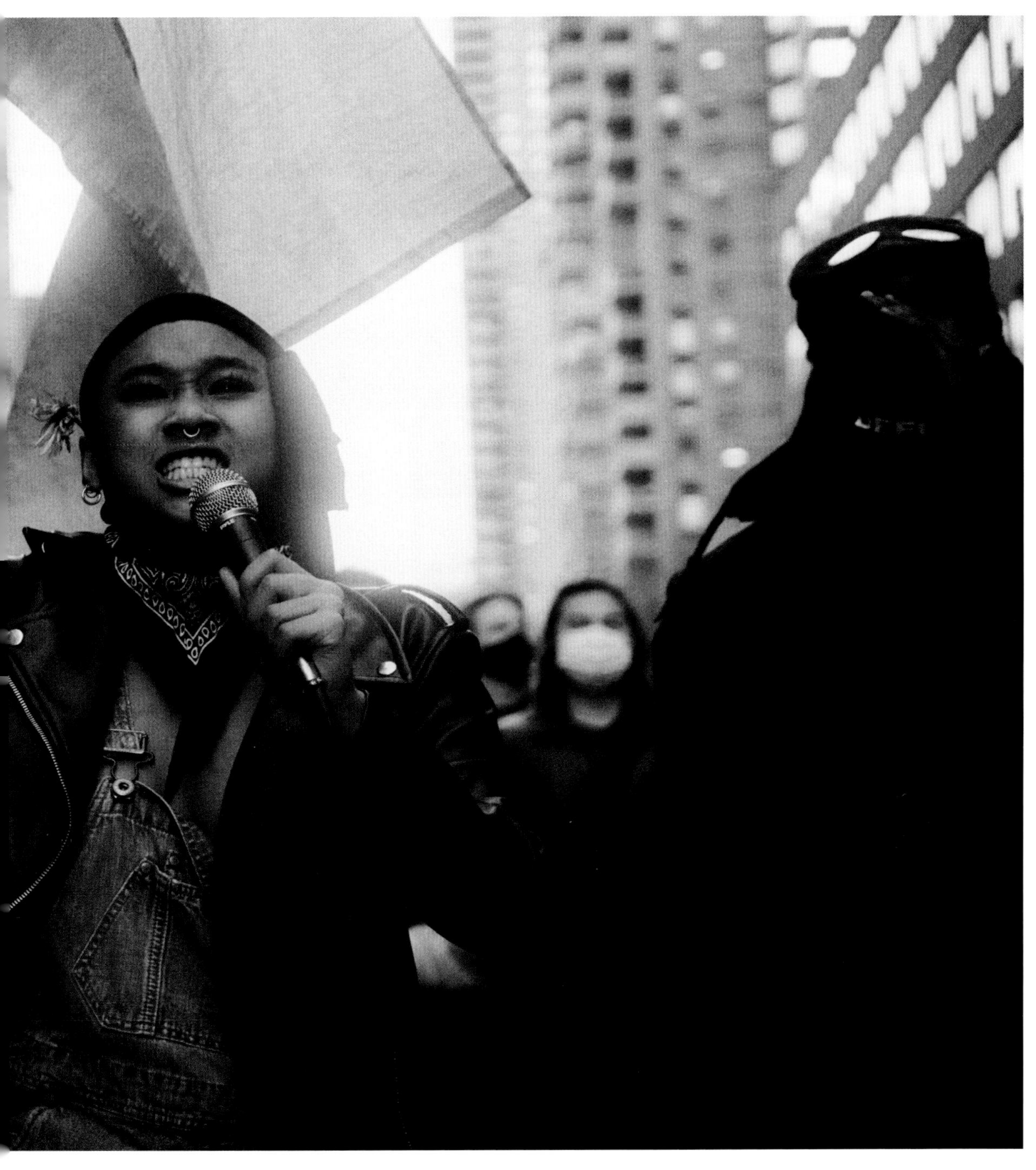

Robert Hamada
Justice for Breonna Taylor
March 2021

Meaningful change starts within, in the depth of our beings, because only our individual transformation has the power to create a new reality. After all, we are all souls living a human experience and walking each other home.

—Souls of a Movement

Caroline Mardok
Who Will Say Their Names
November 2020

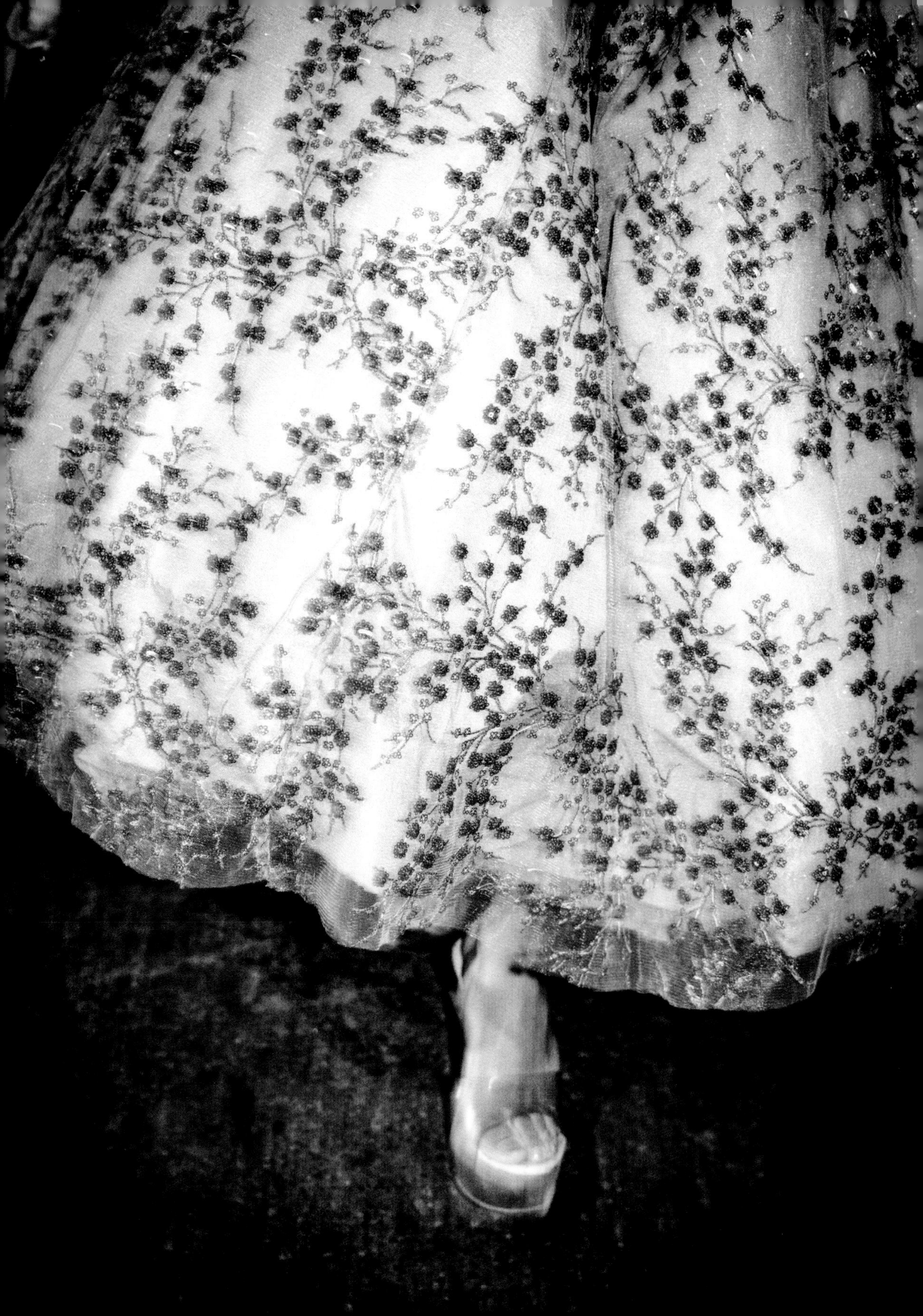

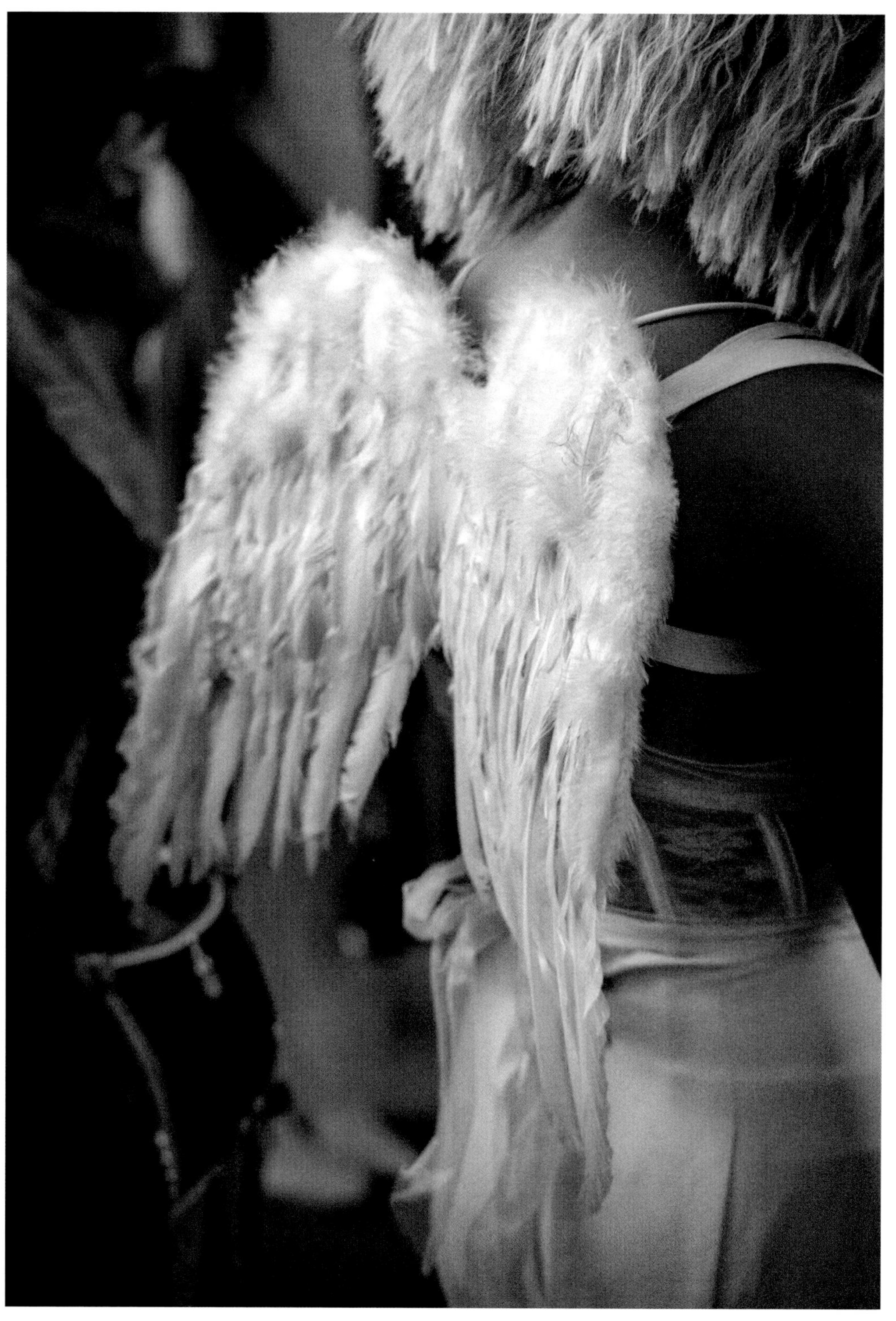

Snake Garcia
Black Angels Ball
October 2020

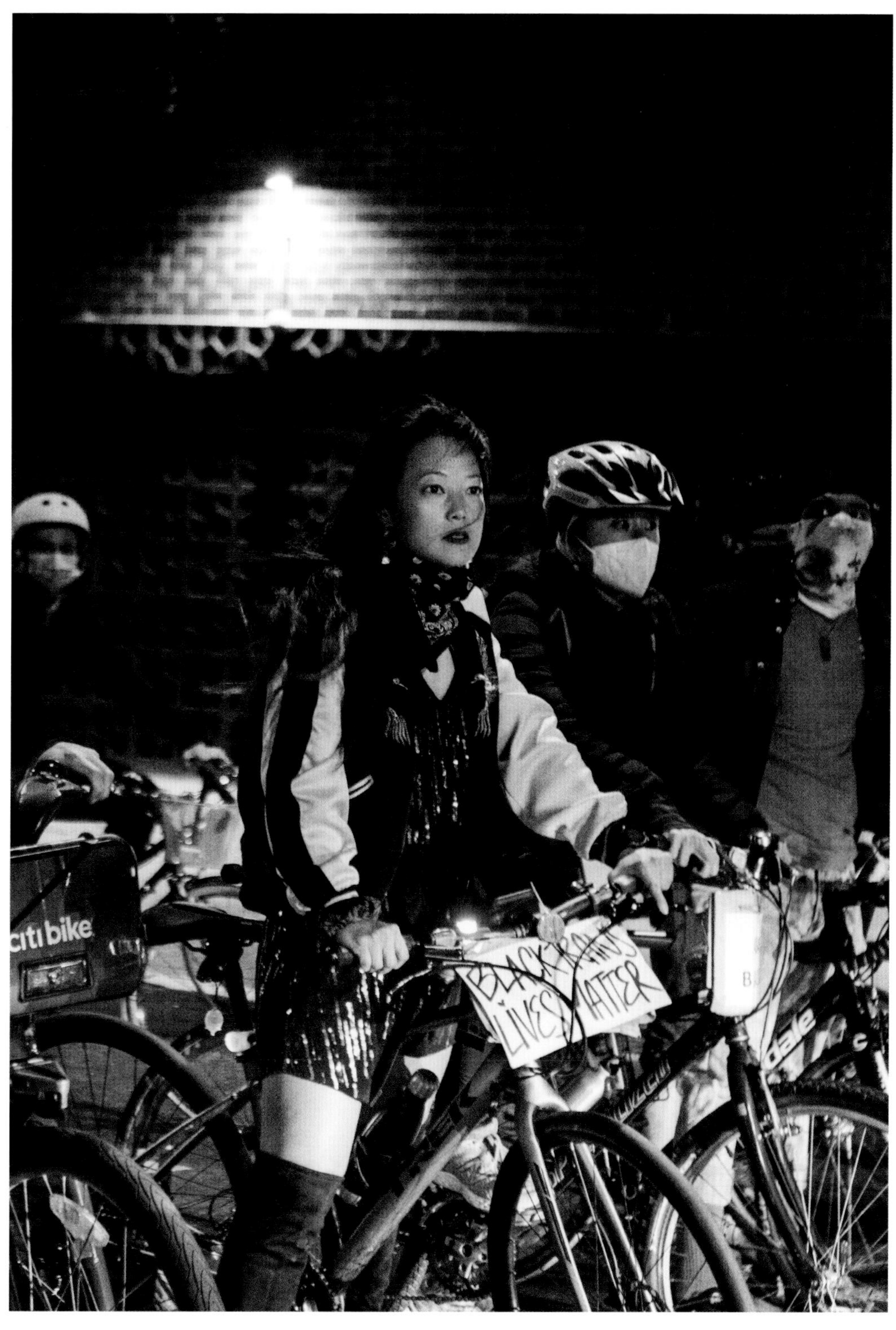

Snake Garcia
Icons Liberation Ball
October 2020

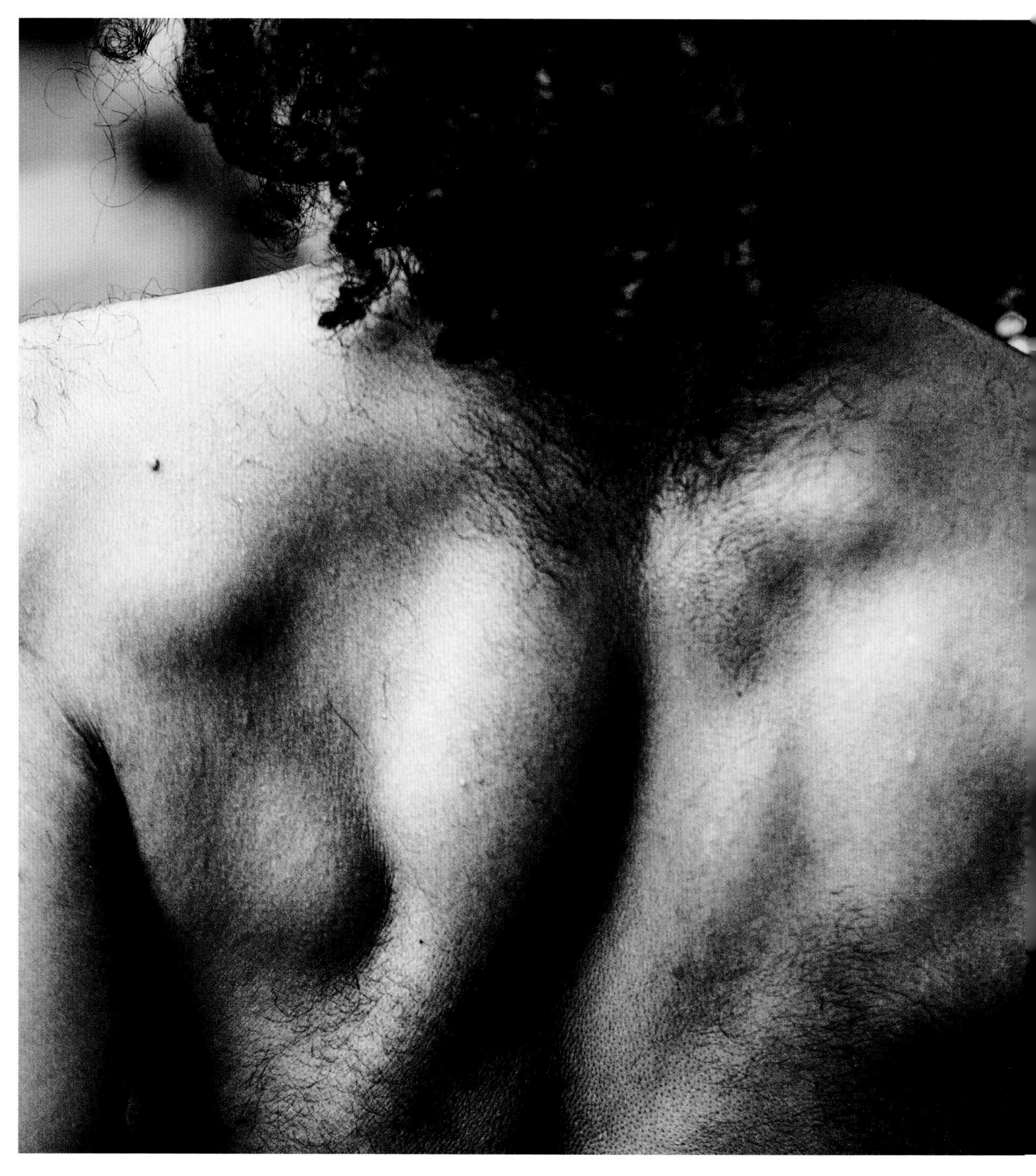

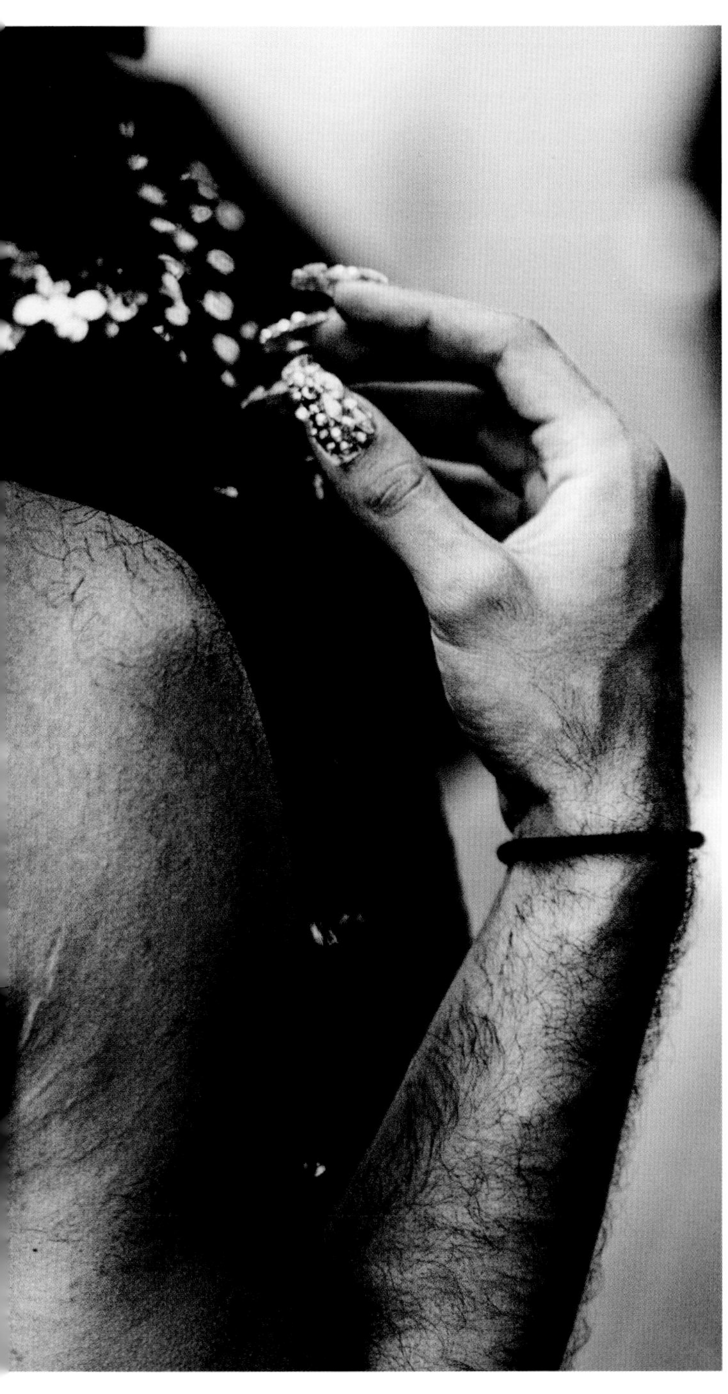

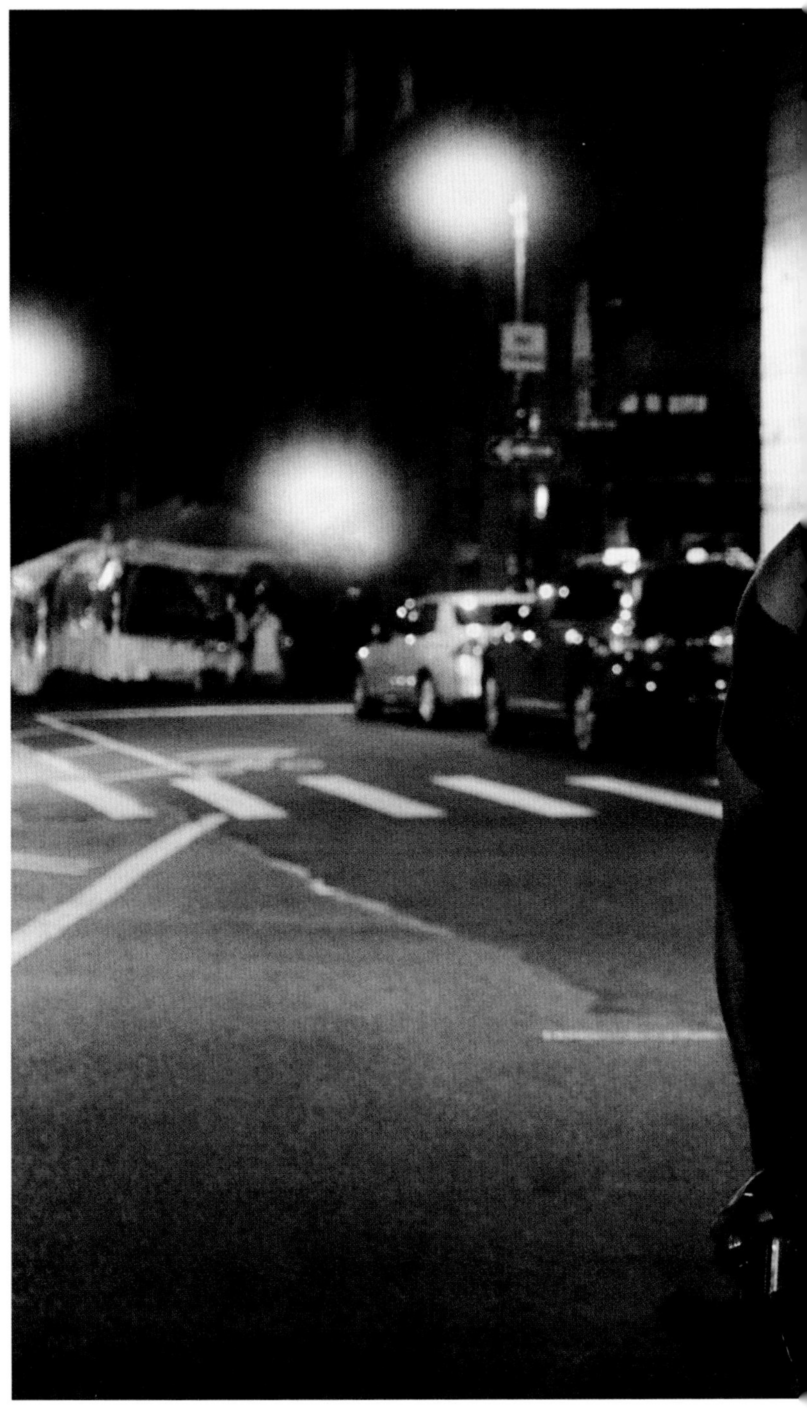

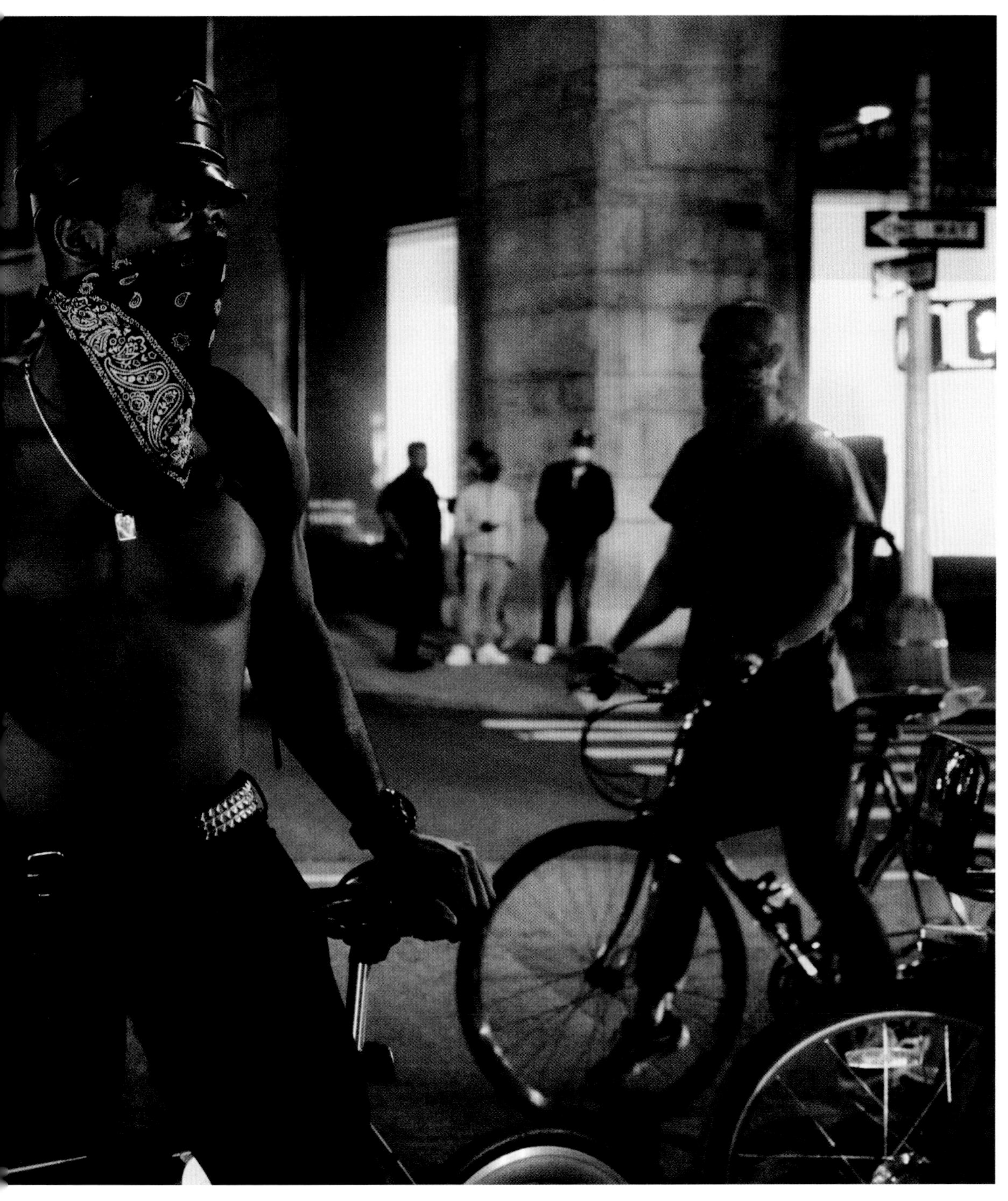

Robert Hamada
Liberation Not Deportation
October 2020

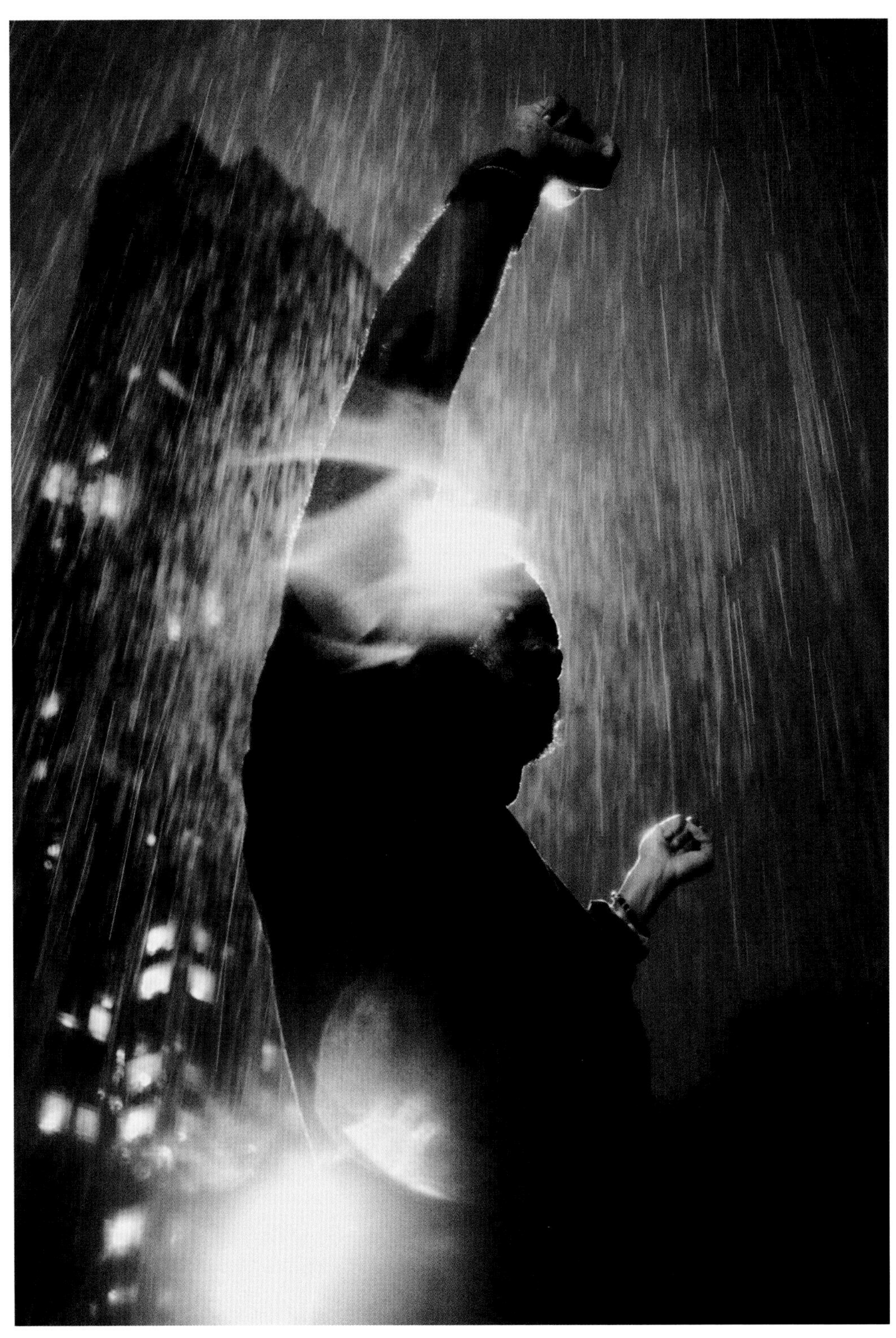

Robert Hamada
Justice for Daniel Prude
September 2020

The Stonewall riots were over fifty years ago, and we cannot continue to rely on failed institutions and antiquated belief systems. The Stonewall Protests created visibility and space for Black trans people, who deserve their place in history and whose messages should serve as inspiration for a more inclusive future.

—Robert Hamada

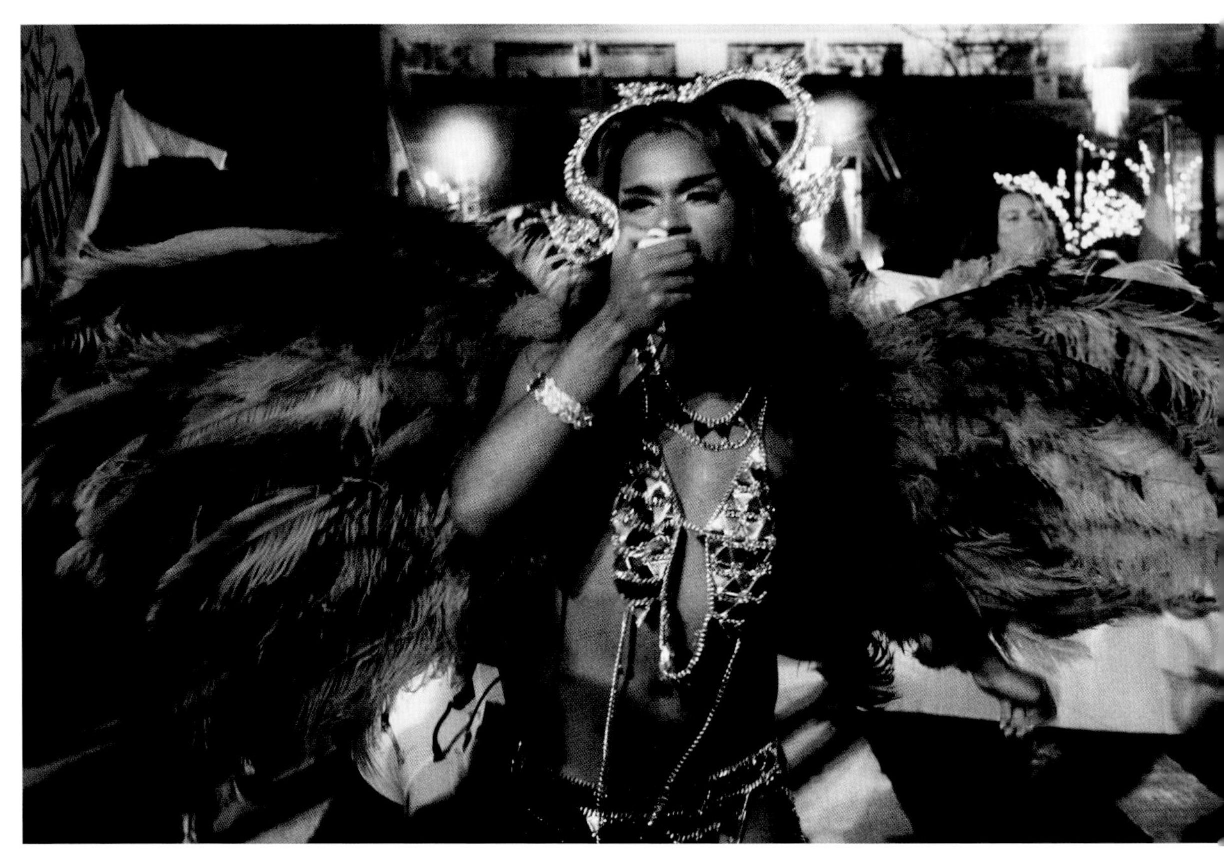

Robert Hamada
The Last Ball of 2020
December 2020

Erica Lansner
Drop the Charges
January 2021

Sean Waltrous
Black Angels Ball
October 2020

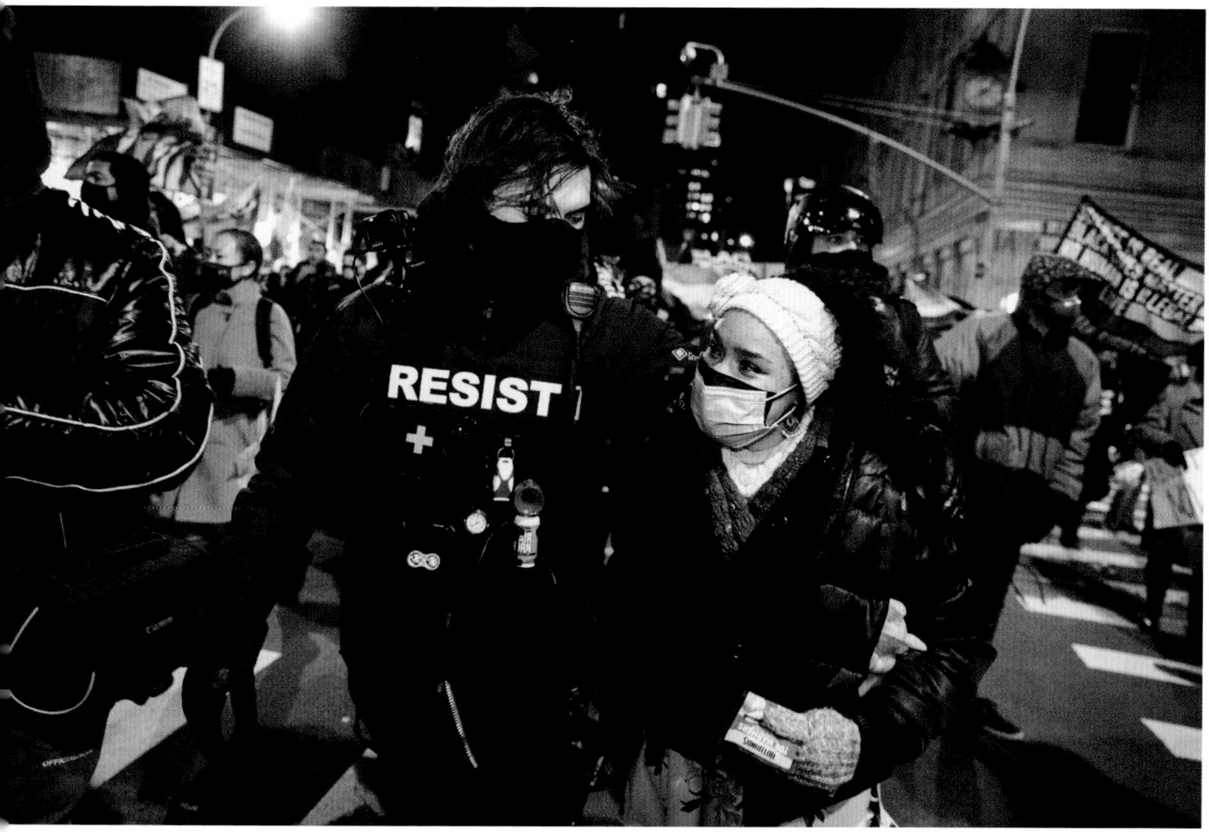

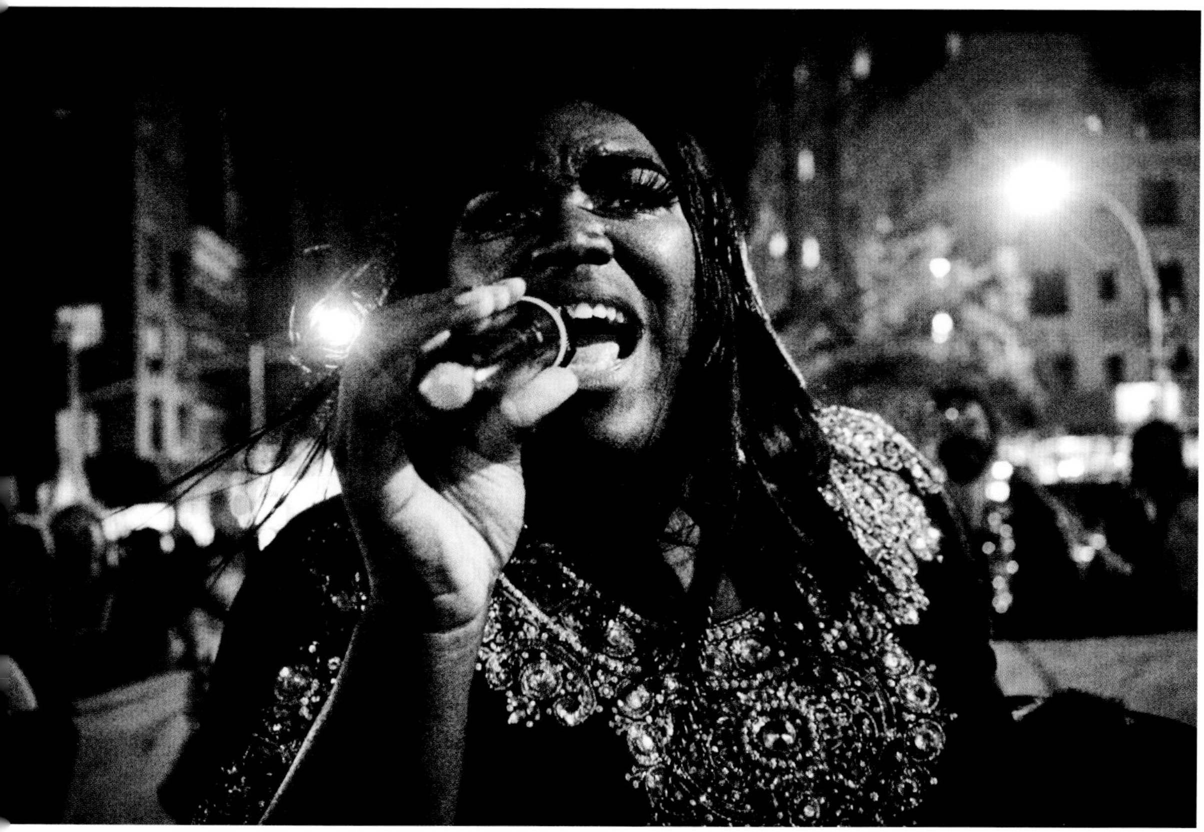

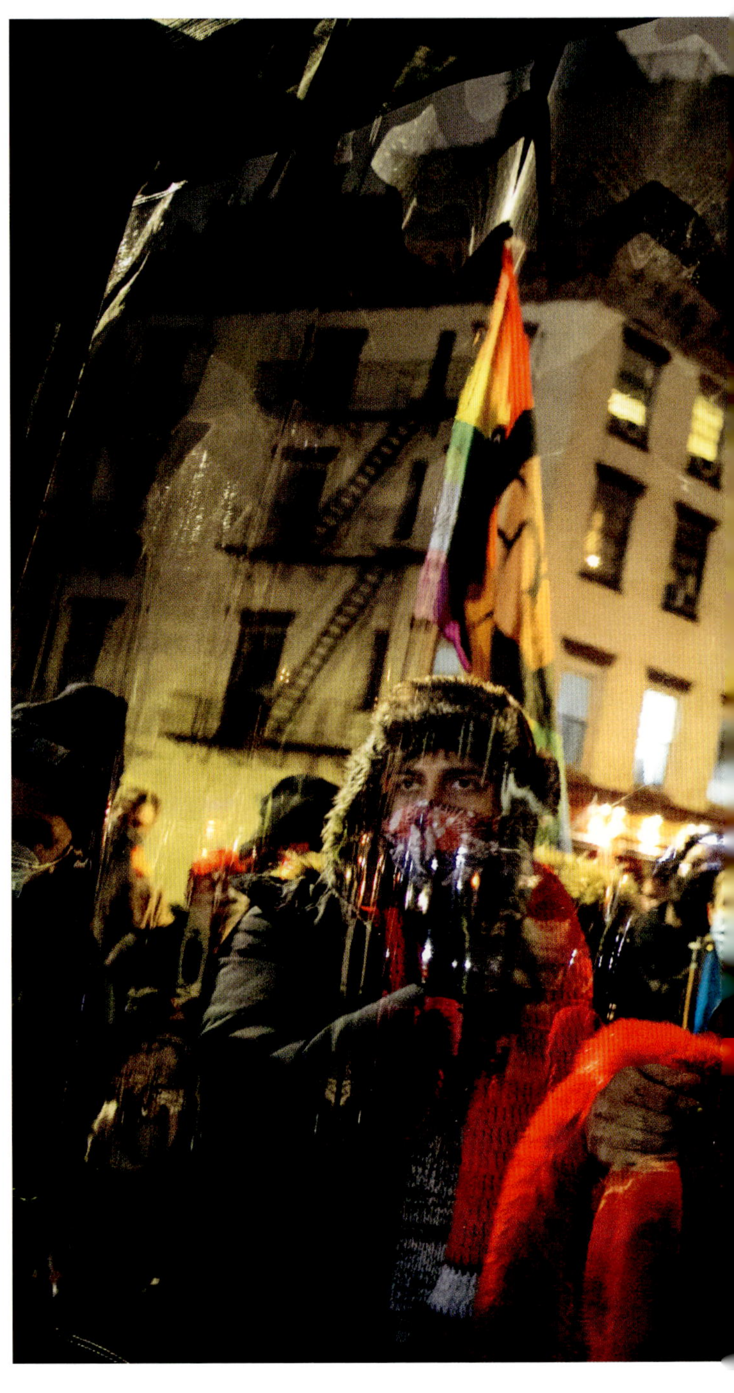

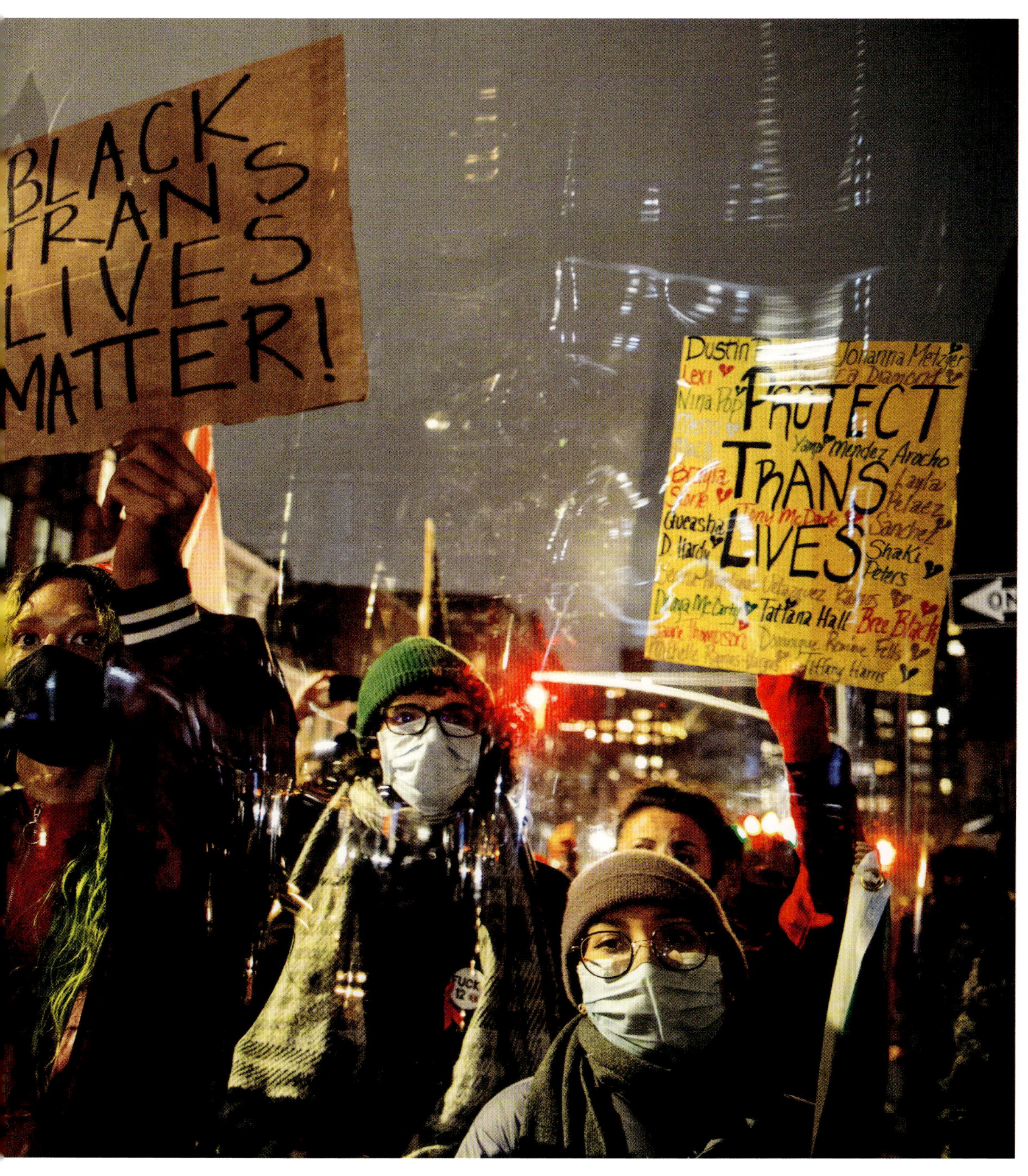

Erica Lansner
Love Liberation: End the Stigma
December 2020

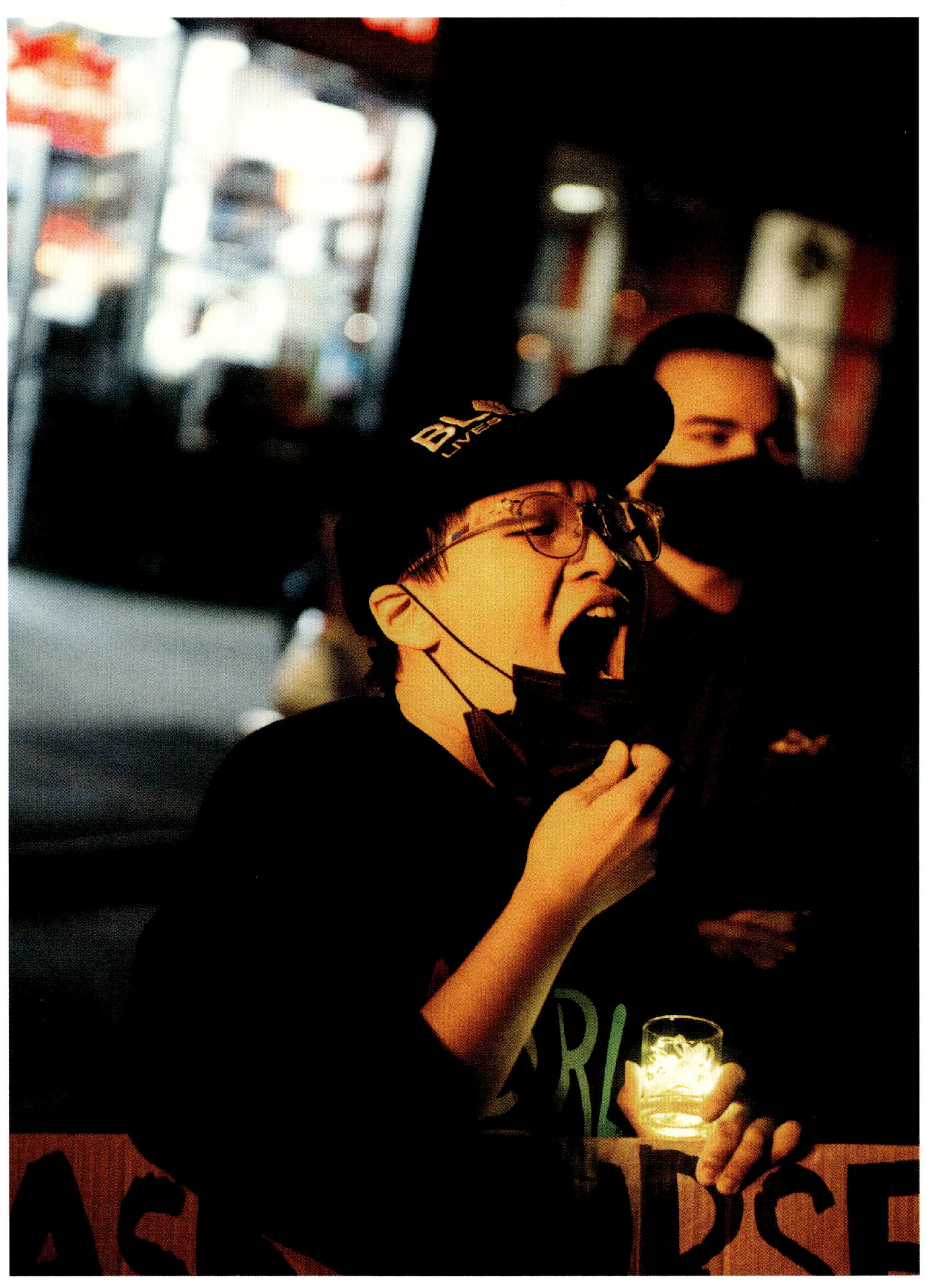

Ryan McGinley
Icons Liberation Ball
October 2020

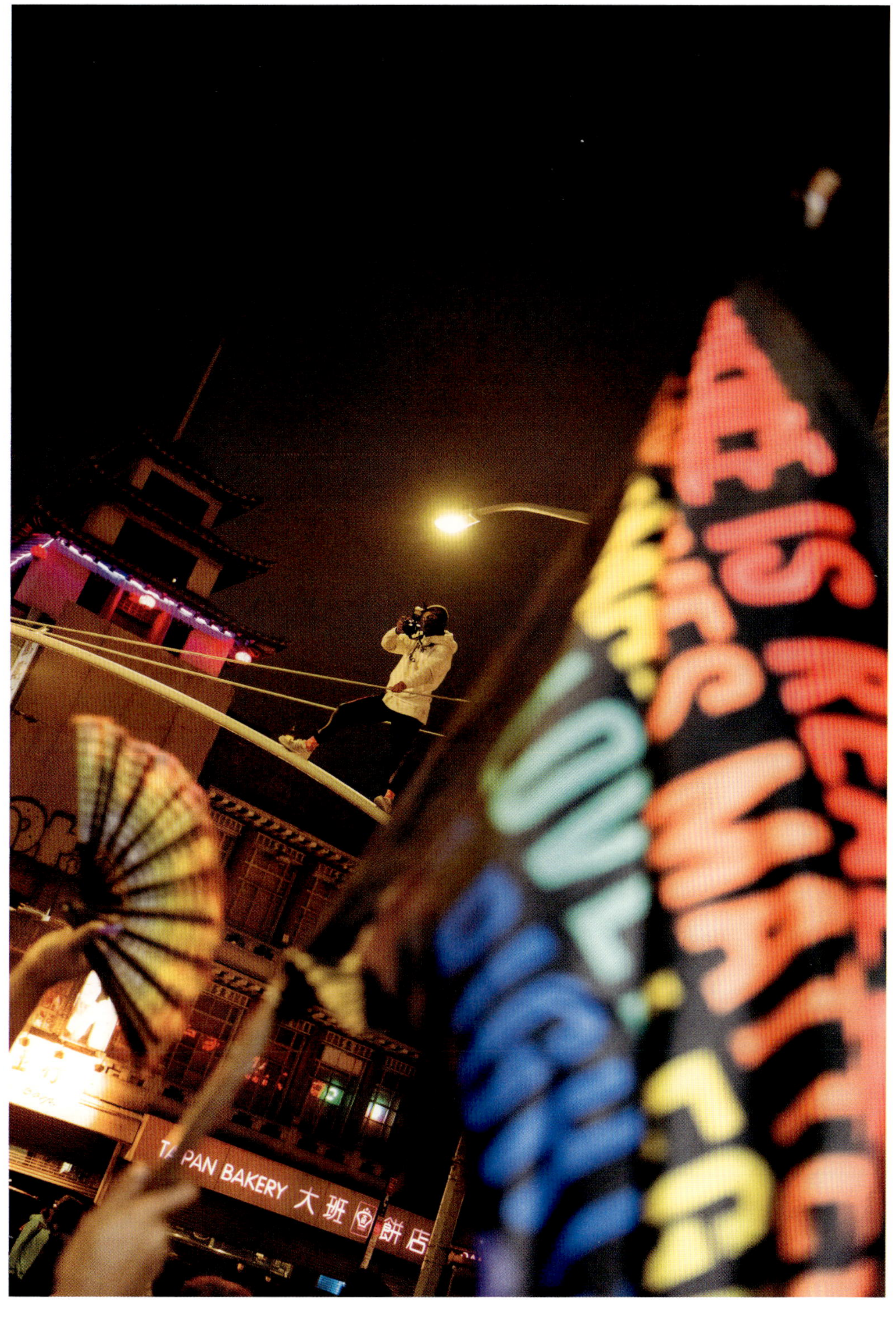

Ryan McGinley
Black and Asian Solidarity
March 2021

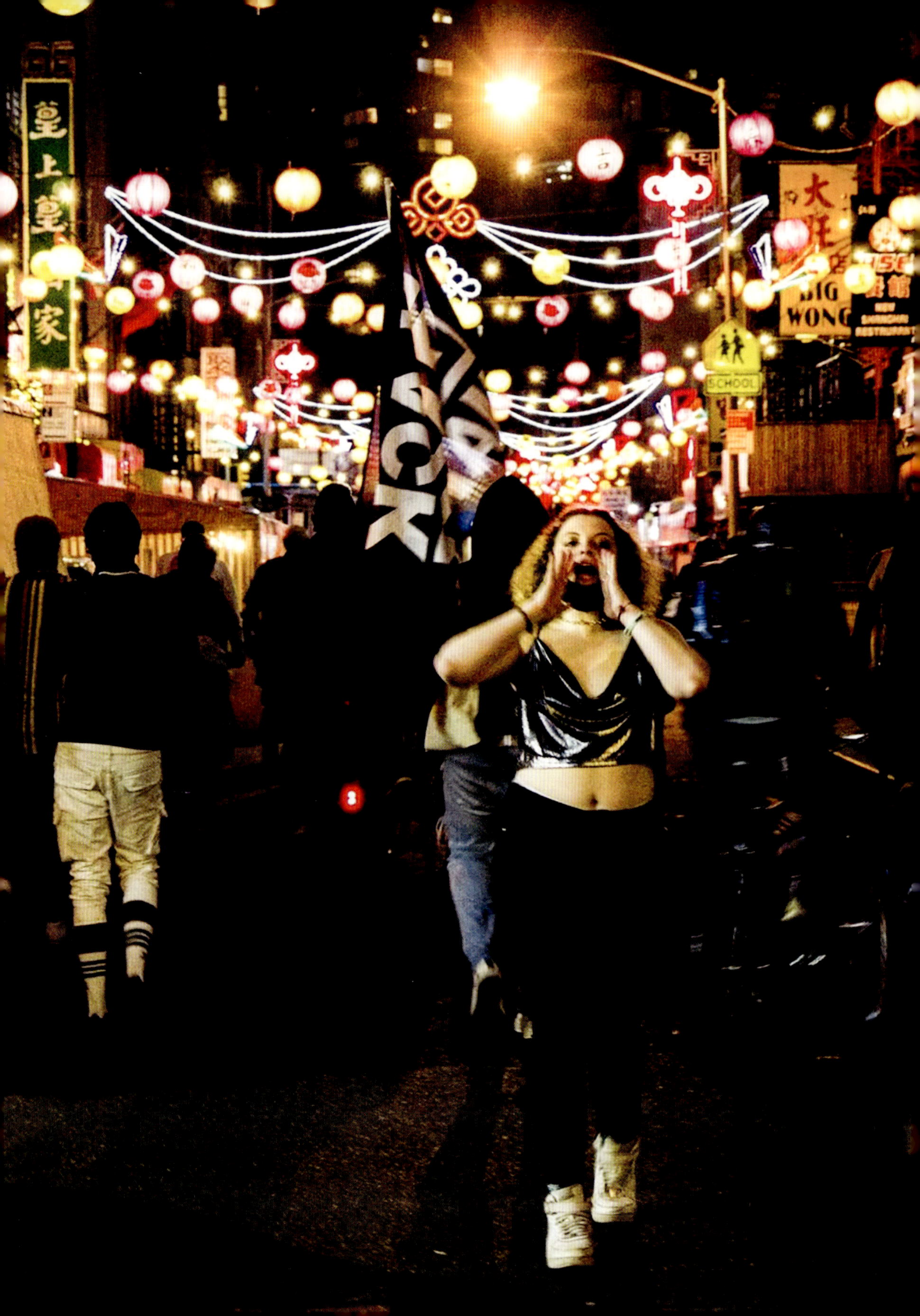

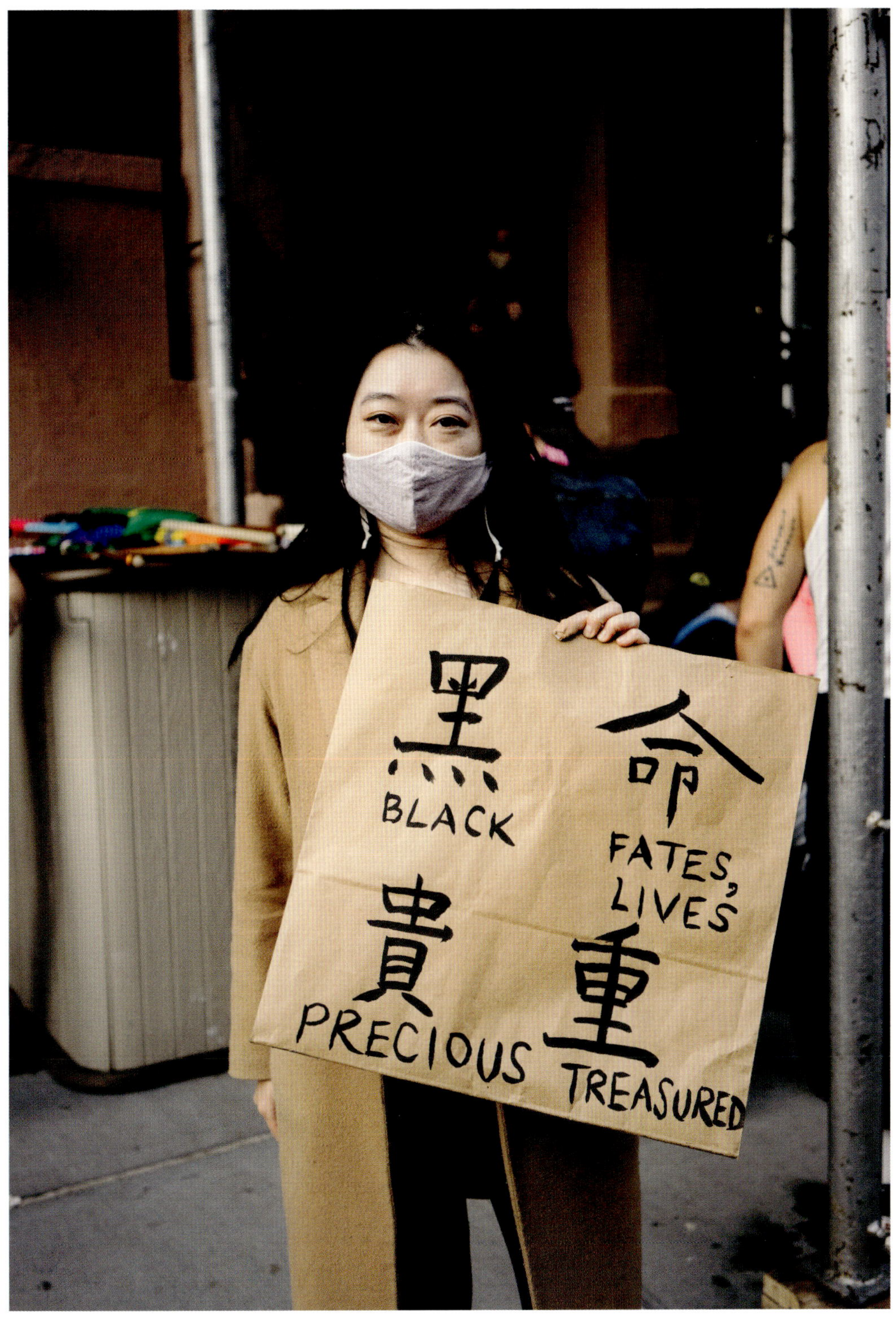

Madison Swart
Black and Asian Solidarity
March 2021

Cindy Trinh
Black and Asian Solidarity
March 2021

New Yorkers of all kinds gathered at Stonewall; together we wrote a Declaration of Interdependence. I know the power of authoring one's own story to tell it directly and undiluted to the world. To be seen is to be acknowledged; to be seen is to be.

—David Zung

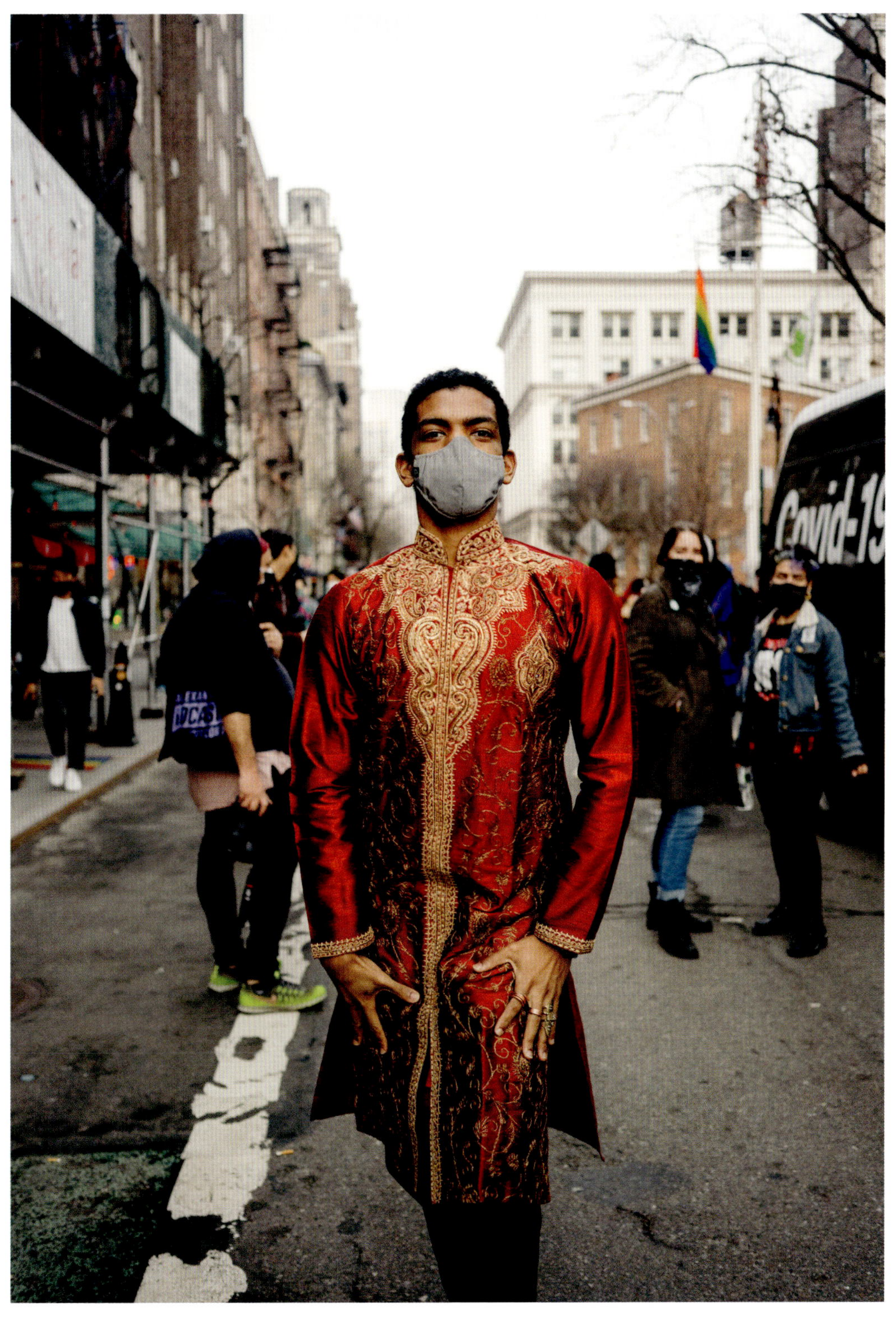

Cindy Trinh
Black and Asian Solidarity
March 2021

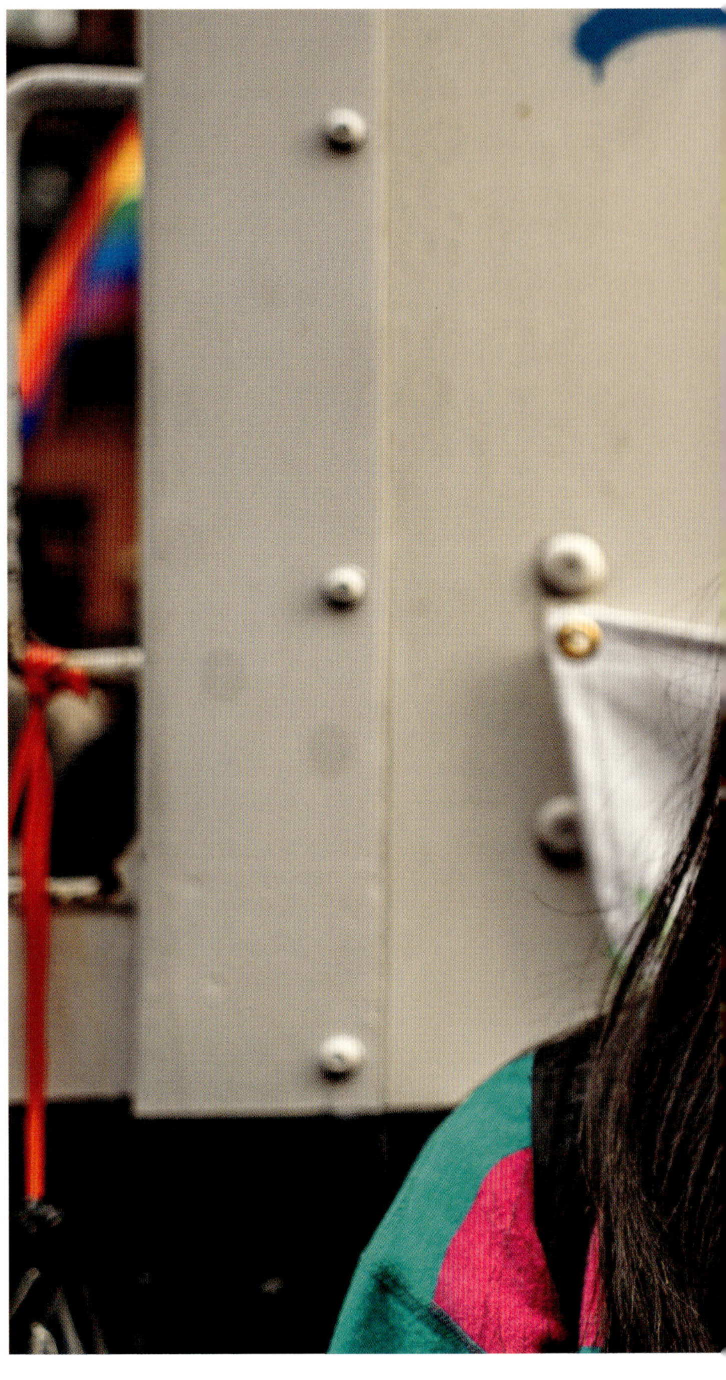

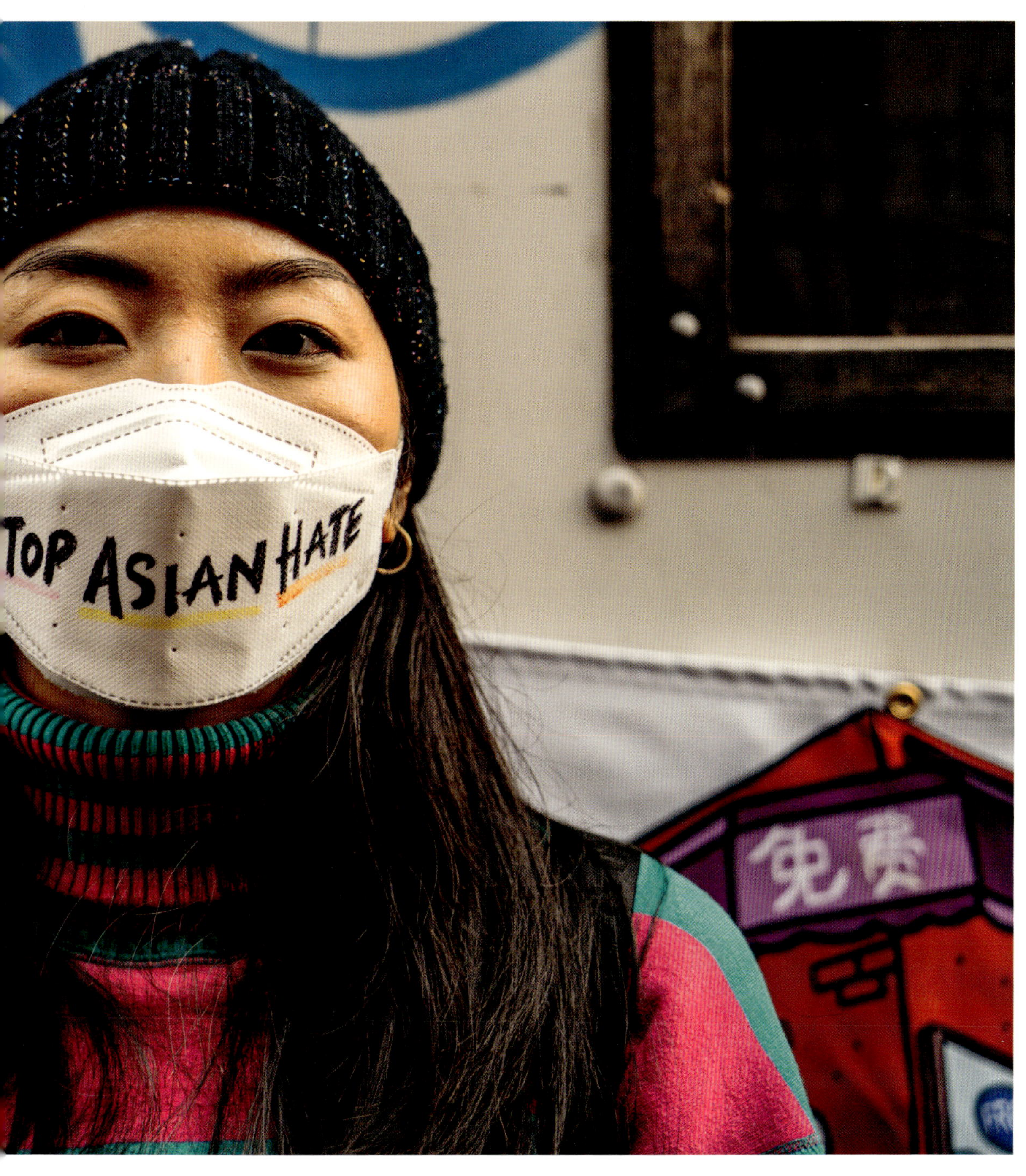

Daniel Lehrhaupt
Black and Asian Solidarity
March 2021

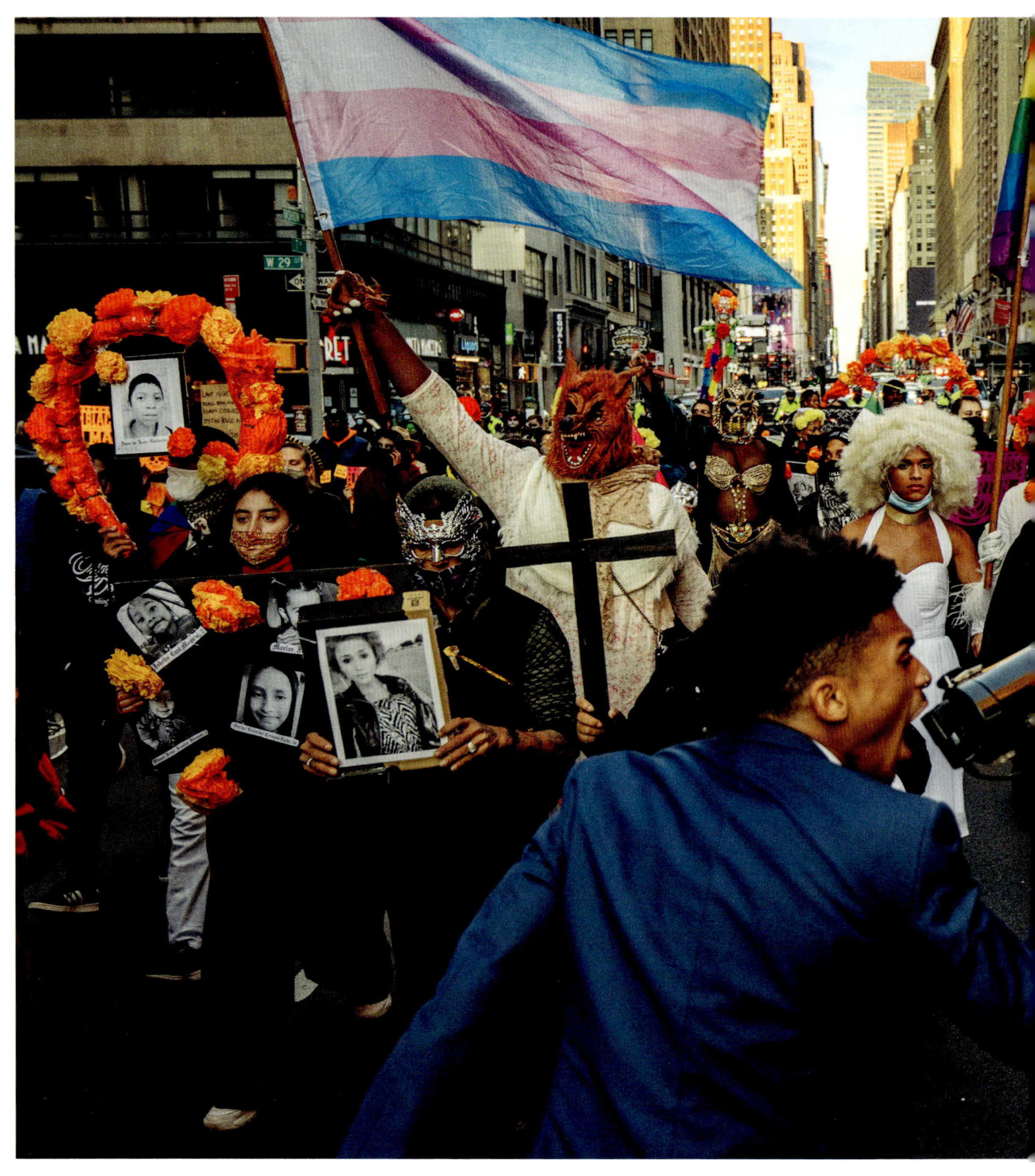

Stas Ginzburg
October 2020

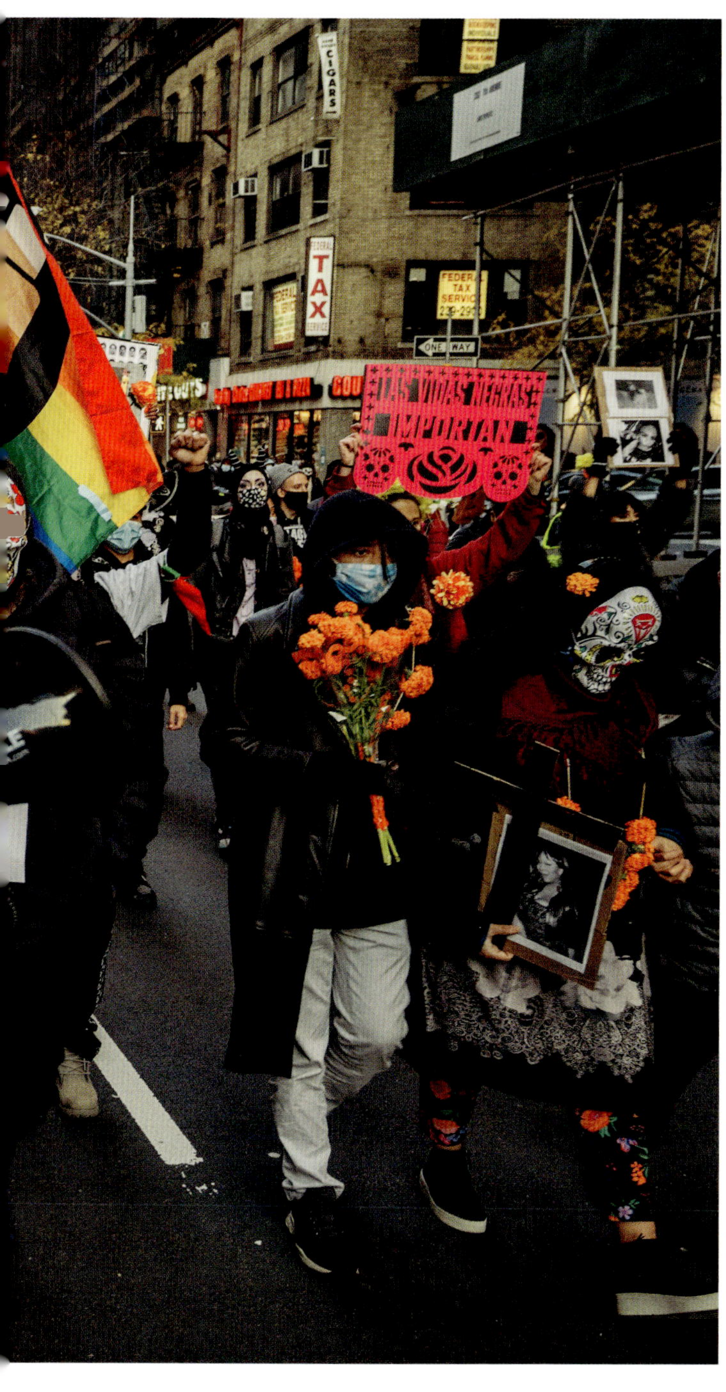

In this space, I began to feel a sense of community like I never had before. Learning about the overlapping systematic oppression faced by Black trans women ingrained in me how none of us are truly free until the Black TGNB community is centered in the fight for liberation.

—Snake Garcia

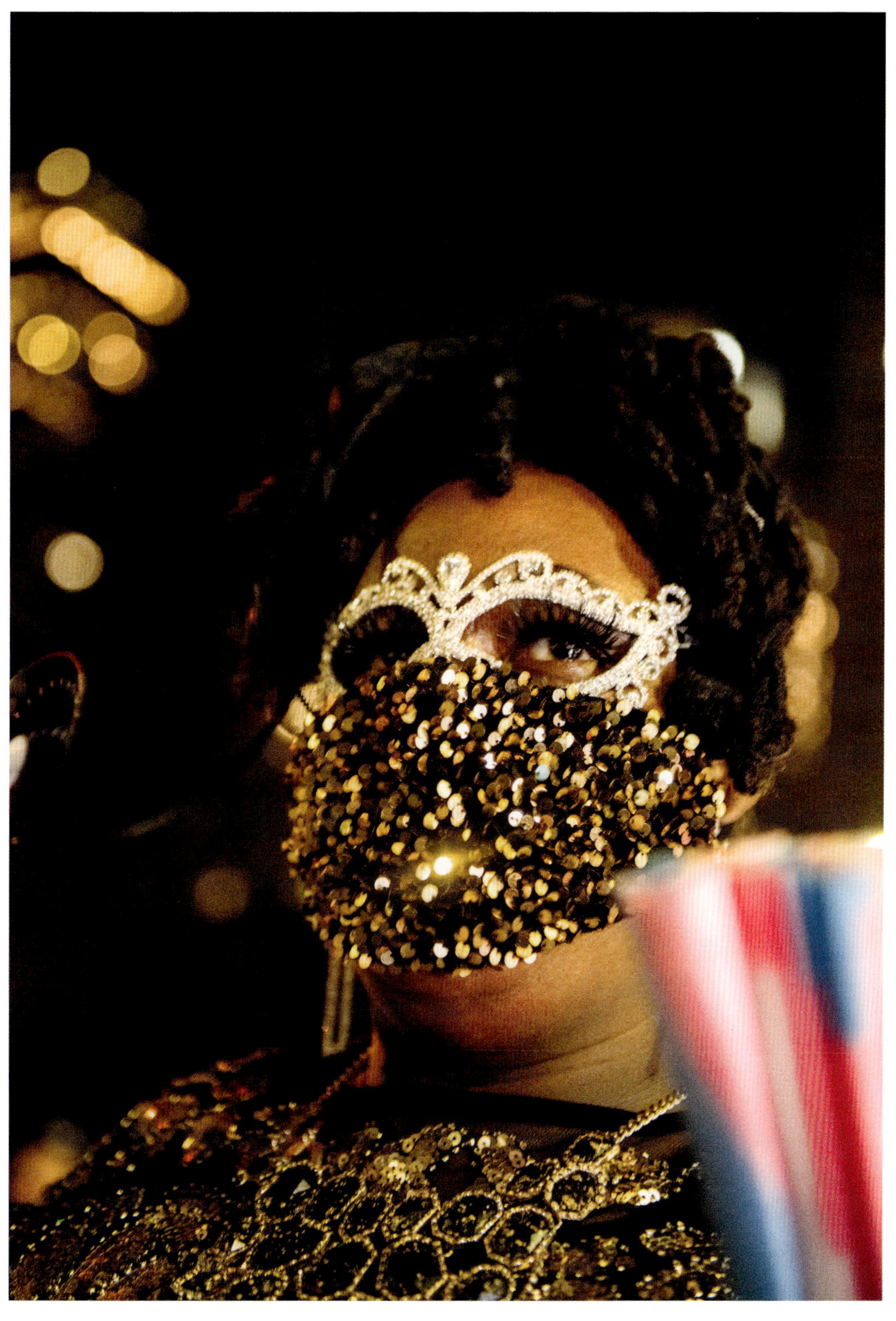

Ryan McGinley
Illumination Ball
October 2020

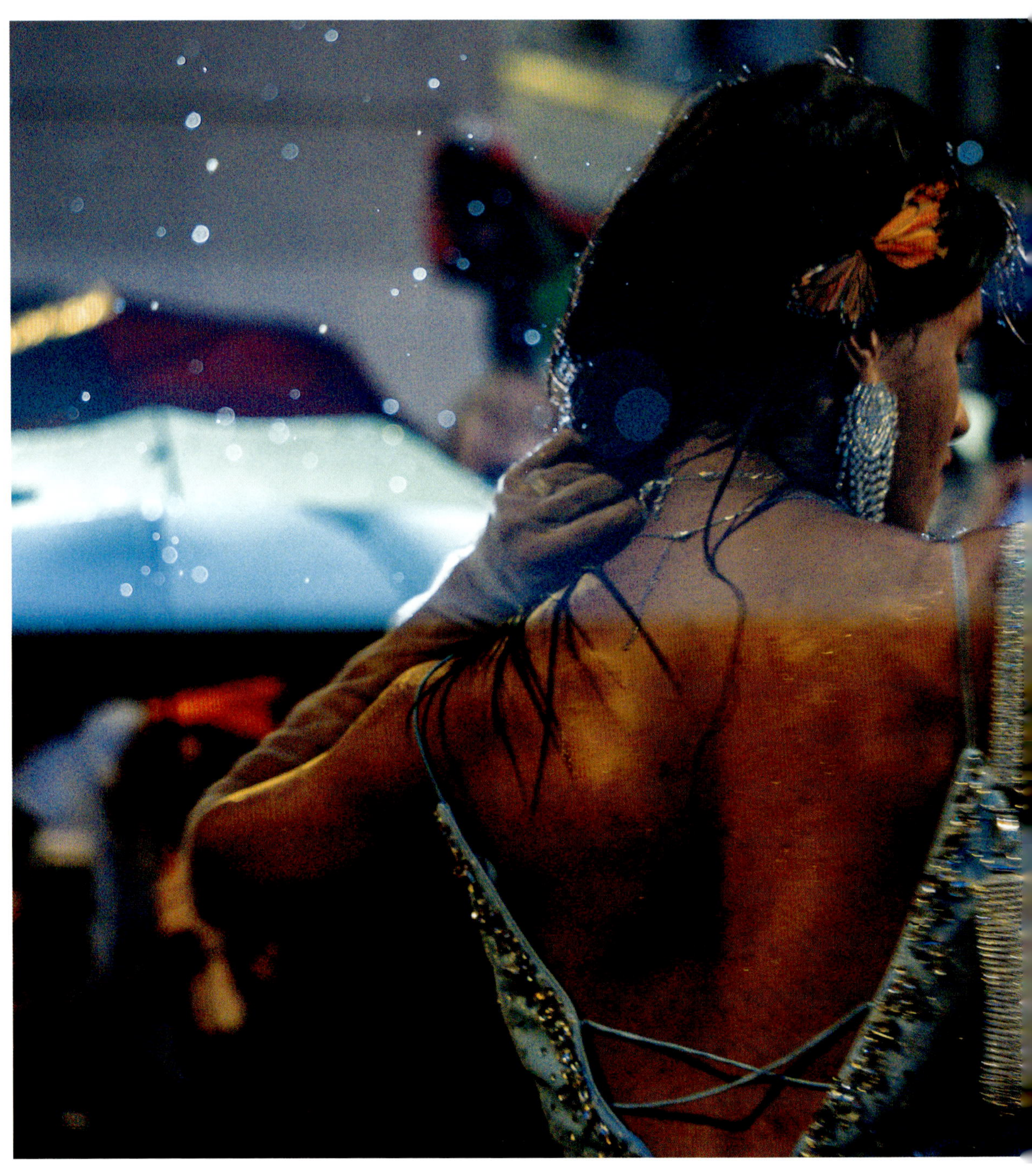

Daniel Lehrhaupt
We Are Pride
June 2021

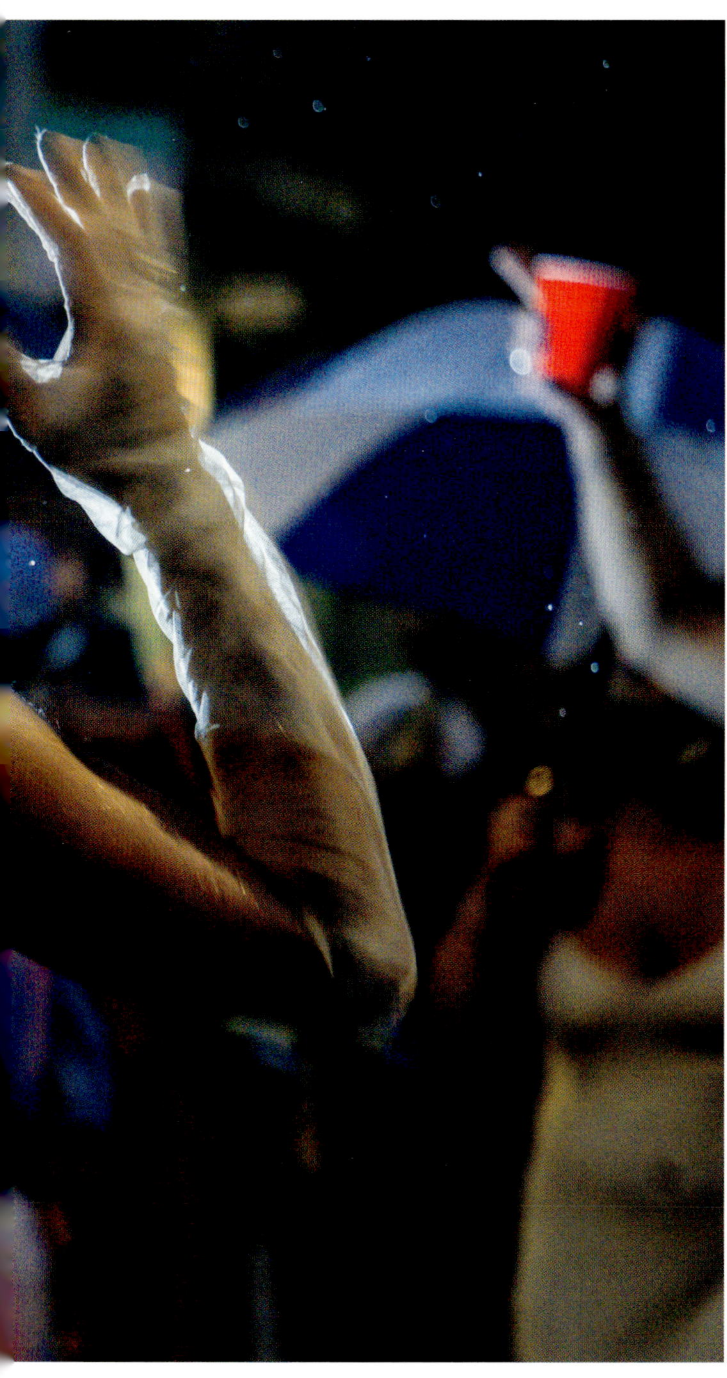

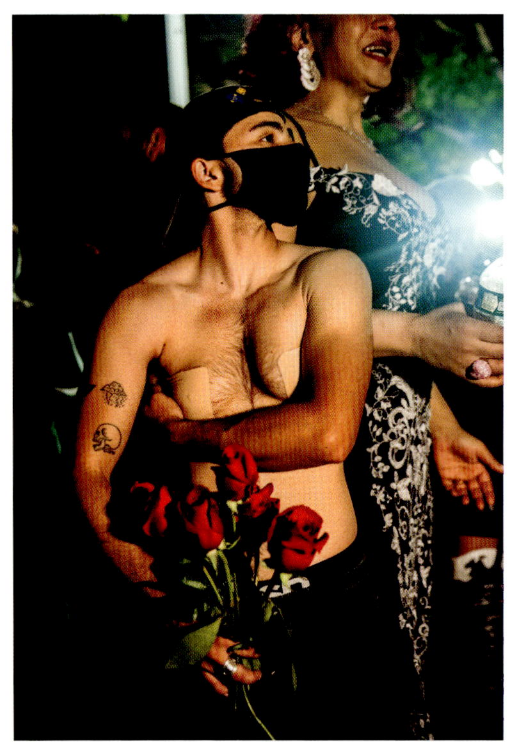

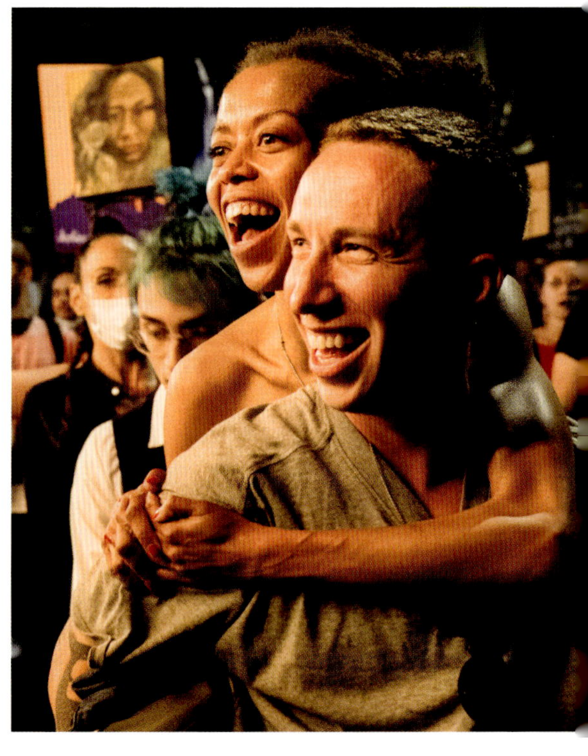

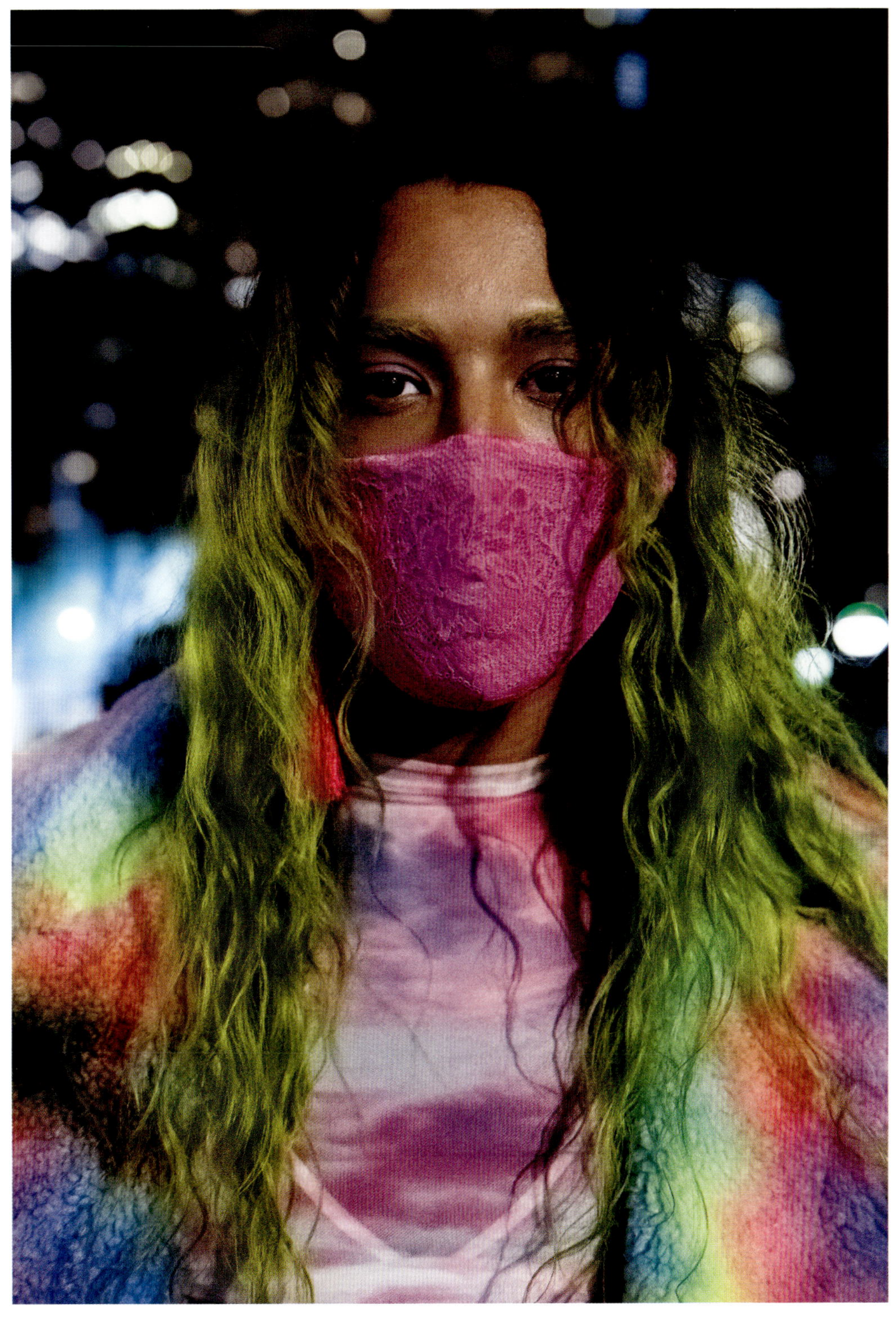

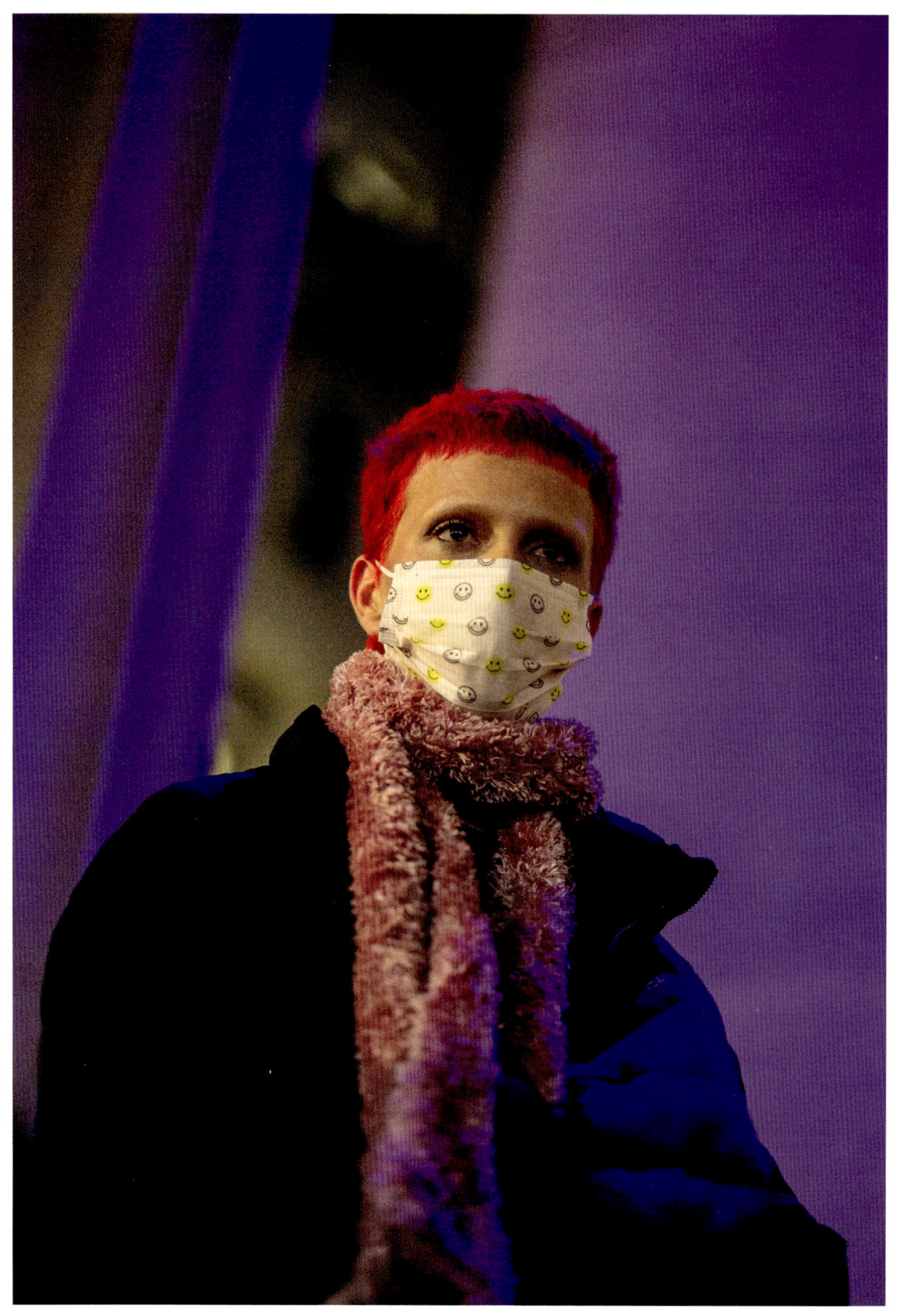

Erica Lansner
Drop the Charges
January 2021

While attending these beautiful protests about Black Trans Liberation, I learned history that I never learned in school. As a photographer, I want to show the positivity and celebration that comes from protests.

—Katie Godowski

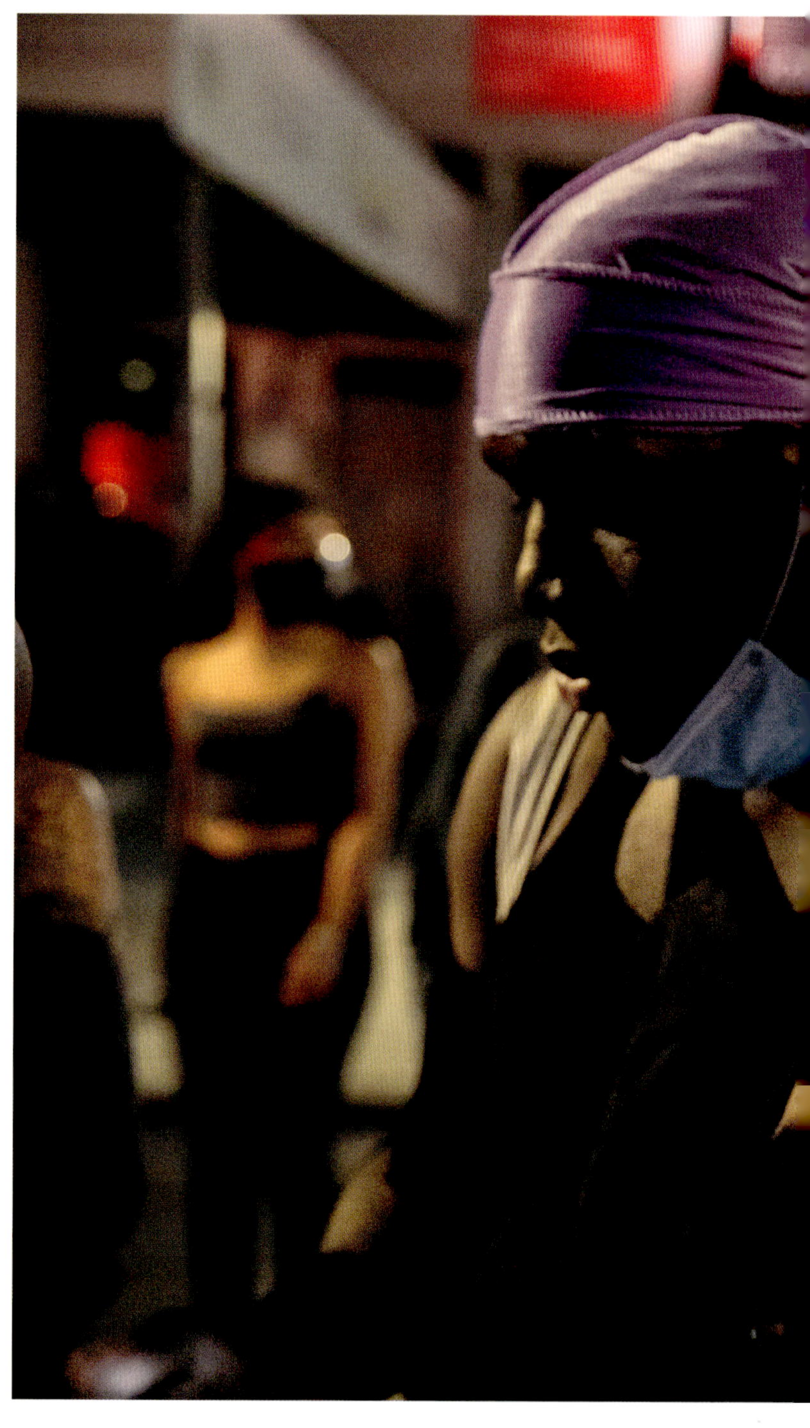

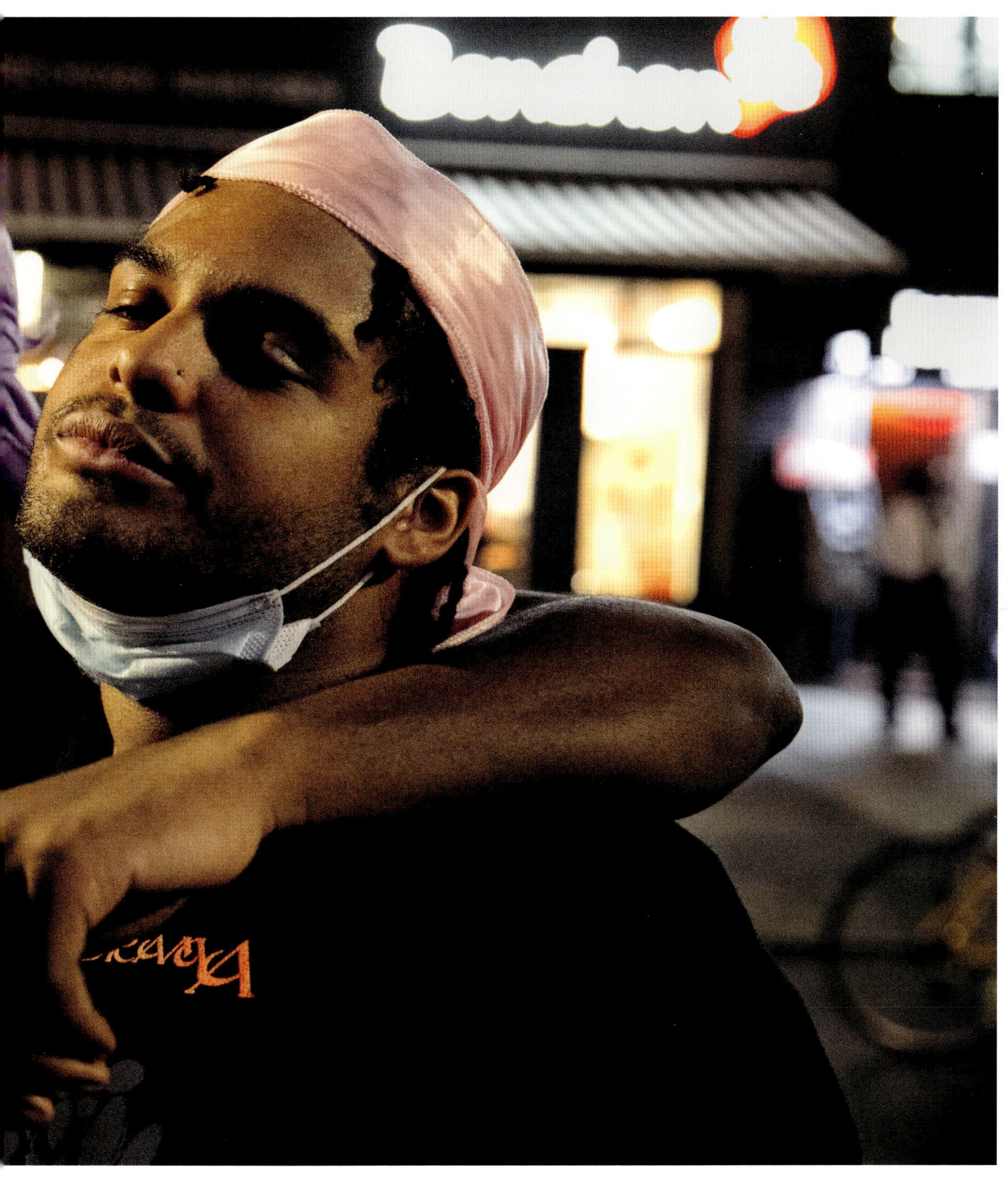

Erica Lansner
Black Angels Ball
October 2020

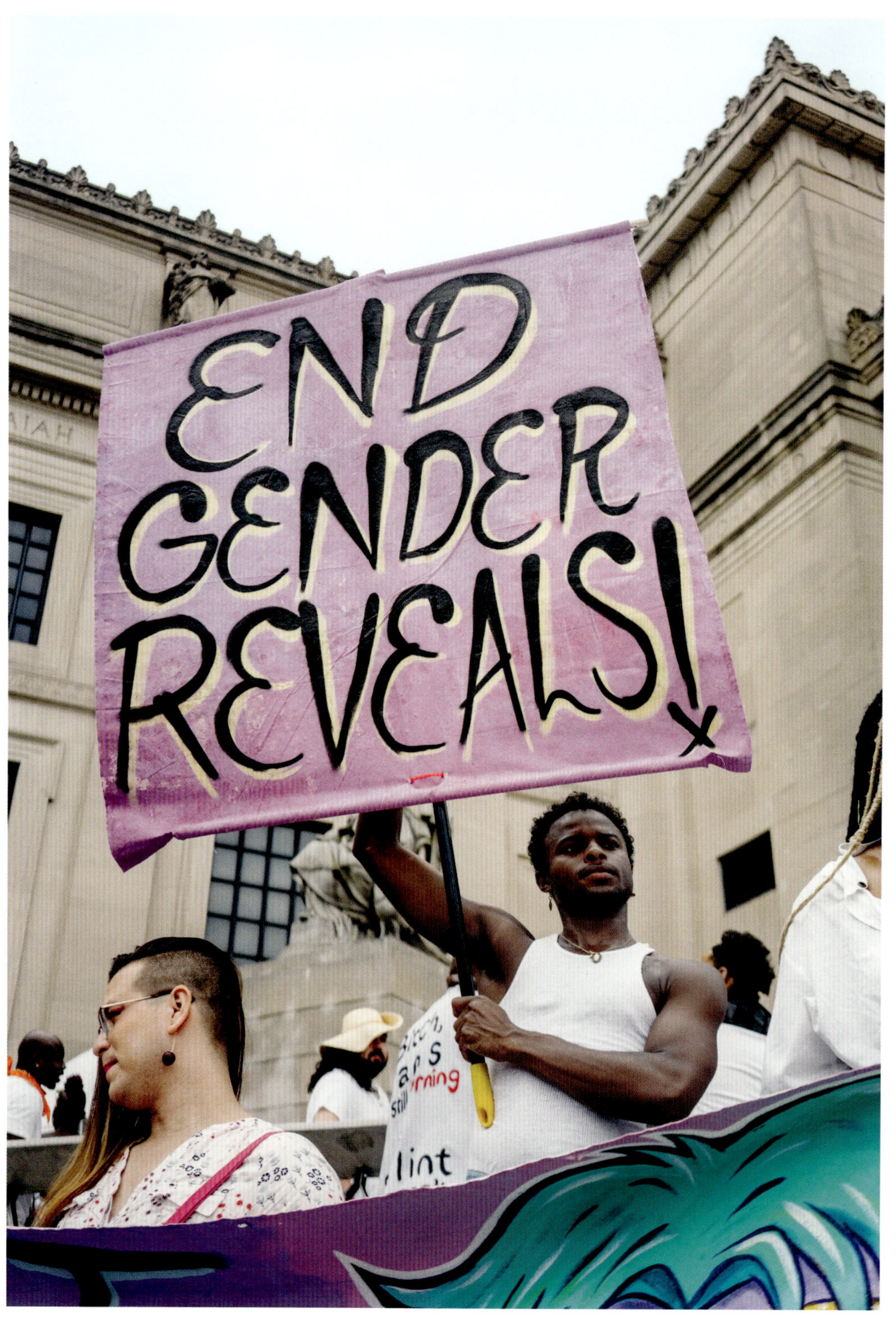

Cindy Trinh
Brooklyn Liberation March
June 2021

Through joy, pain, triumph, and challenge, the movement has achieved a goal of changing the way we have conversations, the way we fight for and defend our Black trans and nonbinary siblings, and the way we think about the world around us through the lens of others.

—Sean Waltrous

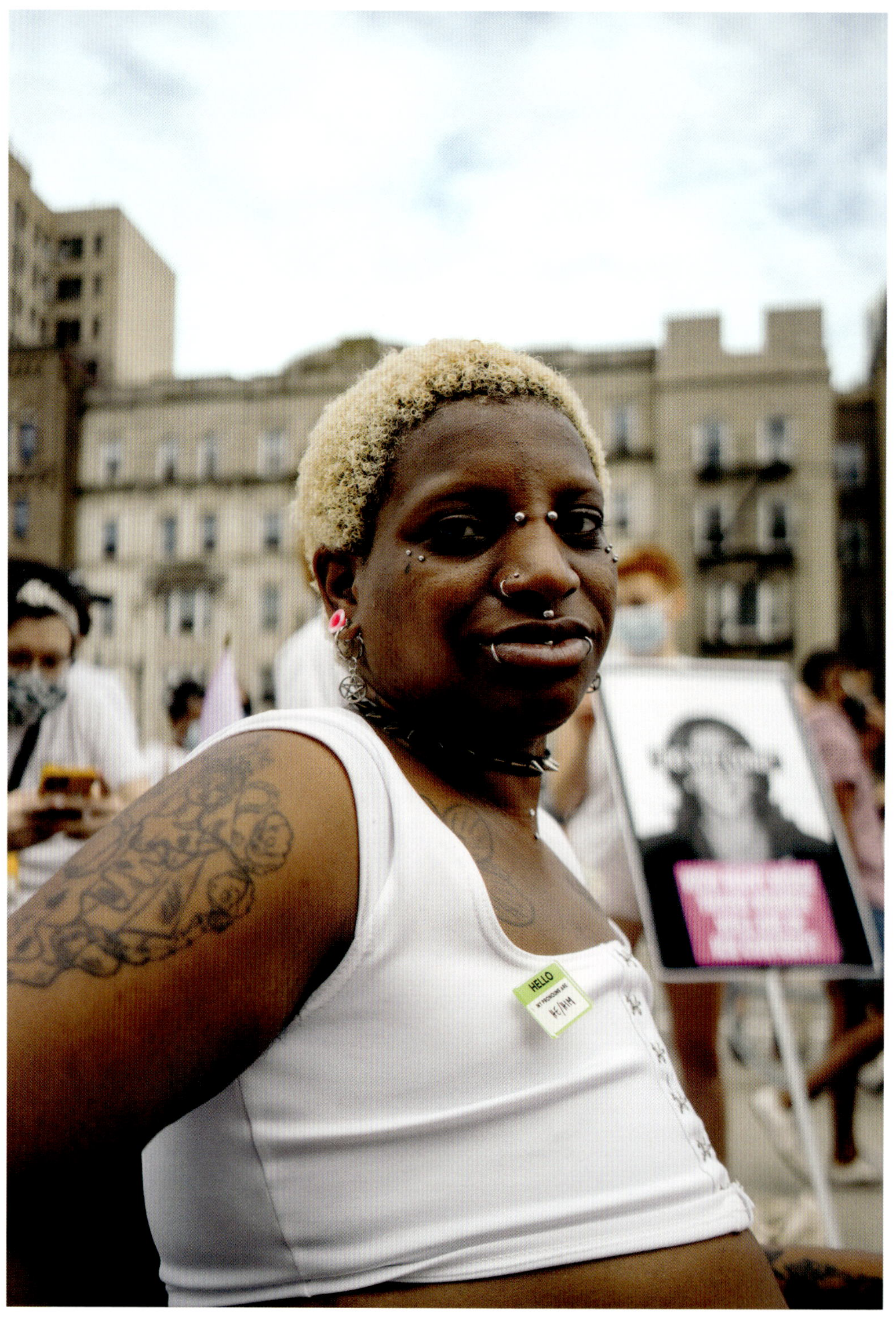

Cindy Trinh
Brooklyn Liberation March
June 2021

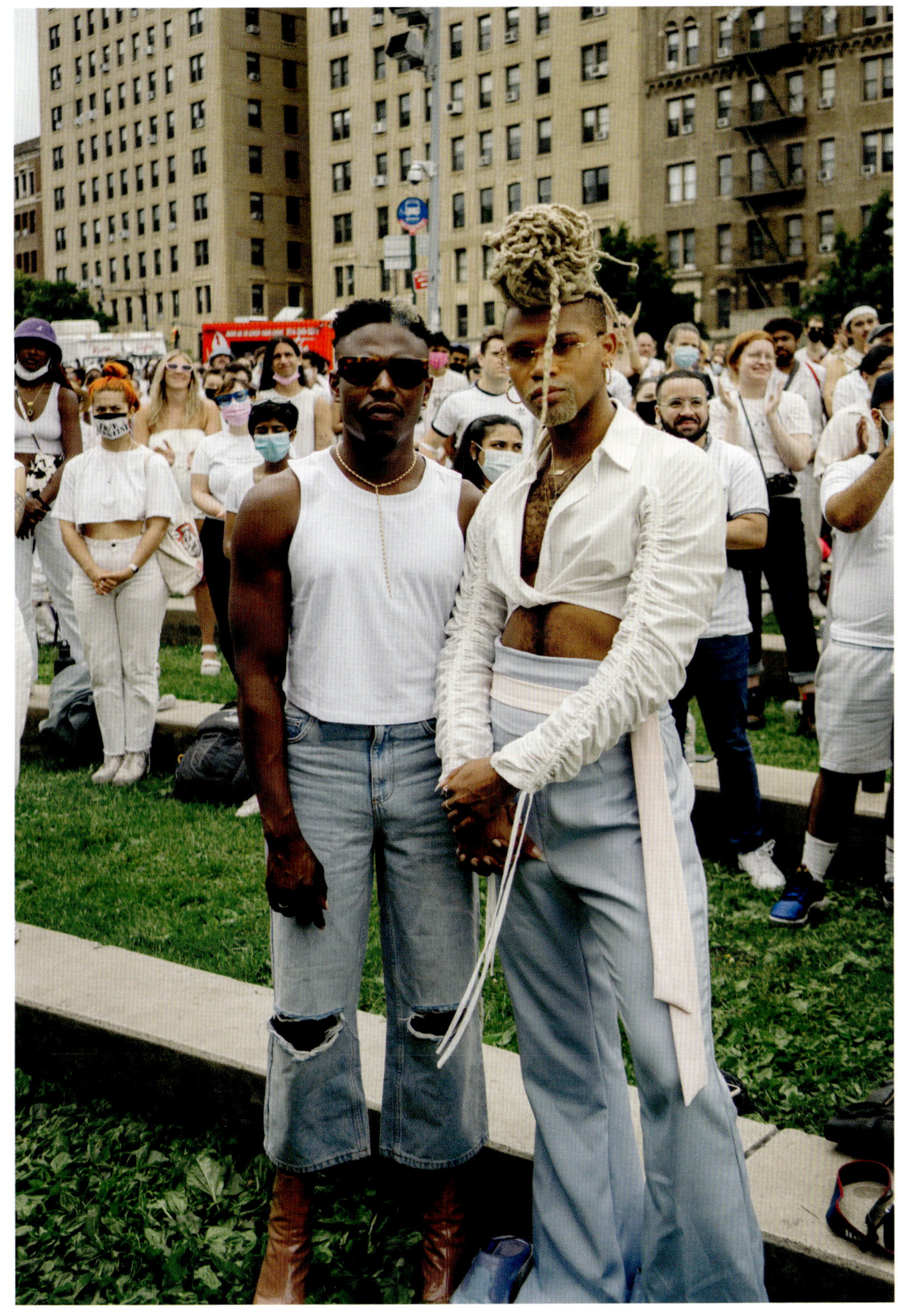

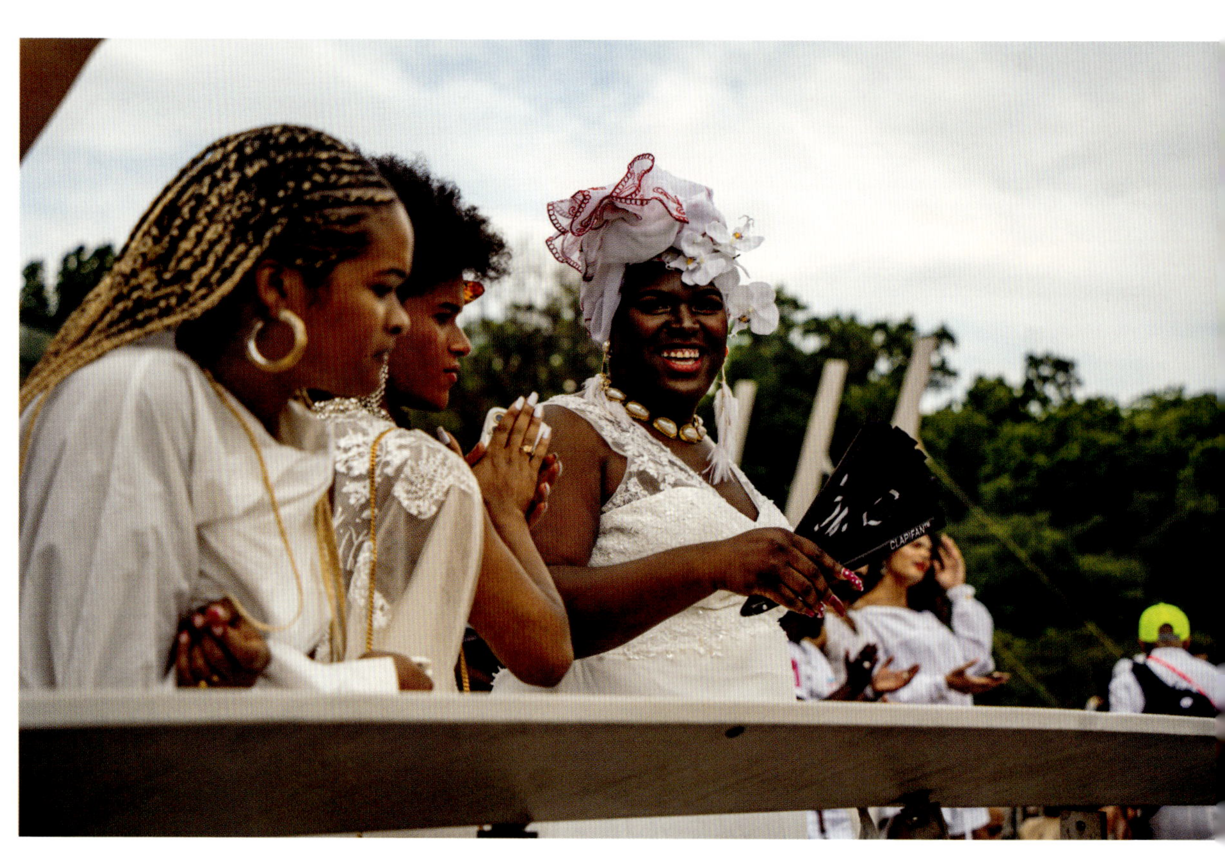

ABOVE AND OPPOSITE BOTTOM:
Daniel Lehrhaupt
Brooklyn Liberation March
June 2021

Caroline Mardok
Brooklyn Liberation March
June 2021

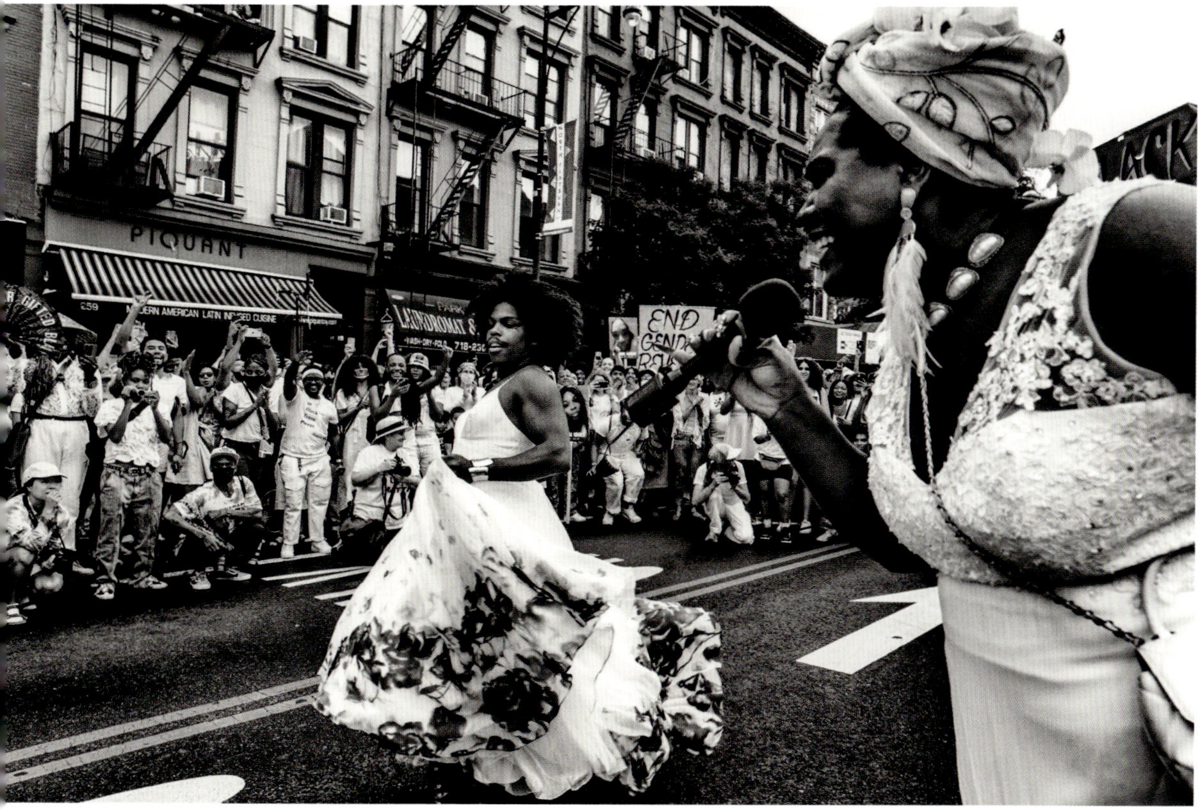
PIQUANT
MODERN AMERICAN LATIN INFUSED CUISINE
END

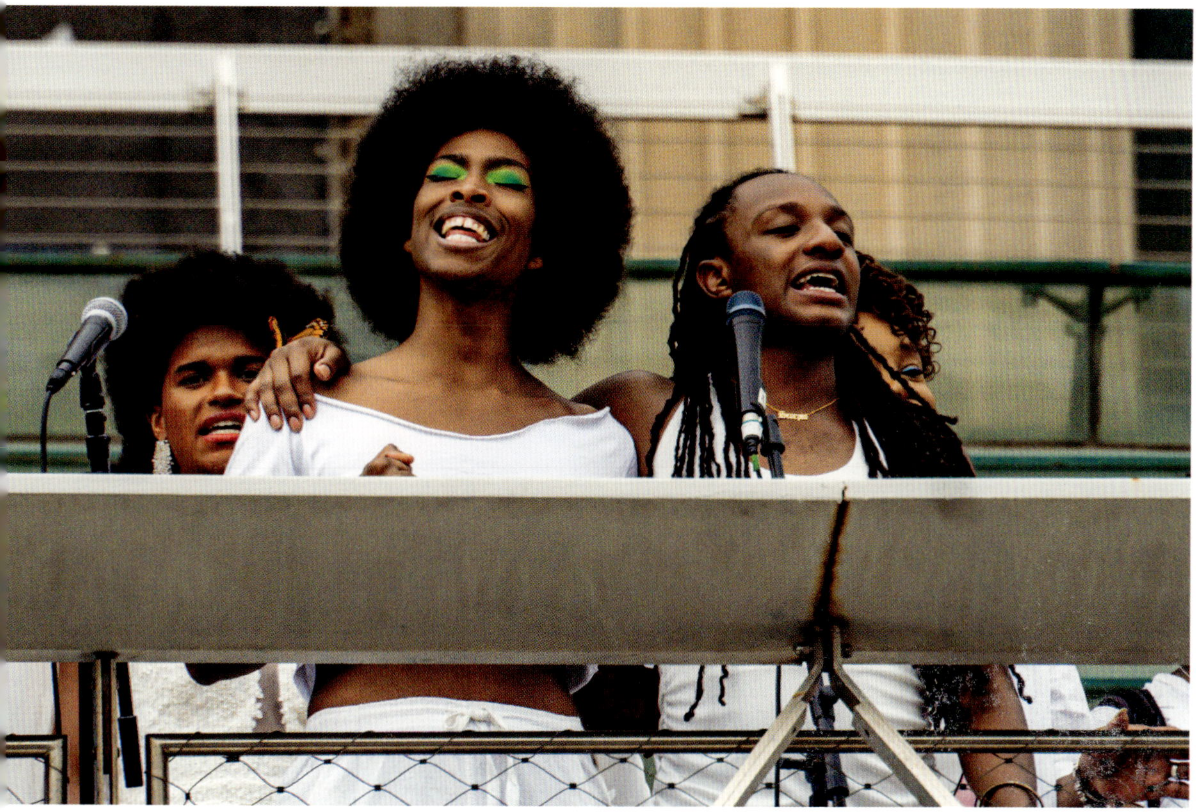

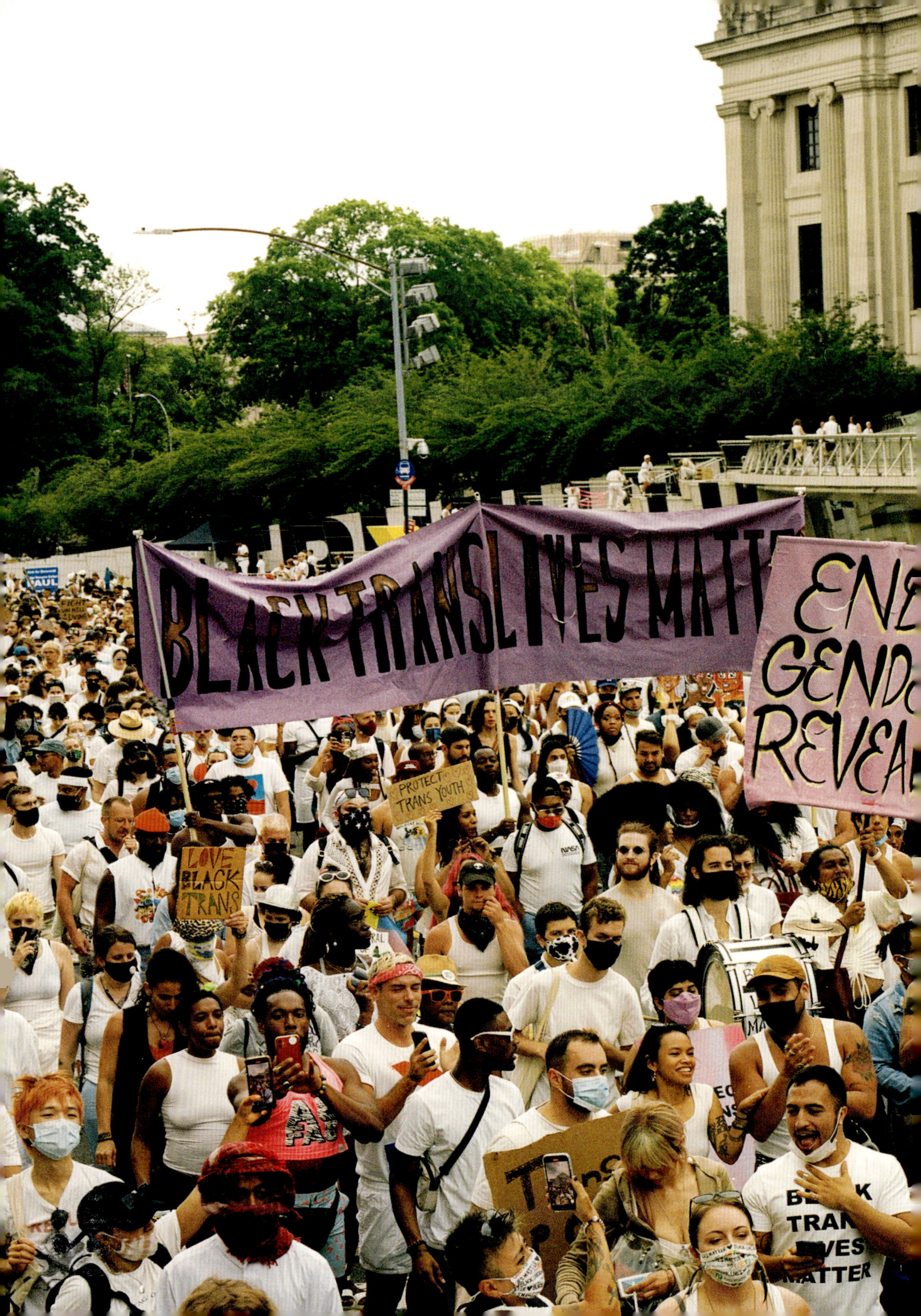

BLACK TRANS LIVES MATTER
ENE
GEND
REVEA
PROTECT
TRANS YOUTH
LOVE
BLACK
TRANS
BLACK
TRANS
IVES
MATTER

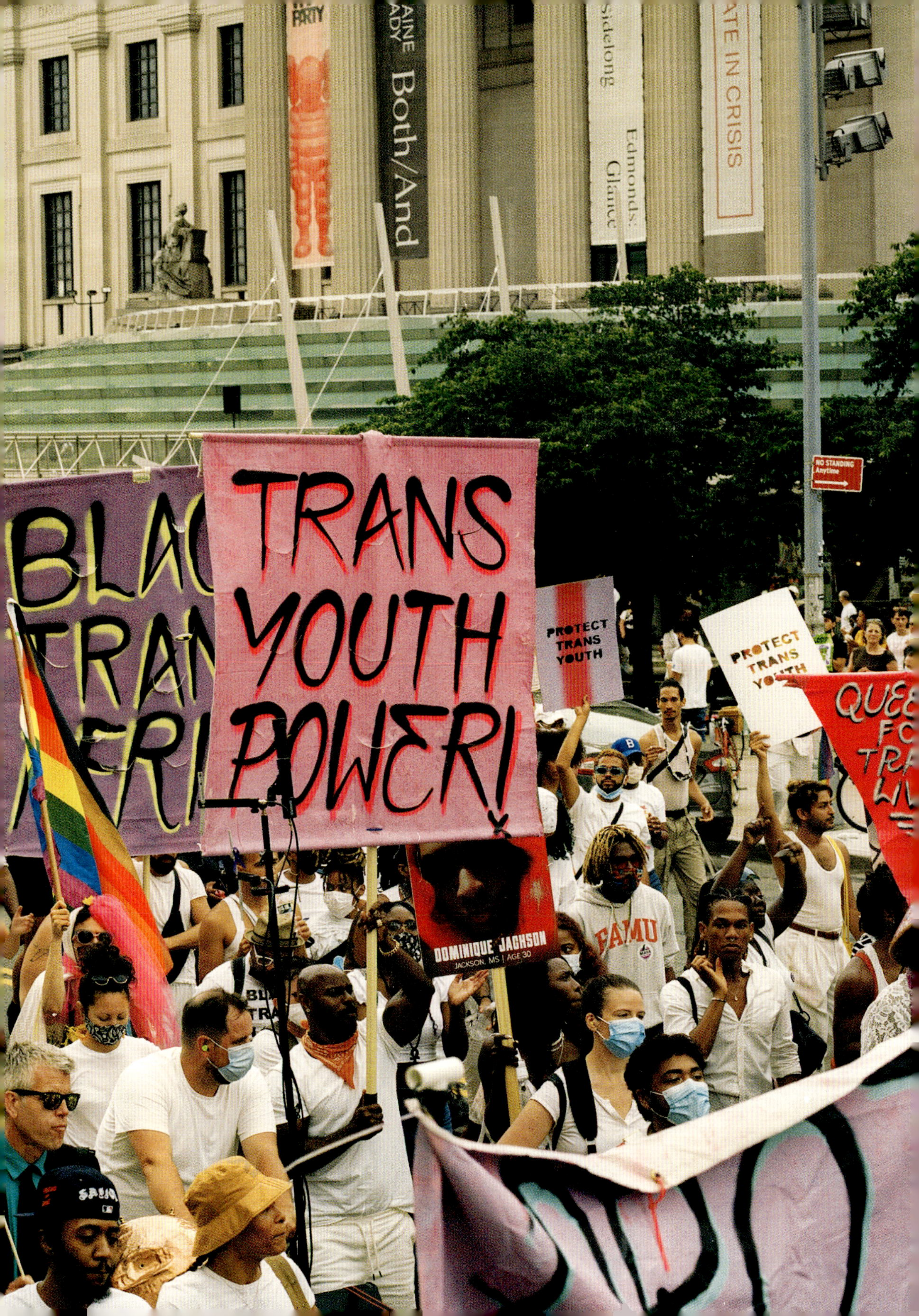
BLAC
TRAN
MERI
TRANS YOUTH POWER!
PROTECT TRANS YOUTH
PROTECT TRANS YOUTH
QUEE
FO
TRA
DOMINIQUE JACKSON
JACKSON, MS | AGE 30
FAMU
NO STANDING
Anytime
PARTY
AINE
ADY
Both/And
Sidelong
Edmonds:
Glance
ATE IN CRISIS

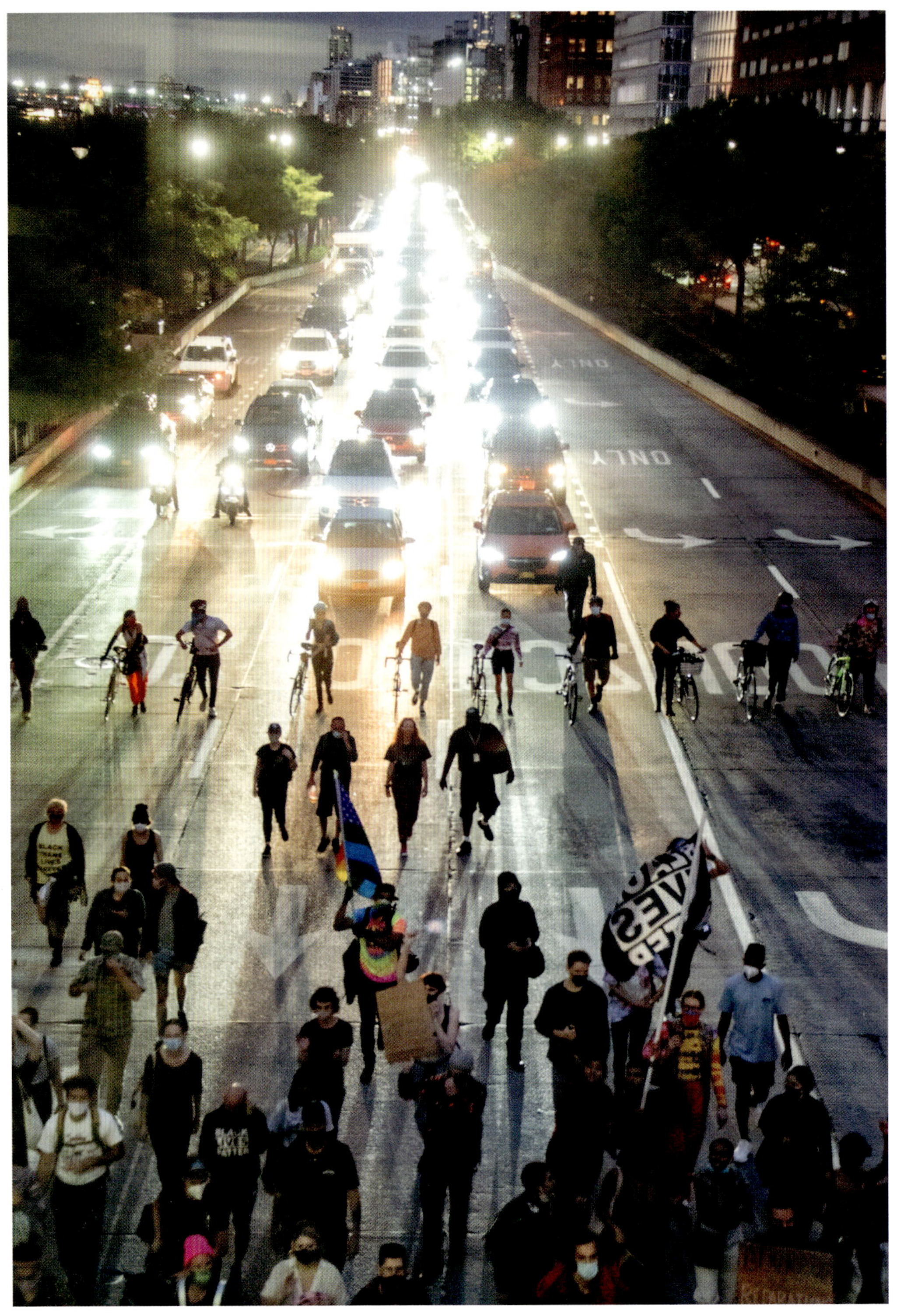

PREVIOUS SPREAD:
Ramie Ahmed
Brooklyn Liberation March
June 2021

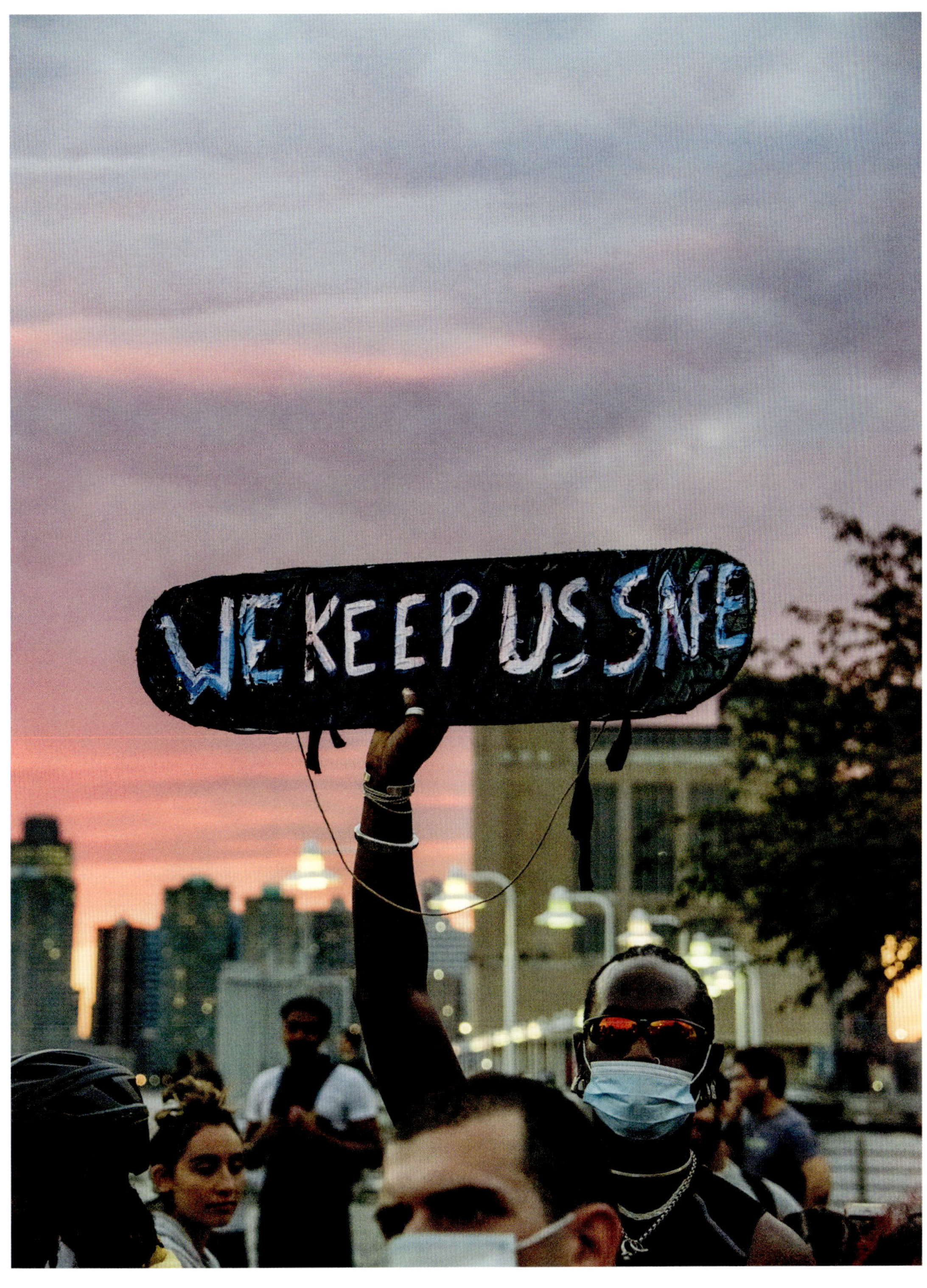

OPPOSITE AND ABOVE:
Ruvan Wijesooriya
Liberation Not Deportation
October 2020

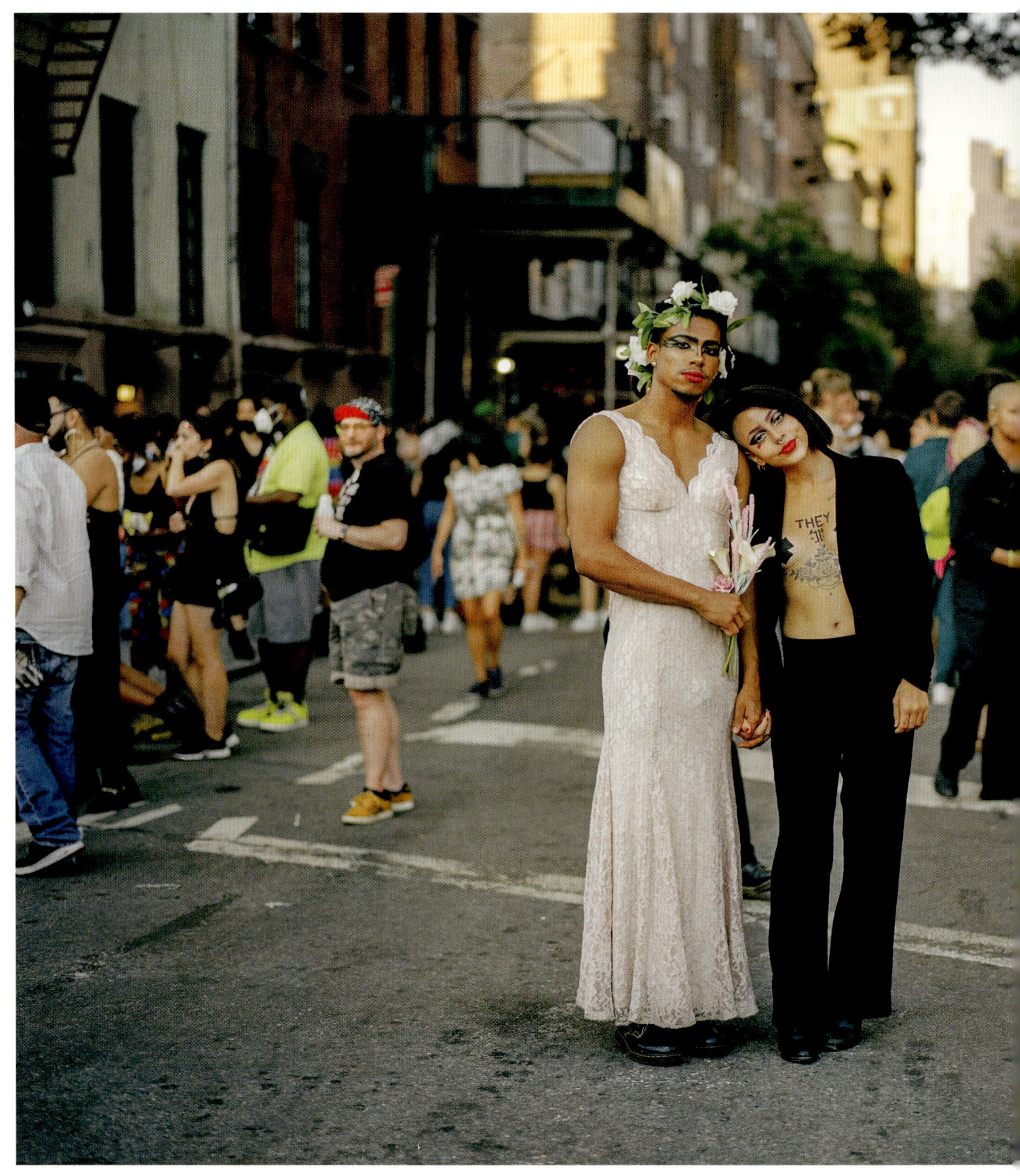

Ramie Ahmed
The Stonewall Protests Anniversary
June 2021

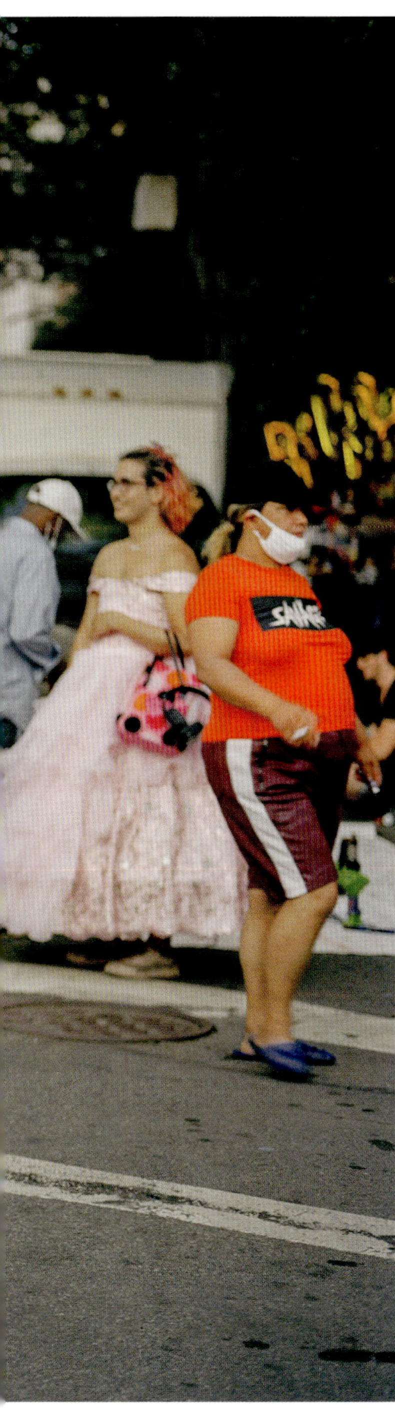

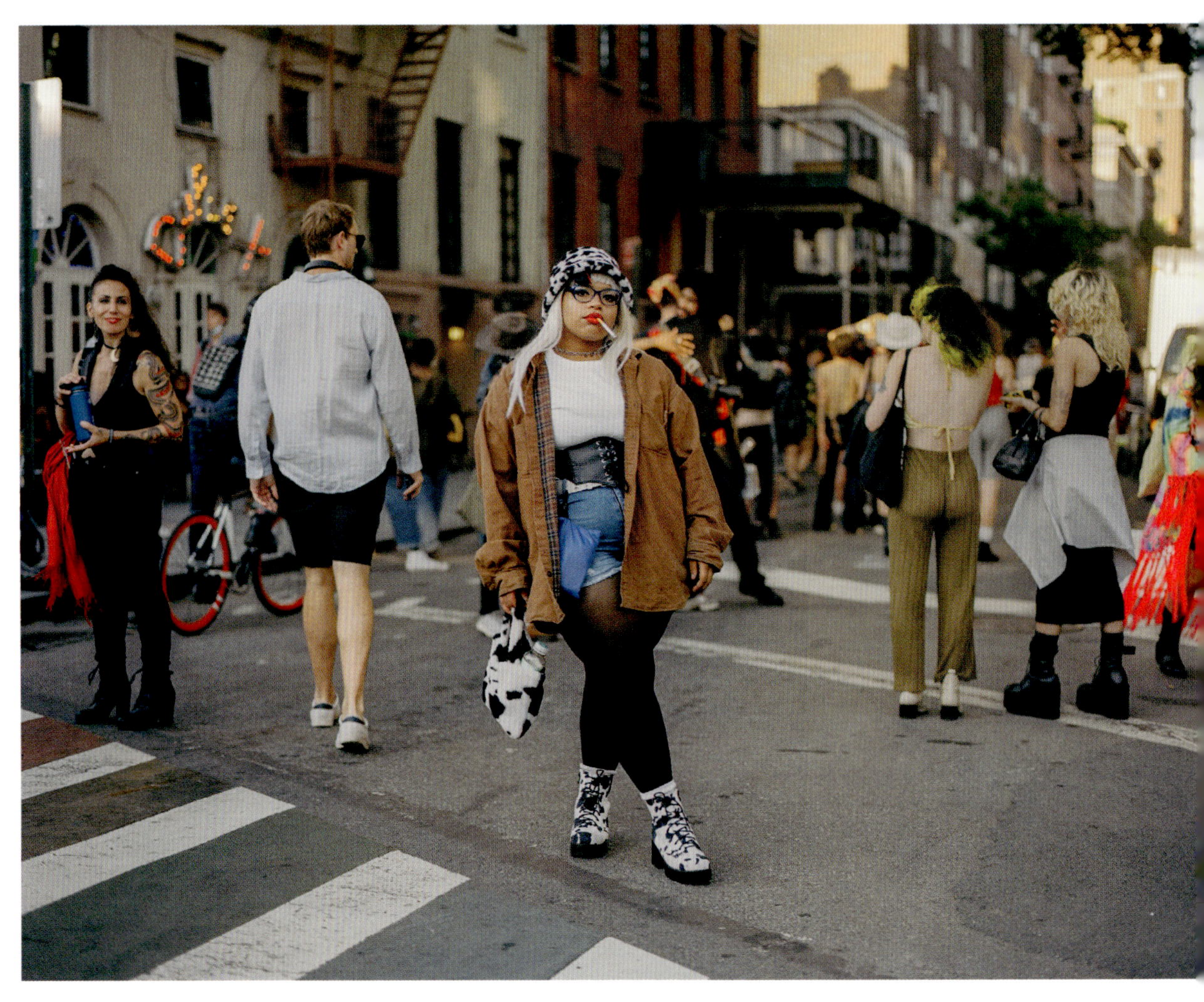

Ramie Ahmed
The Stonewall Protests Anniversary
June 2021

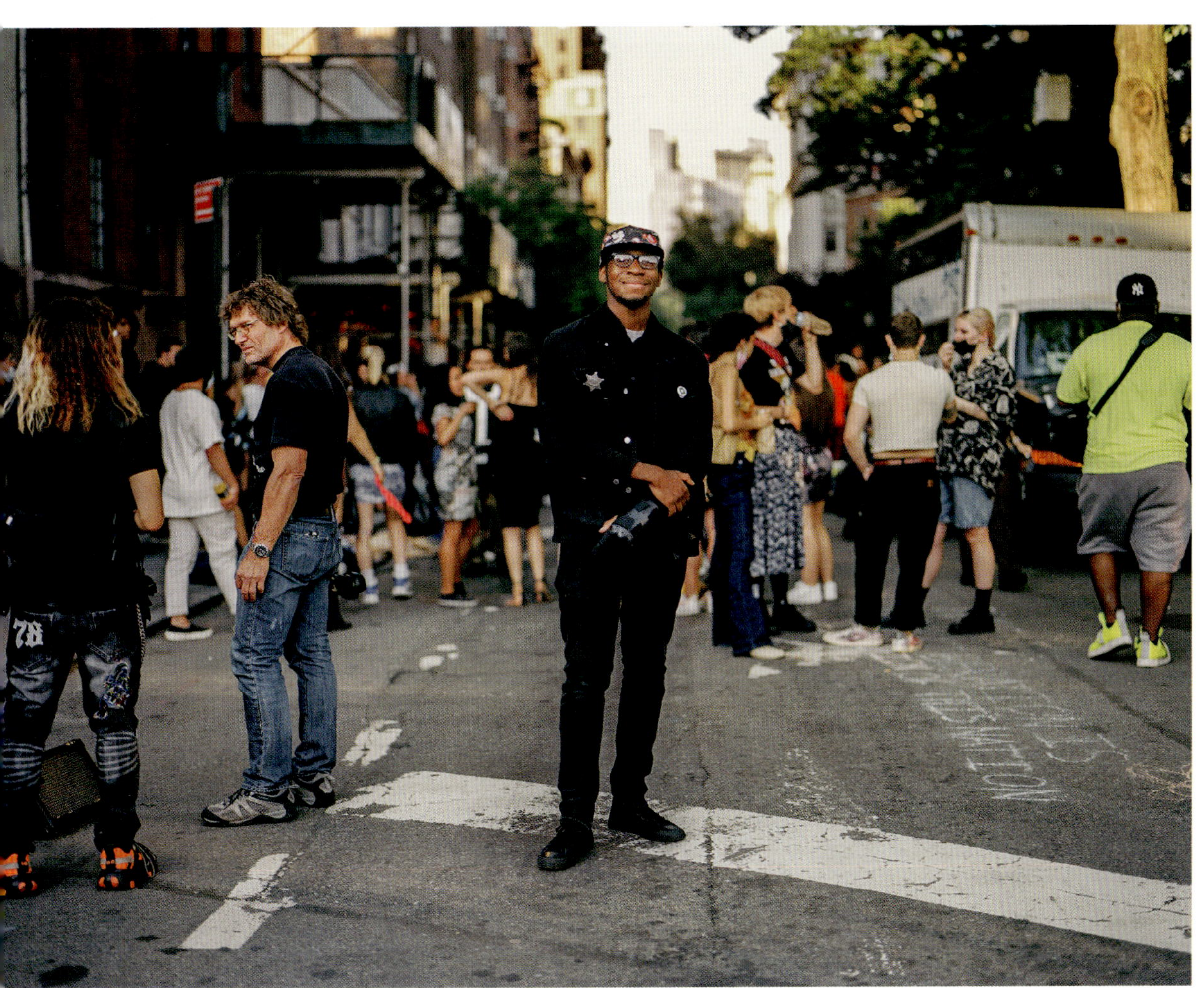

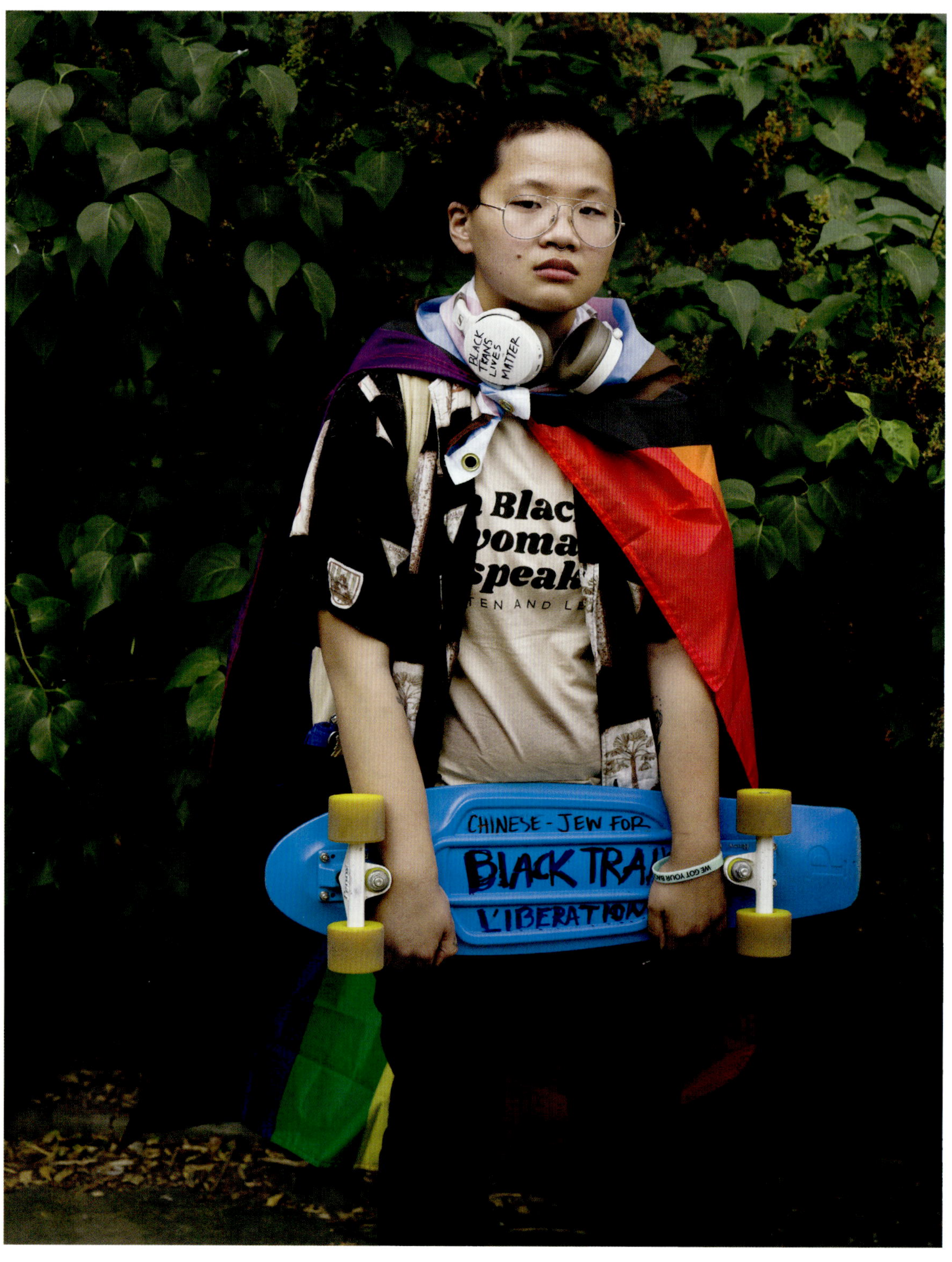

Stas Ginzburg
May 2021

As an activist, I deeply cherish all the connections I've made while doing this work, because to me, community is the most important thing we have in this fight for our liberation.

—Cindy Trinh

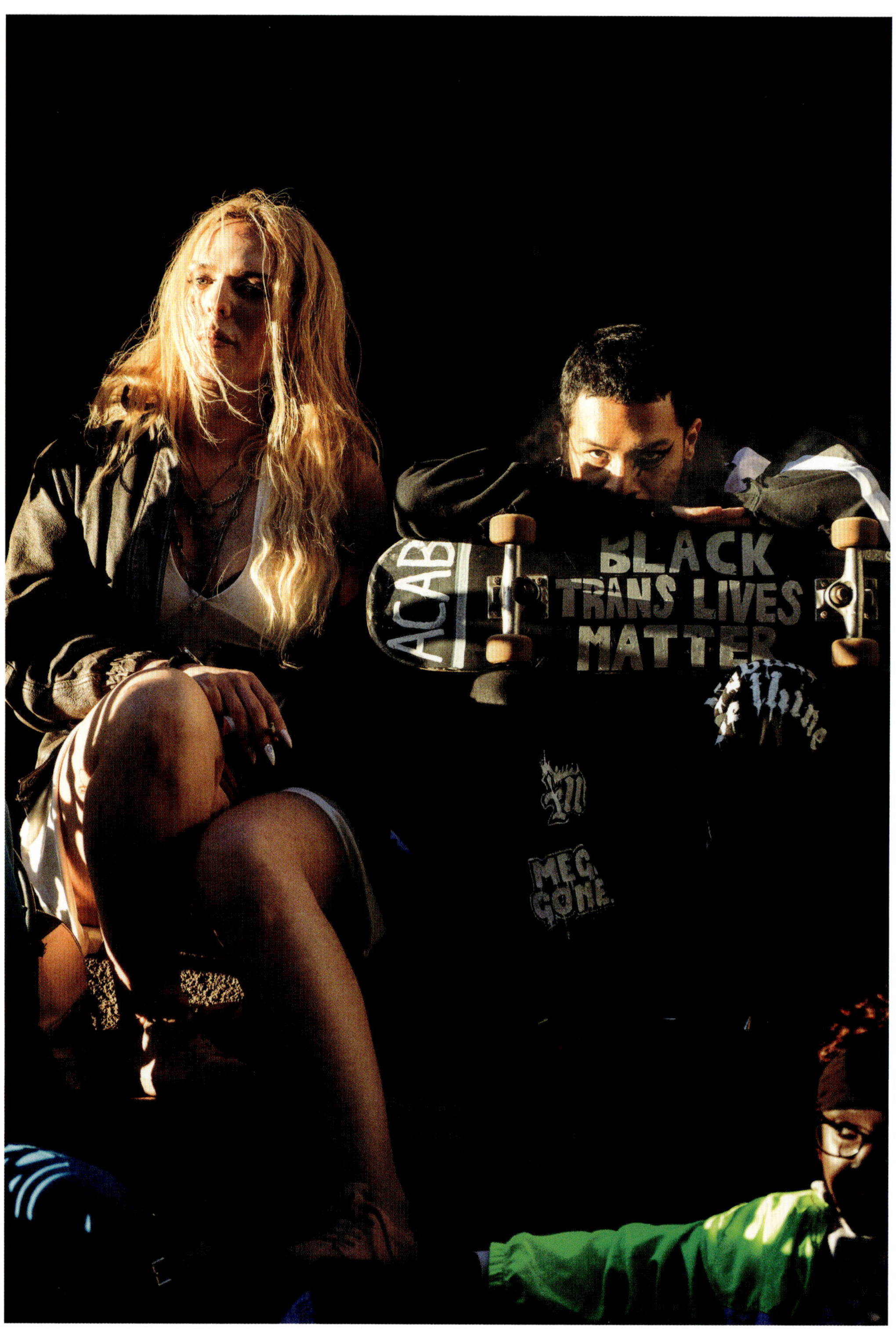

Ryan McGinley
Icons Liberation Ball
October 2020

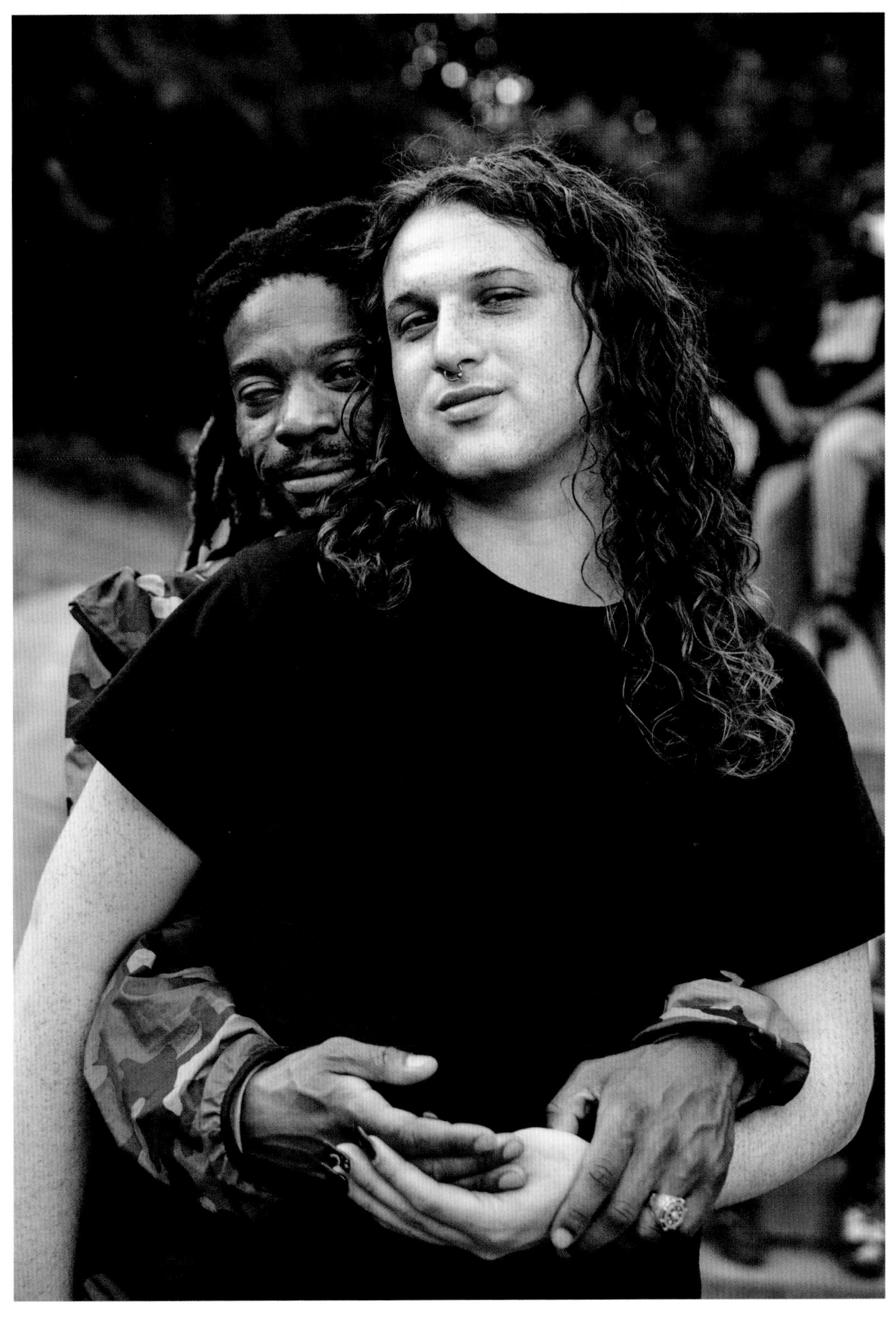

Chae Kihn
End Transgender Violence
June 2021

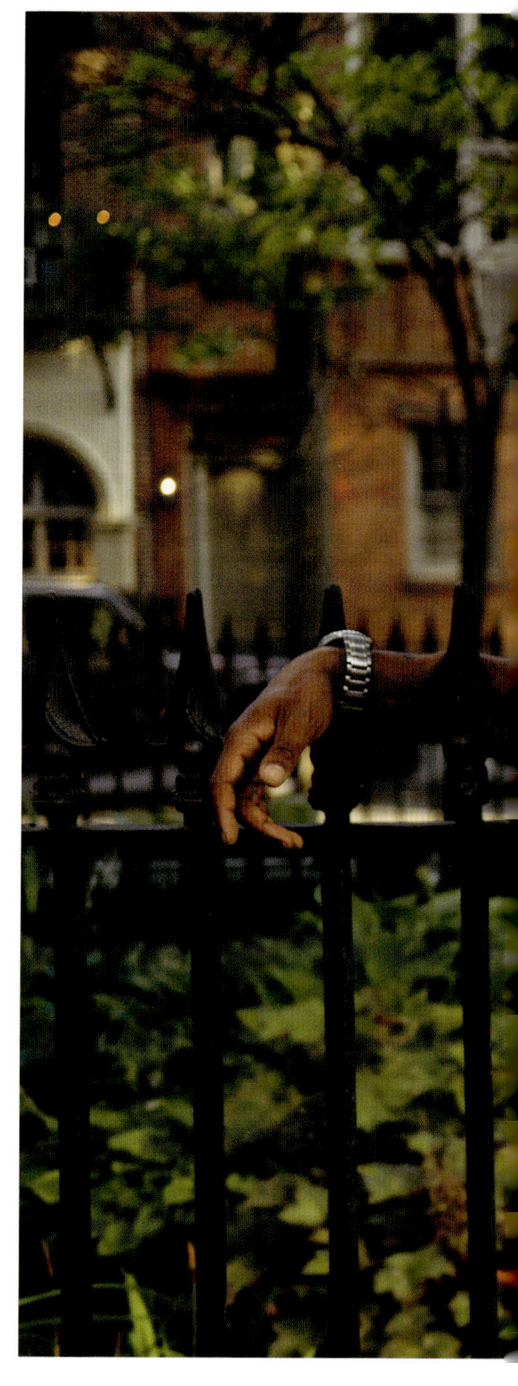

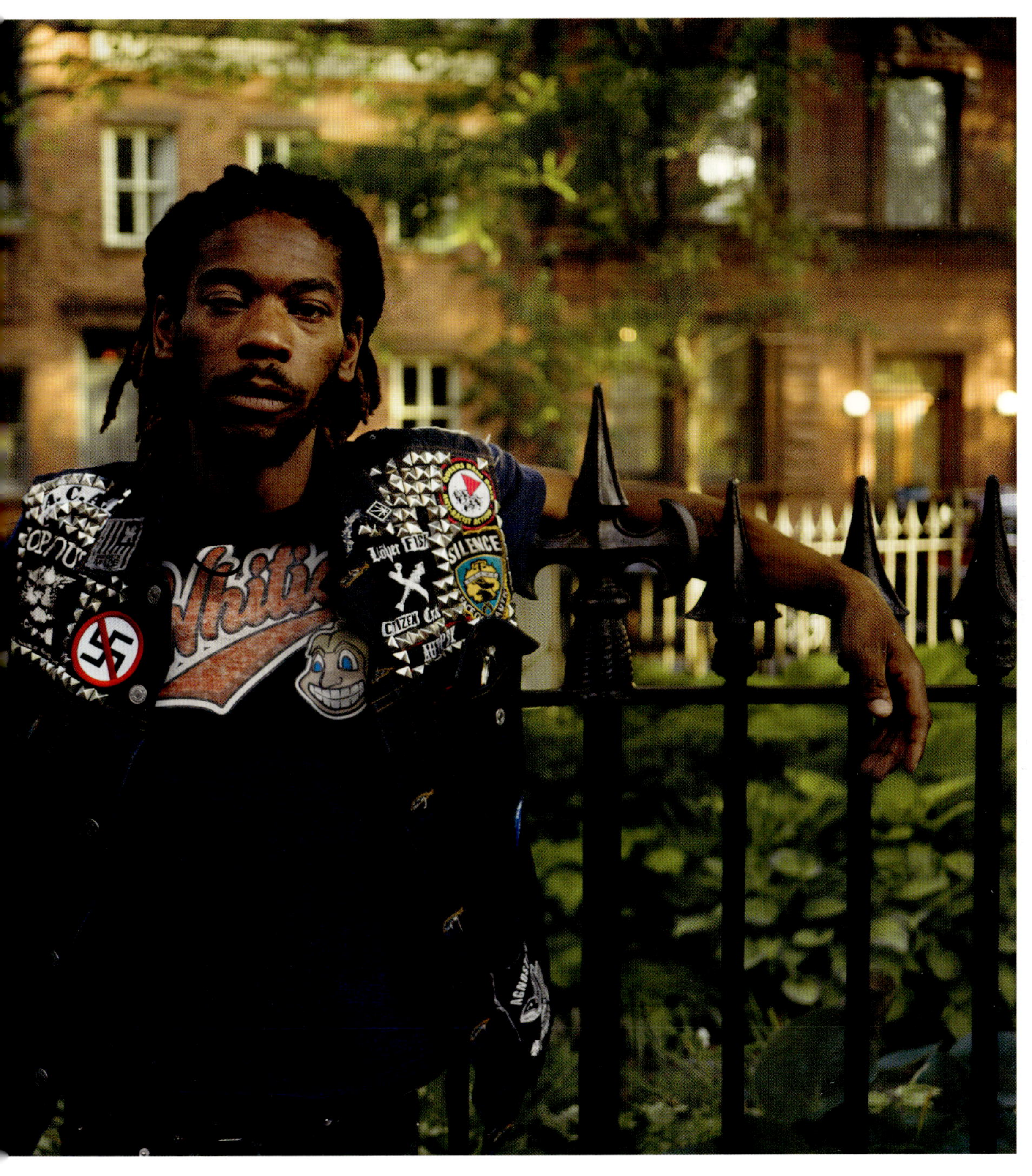

Stas Ginzburg
March for Tony McDade
May 2021

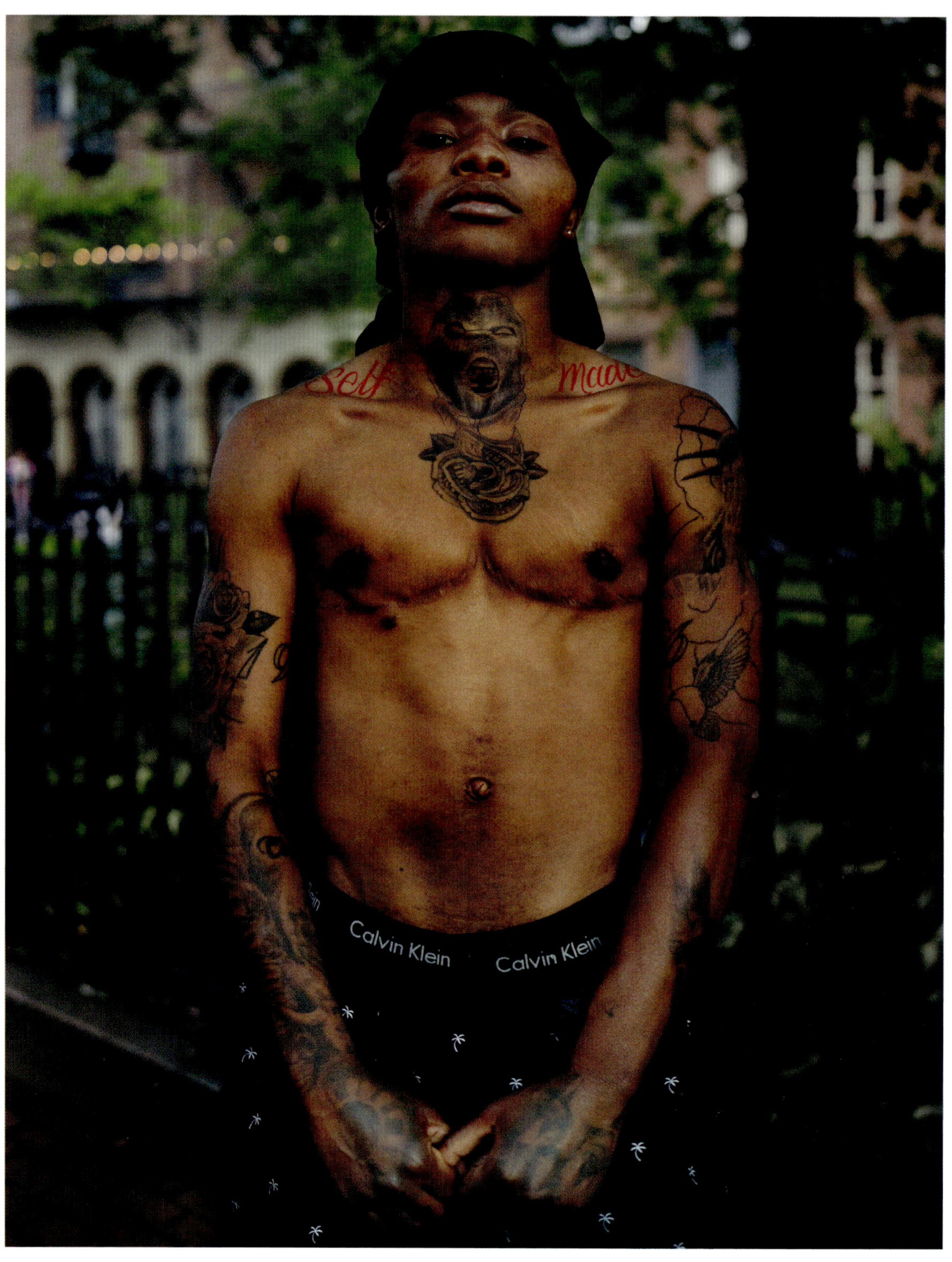

Stas Ginzburg
The Stonewall Protests Anniversary
June 2021

With a camera in hand, not only was I able to experience love and belonging, but I was able to capture love and a community that exists only once in a lifetime. The love that was cultivated here allowed me and many others to grow, to learn. Most importantly it made me realize that my love and my art are my superpowers, and I am able to help others see their irrefutable beauty through photographs.

—Madison Swart

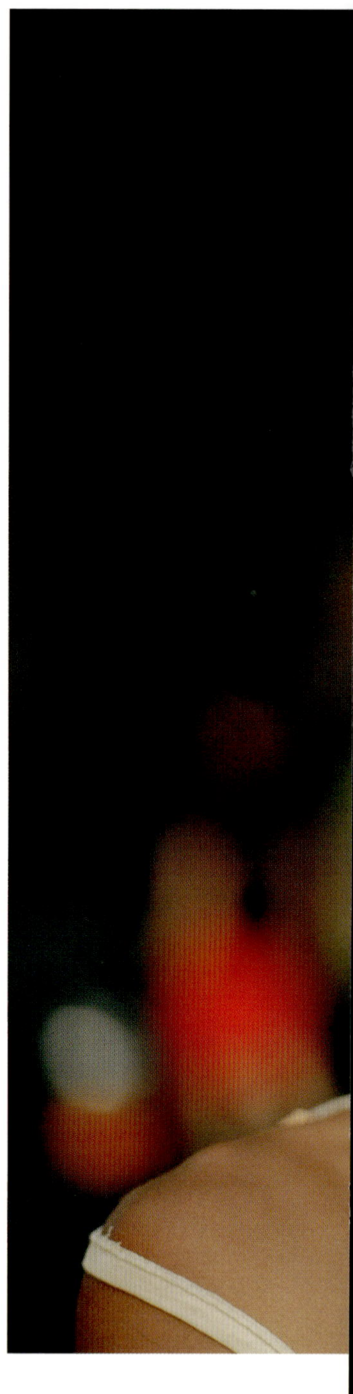

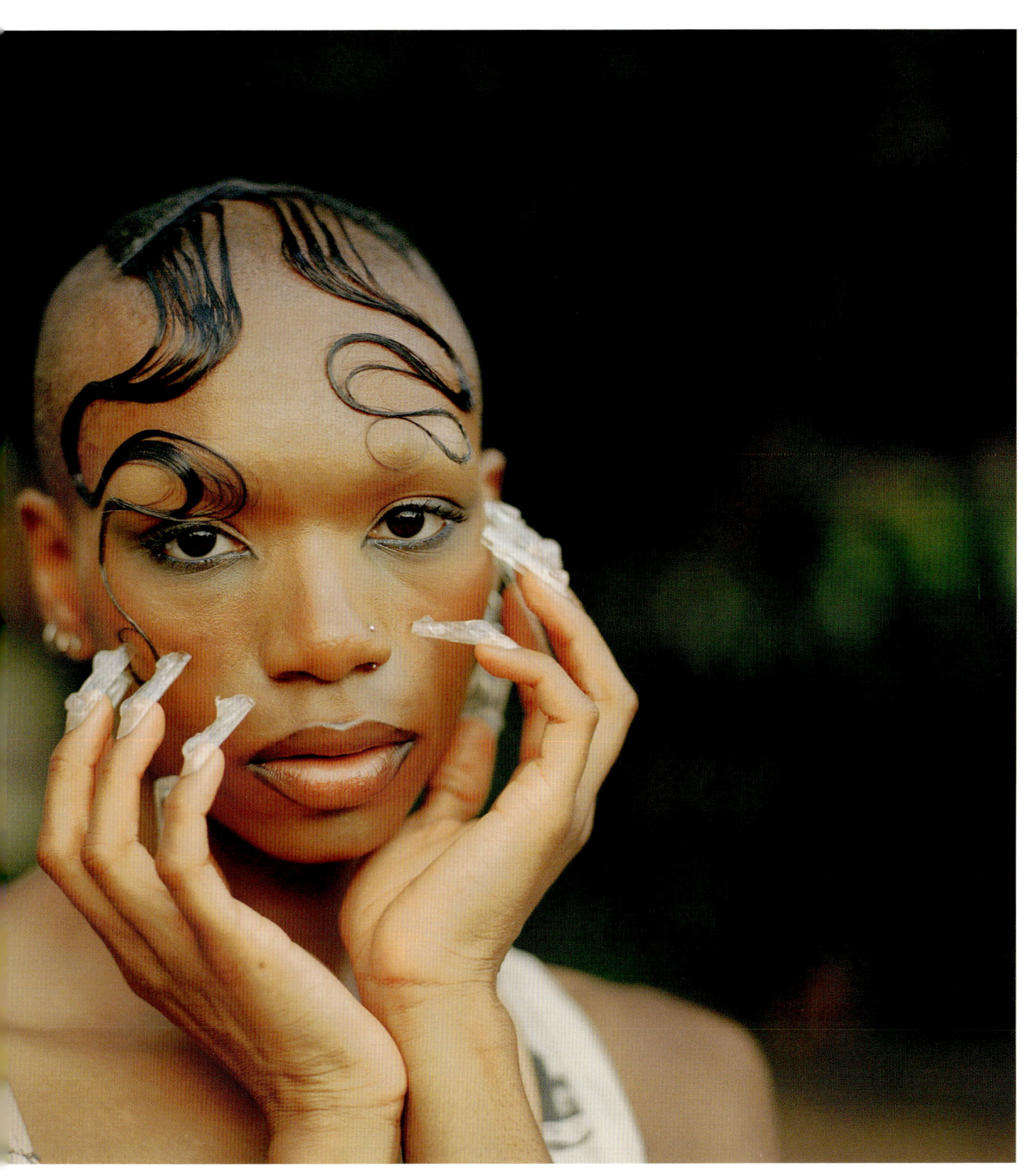

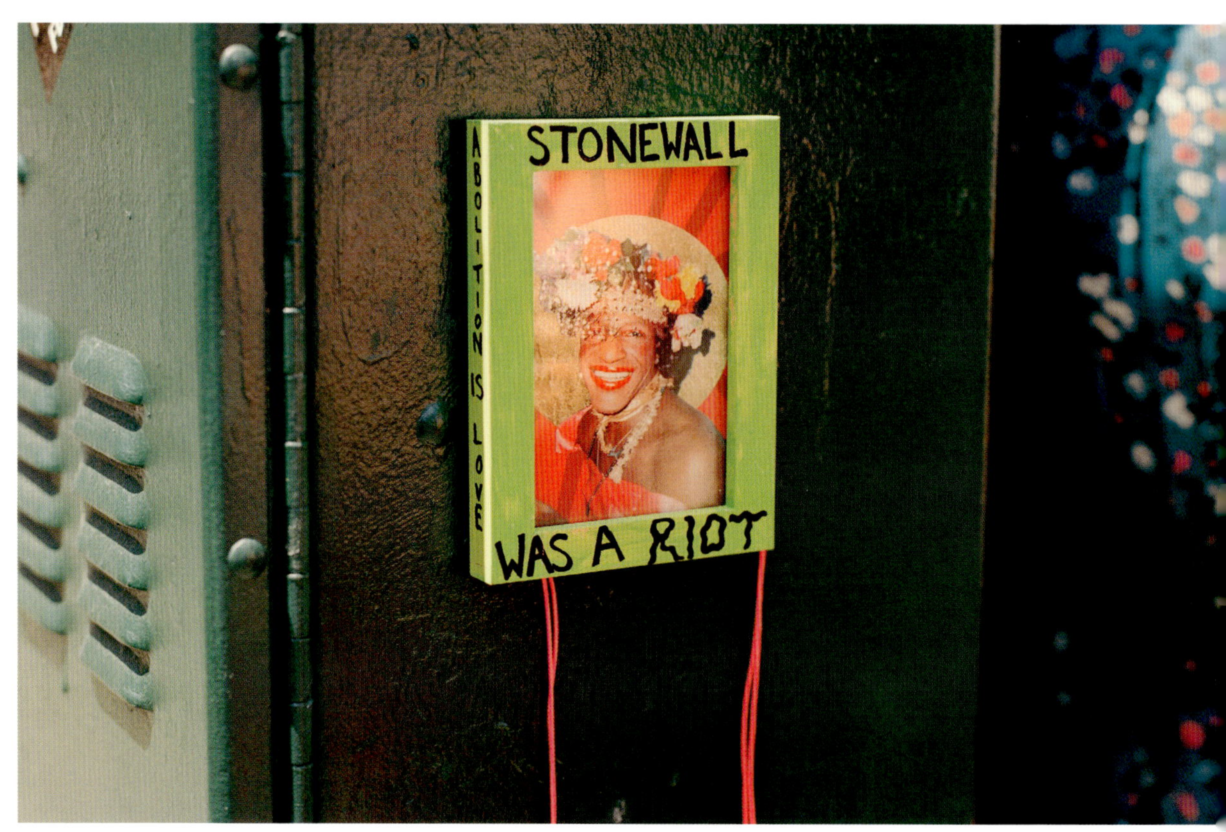

Ramie Ahmed
June 2021

Daniel Lehrhaupt
July 2021

Daniel Lehrhaupt
Community Building Through
Intersectionality
April 2021

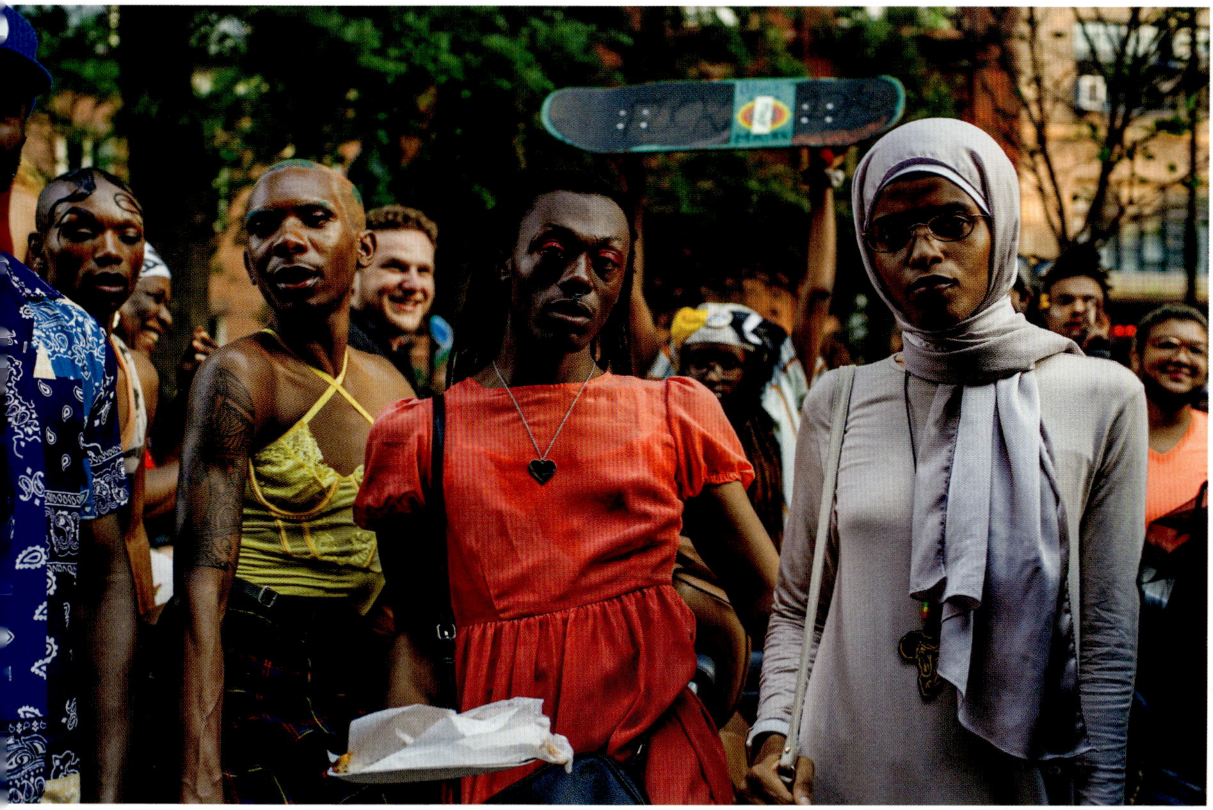

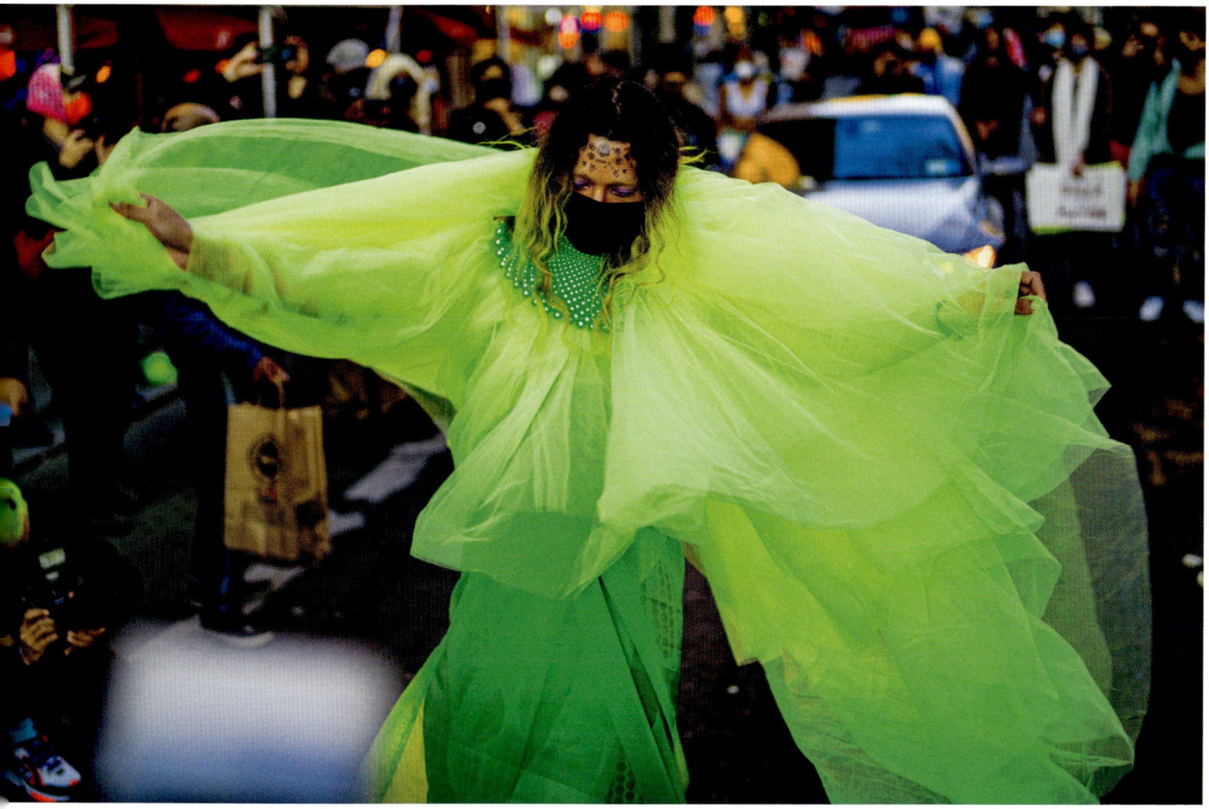

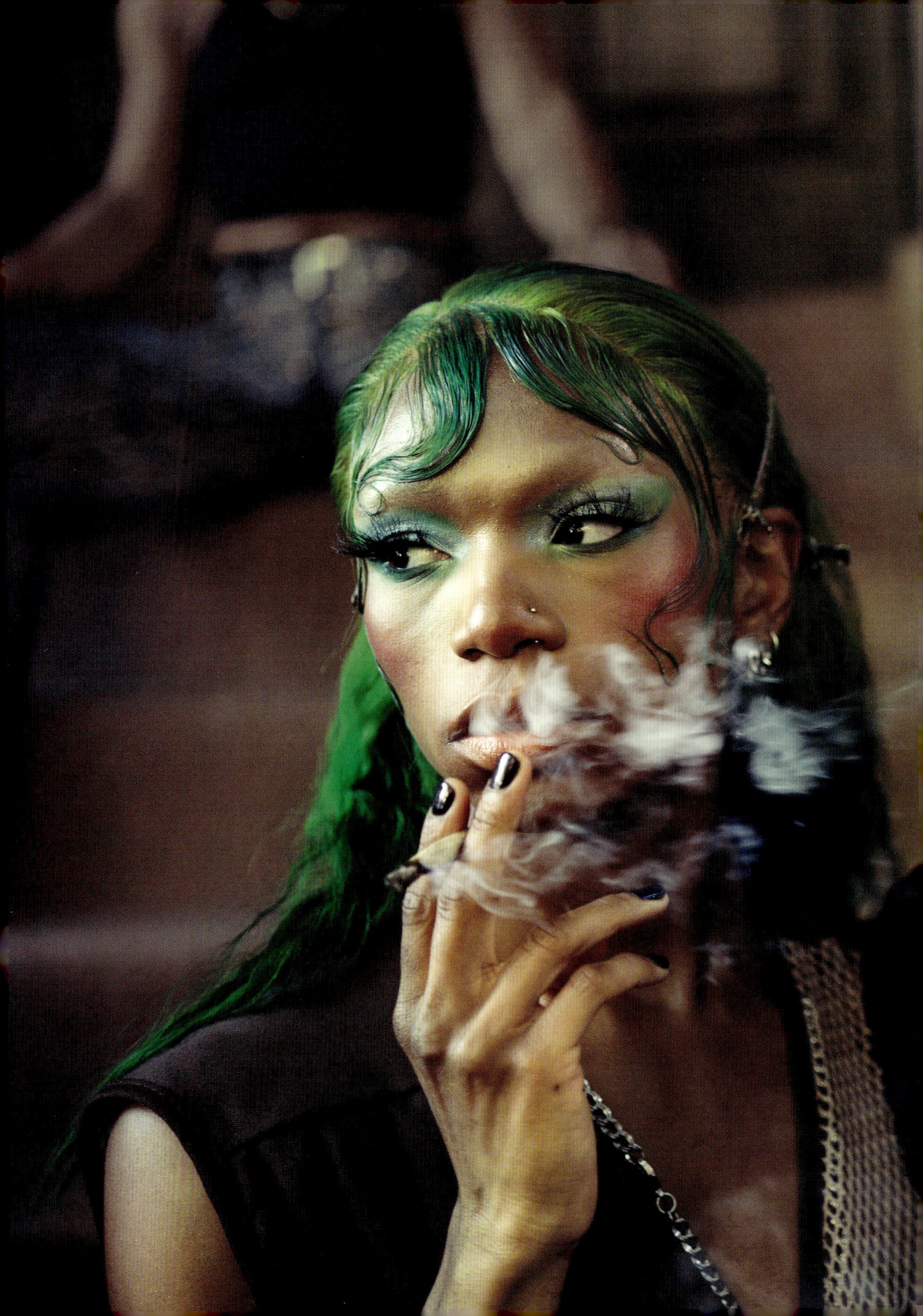

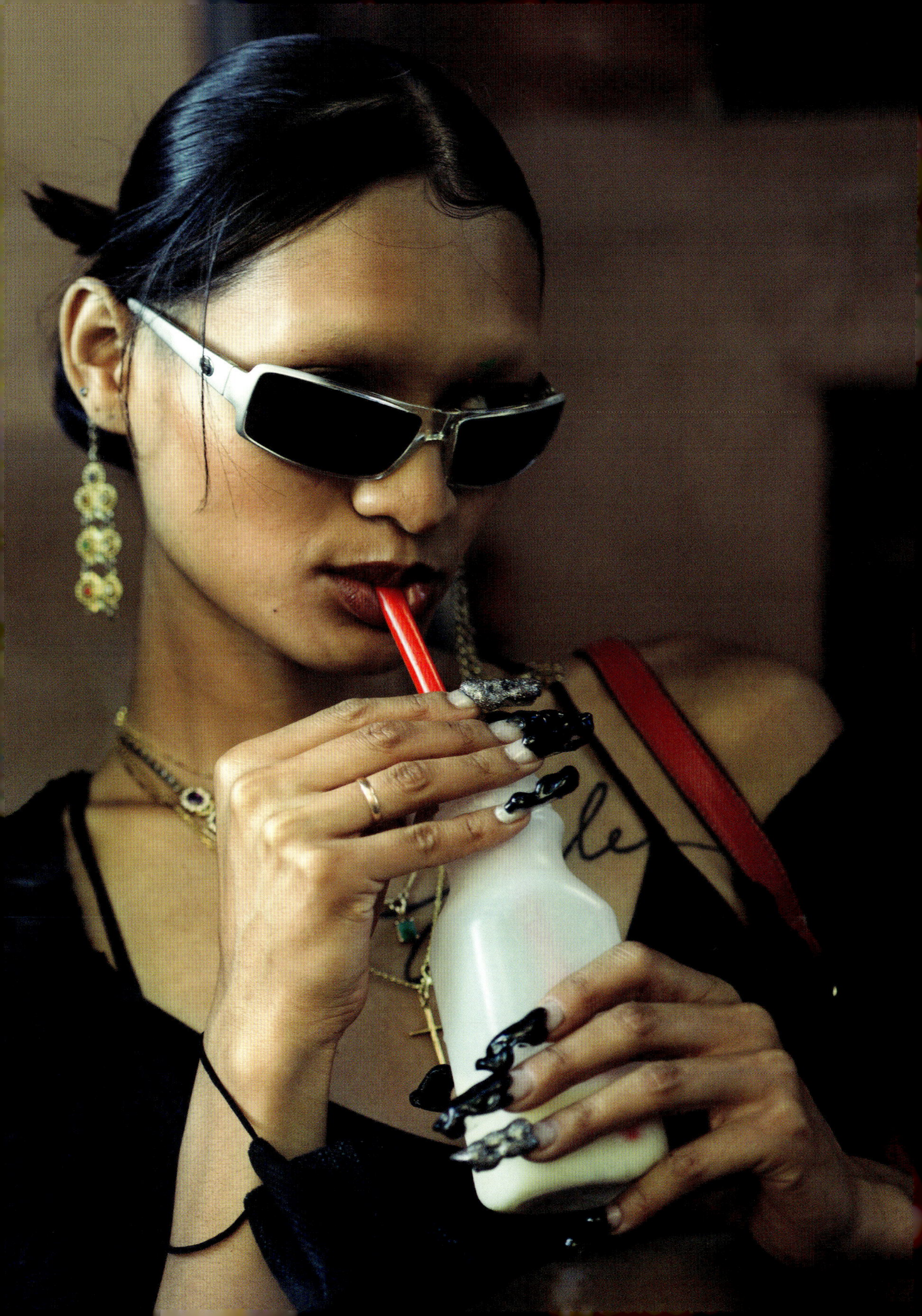

During this year I received one of the most important educations of my life, all the while finding a chosen family and community. Black trans joy is one of the most powerful forces that exists toward achieving Black Trans Liberation.

—Daniel Lehrhaupt

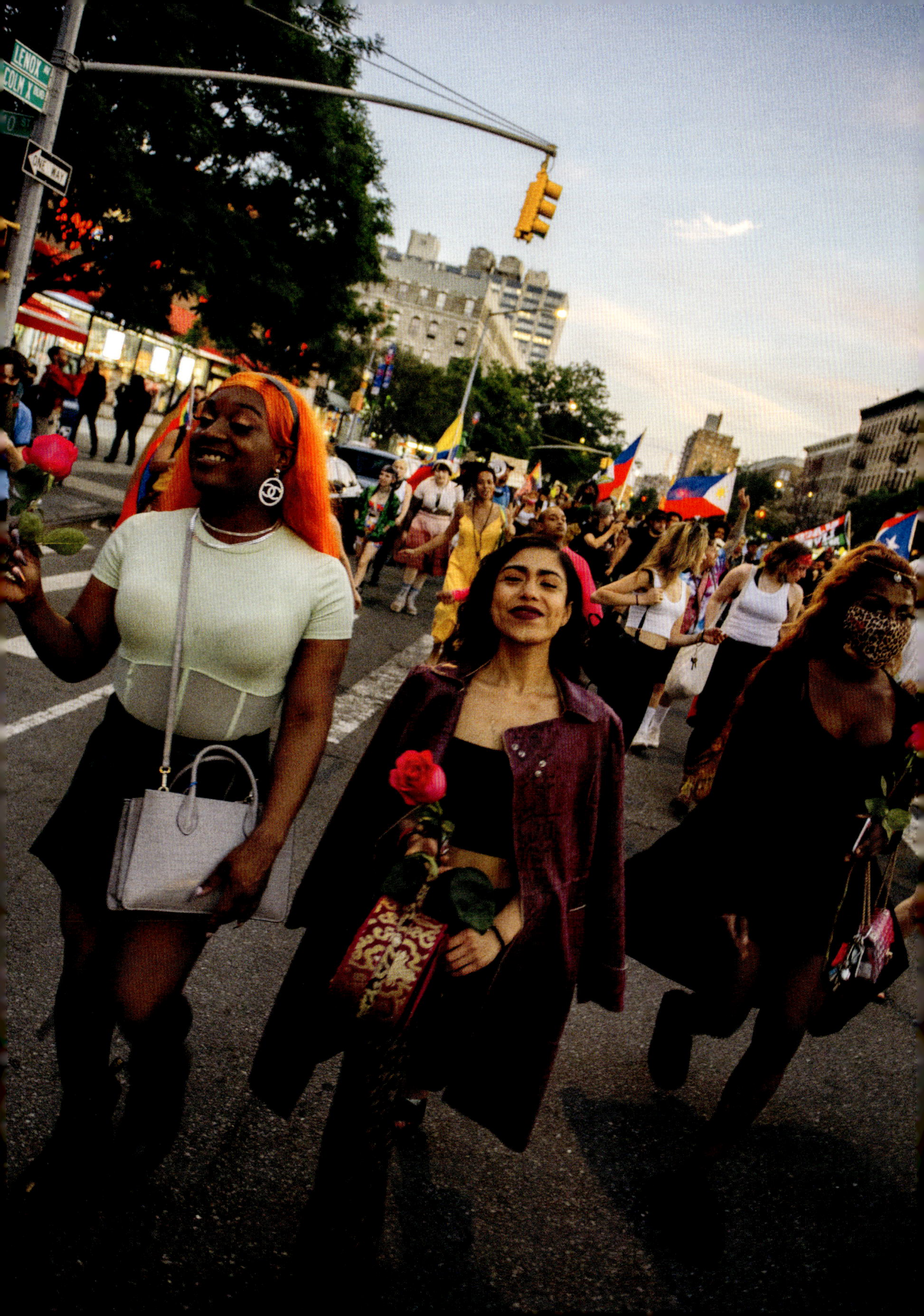

LENOX AV
COLM X BLVD
0 ST
ONE WAY

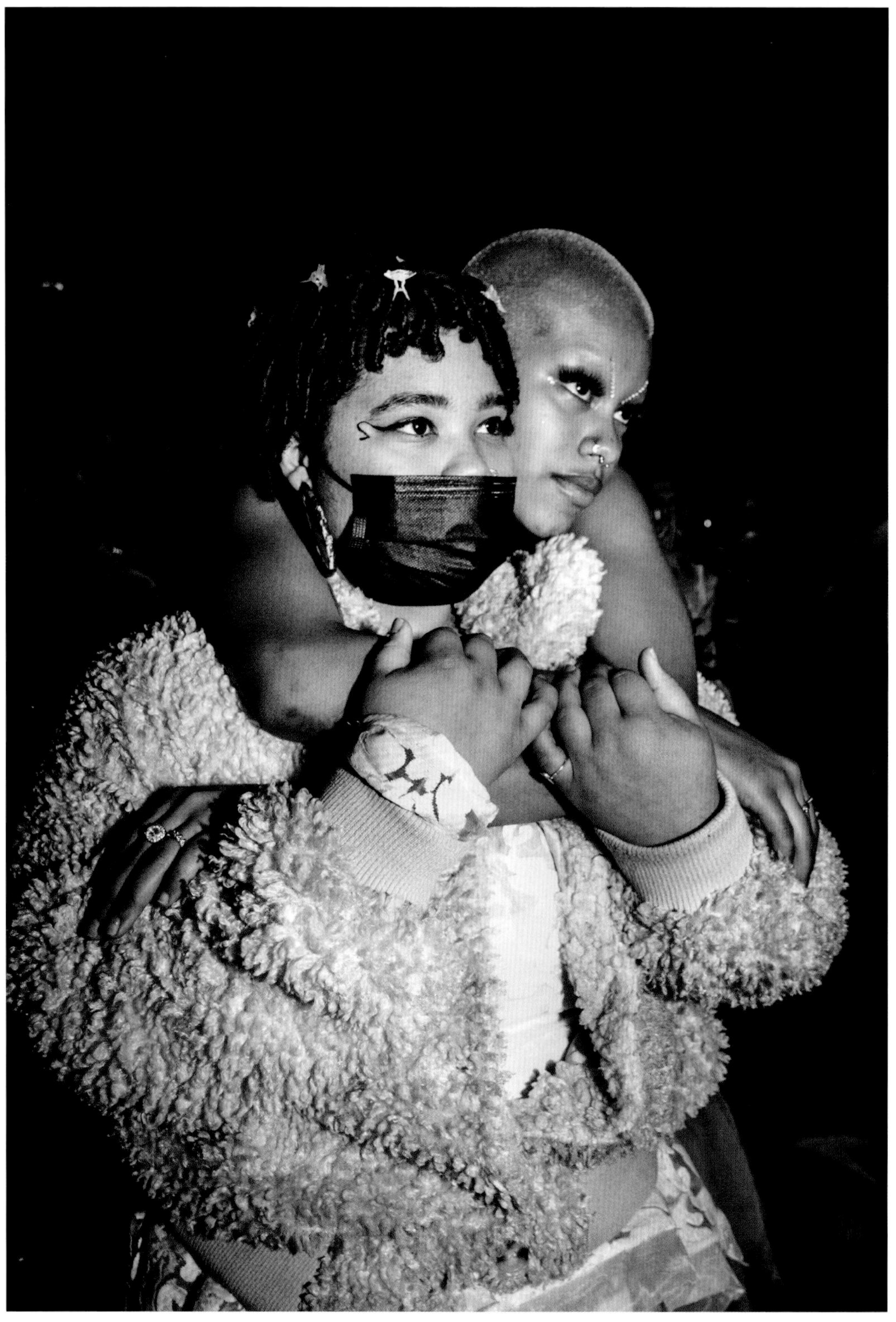

Caroline Mardok
Community Building Through Intersectionality
April 2021

Caroline Mardok
The Stonewall Protests Anniversary
June 2021

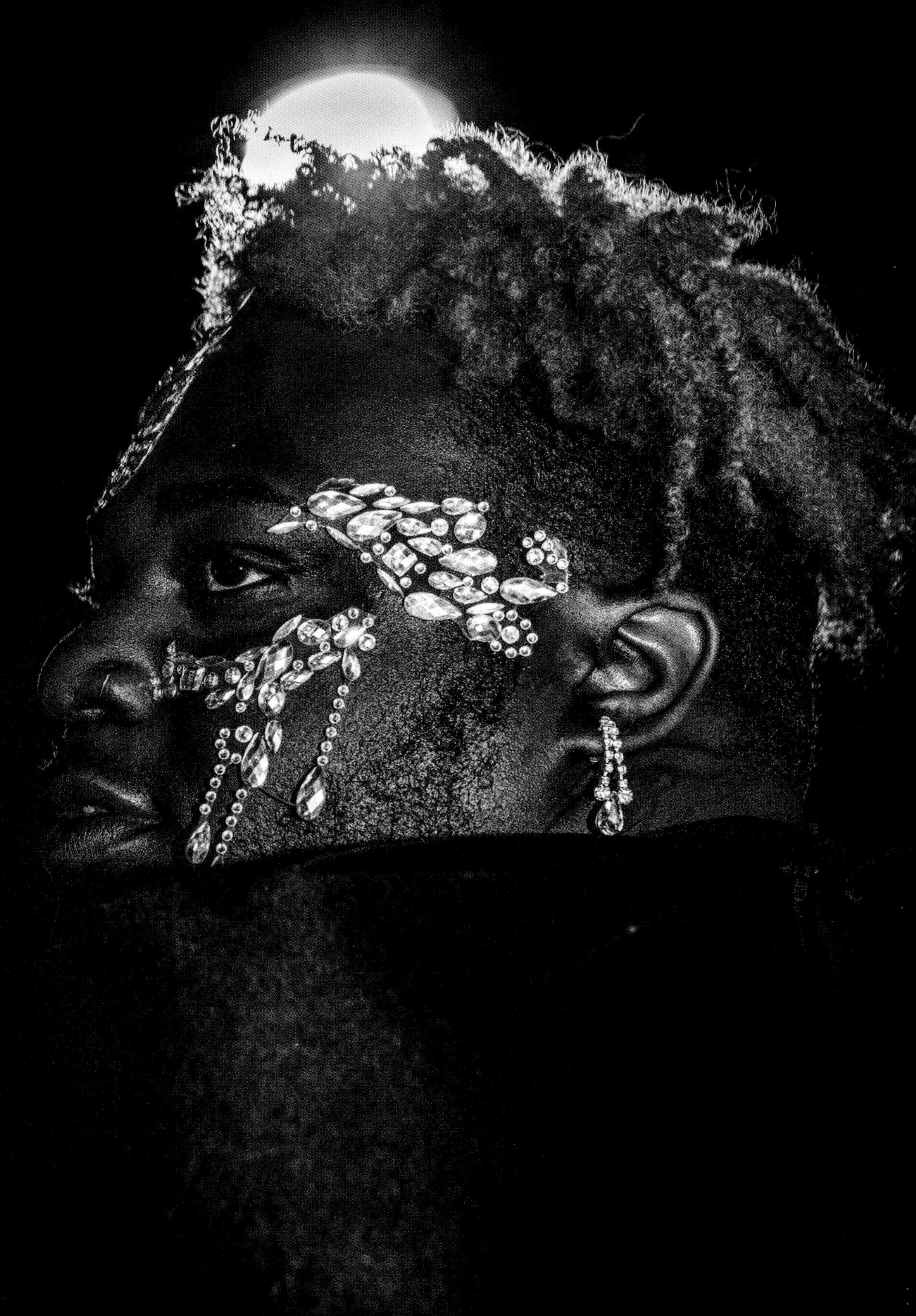

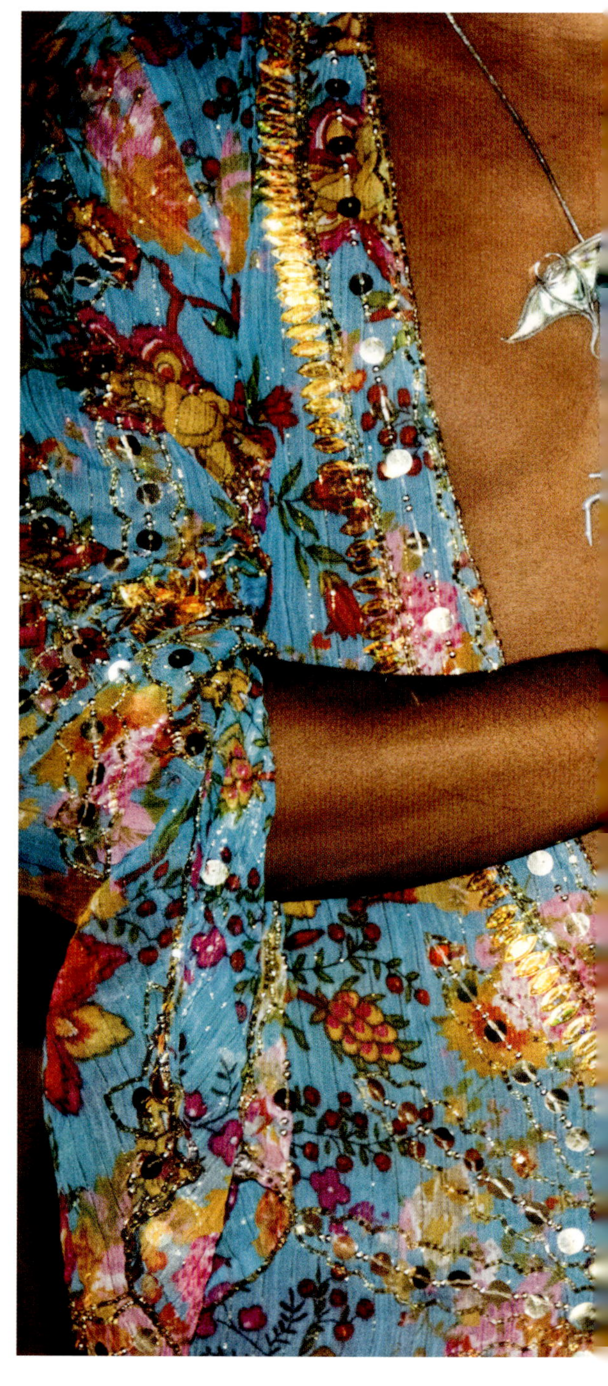

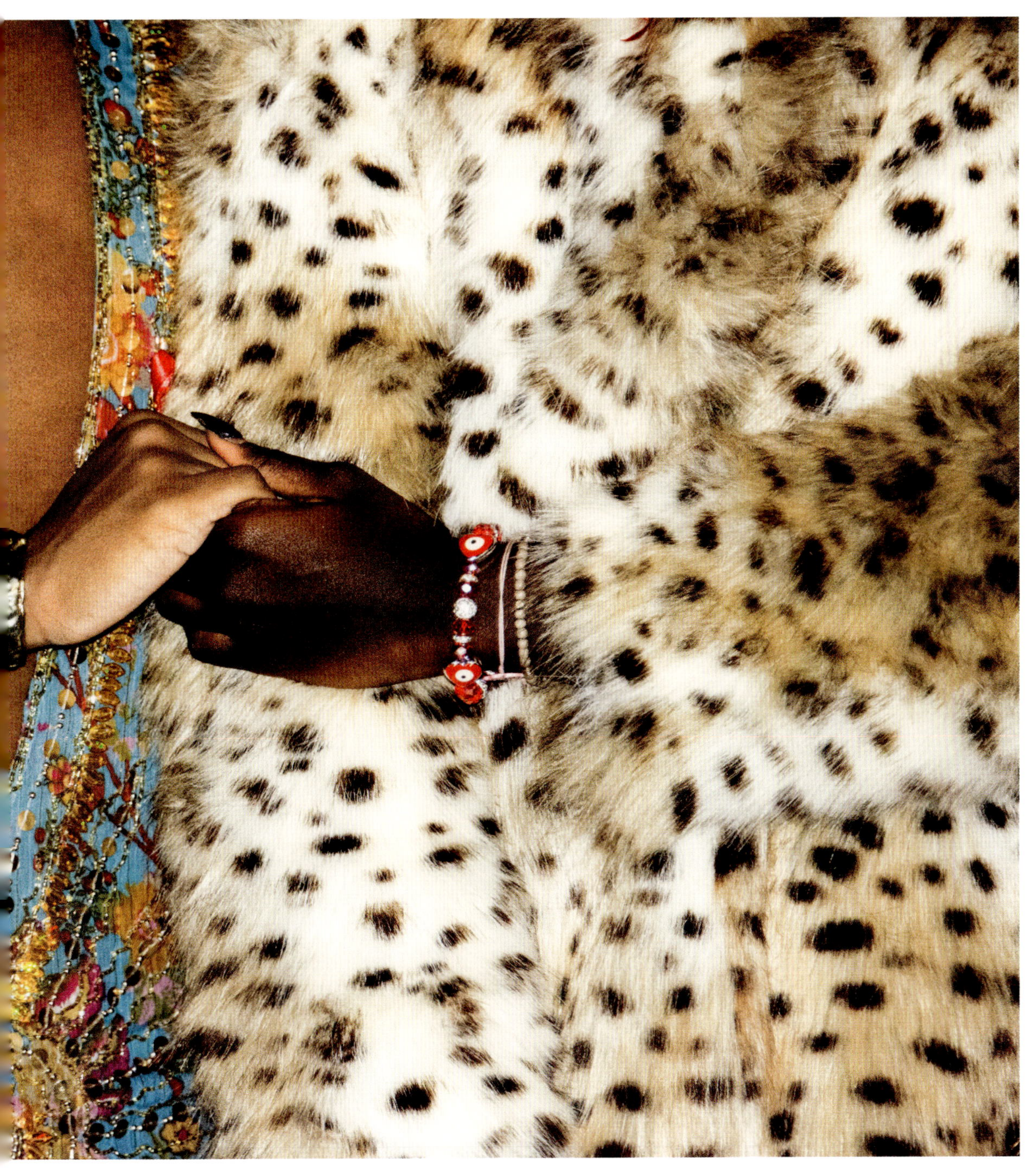

Ruvan Wijesooriya
Say Their Names
December 2020

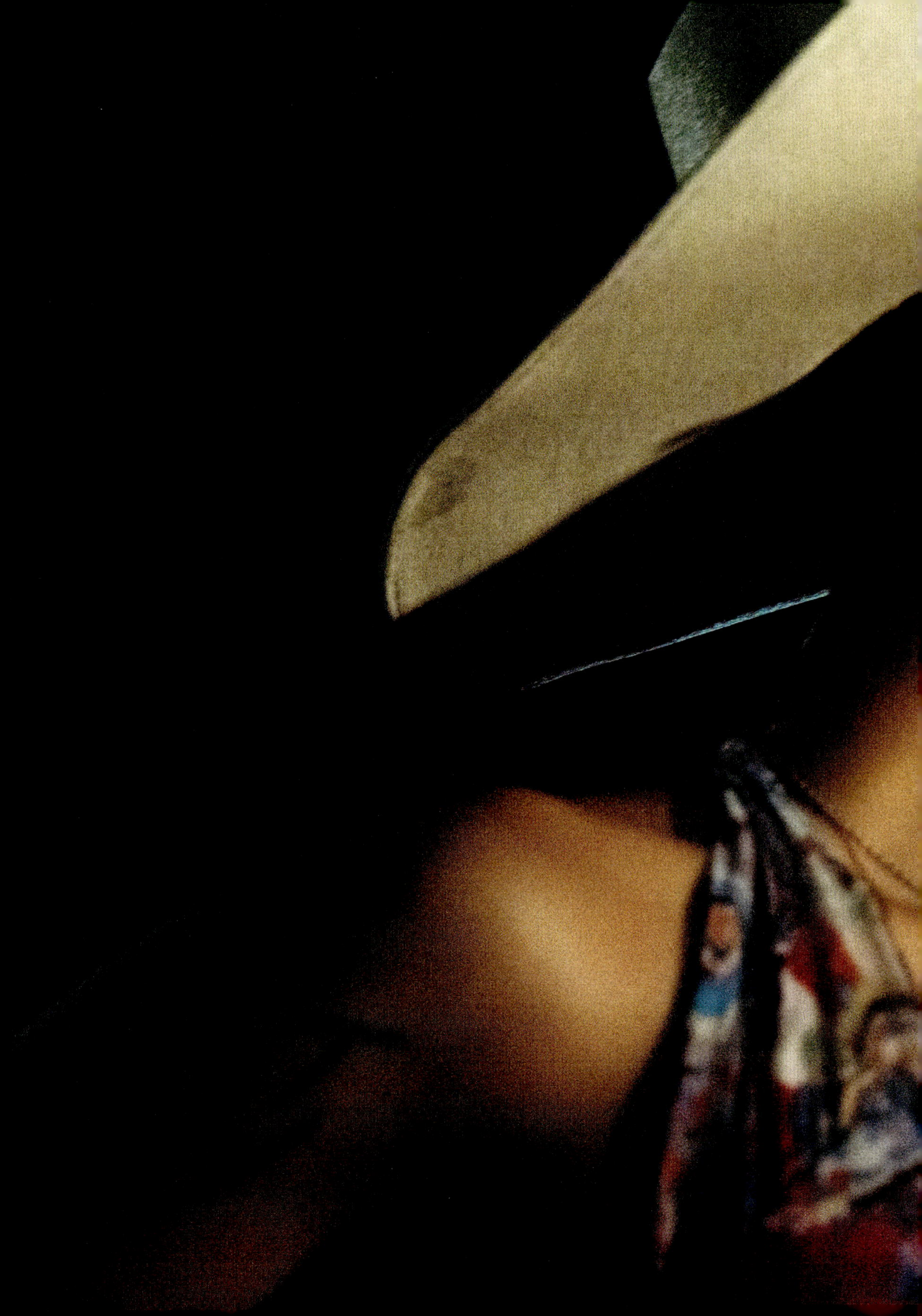

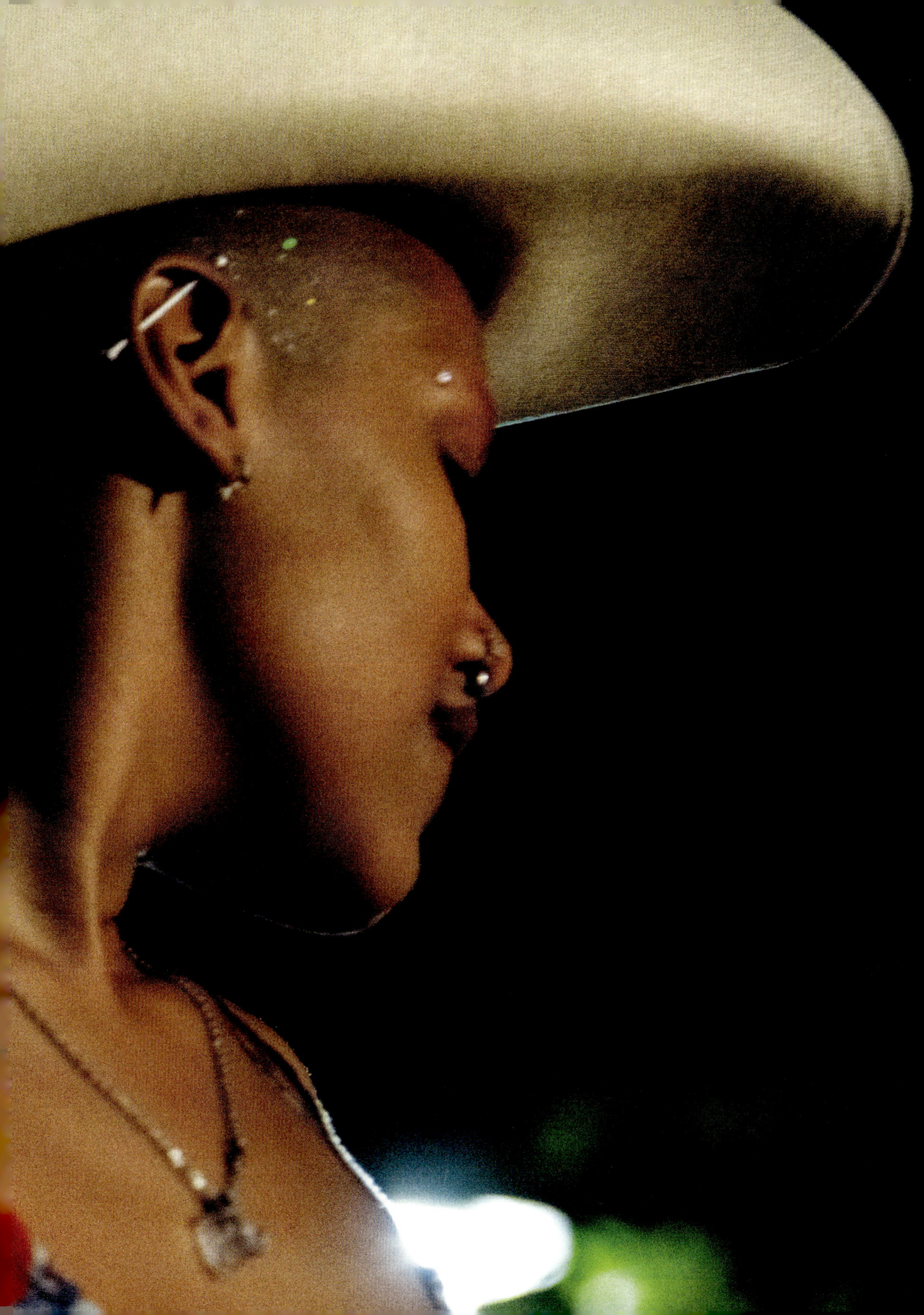

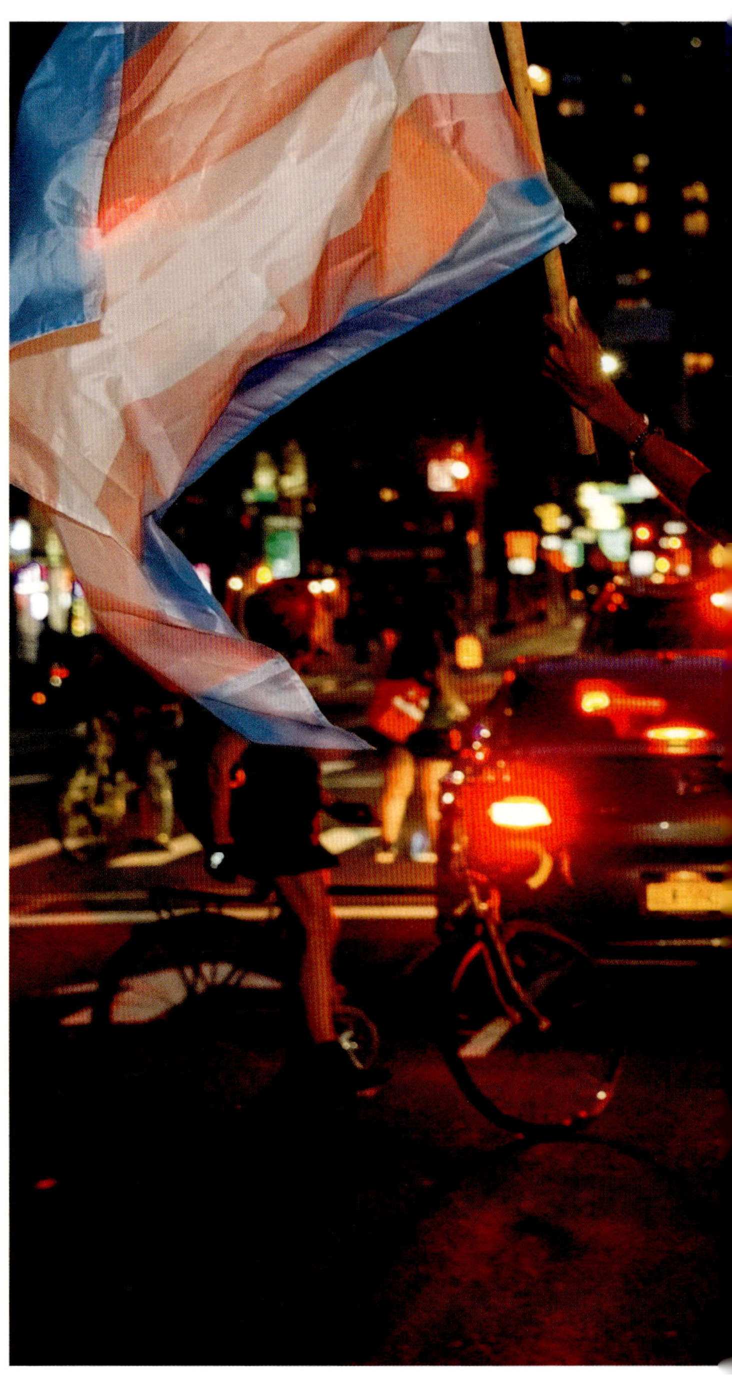

PREVIOUS SPREAD:
Ruvan Wijesooriya
The Stonewall Protests Anniversary
June 2021

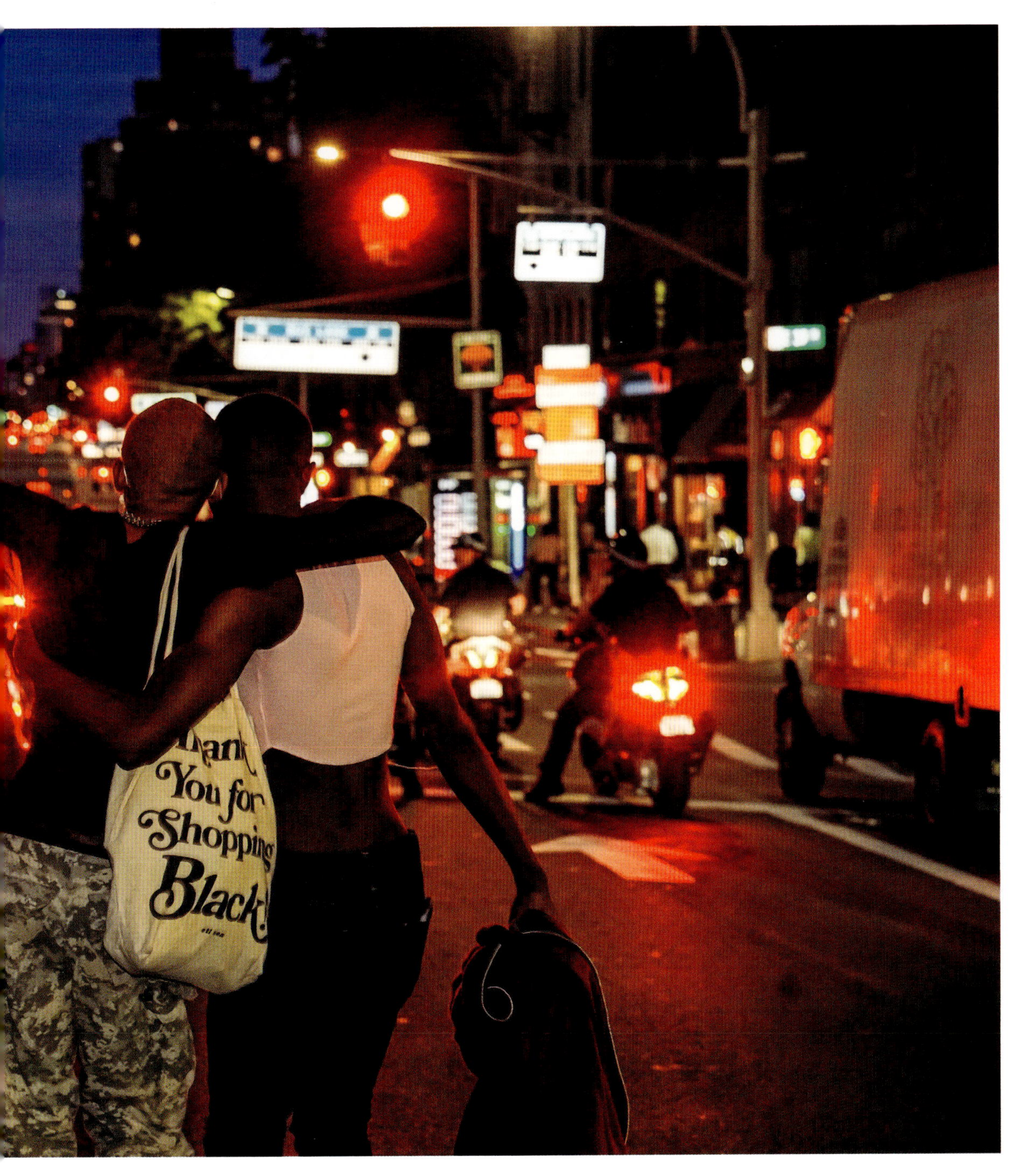

Daniel Lehrhaupt
July 2021

An Ongoing Revolution: Writing a New History at Stonewall
Mikelle Street

Stonewall has always been about community. At the initial 1969 uprising, queer and trans folks rose up to fight back against oppression. The annual commemoration of that event became the New York City Pride march we know today. The LGBTQ+ community has continually returned to the steps outside the Stonewall Inn at pivotal moments. When marriage equality passed nationwide in 2015, hundreds flocked to the block to celebrate. Similarly, when the Pulse massacre occurred in 2016, thousands attended a vigil to grieve among others. In June 2020, Joela Rivera and Qween Jean returned to those steps, yet again, to launch the Stonewall Protests, a fight for trans liberation marked most consistently by a series of weekly actions that wound through lower Manhattan. There, they created a community anew.

You can see part of that community in the images in this book. Though Jean, Rivera, and other trans women feature prominently in positions of power and leadership, the photographic documentation of the events shows the vast diversity of the community they created and cultivated: A community that came to them for education, for reinvigoration, for healing, and for representation. A community that convened every week, come rain, sleet, or snow, that held space, stood in the face of police officers (who occasionally arrested them) and stopped traffic on the West Side Highway. A community that not only demanded that those around them hear their calls for liberation but that the history books take notice. That community also extended to the image makers who were there capturing the movement.

"I am very much a part of the protest every time it's happening," Cindy Trinh, who has been shooting political movements under the Instagram handle @ActivistNYC since 2014, says. "I am marching, and I am chanting too. My work is that of an activist first and foremost." Trinh, like many of the other photographers in this book, chronicled the protests, many times on foot as a part of the action. Others sometimes ran alongside them or hung from light poles and even from the scaffolding of nearby construction. Some, like Josh Pacheco, began with feeling spurred into action by injustices like the deaths of Michael Brown and George Floyd, and photographing these protests became part of their own activism. While the photographers at Stonewall were shooting to record and document, their approach offers new perspective and inquiry to the ways in which this work has been done in the past.

For photographers like Trinh and Erica Lansner, being a part of this lineage meant avoiding documenting clashes with police due to how those visual tropes may be perceived without context: pervasive ideas of police as enforcers of justice could lead to the assumption that protestors did something that needs correction. Instead, Trinh focused their lens on moments of intimacy and softness. "People that come are bringing forth their bodies and their minds and coming from a place of wanting to learn and show that they care," they say. "So I try to capture that, so you see people just in a relaxed state exercising their First Amendment right to peacefully protest."

Pacheco sees existing standards around consent as insufficient, and strives to go further by getting express consent from as many subjects as possible. "I feel like it is immensely crucial to honor consent and respect in this public space that is so vulnerable at all times," they say. "In a heightened state of crisis, panic, and worry, it's vital." As members of the community who are also connected in some way to the issues raised during these actions, the photographers who shot the Stonewall Protests regularly did their work with care for the people they documented.

Those photographers also developed a mutual respect and support for one another, according to Lansner. "We were all there to document this incredible moment in history," she says, "and it felt like you had to show up and share it as well."

This acknowledgment and the recurring nature of the protests eventually caused a shift in the communal relationship between photographers and the larger movement: organizers and attendees began to use the often vibrant, evocative imagery to promote the actions themselves. Those photographs allowed outsiders to see themselves at the events, in the wide swath of faces captured. Seeing those faces and bodies with signs emblazoned with values they shared or basking in the euphoria of the dance breaks—part runway show, part voguing circle—that became a staple of the protests encouraged others to attend. In turn, the proliferation of those images on social media led marchers to dress for the cameras. The result: attendees were presented with a unique opportunity to project how they wished to be remembered to their world as well as the history books—to project a lasting statement of who they were.

"It felt like a responsibility," Lansner says of sharing her photos with the subjects, and allowing them to use them as they needed. A responsibility, Pacheco adds, set by the protestors. At one action, Rivera spoke of the tendency for the organizers to arrive every week in their finery, and for a crush of photographers to shoot them as if they were paparazzi. Once, the organizers even arrived in a convertible with the top down, resembling pageant queens or politicians. "Six days a week, outside of Thursday, I don't feel beautiful," Rivera said into the mic, addressing the assembled crowd before it began winding through the streets of New York. But when she is at the protests with her community, she added, she feels beautiful and dresses as such, completing her vision of herself.

And when she looks back, when others look back, history will remember her as the woman she has always known herself to be, fighting for a community she helped to create.

Afterword
Joela Rivera

The birth of the Stonewall Protests came simultaneously with the resurgence of the Black Lives Matter movement. In the first weeks of the rioting and protesting in June 2020, the need for Black trans activism was deeply felt, because there was no Black Queer Lives Matter, there was no Black Trans Lives Matter. It opened the door to the building that the Black community needs to do within itself, and I believed that with a strong presence—a strong Black presence as we built in the Stonewall community—we could show that Black trans and Black queer culture is Black culture, and that in our community there is space for all of us. A community not only to be Black in, but to be completely free in. That's how it started: with marches every Thursday centering Black trans and Black queer people. We were preaching of abolition, and we were living to be students of abolition. While many people there weren't necessarily abolitionists or didn't know how to practice abolition, they were still a part of our community, because the Stonewall Protests was and is a safe space, a home.

Naturally though, people change, people move on, and the world keeps evolving. We had to get to that next step of Black liberation. We had to evolve. We had to create sustainable ways to keep the Black Lives Matter movement progressing, and that's where we're at right now. However, it's still really beautiful to look back at that year and a half of being outside and really changing the world—it felt so small. But the impact that we all had is amazing, and it's something nobody can take away. I'm so grateful that I was able to be a part of it.

Timeline of Actions

This is a selection of direct actions organized or attended by activists with the Stonewall Protests between June 2020 and July 2021. All actions took place in New York City unless otherwise noted.

Brooklyn Liberation March	June 14, 2020
Stonewall's First March	June 18, 2020
Occupy City Hall	June 26, 2020
Queer Liberation March	June 28, 2020
Vigil for Black Womxn	July 19, 2020
Trans Liberation March	July 24, 2020
March for Black Womxn	July 26, 2020
Black Sex Worker Liberation March	August 1, 2020
The March for Breonna Taylor	August 9, 2020
Stonewall March for Black Queer Lives	August 20, 2020
Marsha's March & 75th Birthday	August 24, 2020
March on Washington 2020, Washington, DC	August 27, 2020
The Commitment March, Washington, DC	August 28, 2020
Justice for Daniel Prude	September 3, 2020
Abolition Is Liberation	September 17, 2020
Be Empowered to Fight Back: Trans Self Defense	September 20, 2020
West Side Highway March: Liberation Extravaganza	September 24, 2020
The Forgotten Children's Youth March	September 26, 2020
Liberation Not Deportation	October 1, 2020
People's March for Roxanne Moore	October 2, 2020
Trans Visibility March	October 3, 2020
Be Empowered to Fight Back: Trans Self Defense	October 4, 2020
Icons Liberation Ball	October 8, 2020
Trans Visibility March	October 9, 2020
Black Angels Ball	October 15, 2020
Illumination Ball	October 22, 2020
People's March for Indigenous Lives	October 27, 2020
Black Royalty Ball	October 29, 2020
BLM Revolution Ball	October 31, 2020
We Choose Freedom	November 5, 2020
Love Legacy Liberation	November 12, 2020

Contributor Bios

Ramie Ahmed is a Black analog and lens-based artist interested in portraiture. He is currently residing in New York.

Lucy Baptiste is a photographer based in Brooklyn. In 2020, she jumped into photojournalism after watching the world mobilize to seek justice for the murder of George Floyd. Baptiste traveled to Minneapolis during the trial of Derek Chauvin to document the community as it waited for the verdict and sentencing of the former Minneapolis police officer.

Budi is a twenty-eight-year-old storyteller and artist based in New York. After receiving a scholarship to study acting in New York, he resigned from his job in Switzerland and moved to the US, graduating during the pandemic in May 2020. After the murders of George Floyd and Breonna Taylor, he borrowed his roommate's camera and started documenting and telling stories through photography. He is Egyptian and is fluent in English, German, Swiss German, Arabic, and French. He can be found on Instagram @bbuudii.

Brandon English is a New York–based visual artist invested in contemporary abolitionist practices as they intersect with vernacular image-making.

Deb Fong is a New York–based photographer whose images have been featured in multiple exhibitions and publications. She is a semifinalist in the 2022 Outwin Boochever Portrait Competition, National Portrait Gallery, Smithsonian Institution, Washington, DC.

Snake Garcia is a nonbinary photographer and activist who documented the 2020 uprisings for racial justice on the streets of New York.

Stas Ginzburg is a multidisciplinary artist and photographer based in Brooklyn. In 2022, a selection of his photographs of protests for racial justice were featured in *Live Pridefully: Love and Resilience within Pandemics* by Caribbean Equality Project at the Queens Museum.

Katie Godowski is a photographer based in New York. Her first published article was in *New York Magazine* in July 2020.

Robert Hamada is a director and photographer based in New York.

Qween Jean is a New York–based activist and costume designer who has designed over fifty shows. In 2020, Jean founded Black Trans Liberation, an organization aiming to provide access and employment resources for trans and gender-nonconforming communities. In 2021, she was artist-in-residence at MoMA PS1, New York.

Chae Kihn is a New York–based artist and photographer with more than fifteen years of experience. She had her first solo show at Umbrella Arts, New York, in 2019 and has been in numerous national and international group shows.

Zak Krevitt is an artist and activist living in Brooklyn. They have led several initiatives to empower trans and queer folks in their local community and around the world. Their photography explores a wide array of queer cultural motifs and has been exhibited internationally.

Erica Lansner is a photojournalist based in New York. She is a contributing photographer to Redux Pictures, New York, and in 2021 won her second Award of Excellence from Pictures of the Year International, presented by the Donald W. Reynolds Journalism Institute, Missouri School of Journalism.

Daniel Lehrhaupt is a queer New York–based artist who has documented electoral politics, protests, and queer life.

Caroline Mardok is an award-winning French American visual artist based in Brooklyn whose work centers on race, gender identity, and activism. In 2021, her photo sculptures honoring Black Lives Matter were displayed in Poe Park, Bronx.

Ryan McGinley is a New York–based artist. His early photos displayed the unseen intersection of queer skateboard and graffiti culture. At the age of twenty-five, he became the youngest artist to have a solo show at the Whitney Museum of American Art, New York. For more than a decade, McGinley has road-tripped throughout the US to create work that incorporates the human body within the American landscape. You can always find him on the streets of New York photographing queer activists fighting for LGBTQ+ rights.

Josh Pacheco is a two-spirit Mexican American artist and photojournalist based in New York and Los Angeles. Their work has been published in the *New York Times* and *Forbes*, among others, and is featured in the PBS documentary *Not Done: Women Remaking America*.

Joela Rivera is an Afro-Caribbean, Transgender Abolitionist and organizer based in New York.

Jarrett Robertson is a Jamaican Irish native of Hell's Kitchen, New York, and lifelong artist. He studied documentary film and photography at City College of New York. He searches his urban environment to find the true and often hidden heartbeat of the city, seeking to capture candid images that uncover intimate truths about society.

Phoenix Robles is a fine-art and documentary photographer and community organizer currently residing in Brooklyn. Her work often centers on populations and communities that have traditionally been silenced, to explore the hidden joys created within resilience and the defiance required to survive oppression. Her work was recently featured in the exhibitions *Inside/Out* at Black Gotham Experience and *The Future Is Female: Art & Activism* at sk.ArtSpace, both in New York.

Souls of a Movement (Carlos von der Heyde) is an Argentine photographer based in New York. Images from his ongoing project *Souls of a Movement* have been showcased in the 2020 exhibition *#ICP Concerned: Global Images for Global Crisis* at the International Center of Photography, New York, and related book; in *Awakening*, the 2020 nationwide billboard campaign organized by For Freedoms, an artist-led platform for civic engagement; and on the social media platforms of Until Freedom, Grassroots Law Project, and Fotografiska New York.

Mikelle Street is a New York–based editor and storyteller. He is the former editorial director of digital for *Out*, the *Advocate*, and *Plus* magazines, as well as creator and host of HBO Max's *The Let Out: A Legendary Podcast*. Street also previously held positions as digital director and senior editor at *Out Magazine* and style editor at *Maxim*. His writing has appeared in the *New York Times*, *Wall Street Journal*, *GQ*, *Vogue, i-D*, and *Aperture*, among others.

Madison Swart is a nonbinary photographer. Her photographs have been featured in *Cosmopolitan*, and in 2021, her work was featured in the exhibition *Brooklyn Resists* at the Brooklyn Public Library's Center for Brooklyn History.

Cindy Trinh is a photographer, visual journalist, and activist who is passionate about social justice and human rights. They are the creator of *Activist NYC*, a documentary photo project about activism and social justice movements in New York.

Sean Waltrous is a Brooklyn-born and -based photographer. His work is frequently featured in *Ubikwist* magazine, and he was recently honored as a Selected artist in *American Photography 38.*

Ruvan Wijesooriya is a New York–based photographer. His Sri Lankan roots help him create a unique approach to photography's visual language and the world around us. Wijesooriya's images often lie at the intersection of activism, fashion, nightlife, and music.

Raquel Willis is an activist, award-winning writer, and media strategist dedicated to Black Trans Liberation. She has written for *Buzzfeed*, *Essence*, *The Cut*, and *Vogue*, among other publications. She will release her debut memoir with St. Martin's Press in 2023.

David Zung is a visual storyteller working in art, filmmaking, and photography. He has taught at Tisch School of the Arts, New York University; Fashion Institute of Technology, New York; and Feirstein Graduate School of Cinema, Brooklyn College.

Acknowledgments

Endless gratitude and sincere thanks to all who added to the richness of this family, from the individuals and organizations to the photographers and documentarians featured within this book and without, whose work to record and preserve is vital for our history and our future. This list is a testament to the idea of collective liberation. Every contribution, every type of offering, is valuable in this fight. All have contributed to the joy, and sustained joy allows us a path to sustained liberation.

Ali Abolition
Ramie Ahmed
Luis Alba
Alfred
Ali
Joshua Allen
Jael Alvarez
Claudine Anrather
Twinkle Aria
Asanni Armon
Ashten
Robyn Ayers
China B
Marquise Vilsón Balenciaga
Lucy Baptiste
Shawn Batey
Bayside BLM
Kimberly Bernard
Blaise Beyhan
Black Chef Movement
Black Trans Femmes in the Arts
Black Trans Travel Fund
Blasian March

Bobbi
Brendan Gonzales Boston
Bridges4Life
Brooklyn Liberation
Budi
Caribbean Equality Project
Kaiya Carlin
Lawrence Carrol
Jaime Cepero
Jonovia Chase
Kat Chen
Adrian Childress
Gary Dean Clarke
Uli Beutter Cohen
James Destiny Cohen
Colectivo Intercultural
    TRANSgrediendo
The collective community
    of bikers
Victor Colletti
Copwatch Patrol Unit
Matthew Courson
Creative Time

Eliel Cruz
Marti Cummings
West Dakota
Jamilla Dartley
Dani Davis
Jes Davis
DDSSIG
Dee
Stacey Derosier
Derrick
Des the Lion
Devin-Norelle
Ella Dior
Doni
Ceyenne Doroshow
Kyle Dunn
Sequan Dyce
Nialah Edari
Kent Edwards
Adam Eli
Brandon English
Camila Falquez
Tahtianna Fermin

FIG
Doerte Fitschen-Rath
Maya Joi Flores
Deb Fong
For The Gworls
Lexii Foxx
Freedom March NYC
Derek French
Luis Galilei
Hennessy Garcia
Snake Garcia
Alon Geva
Stas Ginzburg
GLITS
Morticia Antoinette Godiva
Katie Godowski
Elena María Ketlsen González
Hunter Green
Stephanie Grey Glass
Haiti
Robert Hamada
Hero
Michelle Hope
Intersectional Voices Collective
Mila Jam
Rashid Johnson
Imara Jones
Jules
Justice for George NYC
Kammy-Raé
Alex Kent
Nupol Kiazolu
Chae Kihn
Relly Rebel King
Gia Lisa Krahne
Zak Krevitt
Ntokozo Kunene
Jade Kuriki-Olivo
Linda La
The Lady Deja
Erica Lansner
Jose LaSalle
Iman Le Caire
Daniel Lehrhaupt
Leslie
Brenna Lip
Gia Love
Donja R. Love
Devin Michael Lowe
Lubianka
Chella Man
Caroline Mardok

Alana Jessica Martin
Nikiya Mathis
Anja Matthes
Jessica Linda Matthews
Dan Mayers
Ryan McGinley
Kimberly Mckenzie
Elise McNeal
Kalaya'an Mendoza
Mexicanos Unidos
Chantaé Miller
Chelsea Miller
Morcos Key
Ms. Boogie
Chris Muller
Rodrigo Muñoz
Musicians United NYC
Shakina Nayfack
Neptunite
Brandon Nick
Nicky
Osh Nine
Chidi Nobi
Willie Norris
Edafe Okporo
Okra Project
Uche Onwa
Isaac Ortega
Josh Pacheco
Rowan Papier
Jeannie Jay Park
Paulie
Alani Payne
J. Peck
People's Bodega NYC
People's March
Josephine Fantasia Perez
Micah Phillips
Jean-Manuel Pourquet
Lily Prentice
Queens Liberation Project
Queer Detainee Empowerment
    Project
Aletheia Rael
Sara Ramirez
Ranger Rick
Nah Rebel
Reuniting of African
    Descendants
Riders4Rights
Jarrett Robertson
Phoenix Robles

Cam K Rouzaud
Safety team & medics
Sanitation Nation
Secure the Bag Safety
Sky
Larry Malcolm Smith Jr.
B. Hawk Snipes
Sound team
Travis Speck
Dréya St. Clair
Ianne Fields Stewart
Stove
Strategy for Black Lives
Mikelle Street
Subway DJ
Madison Swart
Sylvia Rivera Law Project
Aloaye Tisor
Nala Simone Toussaint
Trannilish
Dee TrannyBear
Trans Asylias
Cindy Trinh
Glori Tuitt
Brandyn Lee Tulloch
Uptown Revolutionaries
Lady Jasmin Van Wales
Nina Vartanian
Vineeta
Carlos von der Heyde
Jay Walker
Sean Waltrous
Warriors in the Garden
Megan Watson
Ronald Weaver II
Nia "A" White
Whitney White
Brent Whiteside
Ruvan Wijesooriya
Kiara Williams
Raquel Willis
Lydia Witt
Jay Wu
Rebecca Wu-Norman
Äscen X
Angelica Christina
    Xtravaganza
Yves
Rohan Zhou-Lee
David Zung

Revolution Is Love: A Year of Black Trans Liberation

Featuring images and text by 24 photographers
Text contributions by Qween Jean, Joela Rivera,
Mikelle Street, and Raquel Willis

Front cover: Caroline Mardok
Interior front cover: Zak Krevitt
Interior back cover: Souls of a Movement
Frontispiece: Ruvan Wijesooriya

Editor: Taia Kwinter
Designer: Morcos Key
Production Director: Minjee Cho
Production Manager: Andrea Chlad
Production Consultant: Thomas Bollier
Assistant Editor: Emily Patten
Senior Text Editor: Susan Ciccotti
Copy Editor: Claire Voon
Proofreader: Isla Ng
Community Liaison: Ruvan Wijesooriya

**Additional staff of the Aperture book
program includes:**
Sarah Meister, Executive Director; Lesley A.
Martin, Creative Director; Karina Eckmeier,
Designer; Kellie McLaughlin, Chief Sales
and Marketing Officer; Richard Gregg,
Sales Director, Books; Giada De Agostinis,
Communications and Public Programs Manager;
Isabelle Friedrich McTwigan, Director of Brand
Partnerships

Special thanks:
This project was made possible, in part, with
generous support from David Dechman
and Michel Mercure, in honor of Slobodan
Randjelović; Elaine Goldman; and Michael Hoeh.

Aperture's programs are made possible, in part,
by the New York State Council on the Arts with
the support of the Office of the Governor and the
New York State Legislature.

Image credits:
pp. 24–25, 178–79, 182–85, 194–96 courtesy Ramie
Ahmed; pp. 78–79 courtesy Lucy Baptiste/Flicks
By Lucy; pp. 26, 67, 90–91, 94–95 courtesy Budi;
p. 103 courtesy Brandon English; pp. 60–61, 130,
167 courtesy Deb Fong; pp. 53, 111–12, 140–41
courtesy Snake Garcia; pp. 39, 54–55, 72, 97,
128–29, 160–61, 186, 190–92, 198–99 courtesy Stas
Ginzburg; p. 33 courtesy Katie Godowski; pp.
62–63, 104–6, 108–9, 136–37, 144–46, 148 courtesy
Robert Hamada; pp. 28, 74–75, 106, 118–19, 189
courtesy Chae Kihn; pp. 42–45, 69 courtesy Zak
Krevitt; pp. 50, 119, 131, 149, 150–51, 168, 170–71
courtesy Erica Lansner; pp. 58–59, 70–71, 92–93,
158–59, 164–65, 176–77, 197, 208–9 courtesy Daniel
Lehrhaupt; pp. 76, 80, 89, 139, 177, 202–3 courtesy
Caroline Mardok; pp. 18–20, 35, 46, 49, 51, 68,
82–4, 87, 96, 152–3, 163, 188, 201 courtesy Ryan
McGinley; p. 122 courtesy Josh Pacheco; p. 86
courtesy Jarrett Robertson; pp. 107, 132, 134–35
courtesy Phoenix Robles; pp. 29, 31, 34, 36–37,
40, 113–16, 126–27, 142–43 courtesy Souls of a
Movement (Carlos von der Heyde); pp. 22–23, 27,
32–33, 47, 154, 166 courtesy Madison Swart; pp.
41, 120–21, 155, 157, 172, 174–75 courtesy Cindy
Trinh/ActivistNYC; pp. 64–65, 77, 124–25, 149
courtesy Sean Waltrous; pp. 52, 57, 98, 100–1, 166,
180–81, 204–7 courtesy Ruvan Wijesooriya; p. 85
courtesy David Zung

First edition, 2022
Printed by Midas in China
10 9 8 7 6 5 4 3 2 1

Library of Congress Control Number: 2022905393
ISBN 978-1-59711-530-8

To order Aperture books, or inquire about
gift or group orders, contact:
+1 212.946.7154
orders@aperture.org

For information about Aperture trade
distribution worldwide, visit:
aperture.org/distribution

aperture
548 West 28th Street, 4th Floor
New York, NY 10001
aperture.org

Aperture, a not-for-profit foundation, connects
the photo community and its audiences with the
most inspiring work, the sharpest ideas, and with
each other—in print, in person, and online.